INTERIOR DETAILING

IN CONTRACT WORKS

BY JIMMY F. DOCTOR

ORO EDITIONS

ORO
EDITIONS

Publishers of Architecture, Art, and Design
Gordon Goff: Publisher
www.oroeditions.com
info@oroeditions.com
Published by ORO Editions

Text by Jimmy Doctor
Edited by Rebecca Morris
Book Design by Brooke Biro
Managing Editor: Jake Anderson

10 9 8 7 6 5 4 3 2 1 First Edition

ISBN: 978-1-940743-69-1

Color Separations and Printing: ORO Group Ltd.
Printed in China.

ORO Editions makes a continuous effort to minimize the overall carbon footprint of its publications. As part of this goal, ORO Editions, in association with Global ReLeaf, arranges to plant trees to replace those used in the manufacturing of the paper produced for its books. Global ReLeaf is an international campaign run by American Forests, one of the world's oldest nonprofit conservation organizations. Global ReLeaf is American Forests' education and action program that helps individuals, organizations, agencies, and corporations improve the local and global environment by planting and caring for trees.

TABLE OF CONTENTS

Balinese wall sculpture in local stone for a house in Jakarta.

THIS BOOK IS DEDICATED TO

My late parents
Mr. Framroze E. Doctor and
Mrs. Cooma F. Doctor

Because of them I am where I am today
and this book has been possible.

With thanks also,
to my family

Wife
Nelly (Nee Manecksha)

Children
Ruzeen, Dushan, Zileena, and Fred

And grandchildren
Suri, Rayan, and Mia

For their support and encouragement in my times of need.

Bedroom desk and TV console.

SPECIAL THANKS

A special thanks to those who have aided in compiling, editing, preparing, photographing, and drawing for this book. Without these individuals, this would not have been possible.

Angie Mui - Owner
Framing Angie Art Gallery Pte Ltd - Singapore
www.framingangie.com
Refer to chapter 17, "Framing of Artworks and Photographs"

Rebecca Morris - Editor

Tan Boon Fong
Red Pixel Studio - Singapore
www.rps.com.sg
Provided all the artist's impressions in the book

K. L. NG
Photographer - Indonesia
Provided all photographs in the book

Lor Mei Nga (Sally)
JFD Designs Pte Ltd - Singapore
Provided all the CAD drawings and manuscript in the book

PREFACE

There is a saying that "every journey begins with a single step".

Well, this is one of those journeys.

To extend the analogy to interior design and architecture one could say that 'with the drawing of a single line, the extension of a thought from the mind, translated through the hand onto paper, can be the germination of a beautiful piece of interior space, or a colossus of an edifice of architecture'.

When I was a teenager studying for my final diploma, I had to make a decision, what to do when I finished high school. My family name happens to be Doctor, so I could have been a medical practitioner, or I could have been a lawyer (my wife says I am good at arguing). But my uncle, the late Mr B E Doctor, who was a leading architect in Bombay in his day, used to sit in his office drawing pretty pictures of buildings and making a lot of money. That gave me the idea of making a fast buck, and, being good at drawing, gave me the incentive to study architecture. Five years later, with a year doing practical training and studies in my uncle's office, I took my final examinations in architecture, and became a qualified architect.

Architecture/interior design is a noble profession. In the good old days, young and naïve as I was, I believed it would be a bed of roses. It is not. But then, it is not a bed of thorns either. They say, "As you sow, so shall you reap". You will gain what you put into your profession, it is all up to you and you alone.

After years in the profession of architecture and interior design, and after learning a lot about these professions from various architects, designers, contractors, craftsmen, etc., I began to ask myself: What should I do about the knowledge that I have gleaned over the years? - Why let it go to waste? Why not, pass it on? And, the germination of an idea came to mind: hence, the production of this book for neophyte designers, which I call, Interior Detailing in Contract Works.

The book is essentially geared towards newly qualified interior designers, interior design students, and architectural students, and possibly also interior contractors and even homemakers. It can be used in art and design schools, interior design offices, building sites and also in homes.

The book contains eighteen chapters, ranging from building and design terminology and abbreviations to dining table settings for formal dining, and to dining table etiquette. Chapter 2 gives the interior designer the basics of writing specifications for furniture and finishes of interior projects. It explains how each piece of furniture and its finishes can be used in a particular interior space and how every piece of furniture can be identified, codified and collated. Chapter 3 provides a similar basis as Chapter 2, but is geared towards decorative lighting fixtures.

Information on window treatment and drapery can be found in Chapter 6, dressing areas and wardrobes in Chapter 9, domestic kitchens in Chapter 11, and dining table settings for formal dining, and dining table etiquette can be found in Chapter 18. All these can be useful for homemakers.

For interior contractors and interior designers, there is detailed information on door scheduling/detailing, and door hardware specification writing in Chapter 7 and wall treatment in Chapter 13. Furniture and case goods design and detailing in Chapter 16 can be of particular help when searching for design and detailing solutions.

For interior designers who are starting out on their own, Chapter 1, which gives general information, will assist in setting up projects, and also provides the information that goes on-to the drawings that they will produce, including notations on copyright.

So, all in all, this book is designed not only for people in the interior design field, but also for those in the interior contracting field and homemakers.

There is a saying in Singapore, and I quote,
"When you share your knowledge, the doors to learning open"
This is the reason for this book.

Jimmy F. Doctor

House in Jakarta, Indonesia.

Bedroom for twin sisters with a king-sized bed, long dressing table with two dressing chairs, and sitting area.

CHAPTER 1

GENERAL INFORMATION

1. Layout of main tracing sheet and sheet indicating drawing information
2. Tracing sheet indicating how plans, elevations, sections and details should be organized
3. Abbreviations of building terminology
4. Architectural symbols
5. Electrical symbols
6. Light fitting symbols
7. Interior coding symbols
8. Coding of furniture items and documentation
9. Coding of light fitting items and documentation
10. Coding of materials and finishes and documentation
11. Coding of artwork, wall hangings, wall treatments, sculptures, etc.
12. Coding of drapery and window treatment items
13. Symbols and reference markings on drawings

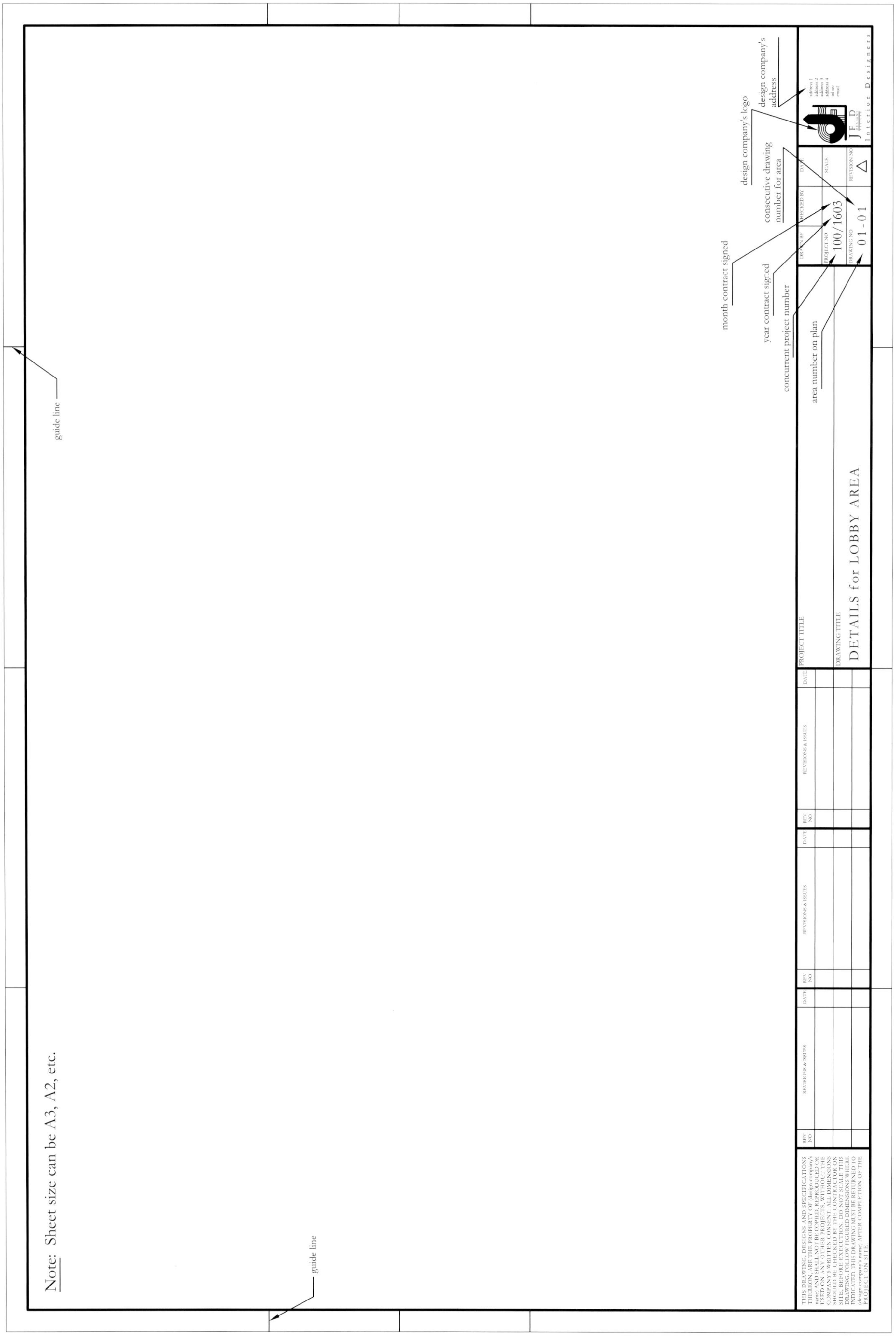
Note: Sheet size can be A3, A2, etc.
guide line
guide line
month contract signed
year contract signed
concurrent project number
area number on plan
consecutive drawing number for area
design company's logo
design company's address
100/1603
01-01
DETAILS for LOBBY AREA

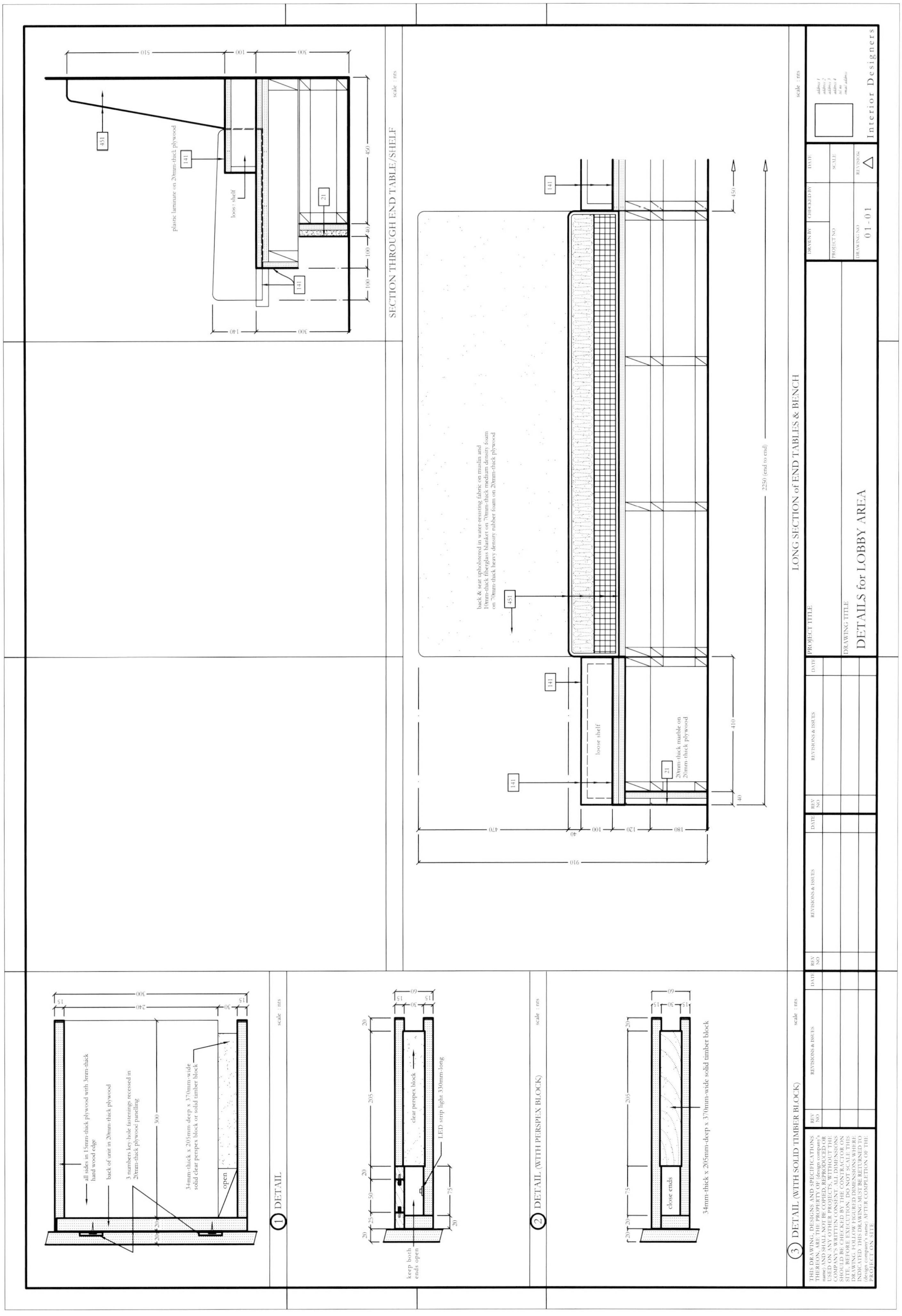
SECTION THROUGH END TABLE/SHELF
LONG SECTION of END TABLES & BENCH
1 DETAIL
2 DETAIL (WITH PERSPEX BLOCK)
3 DETAIL (WITH SOLID TIMBER BLOCK)
DETAILS for LOBBY AREA
01-01
Interior Designers

ABBREVIATIONS OF BUILDING TERMINOLOGY

access door	acc. dr.	diameter	dia.
access panel	acc. pnl.	direct current	dc.
acoustic plaster	acou. pl.	distance	dist.
above finished floor	aff. or AFF.	ditto	" or dit.
air conditioning	air con.	down	dn.
altitude	alt.	dozen	doz.
alternate current	ac.	drain	dr.
aluminum	alum.	drawing	dwg.
apartment	apt.	duplex	dx.
approved	apd.	duplicate	dupl.
architect	arch.	electric	elec.
automatic	auto.	elevation	elev.
basement	bsmt.	emergency	emer.
bevelled	bvd.	enclosure	encl.
breadth	bdth.	engineer	engr.
broom closet	bc.	entrance	ent.
bulletin board	blt brd.	equal	eq.
cabinet	cbt.	equipment	equip.
caulking	clkg.	estimate	est.
cast-iron pipe	cip.	executive	exec.
ceiling	clg.	exhaust duct	ex. dt.
cement	cem.	existing	extg.
center	ctr.	exterior	ext.
center line	℄	feet	ft.
ceramic tile	cer. tl.	finished floor	fin. Flr.
centimeter	cm.	fire hose cabinet	fhc.
chromium plate	cr. pl.	fire hydrant	fhy.
ceiling height	ch.	fireproof	fpr.
circle, circular	crr.	fitting	ftg.
closet	cl.	floor	flr.
column	col.	floor drain	fd.
company	co.	fluorescent	fluor.
concrete	con.	foot/feet	ft.
concrete floor	conc. flr.	fresh air	fa.
construction	const.	galvanised	galv.
contract	cont.	gauge	ga.
contractor	contr.	general contractor	gen. cont.
counter	cntr.	glass	gl.
cover plate	cov. pl.	granite	grnit.
cubic foot	cu. ft.	gypsum	gyp.
cylinder	cyl.	hardware	hdw.

ABBREVIATIONS OF BUILDING TERMINOLOGY

decibel	db.	heater	htr.
detail	det. or dtl.	height	hgt.
horizontal	hor.	hexagonal	hex.
horse power	hp.	plumbing	plmb.
hour	hr.	point	pt.
house	hse.	polish	pol.
inch	"or in.	quantity	qty.
information	info.	quart	qt.
insulation	insul.	radius	rad.
interior	int.	receptacle	recp.
janitor's closet	j. cl.	rectangle	rect.
kiln dried	kldr.	reflector	refl.
kitchen	kit.	refrigerator	ref. or fridge
knocked down	kd.	reinforce	reinf.
laboratory	lab.	repair	rep.
lavatory	lav.	required	req.
length	lgth.	return	rtn.
library	lib.	revision	rev.
linear feet	lin. ft.	right	rt.
linoleum	lino.	riser	r.
living room	liv. rm.	road	rd.
locker room	lkr. rm.	roof drain	rfdn.
machine	mach.	roofing	rfg.
manhole	mh.	room	rm.
manufacture	mfr.	rubber	rub.
marble	mar.	schedule	sch.
maximum	max.	sewer	sew.
mechanical	mach.	sheet	sht.
medium	med.	shelves	shel.
mezzanine	mezz.	sliding	sld.
millimeter	mm.	sink	s or sk.
miscellaneous	misc.	sleeve	slv.
moulding	mldg.	socket	soc.
number	no.	specifications	specs.
not to scale	n.t.s.	square foot	sq. ft. or ft^2.
octagonal	oct.	stainless steel	st. stl.
office	off.	staircase	str.
opening	opng.	standard	std.
opposite	opp.	station	sta.
painted	ptd.	steel	stl.
pantry	pty.	stone	stn.

ABBREVIATIONS OF BUILDING TERMINOLOGY

partition	ptn.	storage	stg.
passenger	passng.	store closet	st. cl.
percent	% or pc.	toilet	T or tlt.
pipe shaft	ps.	tongue and groove	t & g.
plaster	plas.	transom	tran.
plastic	plstc.	tread	t or tr.
plate	pl.	typical	typ.
street	st.	urinal	ur.
structural	strl.	vacuum	vac.
substitute	sub.	variable	var.
support	suppt.	varnish	varn.
suspend	susp.	ventilation	vent.
switch	sw.	vertical	vert.
switchboard	sw. db.	vestibule	vest.
symbol	sym.	volume	vol.
system	sys.	washroom	wrm.
tangent	tan.	water closet	w.c.
technical	tech.	width	wth.
telephone	tel.	window	wdw.
temperature	temp.	wood	wd.
terminal	term.	wrought iron	w.i.
terrazzo	terz.	yard	yd.
thermostat	thermos.	year	yr.
thick or thickness	thk.		

ARCHITECTURAL SYMBOLS

Masonry wall

Steel, iron, metal, etc.

Concrete

Earth

Marble

Gypsum plaster ceiling, etc.

Plaster on masonry wall

Dressed or finished wood

Rough wood, stud, etc.

Glass (plan, section)

Glass (elevation)

Plywood

Glass window

Steel channel

Steel I section

Steel angle

Insulation

Wood door and frame

Door swing and hinged end

Starting point floor/wall tiles

ELECTRICAL SYMBOLS

- Single switched convenience outlet
- Double switched or duplex convenience outlet
- Weatherproof convenience outlet
- Fan outlet
- Exit light outlet
- Blank outlet
- Junction box
- Single convenience switched outlet, recessed in floor
- Clock outlet
- Cooking range outlet
- Outside telephone & landline outlet
- Internal telephone outlet
- Telephone switchboard
- Push button outlet
- Buzzer
- Door or call bell
- Dimmer switch
- Single pole (one-way) switch
- Double pole (two-way) switch
- Three-way switch
- Automatic door switch
- Key operating switch
- Switch with pilot light
- Micro switch on door or in tight locations
- Special outlet for Broadband (internet)
- Facsimile outside line
- TV antenna outlet
- Shaver outlet, international voltage
- Hairdryer point

Tip: Outlets should be mounted 250mm-AFF, or as noted on plan. Switches should be mounted 1200mm-AFF.

LIGHT FITTINGS SYMBOLS

- Recessed downlight
- Surface-mount downlight
- Recessed directional downlight
- Surface-mount directional downlight
- Ceiling-mounted large exposed light
- Ceiling-mounted small exposed light
- Wall-mounted picture light
- Wall-mounted decorative light
- Floor lamp
- Table lamp
- Up light
- Fluorescent lamp
- Closet lamp
- LED continuous strip light
- Chandelier
- Hanging pendant fittings
- Ceiling-mounted fan
- Wall-mounted fan
- Track lights
- Exit light
- Wireless camera
- Alarm bell

INTERIOR CODING SYMBOLS

F 01, F 02, F 03	Furniture numbers on project - indicated on layout plan
L 01, L 02, L 03	Light fitting numbers on project - indicated on ceiling/lighting plans
103, 201, 301	Materials and finishes items on project (drapery, window treatment) included - indicated on plans, elevations, sections
A 01, A 02, A 03	Artwork numbers on project (artwork, wall hanging, sculpture, wall treatment, etc.) - indicated on plans, elevations
R 01, R 02, R 03	Rugs, loose carpets, etc. Numbers on project - indicated on layout plans
CH2500	Ceiling height in mm, above finished floor - indicated on ceiling plans, elevations, sections, and details

CODING OF FURNITURE ITEMS AND DOCUMENTATION

1. Every item of furniture on the project needs to be individually coded, with a consecutive number put in a hexagon, with a prefix 'F', e.g. **F⟨01⟩ F⟨02⟩ F⟨03⟩ etc.**
2. When each furniture item has been numbered prepare a Furniture Schedule. When each furniture item has been compiled in the Furniture Schedule prepare a Furniture Specification Sheet, which give all the information on that particular piece of furniture, including what the furniture looks like, the finish etc.
3. This is followed by materials and finishes specifications such as like timber, metal, fabrics, etc.
4. This is then bound in a book form, with a list of furniture and finishes suppliers attached at the front of the booklet.
5. This booklet then forms part of the Furniture Supply and Install Contract. You can go forth tendering with this booklet.
6. For detail of booklet see page number 27 to 42.

CODING OF LIGHT FITTING ITEMS AND DOCUMENTATION

1. Every piece of light fitting item on the project needs to be individually coded, with a consecutive number put in a hexagonal, with a prefix 'L', e.g. **L⟨01⟩ L⟨02⟩ L⟨03⟩ etc.**
2. After each light fitting item is numbered, prepare a Light Fitting Schedule.
3. After each light fitting item has been compiled in the Light Fitting Schedule prepare a Light Fitting Specification Sheet, which gives all the information on that particular piece of light fitting, including what the fitting looks like, the size, whether it is a recessed, surface mounted, or a hanging fitting, where it can be manufactured or purchased, the finishes on the fitting etc.
4. This is then bound in a book form, with a list of light fitting manufacturers and suppliers, attached at the front of the booklet.
5. This booklet will then form part of the Light Fitting Supply Contract. You can go forth tendering with this booklet.
6. For detail of booklet see page numbers 44 to 50.
7. **Note**: The installation of light fittings for the project will be by the electrical contractor, and the installation of chandeliers by the chandelier supplier.

CODING OF MATERIALS AND FINISHES ITEMS AND DOCUMENTATION

Every piece of material and finishes item used on the project will be individually coded, with a designated number as reflected in the "Master Materials and Finishes Chart", and put in a rectangular box, e.g. [103], [305] or [529] as the case may be.

These boxed numbers can appear on plans for flooring or on a elevation or section, etc., to indicate materials or finishes that are to be used on walls and which will then correspond to the Master Chart. These boxed numbers can also be put on detail drawings to identify the finishes applied on the details. These numbers from the Master Chart should be used in all areas of the project.
As an easy reference for the purchasing agent, prepare a detailed list of materials and finishes suppliers, including the name of company, address, telephone number, email address and person to contact.

SAMPLE MASTER CHART FOR MATERIALS AND FINISHES ITEMS

code nos.	**Materials & Finishes**	code nos.	**Materials & Finishes**
FLOORING and OTHER HARD SURFACES		WALLCOVERINGS	
01 to 30	Marble, granite, ceramic tiles, Mosaic tiles, terrazzo	276 to 300	Vinyl wall covering
31 to 40	Various glass (plain, tinted)	301 to 339	Paper wall covering
41 to 50	Various mirrors (silver, antique)	340 to 379	Fabric wall covering
51 to 65	Vinyl tiles/sheet flooring	380 to 400	Foil wall covering
66 to 80	Rubber, cork, plastic flooring		
81 to 100	Carpets *Note: As rugs will be purchased under furniture items, they should by coded under furniture, in a-⬡ with a prefix "R"⟨01⟩ or R⟨02⟩ etc.*		
TIMBERS, RATTAN, PLASTICS		FABRICS	
101 to 125	Various woods	401 to 429	Fabrics ~ linen & cotton
126 to 140	Rattan and cane	430 to 449	Fabrics ~ silk
141 to 165	Plastic & metallic laminates	450 to 469	Fabrics ~ synthetics
166 to 175	Acrylics	470 to 489	Fabrics ~ velvets
176 to 185	Glass reinforced plastic	490 to 509	Fabrics ~ wool & felt
PAINTS, STAINS & SPECIAL FINISHES		510 to 529	Fabrics ~ sheers
186 to 210	Paints ~ gloss, semi or matt Gold leaf + silver-leaf finish	530 to 559	Leather & suede
211 to 220	Paints ~ lacquers & duco	560 to 579	Vinyl leather & vinyl suede
221 to 235	Stains, varnishes & special finishes		
METALS		TRIMS, BEADS, & SPECIAL GLASS	
236 to 275	Various metals: polished stainless steel, matt stainless steel, polished brass, matt brass, polished chrome, matt chrome, anodized aluminum, nickel-plated, bronze, copper, pewter, etc.	580 to 599 600 to 620 621 to 635	Trims, tassels & braids Beads, glass reeds, etc. Stained glass Etched glass Spray-painted glass

For layout of Materials & Finishes Chart indicating material samples see pages 33–44 for reference.

CODING OF ARTWORK, WALL HANGINGS, WALL TREATMENT, SCULPTURE, ETC.

1. Every item of artwork, wall hangings, wall treatment and sculptures specified on the project need to be individually coded, with a designated number, as reflected in the Artwork Master Chart, and put in a square box, with a prefix "A" e.g. A [01] A [08] A [20] etc., as the case may be.

2. These boxed numbers can appear on plans and elevations, and will then correspond to the numbers in the Master Artwork Chart, which will describe the type of artwork selected by the designer or art work consultant.

3. After each piece of artwork etc. has been given its individual number, all the items will be combined in an Artwork Schedule.

4. This schedule, in the form of a booklet will form part of the Artwork Contract Document.

5. Note: This portion of the project should be kept separate from the Furniture purchasing section, as there will be a separate budget for Artwork.

CODING FOR DRAPERY AND WINDOW TREATMENT ITEMS

1. Every item of drapery, window treatment etc. specified on the project will be individually coded, with a

   designated number in the Master Materials and Finishes chart, and put in a rectangular box, e.g.

   [401] [470] or [510] etc.

2. These boxed numbers appear on plans, elevations and also on separate drapery, window treatment drawings.

3. After each drapery or window treatment is given its individual number on the detail drawings, all items will be complied in a Drapery, Window Treatment Schedule (see page number 38 to 40) and Window Treatment Section.

4. This schedule in the form of a booklet, will form part of the Drapery Contract Document.

5. Note: The installation of tracks, pelmets, etc. will be by the interior contractor. Supply of electrical motors for drapery, where specified, will be supplied and installed by the drapery contractor and, connected by the electrical contractor.

SYMBOLS & REFERENCE MARKINGS ON DRAWINGS

1. When a particular detail has to be annotated, on the same sheet, draw the following symbol, to show where the detail is to be found, e.g. detail of a door frame. Use a larger circle around the area to be detailed, with a smaller circle containing a number in order to differentiate one detail from another on the same sheet.

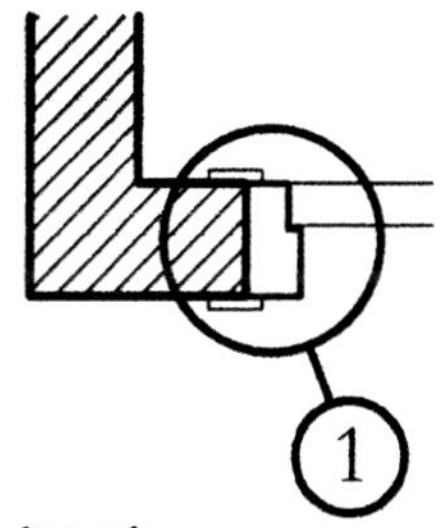

2. When a particular detail has to be annotated on a different sheet, draw the following symbol, to show where the detail is to be found, e.g. detail of a door frame. Use a larger circle around the area to be detailed, with a medium-size circle marked with a horizontal line in the center. At the top of the line put the detail number, and at the bottom of the line put the number of the drawing, where the detail will be drawn.

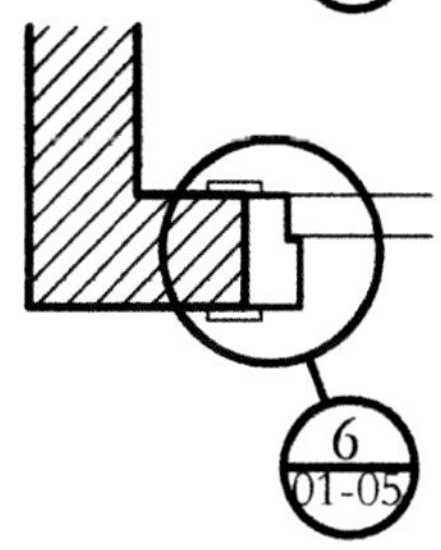

3. When a section is to be indicated on a plan, on the same sheet, draw the following symbol, to show where the section appears on the plan. Indicate a line where the section is taken, with a circle and an arrow. Put a capital letter A, B, C etc. in the circle to identify the section and its location.

4. If a section is to be indicated on a plan, but drawn on another sheet, draw the following symbol to show where the section appears on the plan. Indicate a line with a large circle. Put a capital letter A, B, C etc. at the top end of the circle, and the drawing number of the sheet where the section is drawn, at the bottom end of the circle.

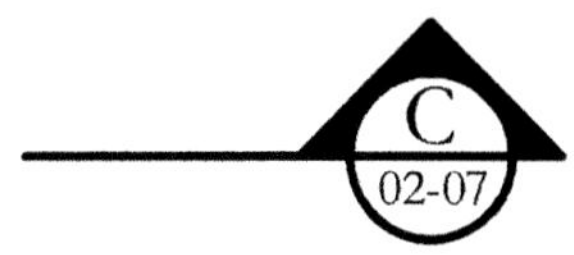

5. When elevations are to be indicated on a plan, the following symbol will apply, a circle with an arrow at the top, and a capital letter in the circle, that applies to the elevation.

6. When elevations are to be indicated on a plan, but drawn on a separate sheet, the following symbol will apply, a large square drawn at 45°, with a smaller square in the center. The four triangles so formed will indicate the elevation references in capital letters, and the smaller square will indicate the drawing number, where the elevations are drawn.

7. Use numerals to indicate detail numbers, and alphabetical capital letters to indicate sections or elevations.

CHAPTER 2

WRITING FURNITURE AND FINISHES SPECIFICATIONS

Preparing a Loose Furniture Schedule Booklet

1. Loose Furniture Schedule (front cover)
    a. Furniture Schedule (loose furniture description)
    b. Furniture Specification and Data Sheet
    c. Data Sheet sample furniture F01 - plan of 2-seat sofa
    d. Data Sheet sample furniture F02 - details of bench and end table (sheet 1)
    e. Data Sheet sample furniture F02 - details of bench and end table (sheet 2)
2. Master Materials and Finishes Chart
    a. Hard surfaces, flooring, etc.
    b. Timbers, rattan and plastics, etc.
    c. Paints, stains and special finishes
    d. Metal
    e. Wallcoverings
    f. Fabrics
    g. Trims, tassels, beads and special glass
3. Fabrics where used with samples of fabrics
4. List of furniture suppliers
5. List of materials/finishes suppliers
6. All furniture layout plans for project indicating furniture numbers

PREPARING A LOOSE-FURNITURE SCHEDULE BOOKLET

1. TITLE SHEET

   To include

   a) Project title

   b) Project location

   c) Project number

   d) Issue date

2. LOOSE FURNITURE SHEET

   To include

   a) Loose-Furniture Description/Schedule Sheets, that will list out all furniture items on the project, starting from F 01 item onwards

   b) Furniture Specification & Data Sheet of F 01

   c) Other data sheets of Item F 01

   d) Follow other furniture items as F 01 above, F 02 onwards

3) MATERIALS AND FINISHES CHART

   To include

   a) 01 onwards for hard surfaces

   b) 101 onwards for various timbers, etc.

   c) 186 onwards for paints

   d) 236 onwards for metals

   e) 276 onwards for wallcovering

   f) 401 onwards for fabrics

   g) 580 onwards for trims, beads, special glass

4) MATERIALS AND FINISHES SAMPLES CHART

   a) provide samples of finishes

5) LIST OF ALL FURNITURE AND MATERIAL SUPPLIERS

6) ALL FURNITURE LAYOUT PLANS ON PROJECT

   a) include all furniture numbers

Refer to pages 27 to 42

LOOSE FURNITURE SCHEDULE

HOUSE

for

MR. & MRS. X Y Z

at

(address)

(name of city)

(name of country)

PROJECT NO: 151/1610 ISSUE DATE: 12.12.2017

LOOSE FURNITURE DESCRIPTION	AREA/LOCATION FIRST STORY	SHEET NO 1 OF PROJECT NO

FURNITURE CODE	STATUS	ITEM DESCRIPTION / SIZE		DATE	REV.	REMARKS
F 01	Client to purchase	Console	W1500 x D450 x H760		△	Entrance Hall
F 02	ditto	Display table	W1350 x D750 x H760		△	Guest Waiting
F 03	spare				△	-
F 04	Client to purchase	Armchair	W720 x D680 x H910		△	Guest Waiting
F 05	ditto	End table	Ø500 x H600		△	Guest Waiting
F 06	ditto	Sofa	W1800 x D680 x H910		△	Guest Waiting
F 07	ditto	Occasional table	W750 x D500 x H420		△	Guest Waiting
F 08	ditto	Display cabinet	W1200 x D500 x H2000		△	Main Staircase
F 09	ditto	King-size bed	W1800 x D2100 x H500		△	Guest Bedroom
F 10	Furniture Contractor	King-size headboard	W2250 x D50 x H1450		△	Guest Bedroom
F 11	ditto	Bedside table	W700 x D500 x H500		△	Guest Bedroom
F 12	ditto	TV unit + dressing table	W2500 x D700 x H760		△	Guest Bedroom
F 13	Client to purchase	Desk chair	W500 x D610 x H875		△	Guest Bedroom
F 14	ditto	Round end table	Ø600 x H710		△	Guest Bedroom
F 15	ditto	Armchair	W650 x D580 x H820		△	Guest Bedroom
F 16	ditto	Mirror	W750 x D50 x H1300		△	Guest Bedroom
F 17	ditto	Round table	Ø450 x H650		△	Media Room
F 18	ditto	Lounge chair	W680 x D660 x H790		△	Media Room
F 19	Furniture Contractor	Three-seat sofa	W2800 x D900 x H920		△	Media Room
F 20	ditto	Occasional table	W1400 x D750 x H480		△	Media Room
F 21	spare				△	-
F 22	Client to purchase	Display table	Ø1200 x H720		△	Living Room
F 23	ditto	Ottoman	W780 x D680 x H480		△	Living Room
F 24	ditto	Desk chair	W570 x D620 x H910		△	Living Room
F 25	ditto	Desk	W1650 x D750 x H760		△	Living Room
F 26	ditto	Lounge chair	W780 x D760 x H1070		△	Living Room
F 27	ditto	Side table	W700 x D610 x H650		△	Living Room

PROJECT TITLE:	REV	REVISIONS/ISSUES	DATE	REV	REVISIONS/ISSUES	DATE
	△			△		
DRAWING TITLE: FURNITURE SCHEDULE	△			△		
	△			△		

TIP - Leave some spare columns for insertion of furniture items that may be added later.

PROTO-TYPE OF DATA SHEET, PAGE No. 1

FURNITURE SPECIFICATION AND DATA SHEET	DESCRIPTION	F	SHEET NO 1 OF / TOTAL QTY

ILLUSTRATION:

space for title of the item to be illustrated

Furniture number from Furniture Schedule

- * *Furniture supplier's number from supplier's schedule.*
- * *Finishes supplier's number, from finishes schedule.*
- * *Furniture's number, from furniture's schedule.*
- * *Finishes code, from finishes schedule.*
- * *Room type will be the different rooms on the project.*

* *Pricing:*
Budget = Established cost of the item.
Quotation = Price obtained from bid on project.
Final Pricing = Negotiated price with appointed bidder.

* *Totals:*
Total quantity of the item, multiplied by the unit's negotiated price, will give the final total price of the item.

SPECIFICATION / DESCRIPTION:

SUPPLIER / MANUFACTURER:	Furniture supplier number	Finishes supplier & finishes code	
MODEL NO:	DIMENSIONS (mm):	ROOM TYPE:	QUANTITY:
		1	
OTHER FINISHES CODE: - - - -	AREA LOCATION:	2	
		3	
PRICING: ☐ BUDGET : $ ☐ QUOTATION : $ ☐ FINAL PRICE : $	TOTAL: TOTAL QUANTITY: TOTAL PRICE: $	4	
		5	
		TOTAL QTY:	

REMARKS/NOTES /SPECIAL INSTRUCTIONS:

Company's address, telephone no., etc.

Company's logo

PROJECT TITLE:	DRAWN BY	CHECKED	DATE	*address 1 address 2 address 3 postal code email address*
	PROJECT NO		SCALE	
DRAWING TITLE:	DRAWING NO		REVISION △	Interior Designers

PROTO-TYPE OF DATA SHEET, PAGE NO 2, 3, ETC.

FURNITURE SPECIFICATION AND DATA SHEET	DESCRIPTION	F	SHEET NO 2 OF TOTAL QTY

ILLUSTRATION:

REMARKS/NOTES/SPECIAL INSTRUCTIONS:

Company's address, telephone no., etc.

Company's logo

PROJECT TITLE:	DRAWN BY	CHECKED	DATE	*address 1* *address 2* *address 3* *postal code* *email address*
	PROJECT NO		SCALE	
DRAWING TITLE:	DRAWING NO		REVISION △	Interior Designers

DATA SHEET	DESCRIPTION FURNITURE SPECIFICATION	F 02	SHEET NO 1 OF 2 TOTAL QTY

ILLUSTRATION:

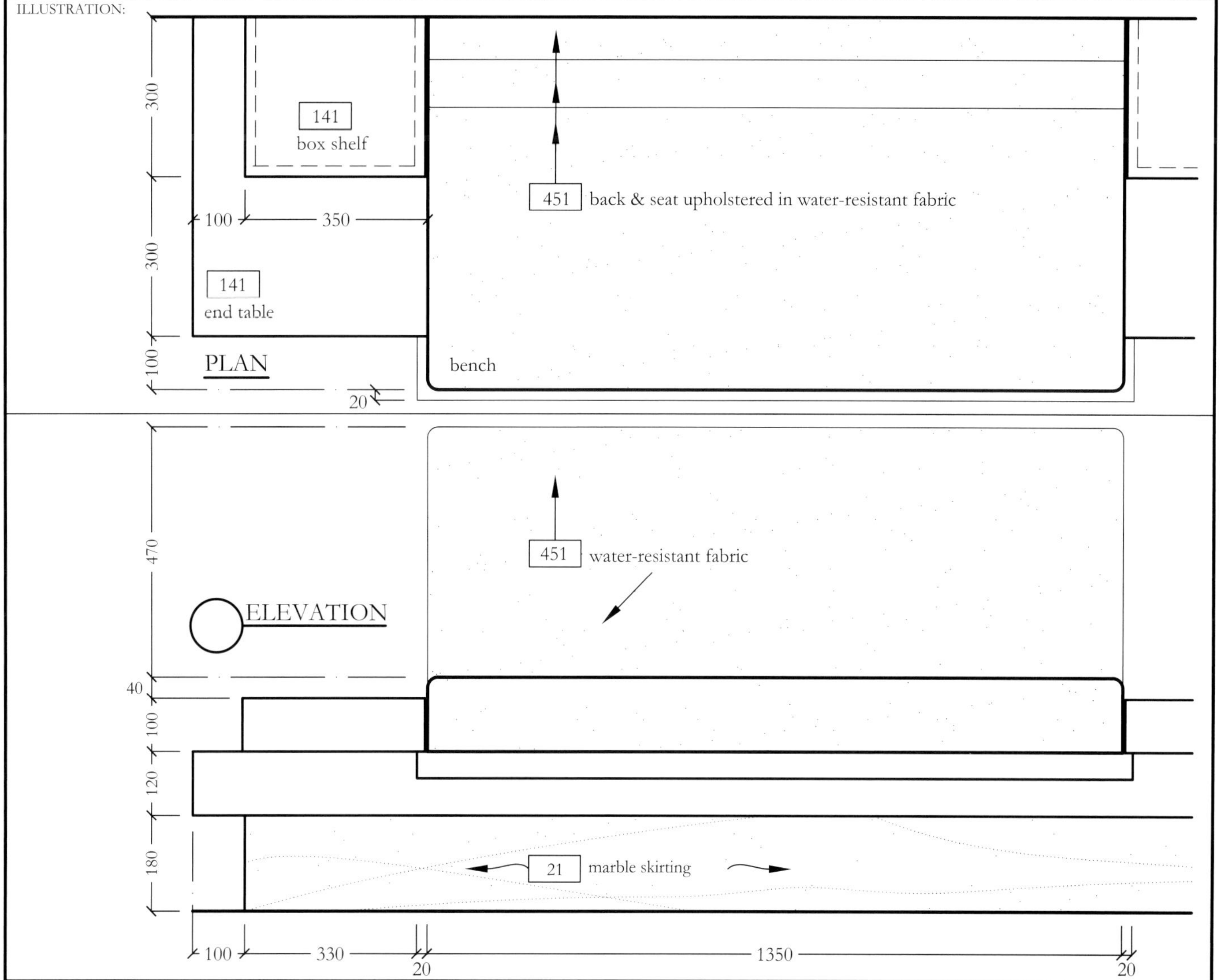

SPECIFICATION / DESCRIPTION:

SUPPLIER / MANUFACTURER:	Furniture supplier number: 09	Finishes supplier & finishes code: 10, 12, 451, 141

MODEL NO:	DIMENSIONS (mm):	ROOM TYPE:	QUANTITY:
custom made	L2250 (o/a) D700 H910	1 Master bathroom	1
OTHER FINISHES CODE: 21, -, -, -	AREA LOCATION:	2	
		3	
PRICING: ☐ BUDGET : $ ☐ QUOTATION : $ ☐ FINAL PRICE : $	TOTAL: TOTAL QUANTITY: TOTAL PRICE: $	4	
		5	
		TOTAL QTY:	1

PROJECT TITLE:	DRAWN BY	CHECKED	DATE	*address 1* *address 2* *address 3* *postal code* *email address* Interior Designers
	PROJECT NO		SCALE	
DRAWING TITLE: PLAN AND ELEVATION OF BENCH AND END TABLES (for bathroom/gymnasium)	DRAWING NO		REVISION △	

DATA SHEET	DESCRIPTION FURNITURE SPECIFICATION	F 02	SHEET NO 2 OF 2 TOTAL QTY

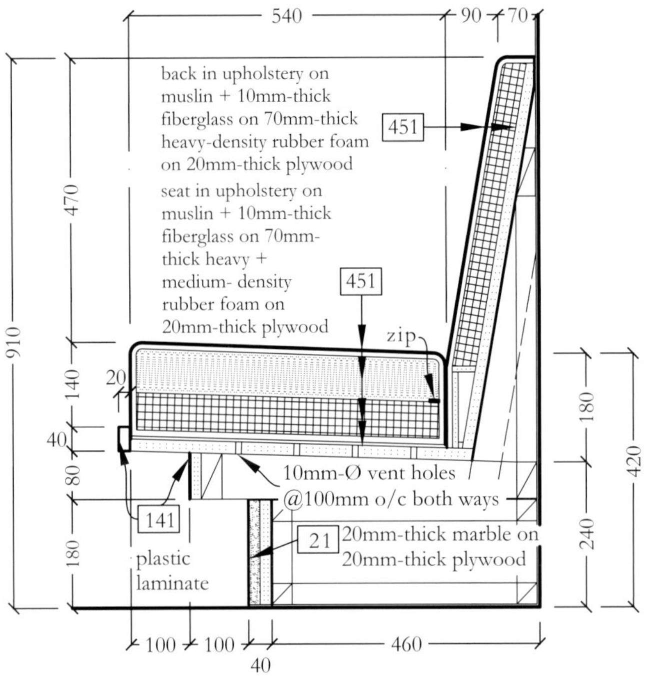

SECTION THROUGH BENCH

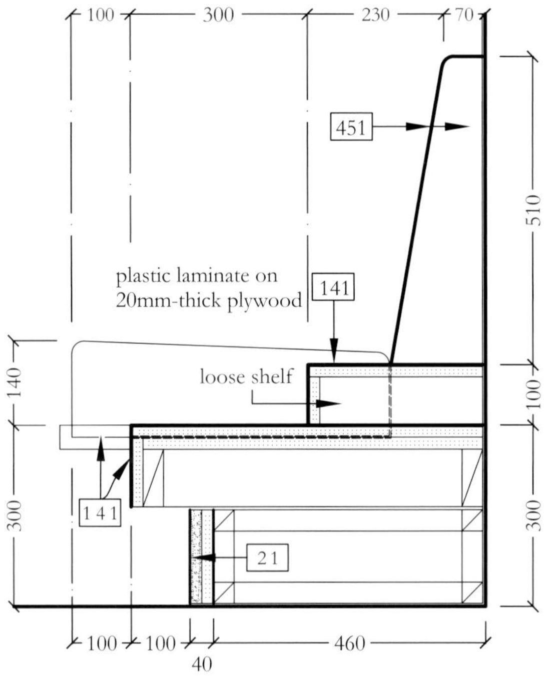

SECTION THROUGH END TABLE/SHELF

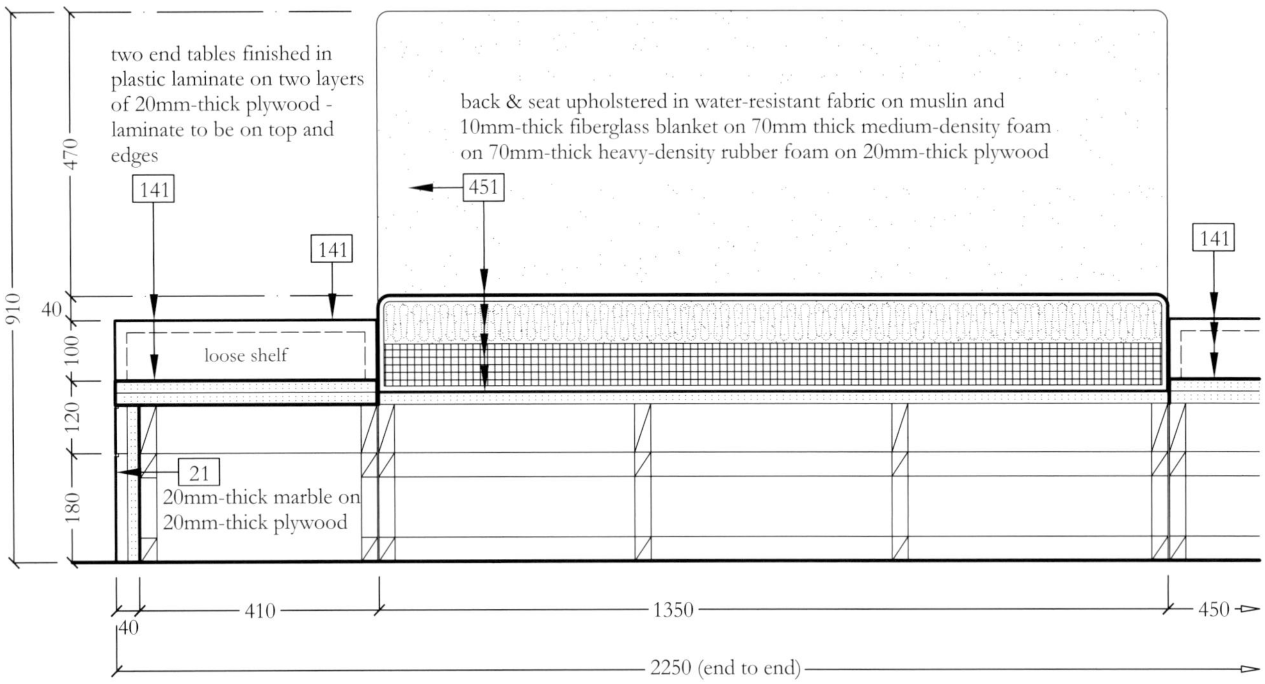

LONG SECTION OF END TABLES & BENCH

PROJECT TITLE:	DRAWN BY	CHECKED	DATE	address 1 address 2 address 3 postal code email address
	PROJECT NO		SCALE	
DRAWING TITLE: DETAILS OF BENCH AND END TABLES (for bathroom/gymnasium)	DRAWING NO		REVISION △	Interior Designers

MASTER MATERIALS & FINISHES CHART	DESCRIPTION HARD SURFACES, FLOORING, ETC.	SHEET NO 1 OF 8 PROJECT NO

FINISHES CODE	SPECIFICATIONS	AREA OF USE	LOCATION	SUPPLIED BY	REMARKS
01	Arabescato Arni 20mm thick, marble	Floor	Living Room Dining Room Lobby	Interior Contractor	Polished finish
02	Granito Rosa Di Baveno 20mm thick, granite	Counter top	Main Kitchen	ditto	Polished finish - Bullnose edge
19	Moasic tiles BDH 040 size - 300mm square	Shower floor	Guest Bathroom 1	ditto	White grout
21	Ceramic tiles SWC 15902 size - W150mm L900mm	Floor	Balcony	ditto	Laid Herringbone pattern - see plan
26	Black Absoluto 20mm-thick, granite	Counter top	Master Bathroom	ditto	Polished finish - Bullnose edge
65	Carpet tiles range: METZ colour: STORM, 327/D4012 textured, patterned, loop size - W460mm L460mm	Floor	Bedroom 2 Bedroom 3	Carpet supplier	Laid wall to wall light blue colour
81	Woven axminster carpet range: MARRAKESH 80% wool, 20% nylon width: 4000mm	Floor	Main Lobby Living Room	Carpet supplier	wall to wall carpet

PROJECT TITLE:	REV	REVISIONS/ISSUES	DATE	REV	REVISIONS/ISSUES	DATE
	△			△		
DRAWING TITLE: MATERIALS AND FINISHES SCHEDULE	△			△		
	△			△		

company name, address, telephone number, fax number, email address

MASTER MATERIALS & FINISHES CHART	DESCRIPTION TIMBER, RATTAN, PLASTICS, ETC.	SHEET NO 2 OF 8 PROJECT NO

FINISHES CODE	SPECIFICATIONS	AREA OF USE	LOCATION	SUPPLIED BY	REMARKS
101	Macassar Ebony high gloss finish	Wall panelling	Living Room Dining Room	Interior Contractor	Veneer on 20mm-thick plywood
102	Bird's Eye Maple - matt finish	Wall panelling	TV Room Master Bedroom	ditto	ditto
103	Burmese Teak - matt finish	Furniture	Living Room Dining Room Bedrooms	ditto	Solid timber - see details
126	Rattan - white wash finish	Furniture	Balcony	Rattan supplier	White washed finish - per approved sample
141	Plastic laminate - colorcore - C0909G - Black high gloss finish	Counter top	Kitchen	Interior Contractor	
142	Plastic laminate - woodgrain - Saw Cut 6053ST, Chalet Oak	Furniture	Master Bedroom	ditto	
176	Glass reinforced plastic	Screen	Dining Room	ditto	

PROJECT TITLE:	REV	REVISIONS/ISSUES	DATE	REV	REVISIONS/ISSUES	DATE
	△			△		
DRAWING TITLE: MATERIALS AND FINISHES SCHEDULE	△			△		
	△			△		

company name, address, telephone number, fax number, email address

MASTER MATERIALS & FINISHES CHART	DESCRIPTION PAINTS, STAINS, SPECIAL FINISHES	SHEET NO 3 OF 8 PROJECT NO

FINISHES CODE	SPECIFICATIONS/MANUFACTURER	AREA OF USE	LOCATION	SUPPLIED BY	REMARKS
186	Wash & Wear White, WW25258L	Ceiling	Living Room Dining Room Bedrooms Lobby	Interior Contractor	matt finish 1 sealer coat + 2 top coats
187	Mouldguard White, PL25664	Ceiling	Bathrooms Kitchen	ditto	matt finish
188	Soft Gold leaf - Accent color	Ceiling	Living + Dining Room coffers	ditto	
189	Wash & Wear Natural Cane, 22617L	Ceiling	Living Room	ditto	matt finish - Accent area 1 sealer coat + 2 top coats
190	Wash & Wear Morning Dew, WW25748L	Walls	Bedrooms	ditto	matt finish - 1 sealer coat + 2 top coats
211	Gloss White, GL101	Doors	All rooms + Kitchen	ditto	high gloss finish - 1 speed undercoat + 2 overcoats of Dulux gloss finish, spray paint
212	Brilliant White, GL 290	Wardrobe + Kitchen cabinet doors	Bedrooms + Kitchen	ditto	high gloss finish - 1 speed undercoat + 2 overcoats of Dulux gloss finish, spray paint
221	Timbertone Honeypine, 16059	Floor	Bedrooms	ditto	on Teakwood - semi gloss finish

PROJECT TITLE:	REV	REVISIONS/ISSUES	DATE	REV	REVISIONS/ISSUES	DATE
	△			△		
DRAWING TITLE: MATERIALS AND FINISHES SCHEDULE	△			△		
	△			△		

company name, address, telephone number, fax number, email address

MASTER MATERIALS & FINISHES CHART	DESCRIPTION METALS	SHEET NO 4 OF 8 PROJECT NO

FINISHES CODE	SPECIFICATIONS	AREA OF USE	LOCATION	SUPPLIED BY	REMARKS
236	Mirror polished stainless steel	Various, including lighting - hardware, furniture	Living Room Dining Room Lobby and other areas hardware	Interior Contractor + Lighting Contractor	
237	Brushed stainless steel	ditto	ditto	ditto	
238	Polished brass	ditto	Lighting - hardware	ditto	
239	Matt brass	ditto	ditto	ditto	
240	Polished chrome	Lighting, hardware screen furniture	ditto	ditto	
241	Matt chrome	ditto	ditto	ditto	
242	Anodized aluminum	Hardware	Living Room Dining Room Bedrooms, Lobby, etc.	Interior Contractor	

PROJECT TITLE:	REV	REVISIONS/ISSUES	DATE	REV	REVISIONS/ISSUES	DATE
	△			△		
DRAWING TITLE: MATERIALS AND FINISHES SCHEDULE	△			△		
	△			△		

MASTER MATERIALS & FINISHES CHART	DESCRIPTION WALLCOVERINGS	SHEET NO 5 OF 8 PROJECT NO

FINISHES CODE	SPECIFICATIONS/MANUFACTURER	AREA OF USE	LOCATION	SUPPLIED BY	REMARKS
276	Textile wallcovering - NFD - 228504 width - 137 cm	Walls	Lift Lobby Entrance Lobby Kitchen	Interior Contractor	sealer coat to be applied before installation of wallpaper.
277	Textile wallcovering Style - SS3307 width - 137 cm	Walls	Corridor	ditto	ditto
278	Textile wallcovering - NFD - 185404 width - 137 cm	Walls	Master Bedroom	ditto	ditto
279	Vinyl wallpaper Goodwall Infinity G12000, Vertical Rib width - 137 cm	Walls	Bedrooms	ditto	ditto
280	Vinyl wallpaper Tahoe - 145.13 width - 130 cm	Walls	Bathrooms Dressing	ditto	ditto
281	Fabric wallcovering MLA - 315 width - 137 cm	Walls	Living Room Dining Room	ditto	ditto
282	Foil wallpaper LY - 19810 C635 width - 91 cm	Walls	Media Room	ditto	ditto
283	Woven grasscloth SDG - 5 width - 91.44 untrimmed	Walls	Bedrooms	ditto	ditto

PROJECT TITLE:	REV	REVISIONS/ISSUES	DATE	REV	REVISIONS/ISSUES	DATE
	△			△		
DRAWING TITLE: MATERIALS AND FINISHES SCHEDULE	△			△		
	△			△		

company name, address, telephone number, fax number, email address

MASTER MATERIALS & FINISHES CHART	DESCRIPTION FABRICS	SHEET NO 6 OF 8 / PROJECT NO

FINISHES CODE	SPECIFICATIONS/MANUFACTURER	AREA OF USE	LOCATION	SUPPLIED BY	REMARKS
401	code: 3229/04 width: 142cm repeat: 135cmH, $95.^{25}$cmV 100% cotton	Furniture	Living Room	Interior Contractor	to be water repellent
402	code: 3229/03 width: 142cm repeat: 135cmH, $95.^{25}$cmV 100% cotton	Furniture	Living Room	ditto	ditto
403	code: 2080/06 - Orange width: 144cm repeat: $64.^{5}$ cmH $54.^{5}$ cmV 80% linen, 20% rayon	Furniture	Guest Waiting Guest Bedroom	ditto	
415	code: 3229/02 width: 142cm repeat: 135 cmH, $95.^{25}$ cmV 100% cotton	Furniture	Living Room	ditto	to be water repellent
416	code: 2178/01, Rice Paper width: 140cm repeat: 1.40cmH, 2cmV 55% linen, 45% cotton	Wall Panelling	Mother's Room	ditto	
417	code: 2166/01, Delphinium width: 142cm repeat: 70cmH, 47cmV 60% cotton, 40% linen	Furniture	Master Bedroom	ditto	
430	code: 3244/01 width: 142cm repeat: 142cmH, 62cmV 22% silk, 54% linen, 24% cotton	Curtain	Living Room Guest Waiting	ditto	see detail drawings
450	code: 2163/03, Navy design width: 133 cm repeat: 7cm H 100% solution dyed polypropylene	Wall Panelling	Media Room	ditto	see detail drawings
451	code: 2163/01, Rice paper design width: 133 cm repeat: 7 cm H 100% solution dyed polypropylene	Furniture	Guest Waiting	ditto	
452	design: 2163/05, Baby blue design width: 133 cm repeat: 7 cm H 100% polypropylene	Curtain	Master Bedroom	ditto	see detail drawings
453	design: Piano/Acacia colour: 06 - Horizon width: 319 cm, repeat: $4.^{5}$cm H 100% Polyester	Sheer	Master Bedroom	ditto	ditto
510	code: 3339/01 width: 350 cm repeat: 58 cmH, $64.^{4}$ cmV 62% linen, 21% polyester, 17% nylon	Sheer	Living Room	ditto	ditto

PROJECT TITLE:	REV	REVISIONS/ISSUES	DATE	REV	REVISIONS/ISSUES	DATE
	△			△		
DRAWING TITLE: MATERIALS AND FINISHES SCHEDULE	△			△		
	△			△		

company name, address, telephone number, fax number, email address

MASTER MATERIALS & FINISHES CHART	DESCRIPTION TRIMS, TASSELS, BEADS AND SPECIAL GLASS	SHEET NO 7 OF 8 PROJECT NO

FINISHES CODE	SPECIFICATIONS	AREA OF USE	LOCATION	SUPPLIED BY	REMARKS
580	Cut Fringe code: 33063 - Samourai colour: 9669 H. 65 mm	Drapery	Living Room Dining Room	Interior Contractor	
581	Scalloped Fringe code: 33304 - Samourai colour: 9905 H. 55 mm	ditto	Master Bedroom	ditto	
582	Tassel Tieback code: 35743 - Samourai colour: 9669 D. 13 mm, L. 95 cm, H. 240 mm	ditto	Living Room Dining Room	ditto	
583	Cord Tieback code: 35079 - Samourai colour: 9905 D. 28 mm, L. 110 cm	ditto	Master Bedroom	ditto	
584	Spray Painted Glass Special Design TH. 10 mm	Screen	Entrance Lobby	ditto	

PROJECT TITLE:	REV	REVISIONS/ISSUES	DATE	REV	REVISIONS/ISSUES	DATE
	△			△		
DRAWING TITLE: MATERIALS AND FINISHES SCHEDULE	△			△		
	△			△		

company name, address, telephone number, fax number, email address

MASTER MATERIALS AND FINISHES CHART	DESCRIPTION FABRICS - WHERE USED/WITH SAMPLES OF FABRIC	SHEET NO 8 OF 8 PROJECT NO

CODE NO	FURN CODE	SPECIFICATIONS/WHERE USED	LOCATION	SUPPLIED BY	REMARKS	SAMPLE
401	F 23 F 26 F -	collection: CHENILLE code: 3229/04 • Ottoman • Lounge Chair	Living Room	Furniture contractor	to be water repellent	to put in fabric samples
403	04 13 15	collection: code: 2080/06 ORANGE • Armchair • Desk Chair • Armchair	Guest Waiting Guest Bedroom	Furniture contractor		
430	F - F - F -	collection: code: 3244/01 • Curtain	Living Room Guest Waiting	Interior contractor	see Drapery drawings	
510	F - F - F -	collection: D'ARTIFICES code: 3339/01 • Sheer	Living Room Guest Waiting	Interior contractor	ditto	
452	F - F - F -	collection: code: 2163/05 BABY BLUE • Curtain	Master Bedroom	Interior contractor	ditto	
453	F - F - F -	collection: PIANO/ACACIA code: 06/HORIZON • Sheer	Master Bedroom	Interior contractor	ditto	

PROJECT TITLE:	REV	REVISIONS/ISSUES	DATE	REV	REVISIONS/ISSUES	DATE
	△			△		
DRAWING TITLE: MATERIALS AND FINISHES SCHEDULE	△			△		
	△			△		

TIP - Leave some spare columns for insertion of furniture items that may be added later.

LIST OF FURNITURE SUPPLIERS (number to be in circle)

supplier no.	supplier's company	supplier's address/details	person to contact
01	ABC Furniture Company	address telephone number email address	detail of person
12	FGH Sofas & Chairs	address telephone number email address	detail of person
25	Miami Furniture Company	address telephone number email address	detail of person

LIST OF MATERIAL/FINISHES SUPPLIERS (number to be in an oval)

supplier no.	supplier's company	supplier's address/details	person to contact
01	ABC Fabric Company	address telephone number email address	detail of person
20	XYZ Paint Company	address telephone number email address	detail of person
31	Marbles from Italy	address telephone number email address	detail of person

DATA SHEET	DESCRIPTION LIVING ROOM (1ST STORY)	SHEET NO 1 OF 3 TOTAL QTY

ILLUSTRATION:

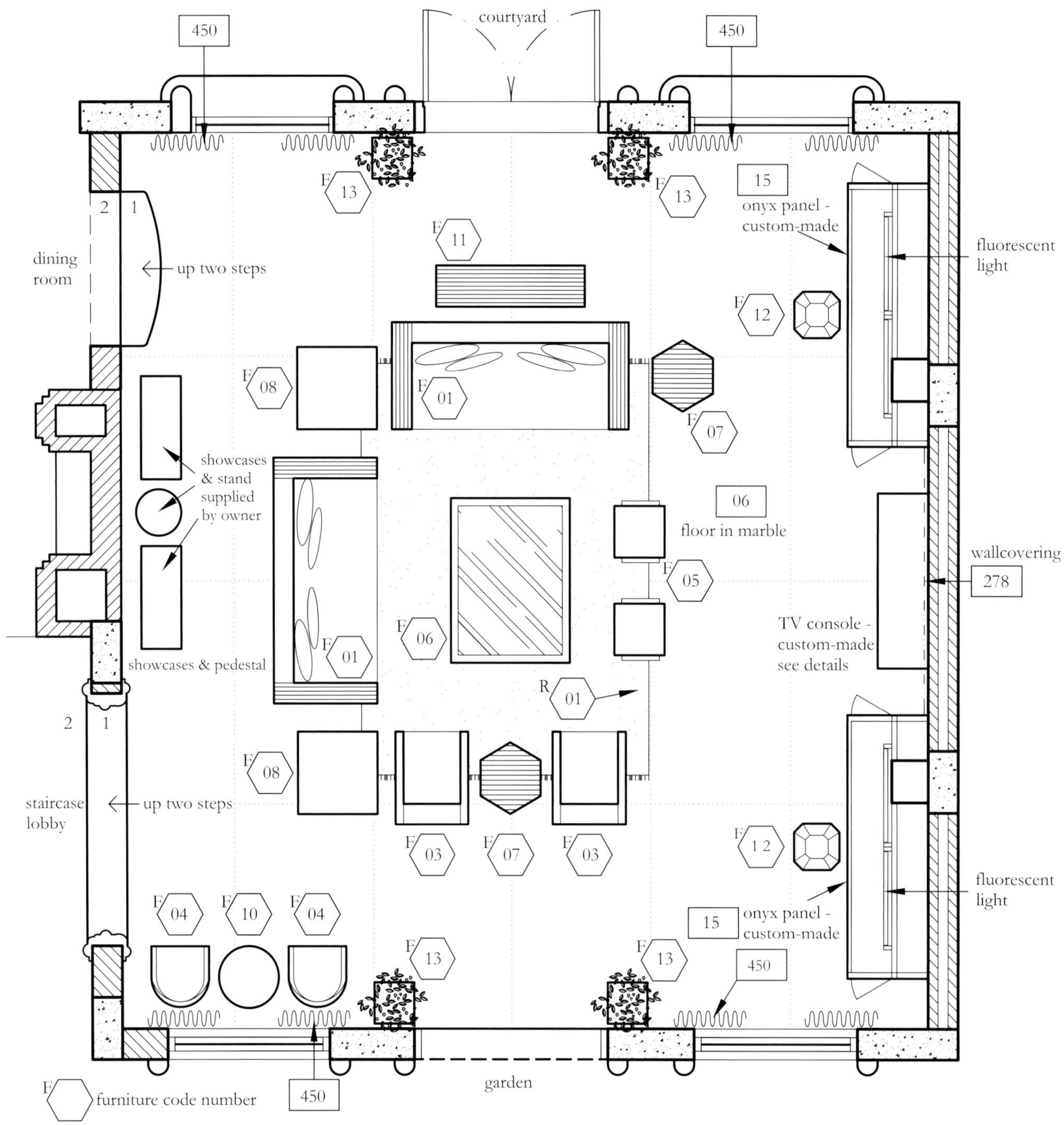

F furniture code number

R rug code number

finishes code number

PROJECT TITLE: HOUSE (2) in JAKARTA, INDONESIA	DRAWN BY	CHECKED	DATE	address 1 address 2 address 3 postal code email address
	PROJECT NO		SCALE	
DRAWING TITLE: FURNITURE LAYOUT PLAN	DRAWING NO 01/01		REVISION △	Interior Designers

CHAPTER 3

WRITING DECORATIVE LIGHTING FIXTURE SPECIFICATIONS

Preparing A Decorative Lighting Fixture Schedule Booklet

1. Title Sheet

    a. Project title
    b. Project location
    c. Project number
    d. Issue date

2. Decorative Lighting Sheet

    a. Decorative light fixture Description/Schedule Sheets that will list out all decorative lighting fixtures on the project, starting from L 01 item and onwards.
    b. Photograph of specified lighting item.
    c. Data Sheet of a designated lighting item, indicating details/dimensions/finishes.

3. List Of All Lighting Suppliers (similar to Furniture Suppliers list)

    a. All decorative lighting fixtures.
    b. All architectural light fixtures numbers from Lighting Designer's drawings.
    c. Include plans indicating dimensions/locations of all fittings.

Refer to pages 44 to 50.

Note: All architectural light fixtures (recessed or surface mounted on ceiling) will be according to lighting designer's drawing and specifications. Refer to lighting designer's drawings and specifications.

DECORATIVE LIGHTING FIXTURE SCHEDULE

HOUSE

for

MR. & MRS. X Y Z

in

(address)

(name of country)

(name of country)

PROJECT NO: 151/1610

ISSUE DATE: 12.12.2017

DATA SHEET DECORATIVE LIGHTING FIXTURE	DESCRIPTION FIRST STORY	L	SHEET NO OF PROJECT NO

LIGHTING CODE	STATUS	ITEM DESCRIPTION	QTY	LOCATION	DATE & REVISION	REMARKS
L 01	purchased by Client	manufacturer: MASIERO - OTTOCENTO model: VE847/PL3/40 size: 400mm-Ø x 80mm-H	01	Lift Lobby	△	ceiling mounted nickel plated clear crystal
L 02	by Lighting Contractor	manufacturer: BRIDGELUX ARRAYS LED model: HALO - 200 - 10W	48	various	△	recessed dimmable - 10 watts, Lumin 740Lm warm white - 3000K
L 03	ditto	manufacturer: HAFELE model: LOOK LED 2020 size: 65-Ø x 14.7mm-H - 3.2W	08	Kitchen + Bar	△	recessed dimmable - 3.2 watts, cool white - 4000K
L 04	ditto	manufacturer: BRIDGELUX ARRAYS LED model: DE - 200 - 7W size: 90-Ø x 77mm-H	17	Kitchen + Bar	△	recessed dimmable - 3.2 watts, cool white - 4000K
L 05	spare	-	-	-	- △	-
L 06	by Lighting Contractor	manufacturer: HAFELE model: LOOK LED 2021 size: 862mm-L x 12.9mm-H - 20.5W	04	Bar behind glass shelves	△	clip-on, attached behind glass, dimmable, nickel plated, 137Lm, 4000K, cool white
L 07	ditto	manufacturer: HAFELE model: LOOK LED 3018 size: 60mm Ø x 520mm long	02	night table - Master Bedroom	△	surface mounted, integrated dimmer on light head - cool white, 4000K - plastic silver
L 08	ditto	manufacturer: DALEN LED REMOTE model: DL - C37T size: 510mm-Ø x 91mm-H	06	Bedrooms	△	surface mounted, 56W, 2800 - 6000K (warm to cool white) - 6 level remote control - 3000Lm
L 15	purchased by Client	manufacturer: VOLTOLINA model: FLORA PLAFONIERA size: 500mm-Ø x 200mm-H	02	Master Bedroom	△	ceiling mounted, 4 x E27 75W, nickel plated, clear glass
L 17	ditto	manufacturer: MASIERO - OTTOCENTO model: VE847/A1 size: 120mm-Ø x 150mm-H	02	Lift Lobby	△	wall light, nickel plated, clear crystal
L 19	by Lighting Contractor	manufacturer: MOISE INC model: SINA-2 size: 88mm-W x 65mm-D x 380mm-H	02	Bath Room	△	2 x E14, 40W metal + opal Glass - ceiling mounted
L 21	purchased by Client	manufacturer: MOROSINI - EVI STYLE model: KARAT S5L size: 148mm-L x 65mm-W x 2000mm-H	01	Dining Corridor	△	Hanging light, fine fittings on one ceiling plate, polished chrome + clear crystal
L 22	ditto	manufacturer: MOROSINI - EVI STYLE model: KARAT PA2	02	Dining Corridor	△	Wall light, polished chrome + clear crystal
L 18	ditto	custom-made chandelier by chandelier supplier	01	Living Room		size: 900mm-Ø x 600mm-H - refer to drawings

PROJECT TITLE:	REV	REVISIONS/ISSUES	DATE	REV	REVISIONS/ISSUES	DATE
	△			△		
DRAWING TITLE: DECORATIVE LIGHTING DESCRIPTION / SCHEDULE	△			△		
	△			△		

company name, address, telephone number, fax number, email address

DATA SHEET DECORATIVE LIGHTING FIXTURES	AREA/LOCATION FIRST STORY	L	SHEET NO 1 OF 1 TOTAL QTY:

to put in pictures of light fittings L 01	L 02	L 03
L 04	L 06	L 07
L 08	L 15	L 17
L 19	L 21	L 22

PROJECT TITLE:	DRAWN BY	CHECKED	DATE	address 1 address 2 address 3 postal code email address
	PROJECT NO		SCALE	
DRAWING TITLE: IMAGES OF SELECTED LIGHTING FIXTURES	DRAWING NO		REVISION △	Interior Designers

DATA SHEET	DESCRIPTION DECORATIVE LIGHTING FIXTURE	L 18	SHEET NO 1 OF 2 TOTAL QTY: 1

ILLUSTRATION:

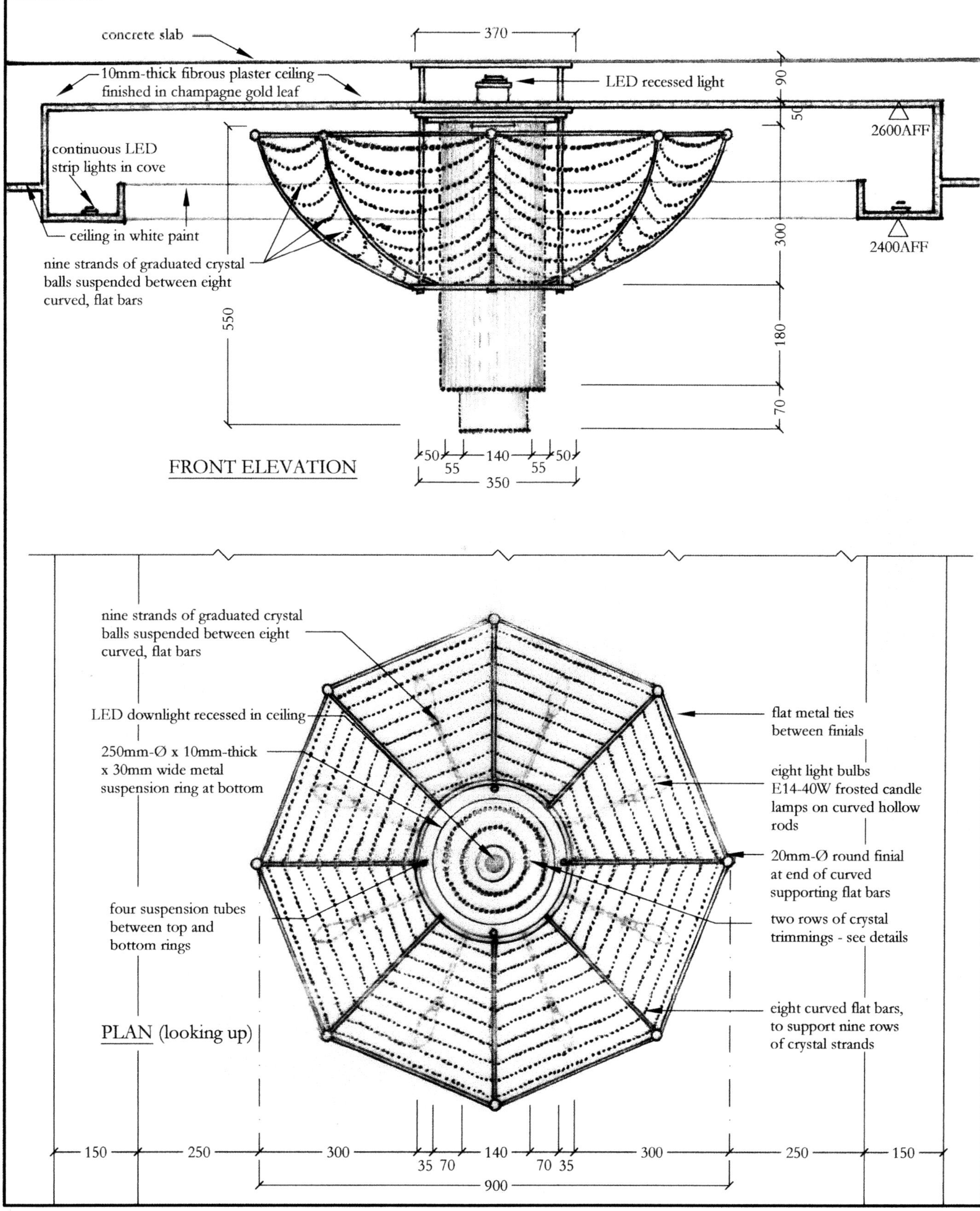

PROJECT TITLE:	DRAWN BY	CHECKED	DATE	address 1 address 2 address 3 postal code email address Interior Designers
	PROJECT NO		SCALE	
DRAWING TITLE: PLAN & ELEVATION of CUSTOM DESIGNED CHANDELIER	DRAWING NO		REVISION △	

DATA SHEET	DESCRIPTION DECORATIVE LIGHTING FIXTURE	L 18	SHEET NO 2 OF 2 TOTAL QTY: 1

ILLUSTRATION:

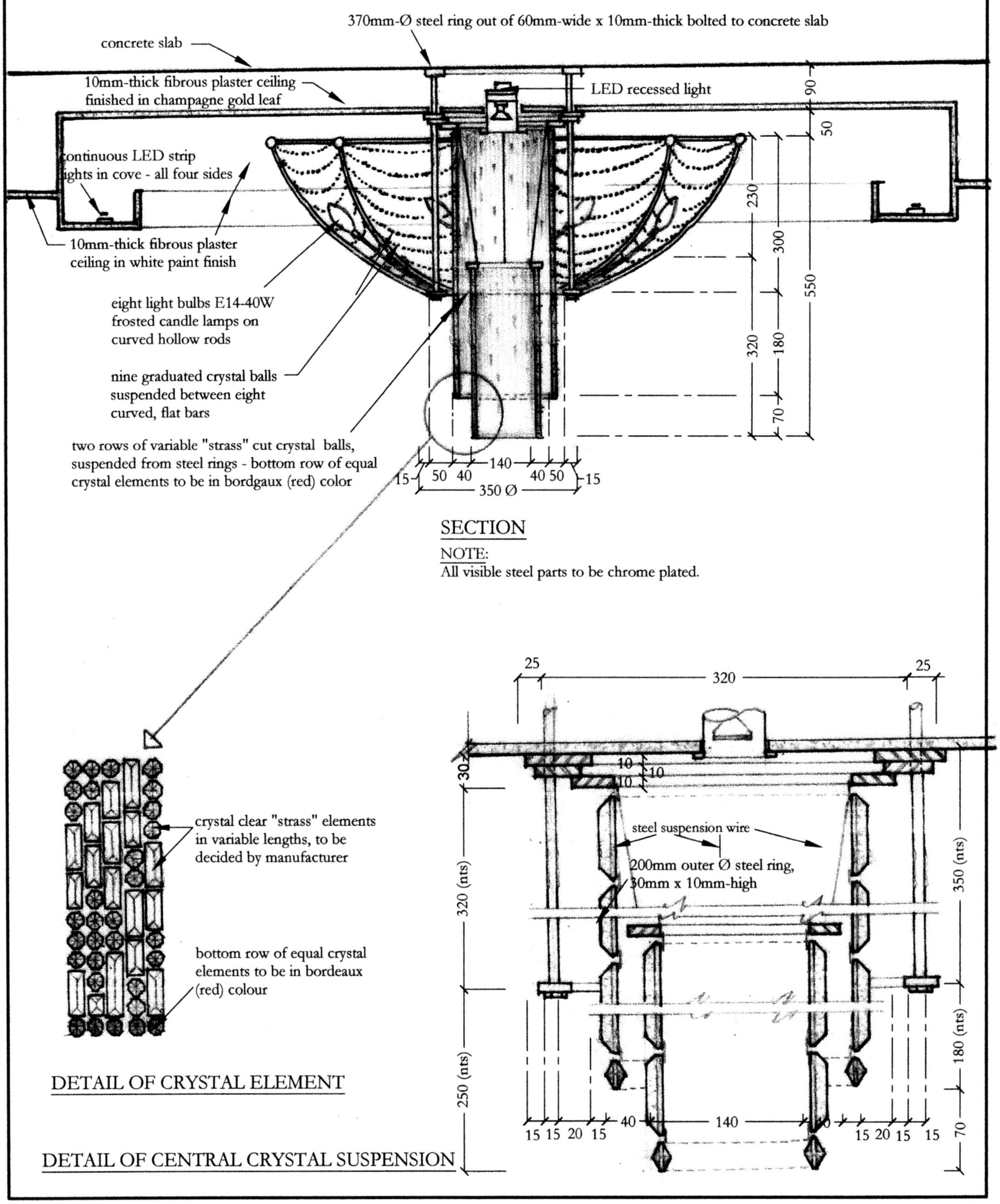

PROJECT TITLE:	DRAWN BY	CHECKED	DATE	address 1 address 2 address 3 postal code email address
	PROJECT NO		SCALE	
DRAWING TITLE: SECTION & DETAILS of CUSTOM DESIGNED CHANDELIER	DRAWING NO		REVISION △	Interior Designers

DATA SHEET	DESCRIPTION CEILING + LIGHTING PLAN		SHEET NO 2 OF 7 TOTAL QTY

ILLUSTRATION:

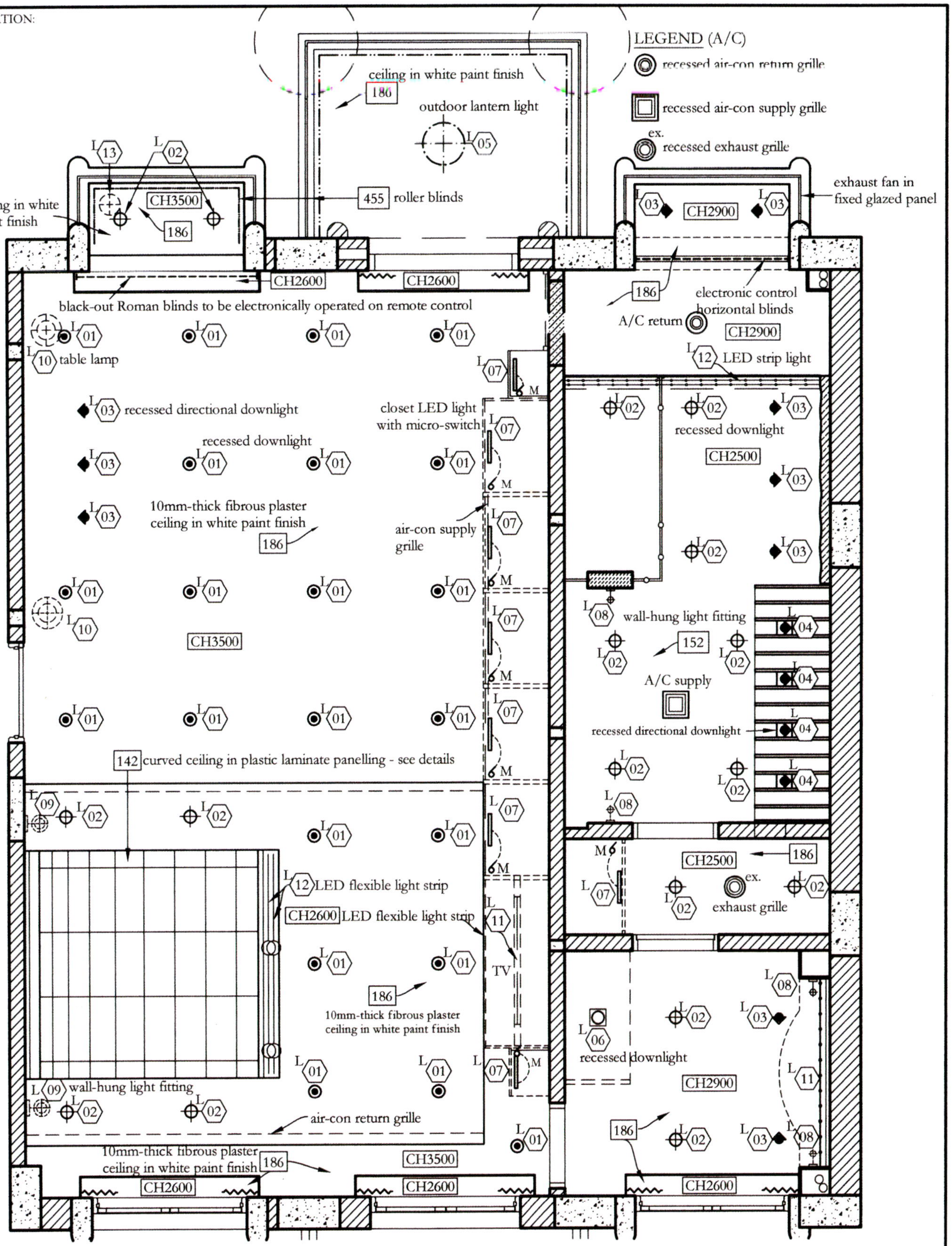

PROJECT TITLE: GRANNY'S SUITE - HOUSE (3) in JAKARTA, INDONESIA	DRAWN BY	CHECKED	DATE	*address 1* *address 2* *address 3* *postal code* *email address*
	PROJECT NO		SCALE	
DRAWING TITLE: REFLECTED CEILING + LIGHTING LAYOUT PLAN	DRAWING NO 01/02		REVISION △	Interior Designers

Detail of a chandelier from a house in Jakarta, Indonesia.

CHAPTER 4

RESIDENTIAL INTERIORS

1. House (2) In Indonesia
    a. Furniture layout plan
    b. Reflected ceiling plan
    c. Elevation A
    d. Photographs - lounge room and bedroom
2. Apartment In Singapore
    a. Furniture layout plan
    b. Reflected ceiling plan
    c. Electrical layout plan
    d. Photograph - living/ dining room
    e. Photograph - living/ dining room

DATA SHEET	DESCRIPTION LIVING ROOM (1ST STORY)		SHEET NO 1 OF 3 TOTAL QTY

ILLUSTRATION:

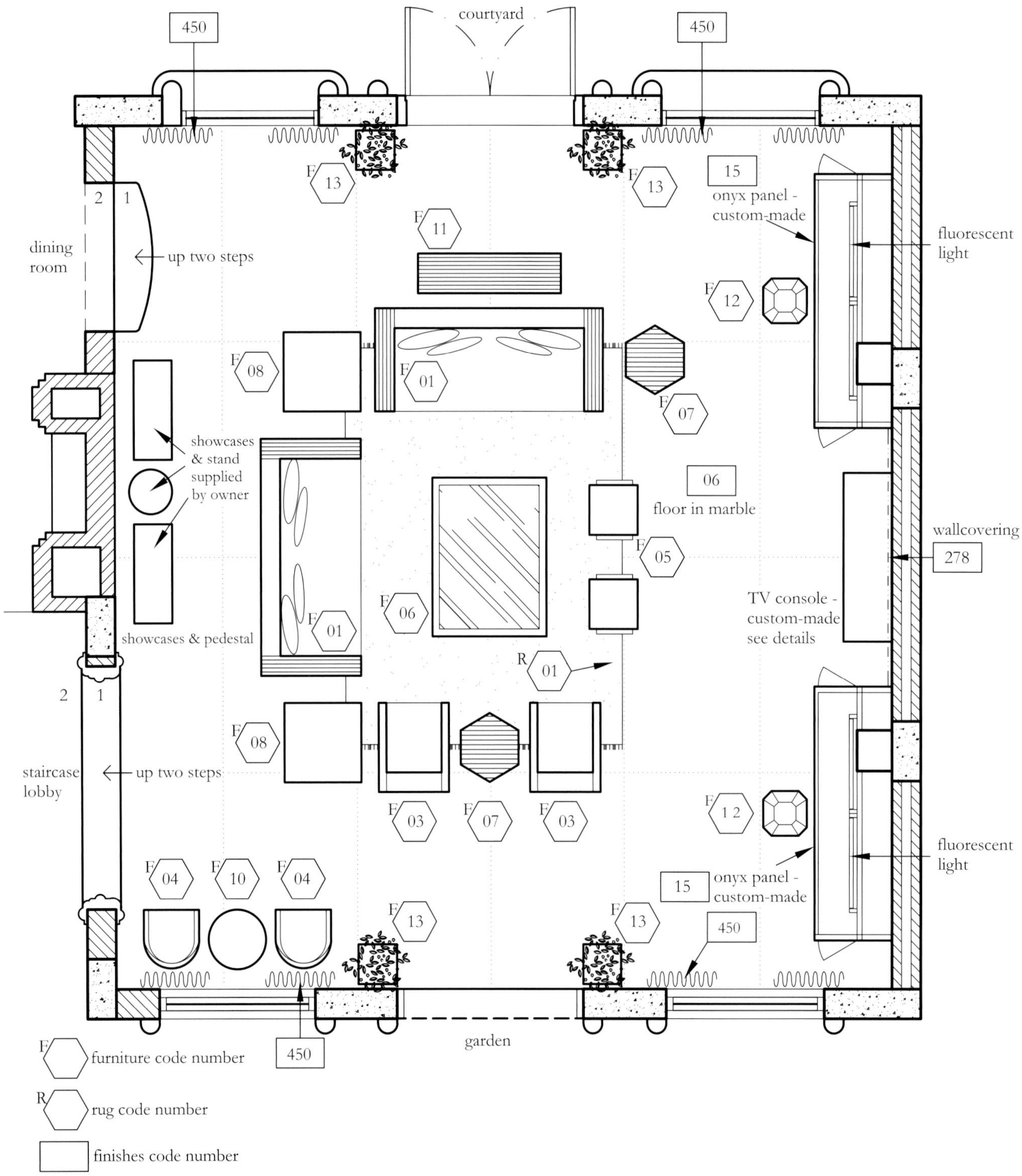

PROJECT TITLE: HOUSE (2) in JAKARTA, INDONESIA	DRAWN BY	CHECKED	DATE	address 1 address 2 address 3 postal code email address Interior Designers
	PROJECT NO		SCALE	
DRAWING TITLE: FURNITURE LAYOUT PLAN	DRAWING NO 01/01		REVISION △	

DATA SHEET	DESCRIPTION LIVING ROOM (FIRST STORY)		SHEET NO 2 OF 3 TOTAL QTY

ILLUSTRATION:

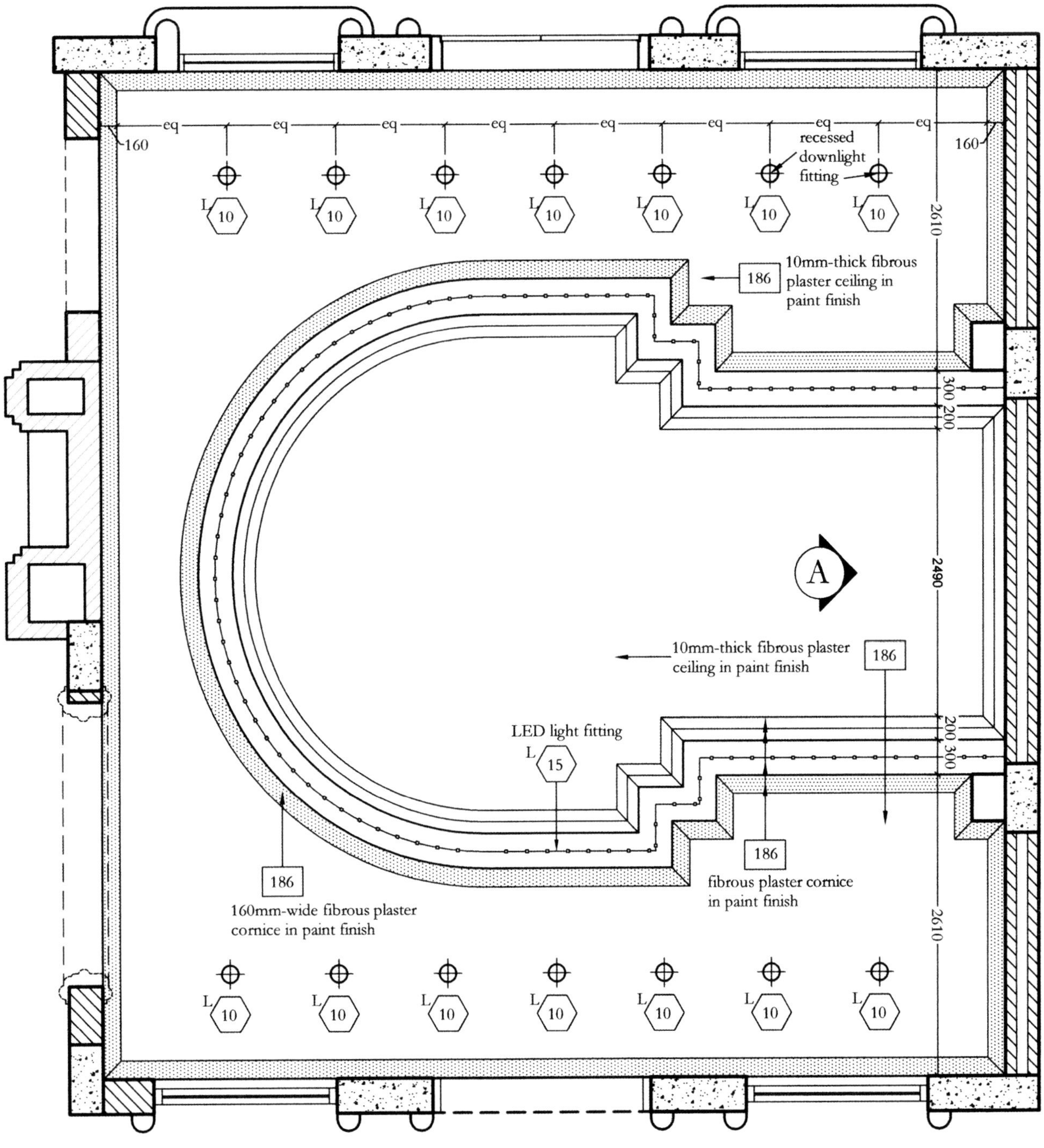

REFLECTED CEILING PLAN

- L ⬡ • light fitting code numbers
- ☐ • finishes code numbers

PROJECT TITLE: HOUSE (2) in JAKARTA, INDONESIA	DRAWN BY	CHECKED	DATE	address 1 address 2 address 3 postal code email address
	PROJECT NO		SCALE	
DRAWING TITLE: REFLECTED CEILING AND LIGHTING LAYOUT PLAN	DRAWING NO 01/02		REVISION △	Interior Designers

DATA SHEET	DESCRIPTION LIVING ROOM (FIRST STORY)	⬡	SHEET NO 3 OF 3 TOTAL QTY

ILLUSTRATION:

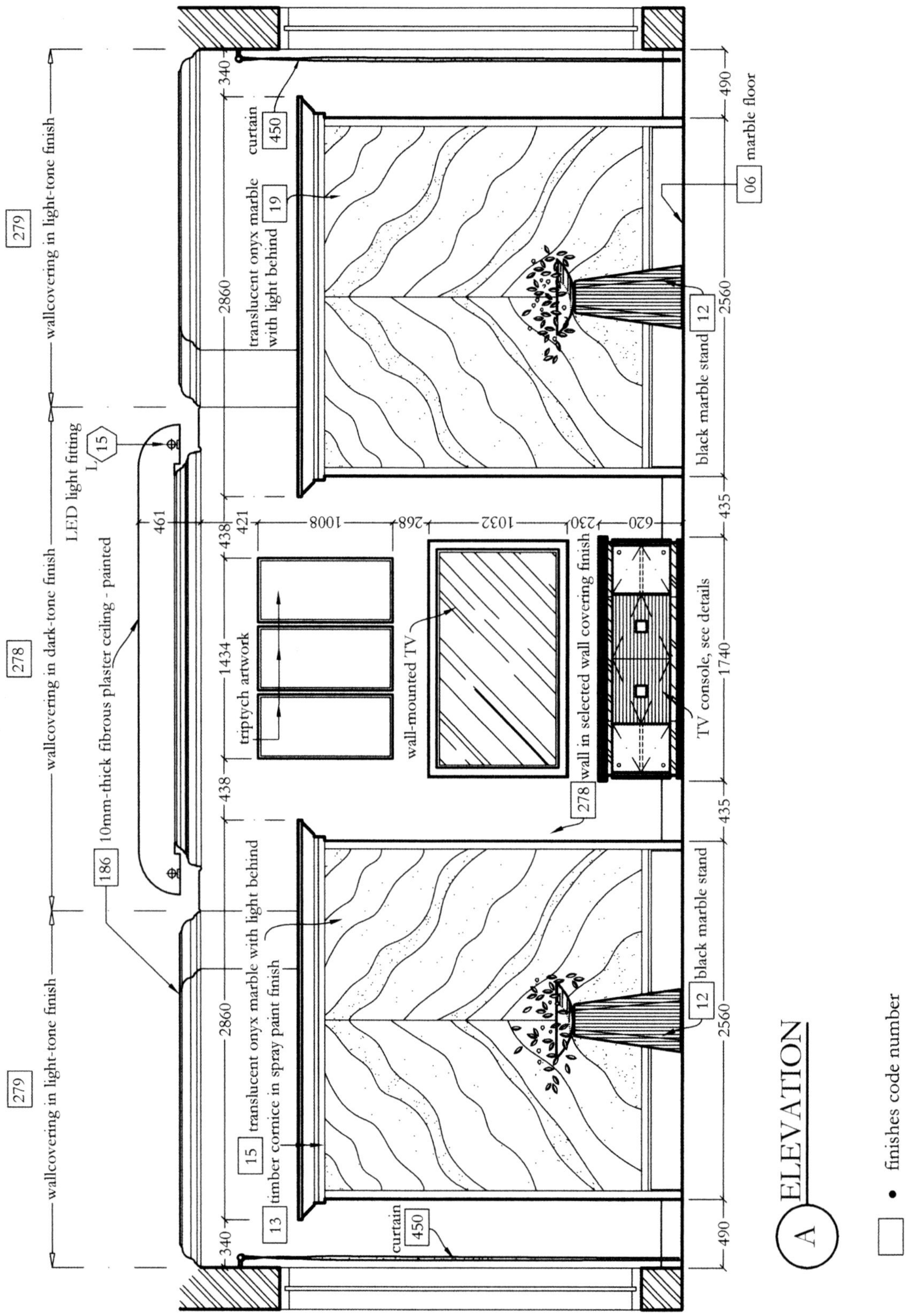

PROJECT TITLE: HOUSE (2) in JAKARTA, INDONESIA	DRAWN BY	CHECKED	DATE	address 1 address 2 address 3 postal code email address
	PROJECT NO		SCALE	
DRAWING TITLE: ELEVATION A	DRAWING NO 01/03		REVISION △	Interior Designers

Lounge area of house in Indonesia.

Bedroom indicating blackout curtains, sheers, dressing table, and TV cabinet for a house in Indonesia.

DATA SHEET	DESCRIPTION FLOOR PLAN	⬡	SHEET NO 1 OF 3 TOTAL QTY

ILLUSTRATION:

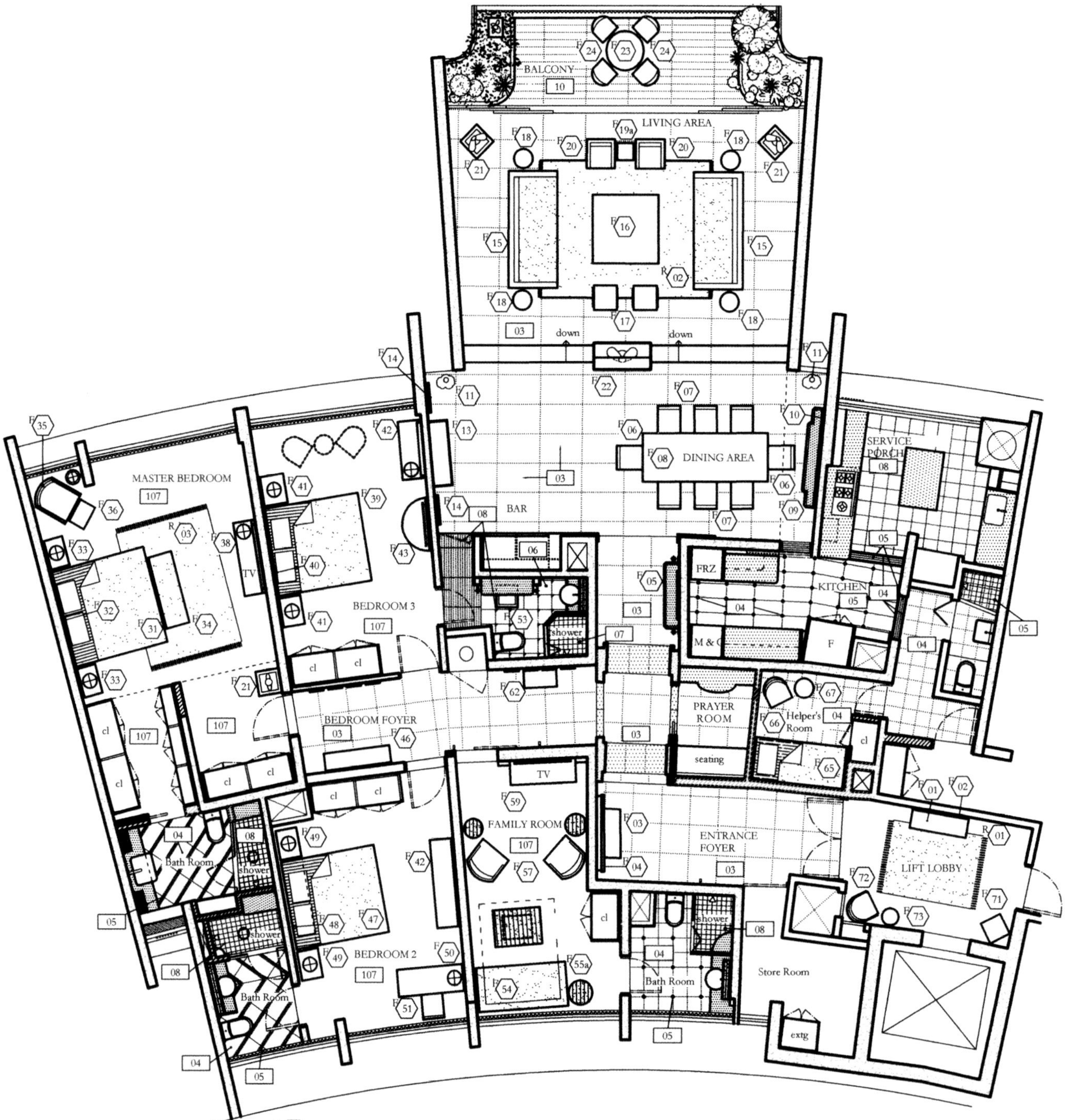

- F ⬡ furniture code number
- R ⬡ rug code number
- ☐ finishes code number

PROJECT TITLE: APARTMENT - SINGAPORE	DRAWN BY	CHECKED	DATE	address 1 address 2 address 3 postal code email address
	PROJECT NO		SCALE	
DRAWING TITLE: FURNITURE LAYOUT PLAN AND FLOOR FINISHES	DRAWING NO 01/01		REVISION △	Interior Designers

DATA SHEET	DESCRIPTION CEILING + LIGHTING PLAN	SHEET NO 2 OF 3 TOTAL QTY

ILLUSTRATION:

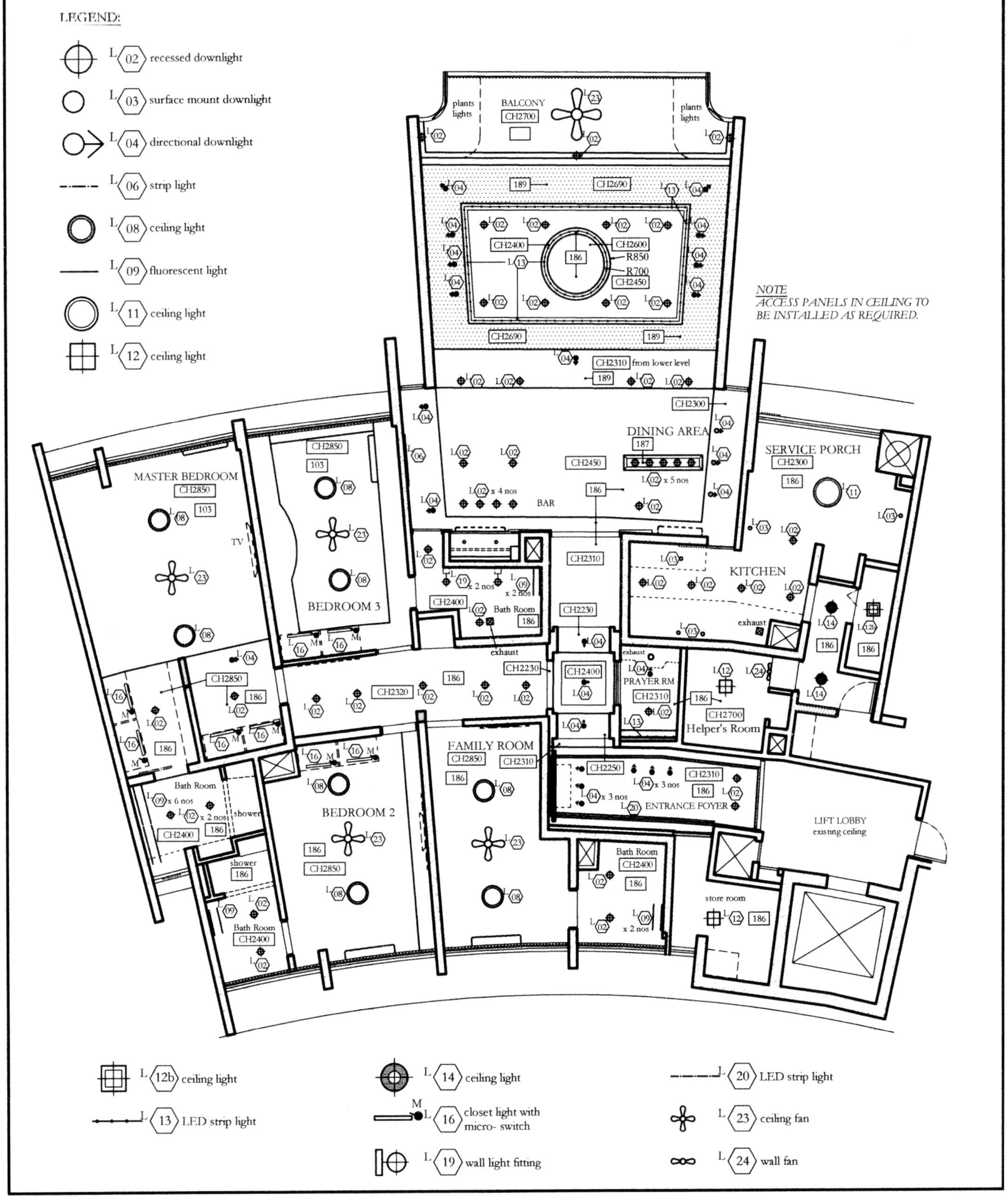

PROJECT TITLE: APARTMENT - SINGAPORE	DRAWN BY	CHECKED	DATE	address 1 address 2 address 3 postal code email address
	PROJECT NO		SCALE	
DRAWING TITLE: REFLECTED CEILING AND LIGHTING LAYOUT PLAN	DRAWING NO 01/02		REVISION △	Interior Designers

DATA SHEET	DESCRIPTION ELECTRICAL PLAN		SHEET NO 3 OF 3 TOTAL QTY

ILLUSTRATION:

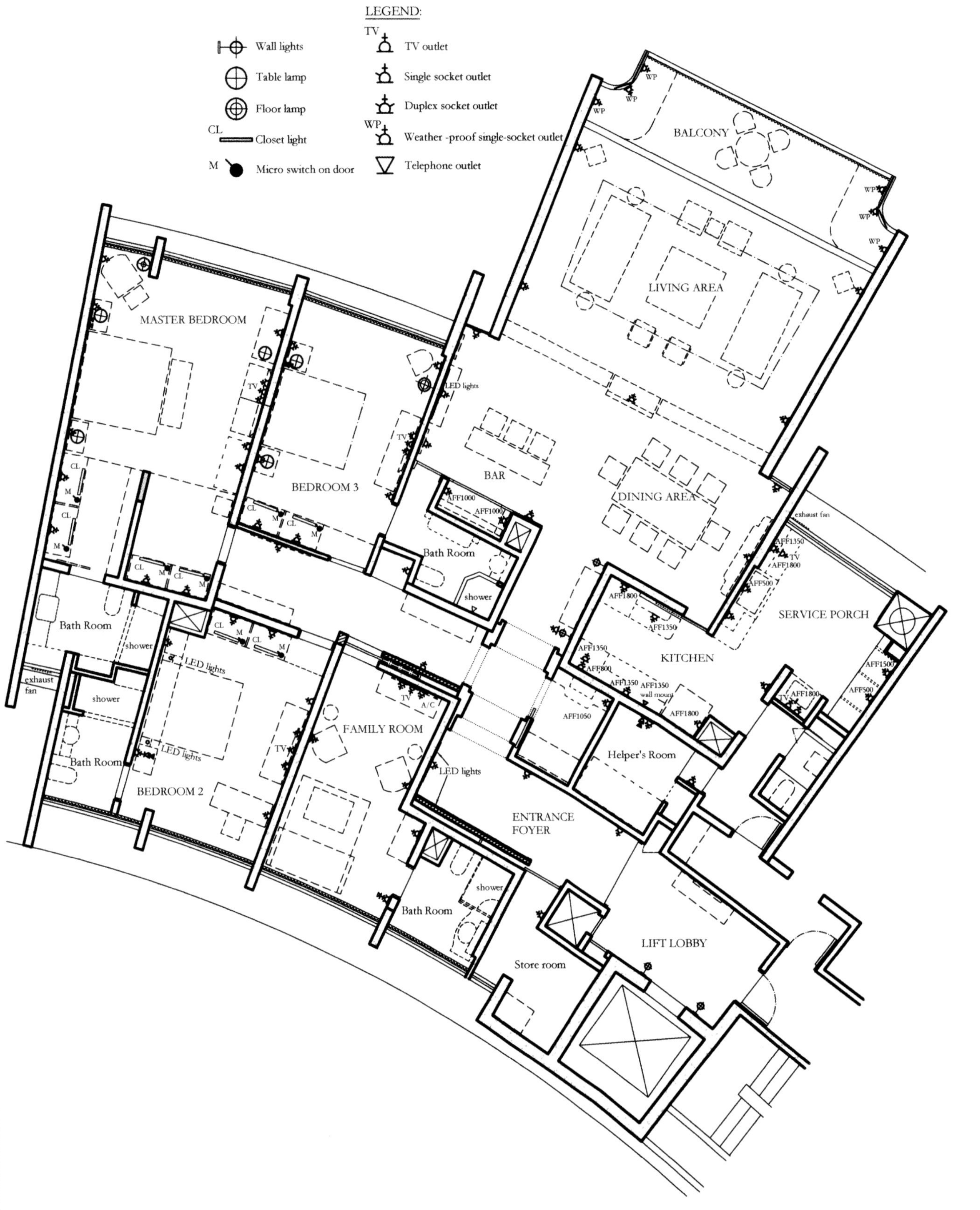

PROJECT TITLE: APARTMENT - SINGAPORE	DRAWN BY	CHECKED	DATE	address 1 address 2 address 3 postal code email address
	PROJECT NO		SCALE	
DRAWING TITLE: ELECTRICAL LAYOUT PLAN	DRAWING NO 01/03		REVISION △	Interior Designers

Living and dining room of an apartment in Singapore (artist's rendering).

Living and dining room of an apartment in Singapore (artist's rendering).

CHAPTER 5

LEISURE AND COMMERCIAL INTERIORS

1. Training Center
    a. Furniture Layout Plan
    b. Dimension Plan
    c. Ceiling and Lighting Plan
    d. Electrical/Phone Points Layout Plan
2. Restaurant (Indonesian Theme)
    a. Interior view
    b. View from entrance
3. Restaurant (Middle Eastern Theme)
    a. Table design
    b. View of interior
    c. Mural depicting restaurant theme
    d. Interior view
    e. Furniture layout plan - restaurant in Beijing, PRC.
    f. Ceiling layout plan - restaurant in Beijing, PRC.
    g. Elevations - restaurant in Beijing, PRC.
4. Orthopedic (1) Clinic
    a. Furniture Layout Plan
    b. Ceiling plan/Lighting/M & E Layout Plan
5. Orthopedic (2) Clinic
    a. Furniture layout plan

DATA SHEET	DESCRIPTION FLOOR PLAN	SHEET NO 1 OF 4 PROJECT NO

ILLUSTRATION:

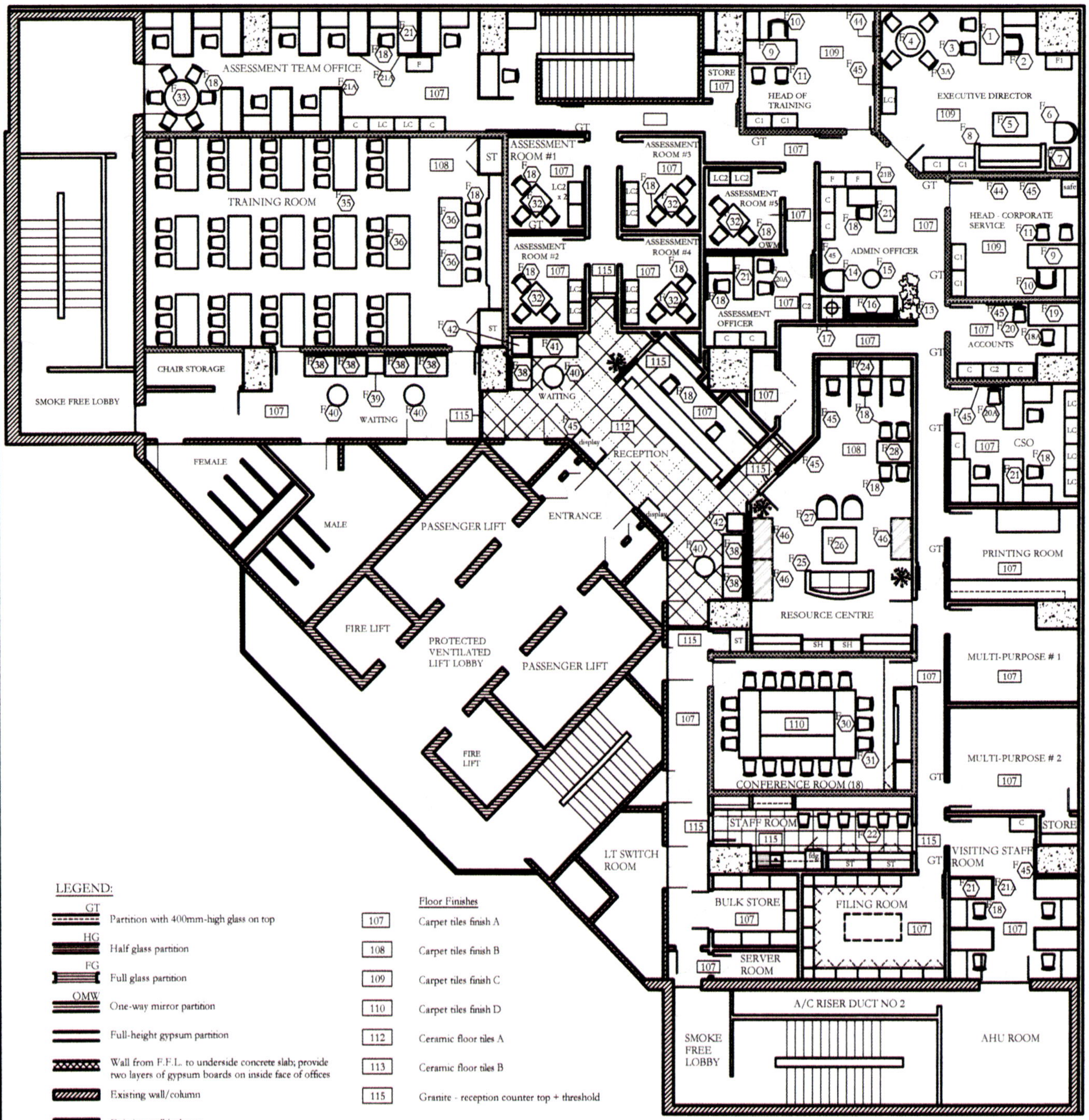

LEGEND:

- GT — Partition with 400mm-high glass on top
- HG — Half glass partition
- FG — Full glass partition
- OMW — One-way mirror partition
- Full-height gypsum partition
- Wall from F.F.L. to underside concrete slab; provide two layers of gypsum boards on inside face of offices
- Existing wall/column
- Existing wall/column

Floor Finishes

107	Carpet tiles finish A
108	Carpet tiles finish B
109	Carpet tiles finish C
110	Carpet tiles finish D
112	Ceramic floor tiles A
113	Ceramic floor tiles B
115	Granite - reception counter top + threshold

REMARKS: All walls to have fiberglass insulation for acoustics and 10mm-thick plasterboard on each side of the metal studs.

PROJECT TITLE: TRAINING CENTER	DRAWN BY	CHECKED	DATE	*address 1* *address 2* *address 3* *postal code* *email address*
	PROJECT NO		SCALE	
DRAWING TITLE: FURNITURE LAYOUT PLAN PLUS FLOOR FINISHES	DRAWING NO 01/01		REVISION △	Interior Designers

DATA SHEET	DESCRIPTION FLOOR PLAN	SHEET NO 2 OF 4 PROJECT NO

ILLUSTRATION:

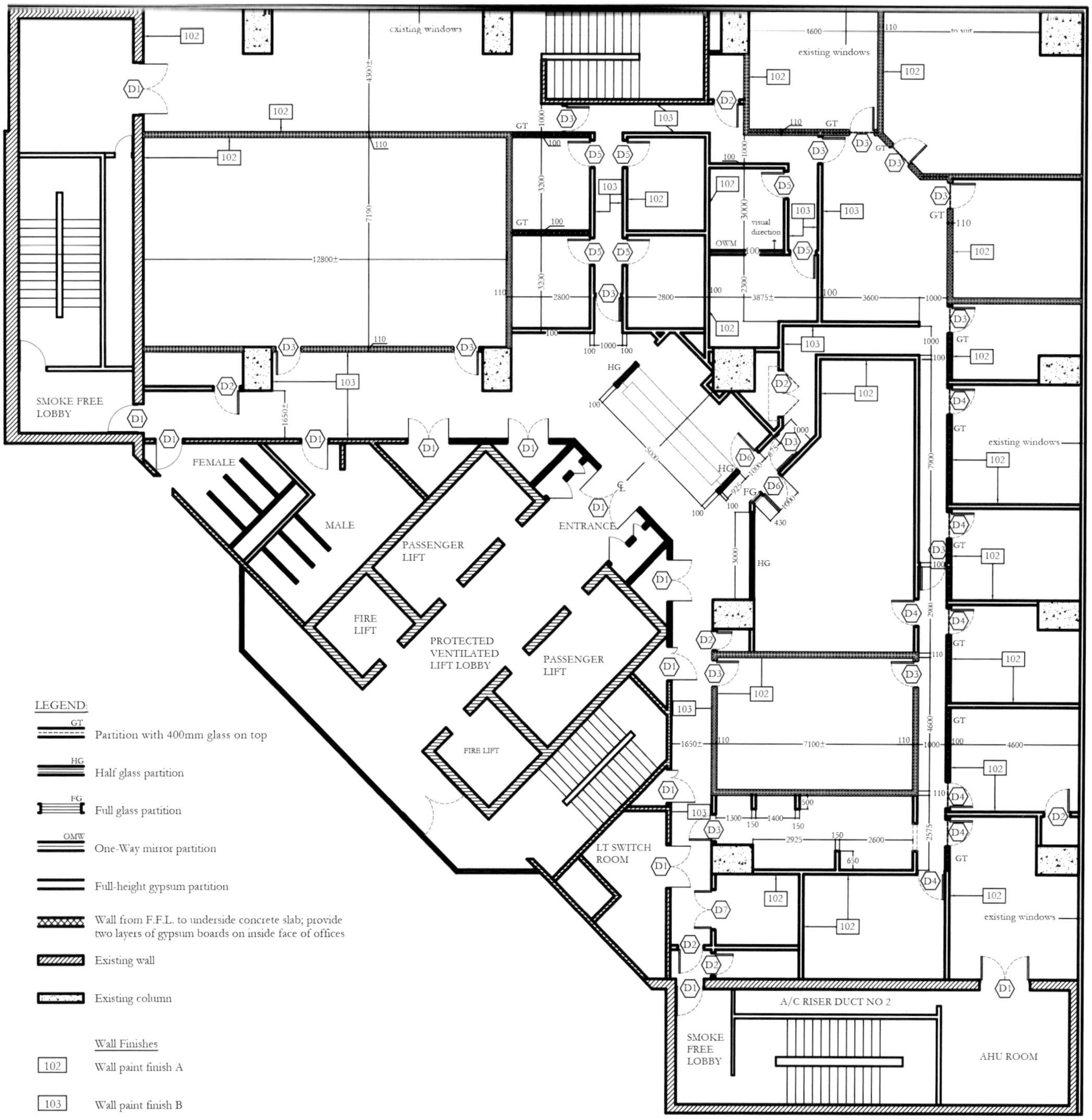

REMARKS: *All walls to have fiberglass insulation for accoustic and all doors to have 1000mm width rough opening.*

PROJECT TITLE: TRAINING CENTER	DRAWN BY	CHECKED	DATE	*address 1 address 2 address 3 postal code email address*
	PROJECT NO		SCALE	
DRAWING TITLE: DIMENSIONS/WALL FINISHES LAYOUT PLAN	DRAWING NO 01/02		REVISION △	Interior Designers

DATA SHEET	DESCRIPTION REFLECTED CEILING PLAN	SHEET NO 3 OF 4 PROJECT NO

ILLUSTRATION:

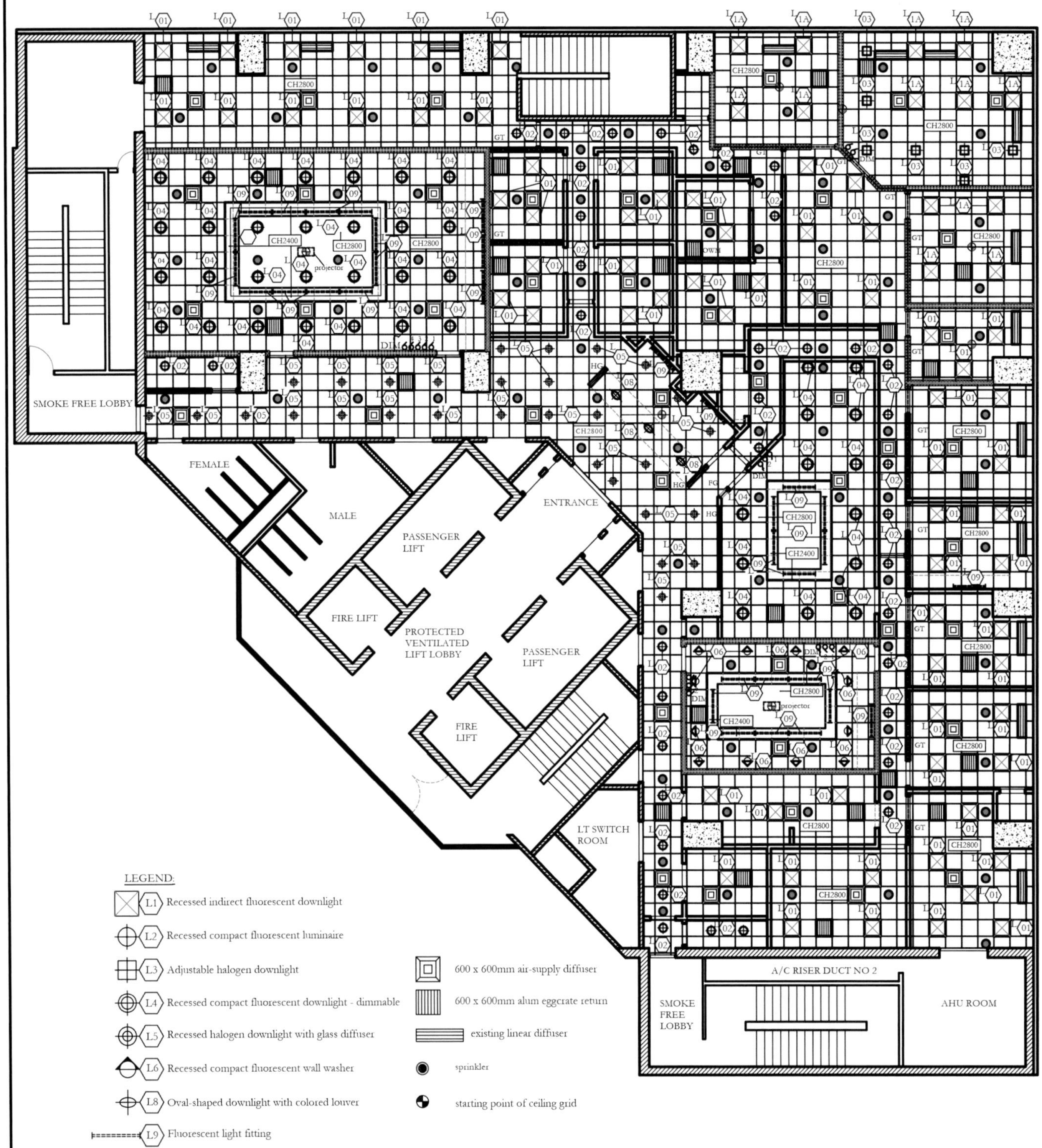

REMARKS: *Dropped ceiling in fire-retardant mineral fiber tiles, 600 x 600 x 15mm-thick; tiles in a lay-in exposed grid system (CH2800).*

PROJECT TITLE: TRAINING CENTER	DRAWN BY	CHECKED	DATE	*address 1* *address 2* *address 3* *postal code* *email address* Interior Designers
	PROJECT NO		SCALE	
DRAWING TITLE: REFLECTED CEILING PLAN PLUS LIGHTING/ AIR-CON / SPRINKLERS	DRAWING NO 01/03		REVISION △	

DATA SHEET	DESCRIPTION FLOOR PLAN	SHEET NO 4 OF 4 PROJECT NO

ILLUSTRATION:

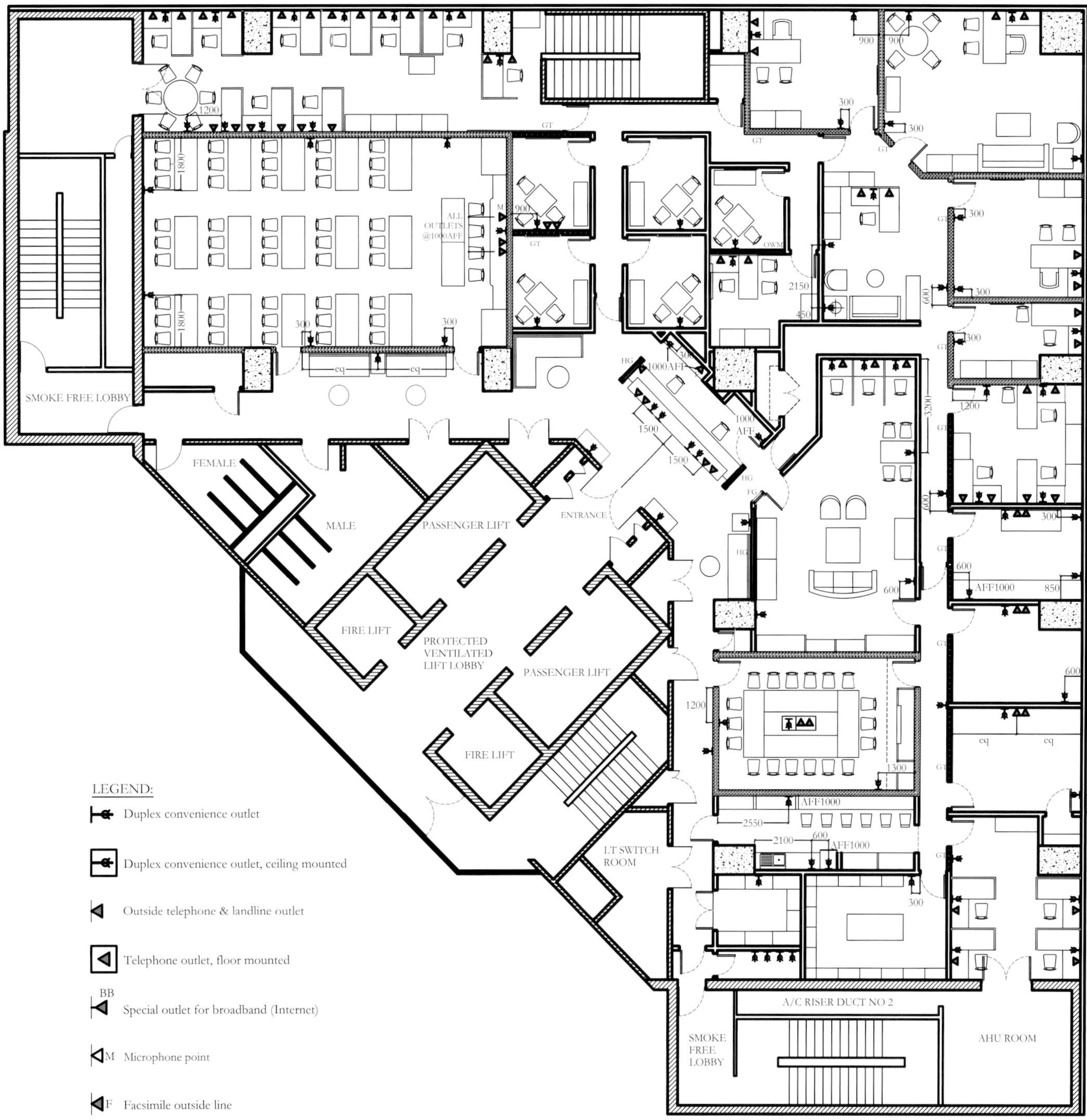

REMARKS: *All outlets are to be mounted 300mm AFF unless otherwise stated.*

PROJECT TITLE: TRAINING CENTER	DRAWN BY	CHECKED	DATE	*address 1* *address 2* *address 3* *postal code* *email address*
	PROJECT NO		SCALE	
DRAWING TITLE: ELECTRICAL/PHONE POINTS LAYOUT PLAN	DRAWING NO 01/04		REVISION △	Interior Designers

Interior view of a restaurant in Singapore.

Entrance view of a restaurant in Singapore.

Detail of table at restaurant in Singapore.

Interior view of a restaurant in Singapore.

Above: Interior view of a restaurant in Singapore.

Right: Mural in restaurant in Singapore.

DATA SHEET	DESCRIPTION RESTAURANT	SHEET NO 1 OF 3 TOTAL QTY:

ILLUSTRATION:

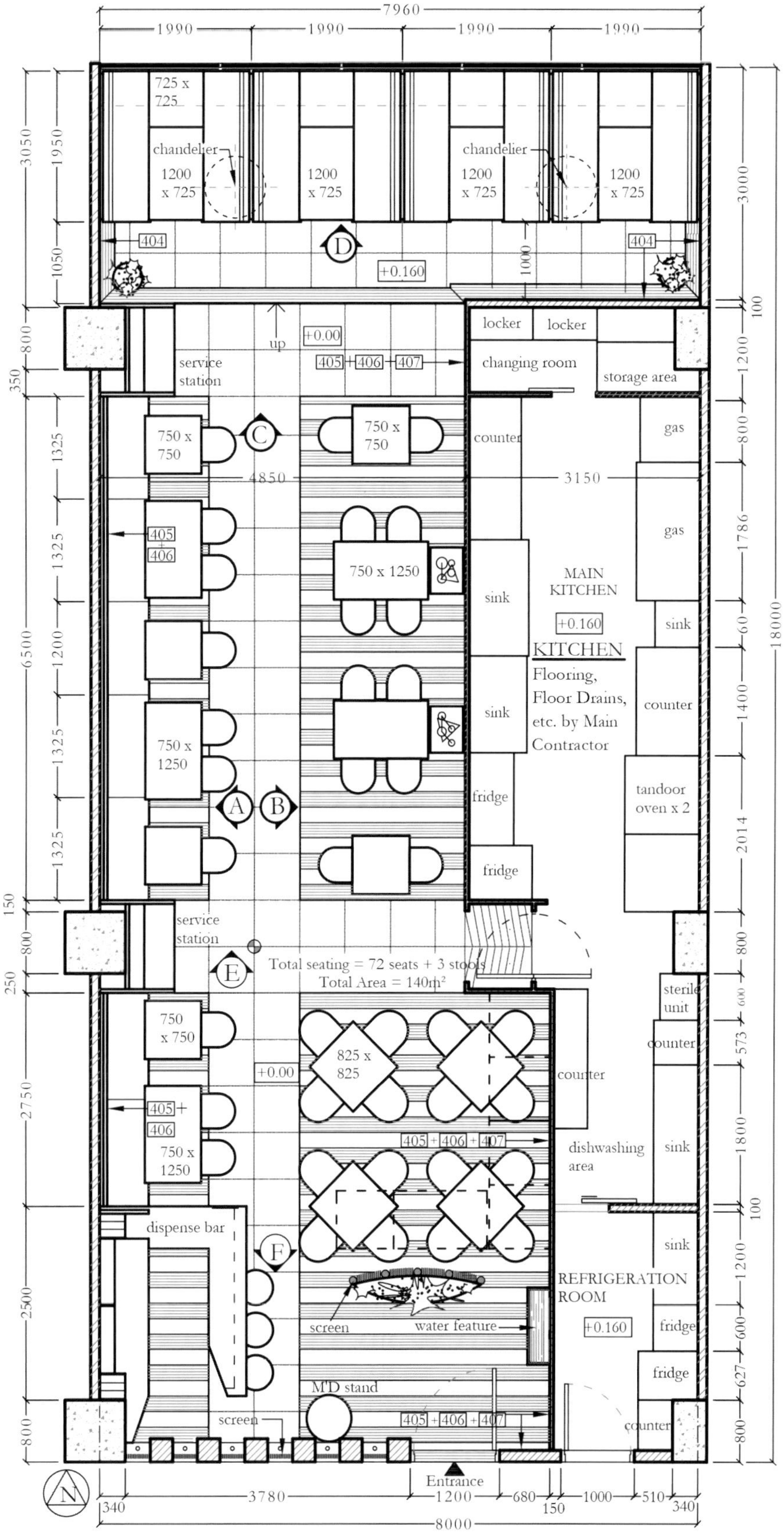

PROJECT TITLE: RESTAURANT IN BEIJING, PRC	DRAWN BY	CHECKED	DATE	address 1 address 2 address 3 postal code email address
	PROJECT NO		SCALE	
DRAWING TITLE: FURNITURE LAYOUT PLAN	DRAWING NO		REVISION △	Interior Designers

DATA SHEET	DESCRIPTION RESTAURANT	SHEET NO 2 OF 3 TOTAL QTY:

ILLUSTRATION:

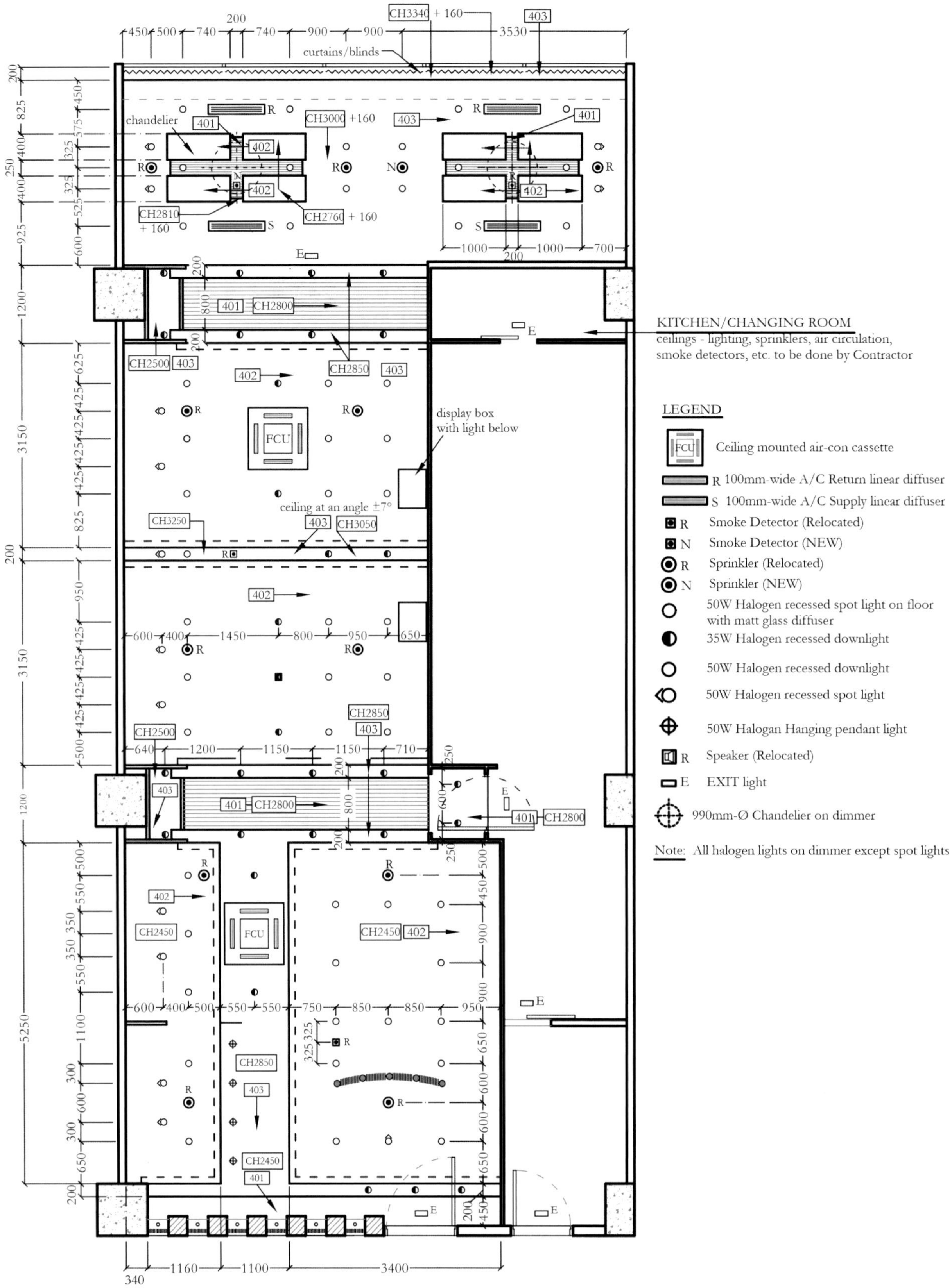

PROJECT TITLE: RESTAURANT IN BEIJING, PRC	DRAWN BY	CHECKED	DATE	address 1 address 2 address 3 postal code email address Interior Designers
	PROJECT NO		SCALE	
DRAWING TITLE: REFLECTED CEILING LAYOUT PLAN	DRAWING NO		REVISION △	

DATA SHEET	DESCRIPTION RESTAURANT	SHEET NO 3 OF 3 TOTAL QTY:

ILLUSTRATION:

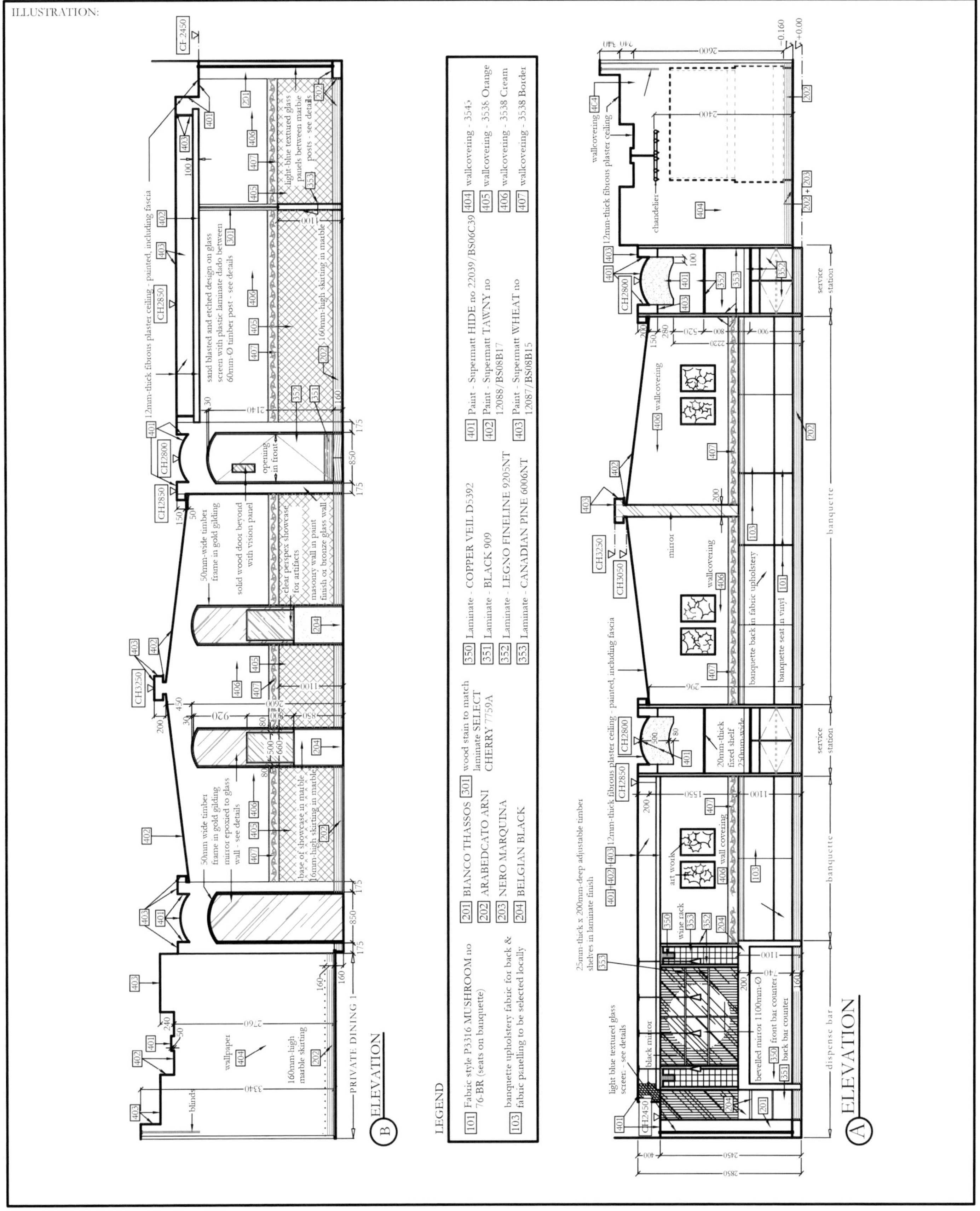

PROJECT TITLE: RESTAURANT IN BEIJING, PRC	DRAWN BY	CHECKED	DATE	address 1 address 2 address 3 postal code email address
	PROJECT NO		SCALE	
DRAWING TITLE: ELEVATIONS A AND B	DRAWING NO		REVISION △	Interior Designers

DATA SHEET	DESCRIPTION CLINIC		SHEET NO 1 OF 2 TOTAL QTY

ILLUSTRATION:

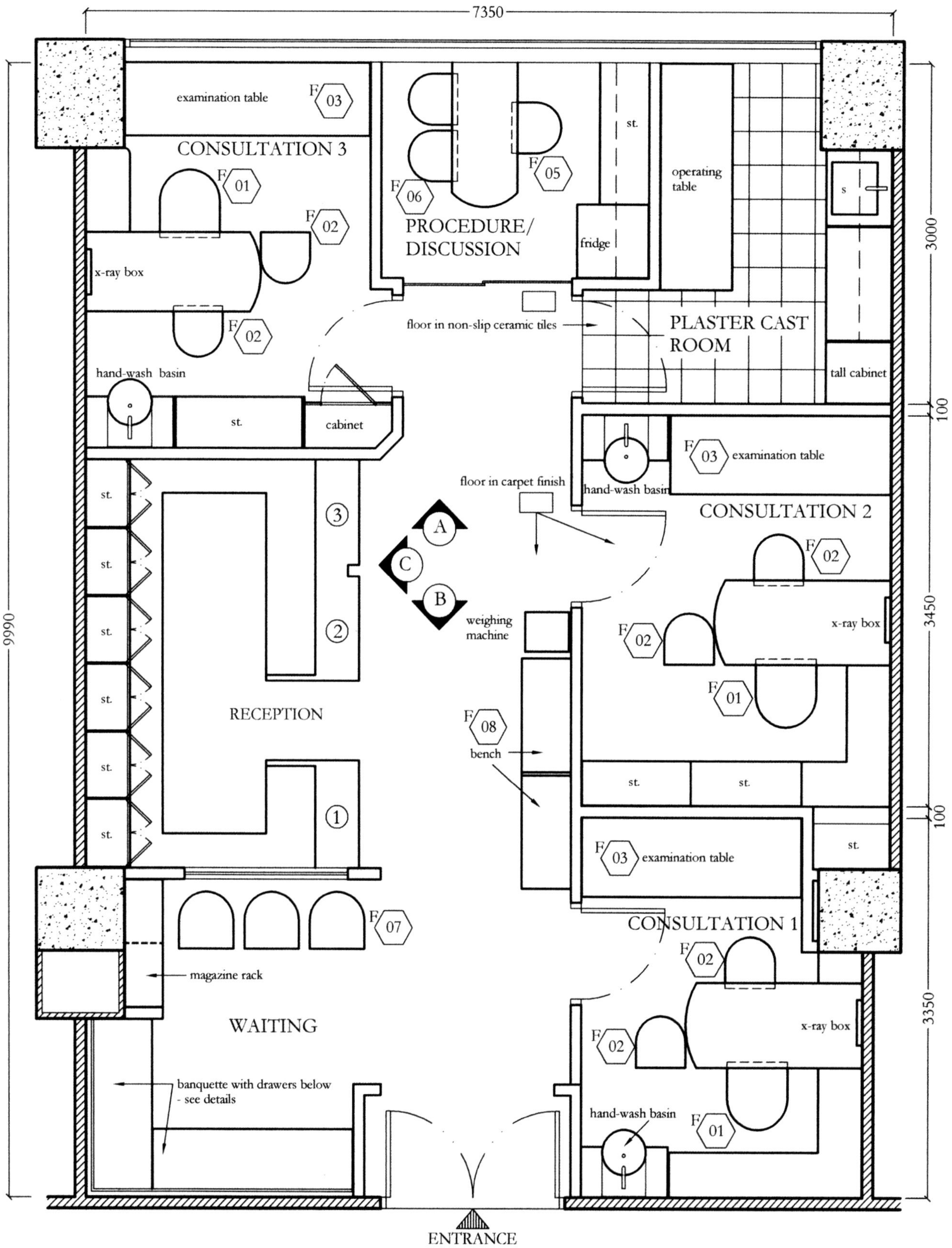

PROJECT TITLE: ORTHOPEDIC CLINIC (1)	DRAWN BY	CHECKED	DATE	address 1 address 2 address 3 postal code email address
DRAWING TITLE: FURNITURE LAYOUT PLAN	PROJECT NO		SCALE	
	DRAWING NO 01/01		REVISION △	Interior Designers

DATA SHEET	DESCRIPTION CLINIC		SHEET NO 2 OF 2 TOTAL QTY

ILLUSTRATION:

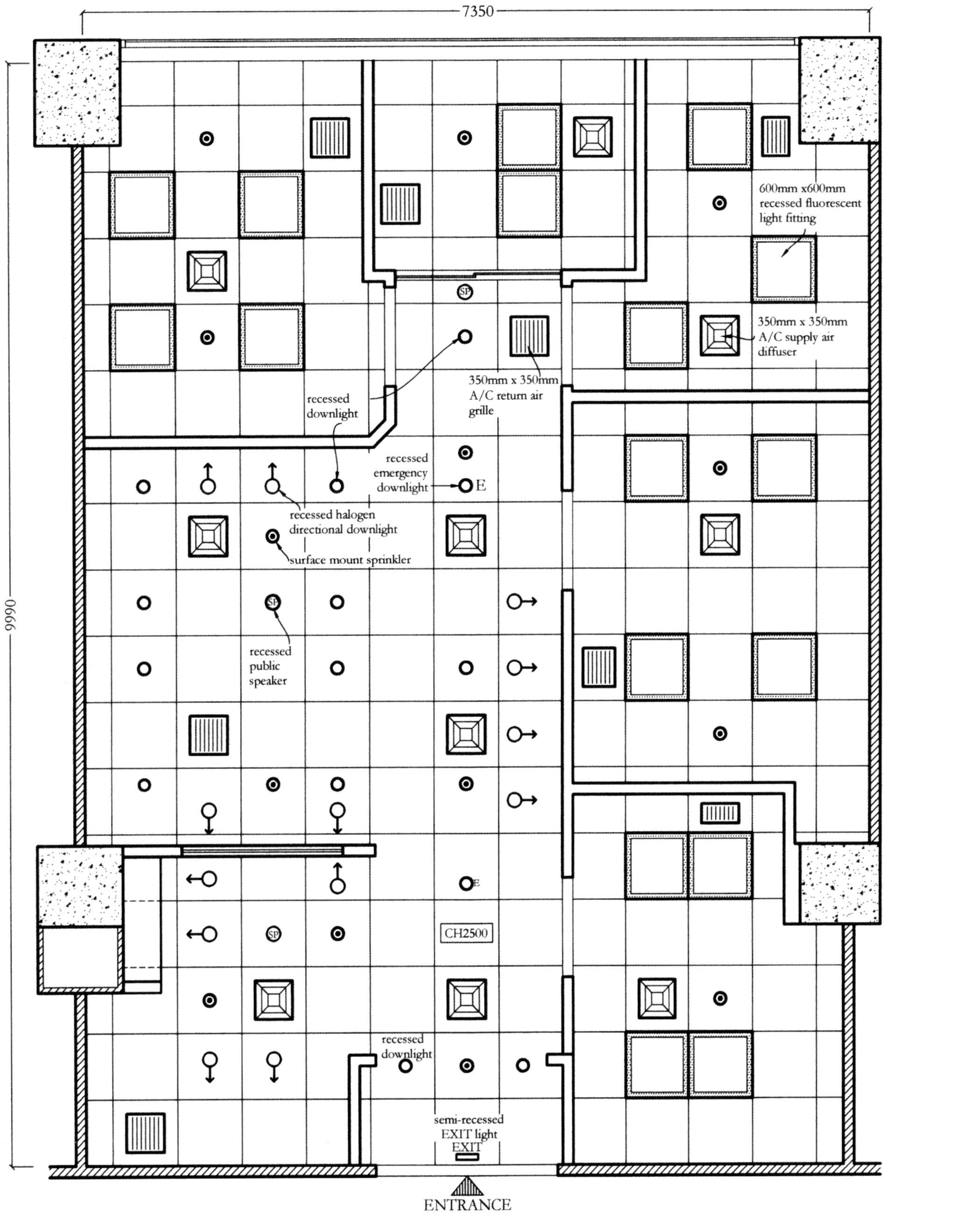

PROJECT TITLE: ORTHOPEDIC CLINIC (1)	DRAWN BY	CHECKED	DATE	address 1 address 2 address 3 postal code email address
	PROJECT NO		SCALE	
DRAWING TITLE: REFLECTED CEILING/LIGHTING/M&E LAYOUT PLAN	DRAWING NO 01/02		REVISION △	Interior Designers

DATA SHEET	DESCRIPTION CLINIC		SHEET NO 1 OF 1 TOTAL QTY

ILLUSTRATION:

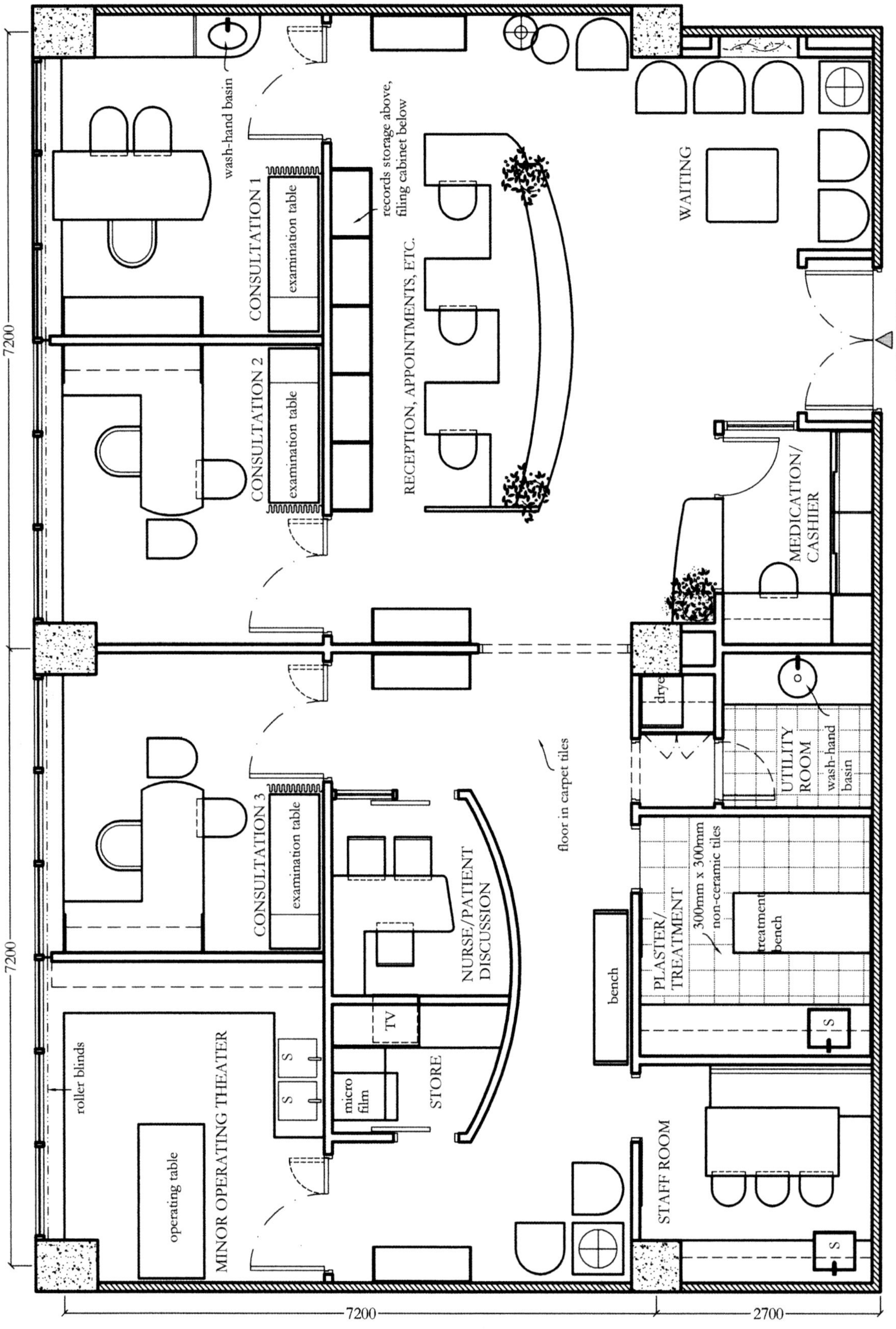

PROJECT TITLE: ORTHOPEDIC CLINIC (2)	DRAWN BY	CHECKED	DATE	address 1 address 2 address 3 postal code email address
	PROJECT NO		SCALE	
DRAWING TITLE: FURNITURE LAYOUT PLAN	DRAWING NO 01/01		REVISION △	Interior Designers

CHAPTER 6

WINDOW TREATMENTS

1. Write-up of window treatments and window dressing
2. Measuring fabric for curtains
3. Elevation plus section of roller blinds
4. Plan plus elevation of valance and Roman blinds
5. Detail through drapery pelmet - section 1
6. Detail through drapery pelmet - section 2
7. Elevation indicating roller blinds, fixed curtain, tie-backs and valance
8. Elevation of window treatment indicating fixed curtain, swag and tail
9. Curtain and valance headings

WINDOW TREATMENTS AND WINDOW DRESSING

Windows are the lifelines of an interior space. If you do not have an opening in an interior space, the space remains in darkness (unless you have artificial light), and is dim and dingy without fresh air (unless you have air-conditioning or bring in forced air). It is up to the designer how big or small to make the opening or window. Dressing up the opening is the biggest challenge for the interior space, and, if done successfully and tastefully, it can become the focal point and mood of the space.

One of the most successful interpretations of a window dressing is the import into the design elements of traditional applications from classical principles, like proportions of width to height of the opening, and the selection of fabric, color, texture, and pattern that will suit the space and relate to the theme of the interior. With any window dressing, the fullness in the width of the curtain will depend on how full a gather is required. With heavier fabric a minimum amount of twice the width of the window is necessary. With a lighter dress fabric, with a minimum amount of two and a half times the width of the window is necessary. With a light weight, sheer fabric, two and a half to three times the width of the fabric, will be necessary. If the curtain is in front of the window opening, a 100mm to 150mm overlap, beyond the edge of the opening is required to allow for blackout. If a curtain or blind is set recessed inside of the window opening, overlap is unnecessary and impractical. Allow the height of the curtain to float 30mm above the finished floor for ease of cleaning the floor, unless the design calls for the curtain to sit on the floor.

Tie-backs, are a very useful detail when designing a curtain, to let in or cut out daylight. When curtains are tied-up against the wall with tie-backs, they give an interesting form to the curtain by creating dramatic swags, and tails. The higher the tie-back is installed, the more daylight will enter the room.

Lining and interlining, form an intrinsic part of a curtain or blind. Expensive dress fabrics should always be lined to give body and weight to the curtain or blind and, most importantly, it protects the fabric from fading due to the sun and inclement weather. Direct sunlight breaks down natural fibers like silk, wool, linen, and cotton. Linings can match the base color of the dress curtain, or can be in a lighter tone of beige, or cream, or white. Swags, tails and valances should always be lined to give them body and stiffness. Sheers and light weight fabrics should not be lined as they are meant to let in diffused light. Sheers should be a blend of silk and polyester, to provide durability, and longer visible life. Weights should always be used on the bottom edges of drapes, including sheers and blinds.

Headings or pleats always define the character of the curtains. There are various kinds of headings, depending on the style of curtain being created. They are "French" or "triple pleat", "goblet pleats", "slot heading" or "pencil pleats", or "gathered headings". Note that unless the window treatment is recessed, the curtain needs to be returned at the sides, for a neat finish, and to cut-off daylight. Roman blinds tend to be architectural in their make-up. They lie flat in front of a window opening, either outside or inside the window niche. They are operated by a single cord passed through rings attached to the back of the blind fabric. Half-round timber dowels are slotted into the fabric from the back at approximately 300mm on centers. If the width of the fabric is less than the width of the window, the fabric has to be joined, and the joint concealed by a contrasting fabric tape.

Following are some of the window treatments that can be adopted for a given interior space. The nomenclature of the various design elements of the curtain treatments is given at the side of the various treatments.

DATA SHEET	DESCRIPTION WINDOW TREATMENT		SHEET NO OF TOTAL QTY:

ILLUSTRATION:

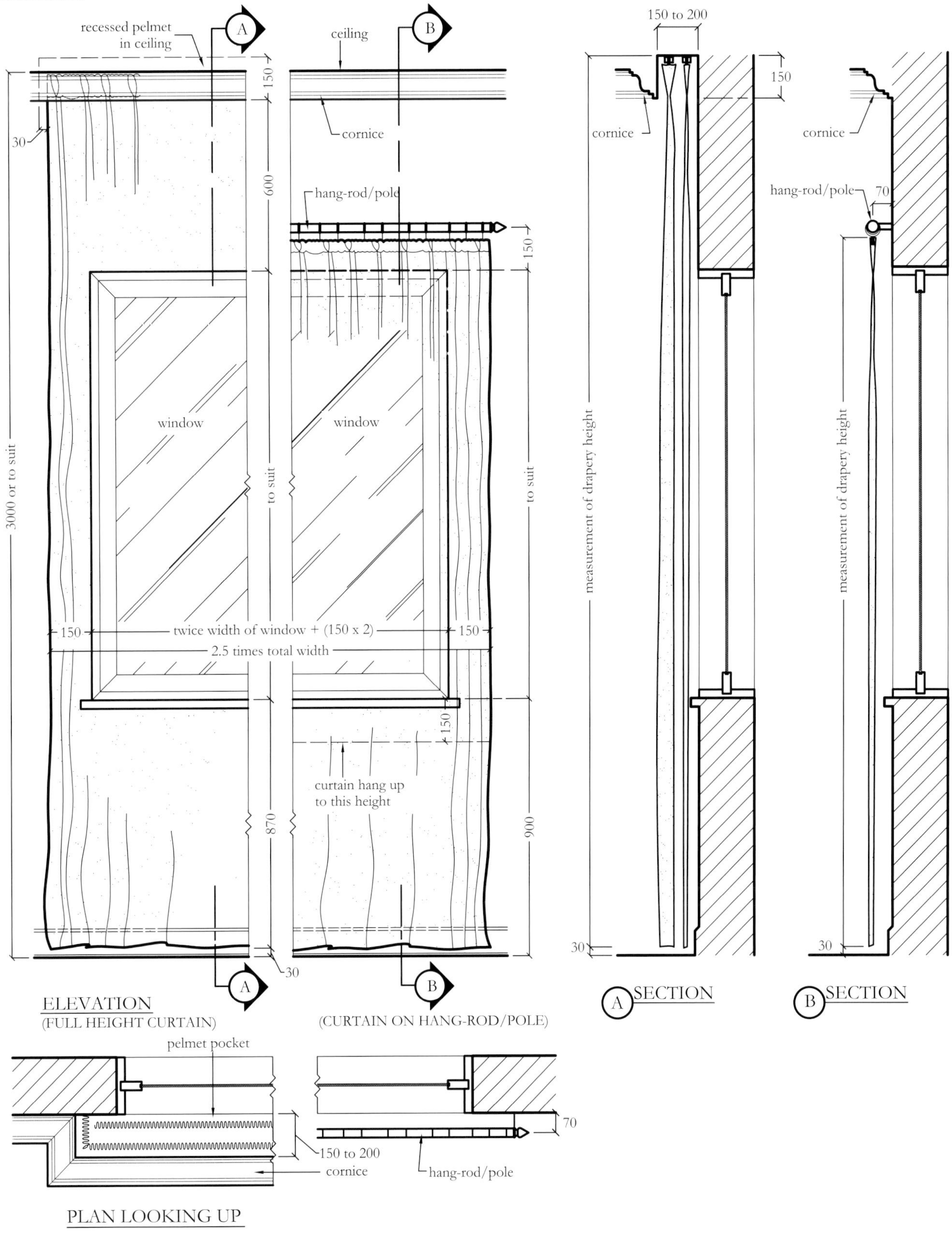

PROJECT TITLE:	DRAWN BY	CHECKED	DATE	address 1 address 2 address 3 postal code email address
	PROJECT NO		SCALE	
DRAWING TITLE: MEASURING FABRIC FOR CURTAINS	DRAWING NO		REVISION △	Interior Designers

DATA SHEET	DESCRIPTION WINDOW TREATMENT	⬡	SHEET NO OF TOTAL QTY:

ILLUSTRATION:

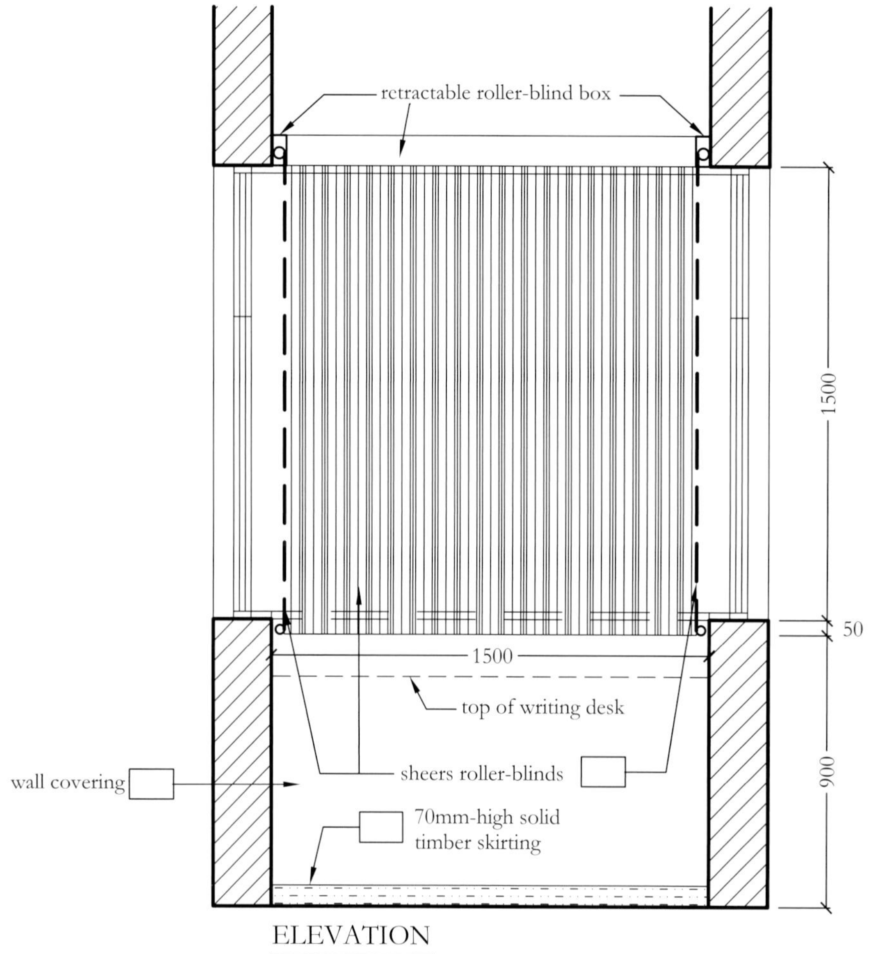

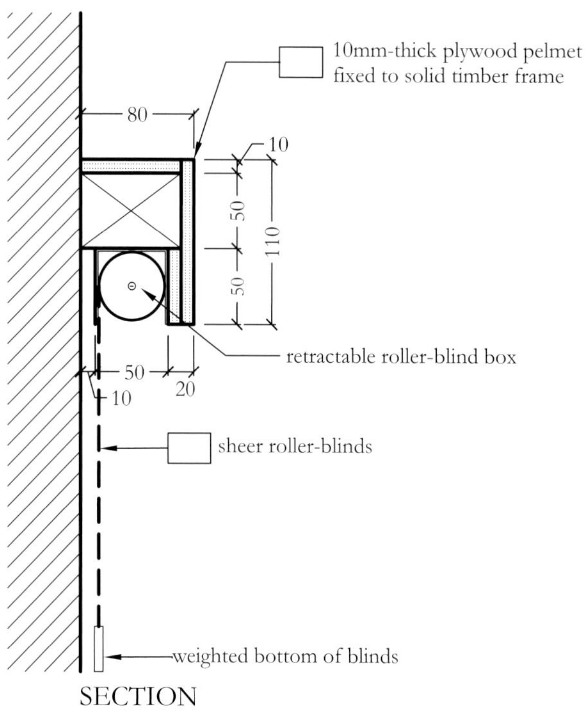

Note: Provide finishes fabric number in rectangular box.

PROJECT TITLE:	DRAWN BY	CHECKED	DATE	address 1 address 2 address 3 postal code email address
	PROJECT NO		SCALE	
DRAWING TITLE: ELEVATION PLUS SECTION OF ROLLER BLINDS	DRAWING NO		REVISION △	Interiors Designers

DATA SHEET	DESCRIPTION WINDOW TREATMENT	SHEET NO OF TOTAL QTY:

ILLUSTRATION:

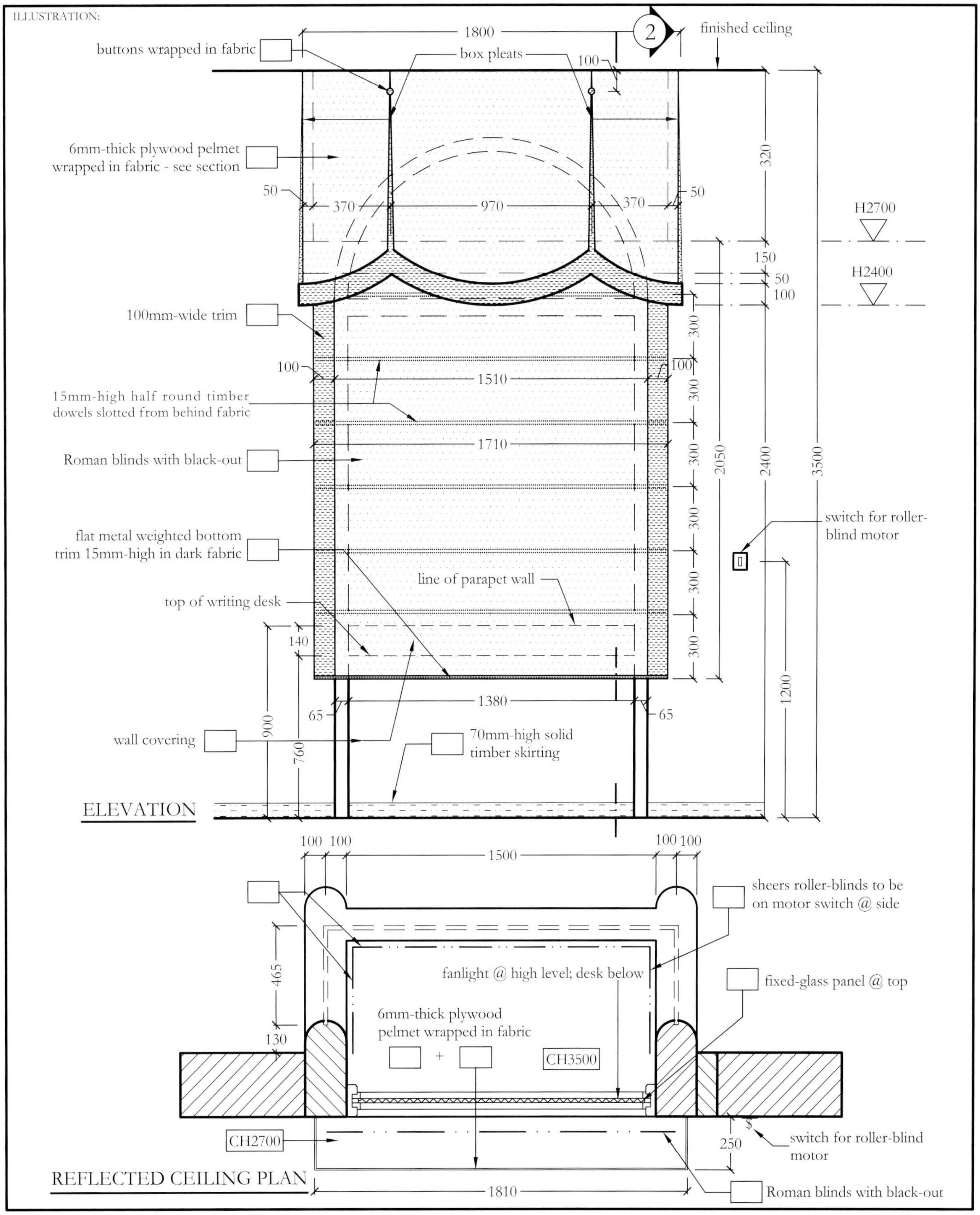

PROJECT TITLE:	DRAWN BY	CHECKED	DATE	address 1 address 2 address 3 postal code email address
	PROJECT NO		SCALE	
DRAWING TITLE: PLAN + ELEVATION OF VALANCE & ROMAN BLINDS	DRAWING NO		REVISION	Interior Designers

Study for a house in Indonesia dress curtains with the tie-backs, sheer curtains, and Roman blinds.

DATA SHEET	DESCRIPTION WINDOW TREATMENT		SHEET NO OF TOTAL QTY:

ILLUSTRATION:

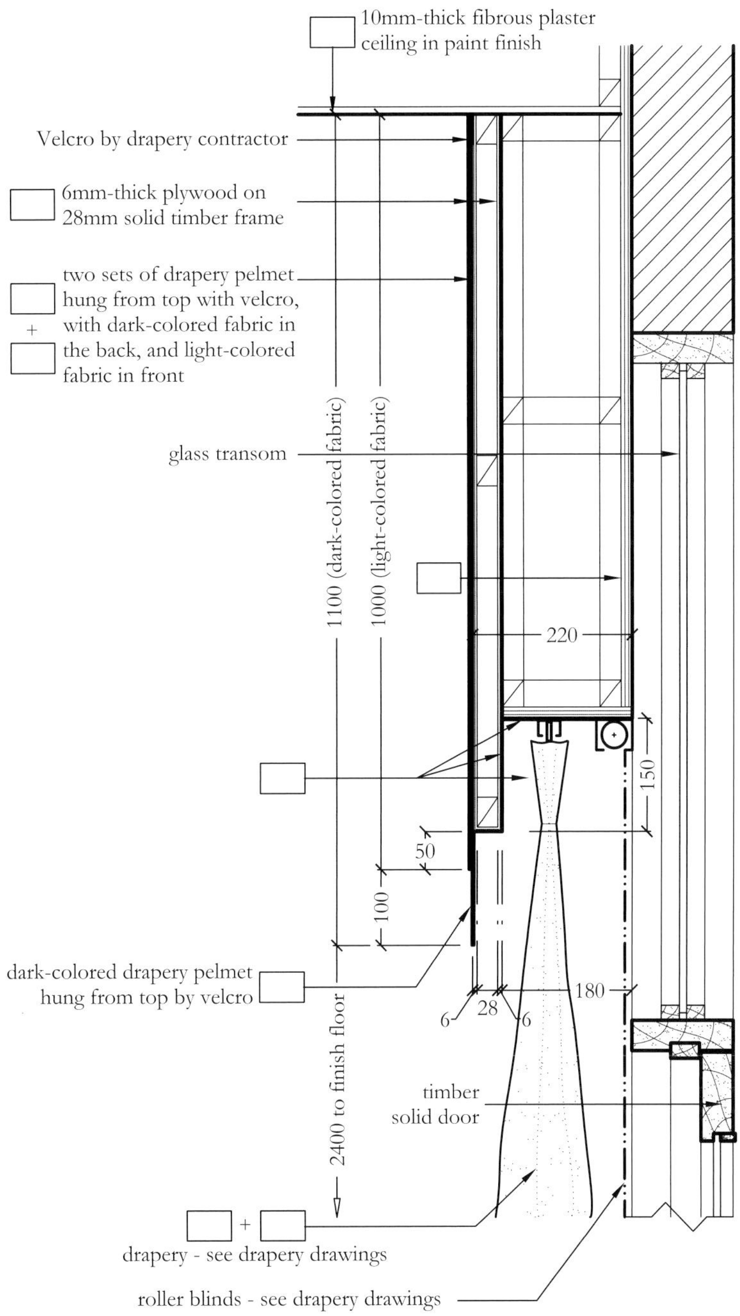

1 SECTION

PROJECT TITLE:	DRAWN BY	CHECKED	DATE	address 1 address 2 address 3 postal code email address Interior Designers
	PROJECT NO		SCALE	
DRAWING TITLE: DETAIL THROUGH DRAPERY PELMET - SECTION 1	DRAWING NO		REVISION △	

DATA SHEET	DESCRIPTION WINDOW TREATMENT		SHEET NO OF TOTAL QTY:

ILLUSTRATION:

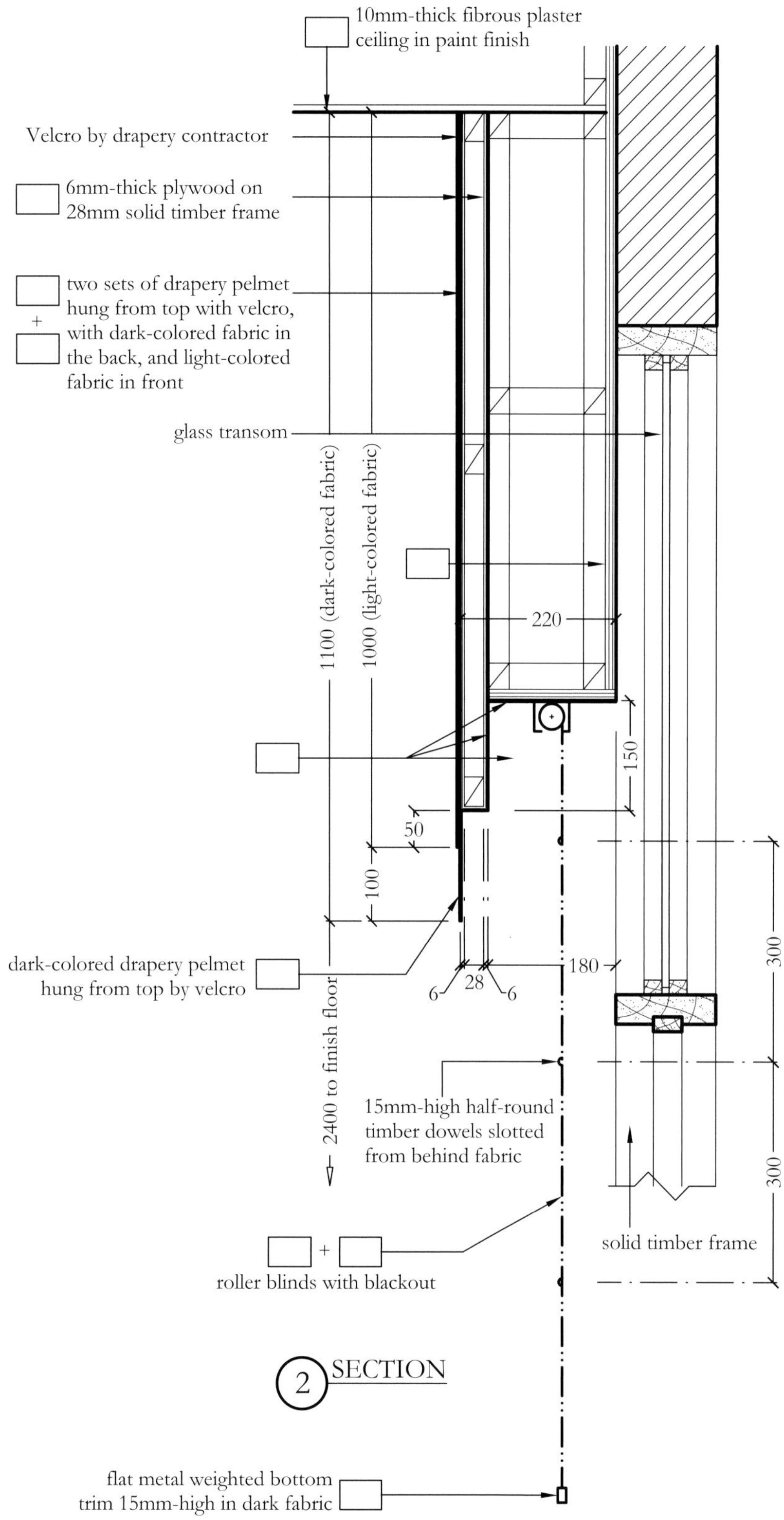

2 SECTION

PROJECT TITLE:	DRAWN BY	CHECKED	DATE	address 1 address 2 address 3 postal code email address Interior Designers
DRAWING TITLE: DETAIL THROUGH DRAPERY PELMET - SECTION 2	PROJECT NO		SCALE	
	DRAWING NO		REVISION	

DATA SHEET	DESCRIPTION WINDOW TREATMENT		SHEET NO OF TOTAL QTY:

ILLUSTRATION:

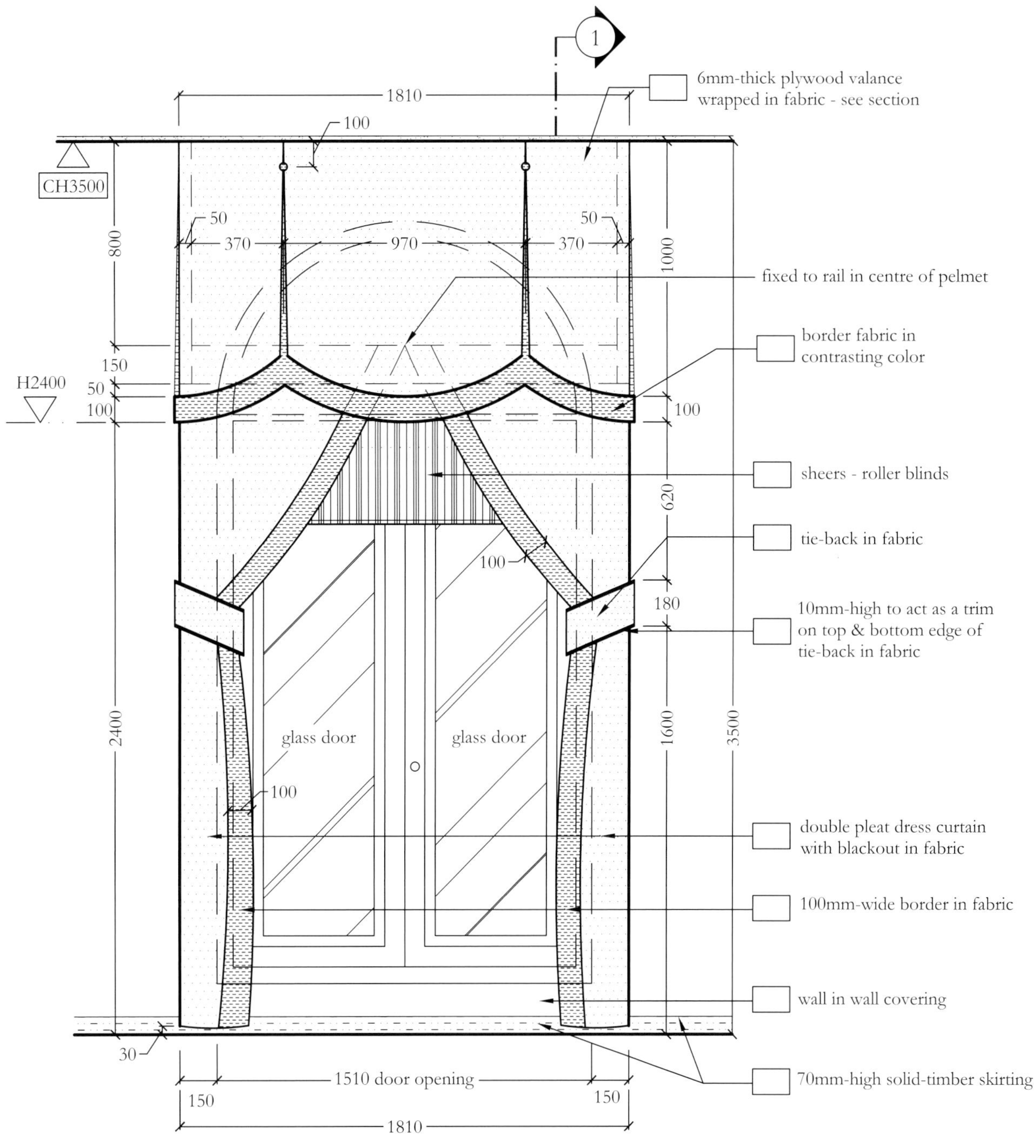

PROJECT TITLE:	DRAWN BY	CHECKED	DATE	address 1 address 2 address 3 postal code email address
	PROJECT NO		SCALE	
DRAWING TITLE: ELEVATION INDICATING ROLLER BLINDS, FIXED CURTAIN, TIE-BACKS, AND VALANCE	DRAWING NO		REVISION	Interiors Designers

Artist's impression of Foyer leading to living/dining rooms for a house in Indonesia.

DATA SHEET	DESCRIPTION WINDOW TREATMENT		SHEET NO OF TOTAL QTY:

ILLUSTRATION:

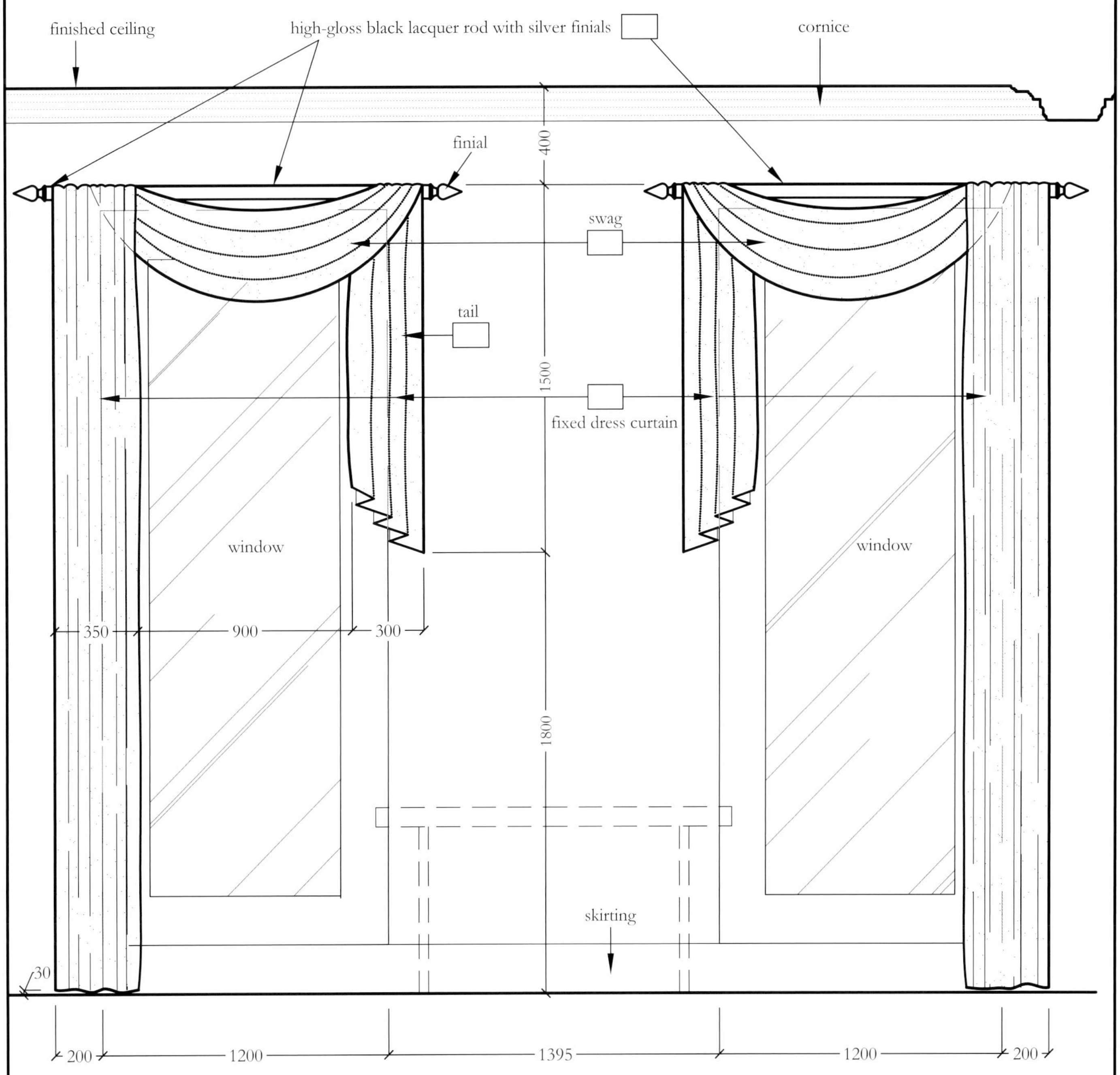

Notes: fixed curtain, swag, and tail to be attached to hanging rod by velcro tapes.

PROJECT TITLE:	DRAWN BY	CHECKED	DATE	address 1 address 2 address 3 postal code email address
	PROJECT NO		SCALE	
DRAWING TITLE: ELEVATION OF WINDOW TREATMENT, INDICATING FIXED CURTAIN, SWAG, and TAIL	DRAWING NO		REVISION △	Interior Designers

DATA SHEET	DESCRIPTION WINDOW TREATMENT		SHEET NO 1 OF 1 TOTAL QTY:

ILLUSTRATION:

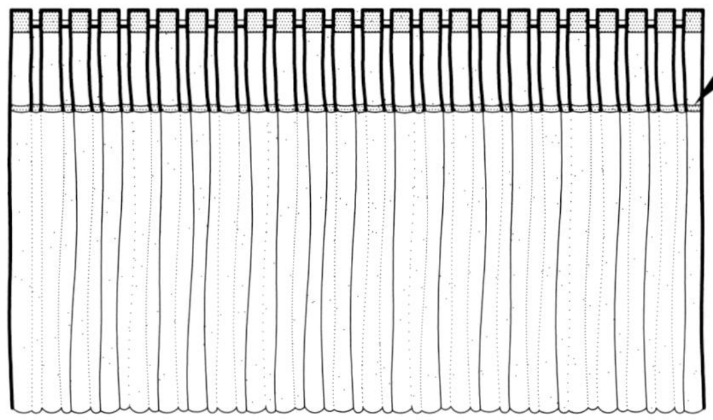

SLOT HEADING or PENCIL PLEATING
(hung on a track)

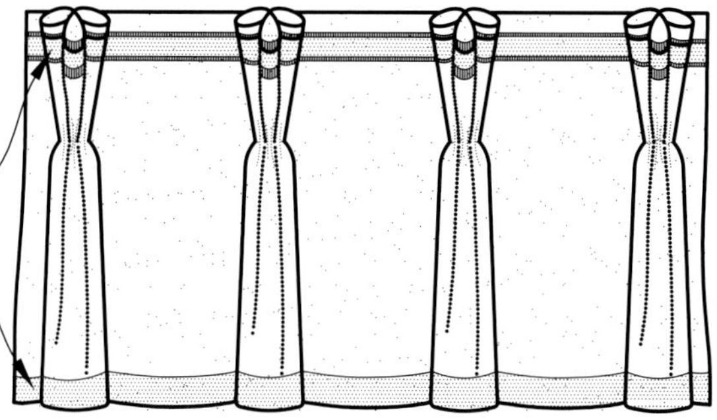

FRENCH OR TRIPLE PLEAT HEADING *(hung on a track)*

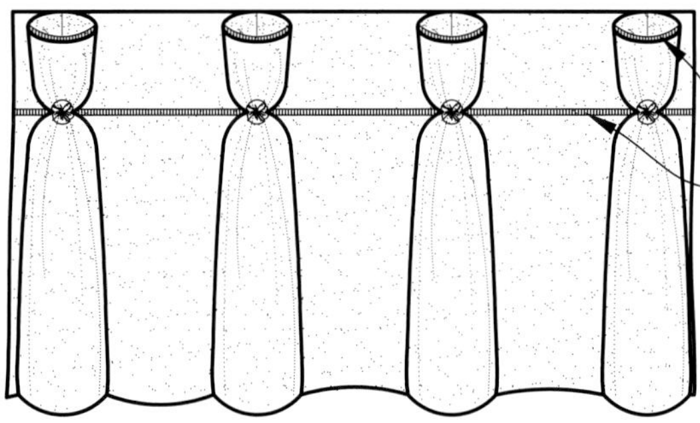

GOBLET HEADING *(hung on a track)*

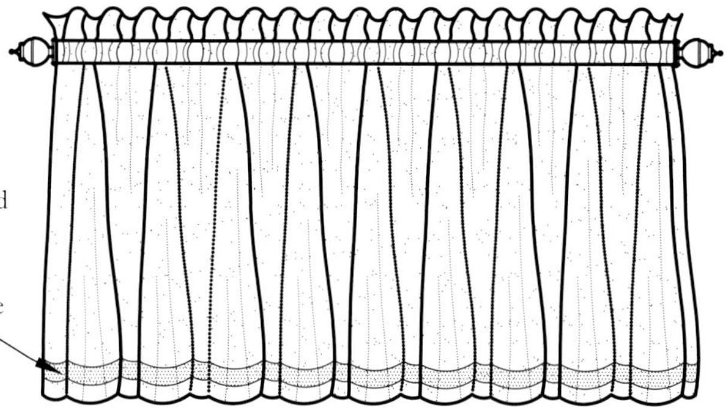

GATHERED HEADING *(pole slotted into fabric, in fixed position)*

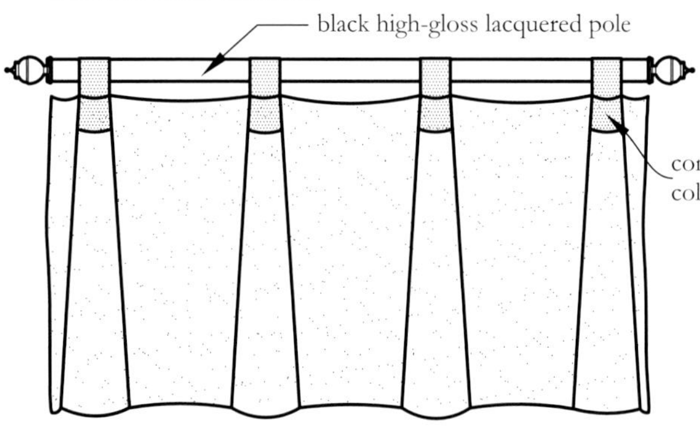

BOX PLEATED CURTAINS
FIXED with LOOPS on POLE

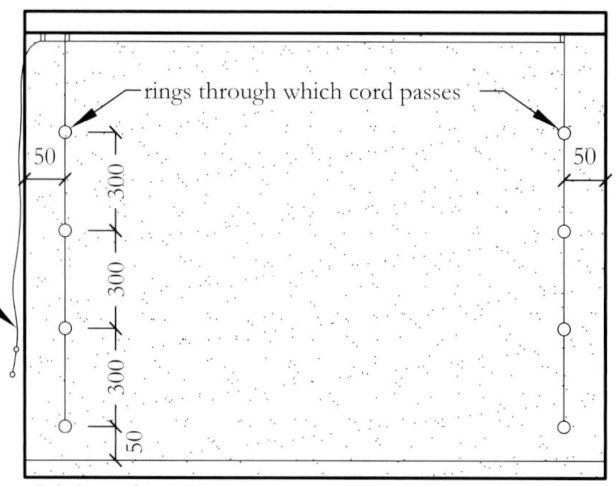

BACK of ROLLER or ROMAN BLIND *(pulled down)*

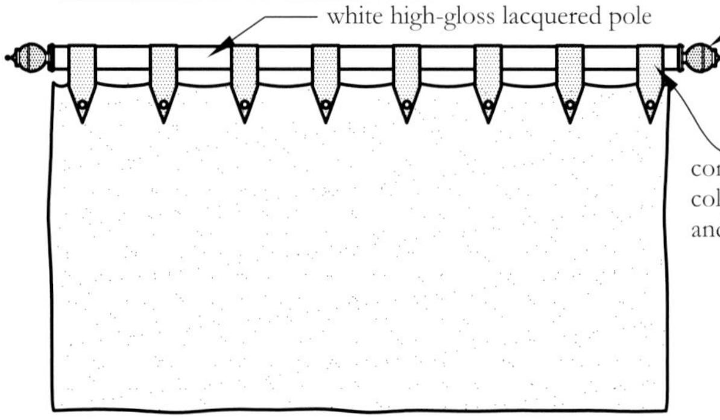

TABS SEWN on CURTAINS for CAFE DRAPES
(hung on pole)

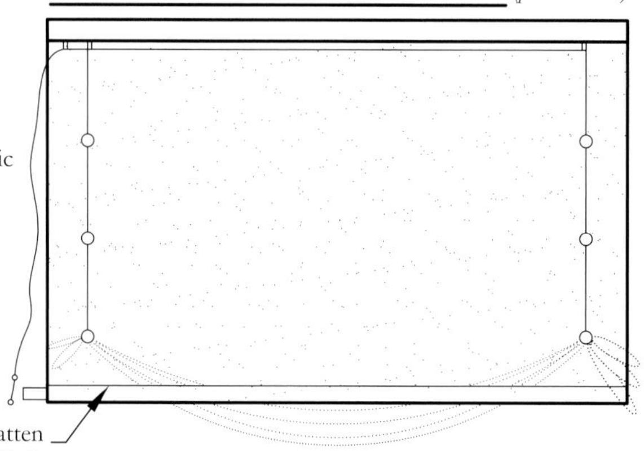

BACK of ROLLER or ROMAN BLIND *(pulled up)*

PROJECT TITLE:	DRAWN BY	CHECKED	DATE	*address 1* *address 2* *address 3* *postal code* *email address*
	PROJECT NO		SCALE	
DRAWING TITLE: CURTAIN AND VALANCE HEADINGS	DRAWING NO		REVISION	Interior Designers

CHAPTER 7

DOOR SCHEDULE, DETAILS, AND HARDWARE SCHEDULE AND SPECIFICATIONS

1. Data sheet - layout plan indicating door numbers
2. Data sheet - door elevations and various types of doors
3. Data sheet - elevation, plan plus section of door D-01
4. Data sheet - detail plan of door D-01
5. Data sheet - detail section of entrance door plus sliding door
6. Data sheet - concealed door in timber paneling front elevation and section
7. Data sheet - concealed door in timber paneling detailed elevation and section
8. Data sheet - concealed door in timber paneling, main plan plus detail plan
9. Data sheet - entrance door with arabesque design, plan plus detail
10. Data sheet - entrance door with arabesque design, elevation
11. Data sheet - entrance door with arabesque design, detail elevation, plan and section
12. Photograph - Restaurant entrance door
13. Data sheet - door schedule, hardware specification

DATA SHEET	DESCRIPTION DOOR SCHEDULE & DETAILS	D	SHEET NO 1 OF 3 TOTAL QTY:

ILLUSTRATION:

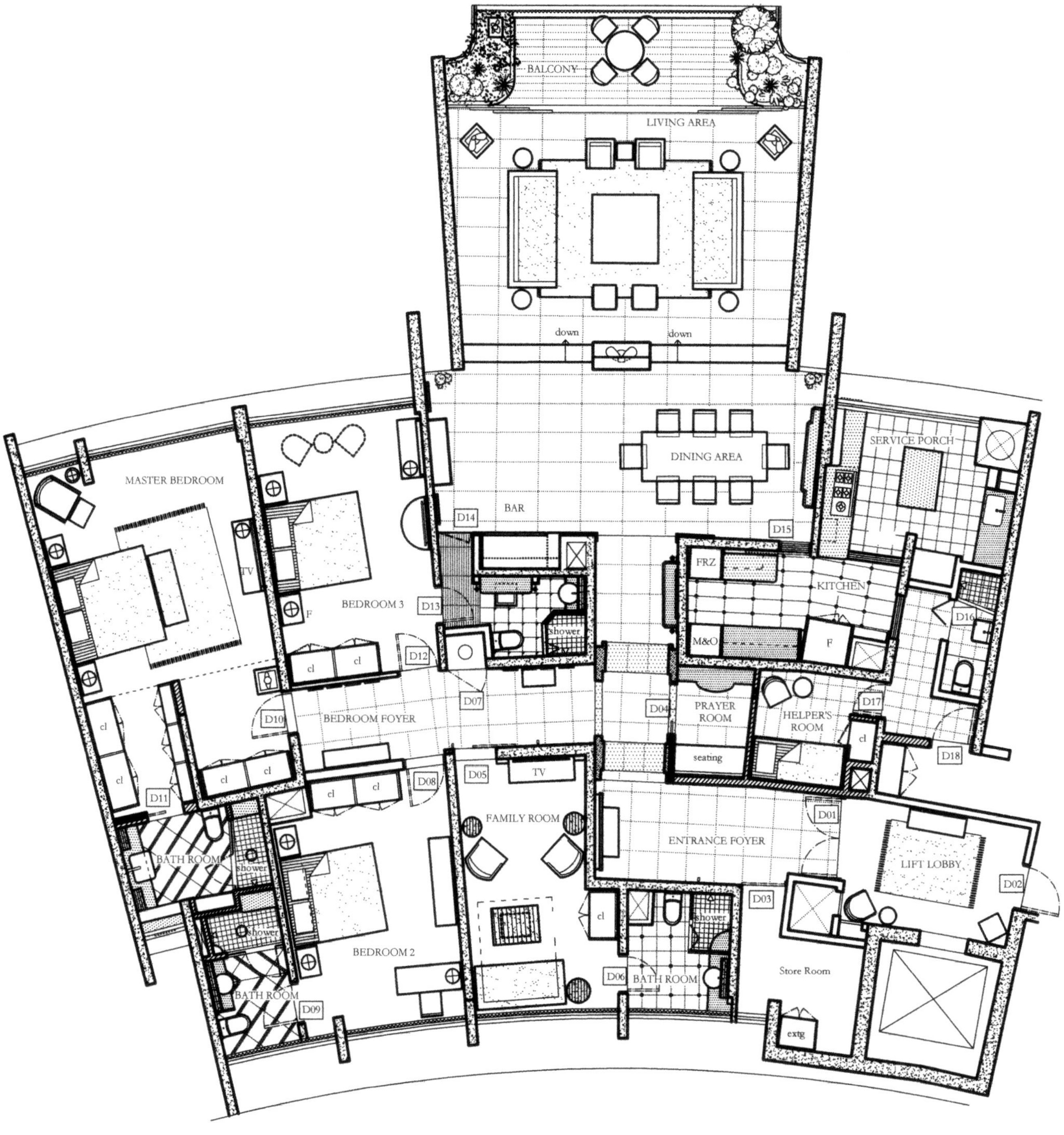

PROJECT TITLE: APARTMENT	DRAWN BY	CHECKED	DATE	address 1 address 2 address 3 postal code email address
	PROJECT NO		SCALE	
DRAWING TITLE: LAYOUT PLAN INDICATING DOOR NUMBERS	DRAWING NO		REVISION △	Interior Designers

DATA SHEET	DESCRIPTION DOOR SCHEDULE & DETAILS	D	SHEET NO 2 OF 2 TOTAL QTY:

ILLUSTRATION:

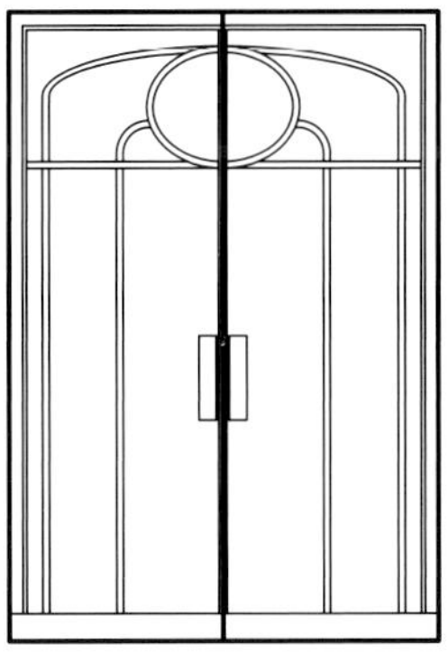

D-01
W1620 H2310
MAIN ENTRANCE
1 no
dwg no:

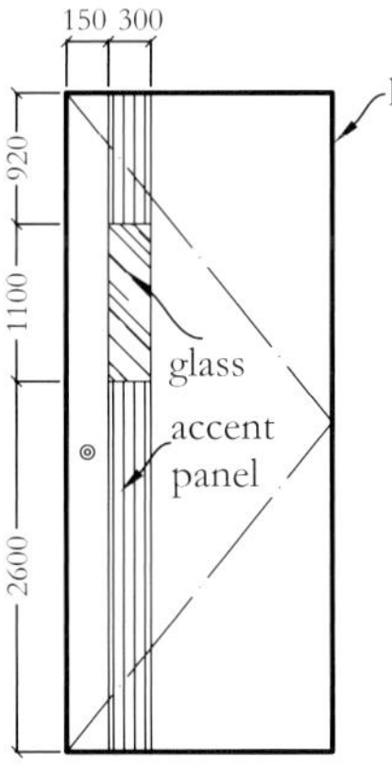

D-02
W950 H2310
LIFT LOBBY
1 no
dwg no:

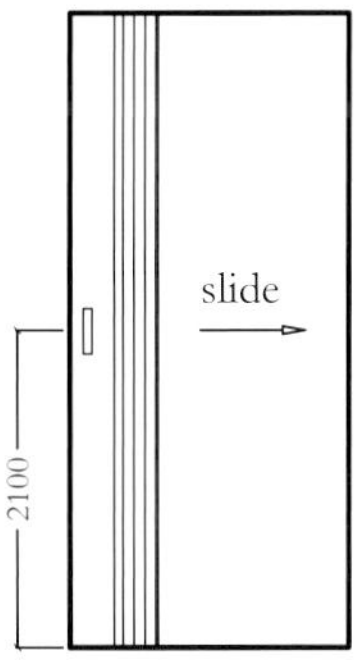

D-03
W950 H2100
STORE ROOM
1 no
dwg no:

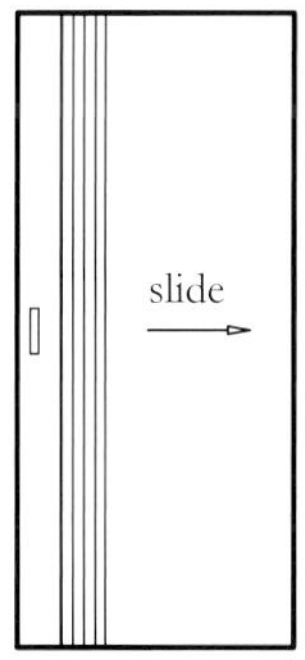

D-04
W950 H2100
PRAYER ROOM
1 no
dwg no:

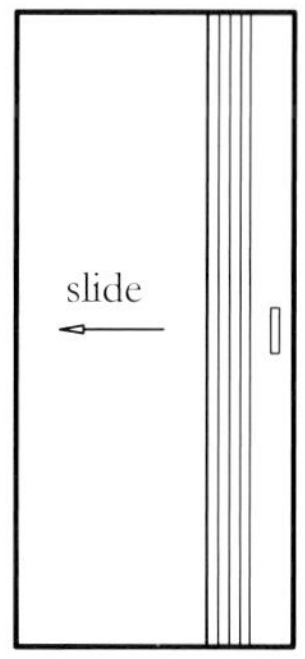

D-05
W950 H2100
FAMILY ROOM
1 no
dwg no:

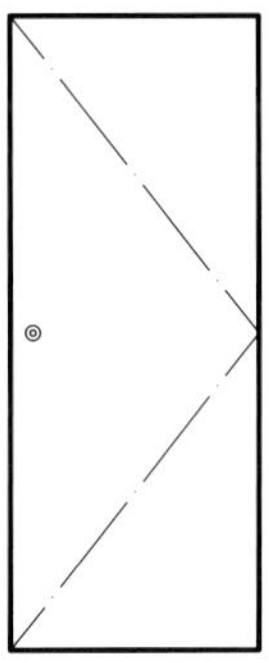

D-06
W850 H2100
BATH ROOM
1 no
dwg no:

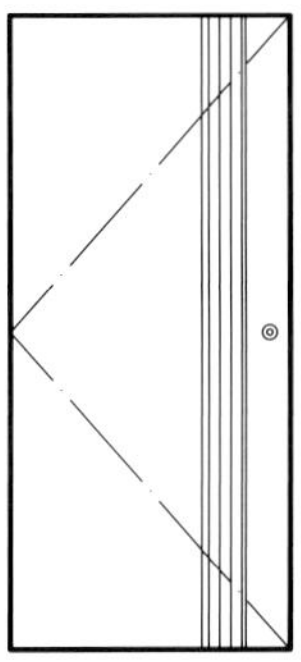

D-07
W950 H2100
BOILER ROOM
1 no
dwg no:

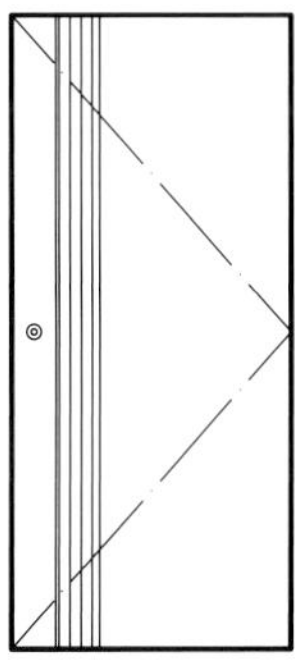

D-08
W950 H2100
BED ROOM 2
1 no
dwg no:

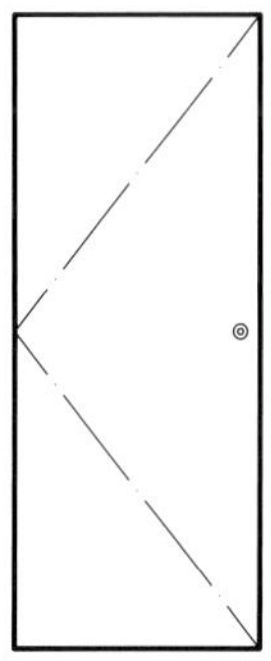

D-09
W850 H2100
BATH ROOM
1 no
dwg no:

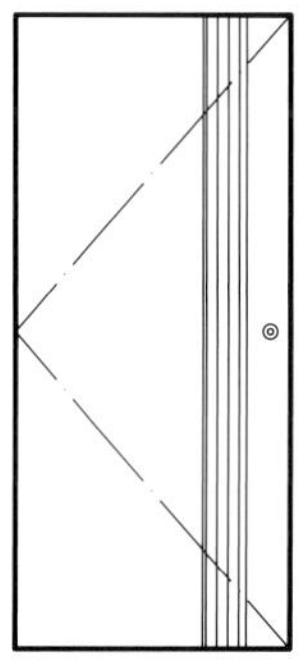

D-10
W950 H2100
MASTER BED ROOM
1 no
dwg no:

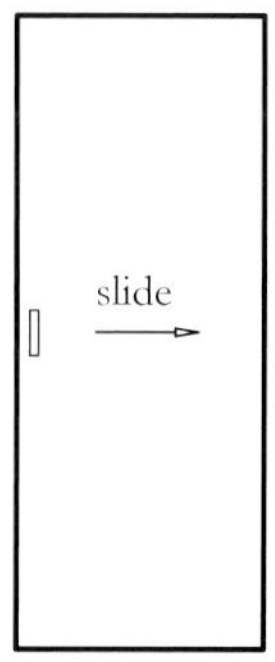

D-11
W850 H2100
BATH ROOM
1 no
dwg no:

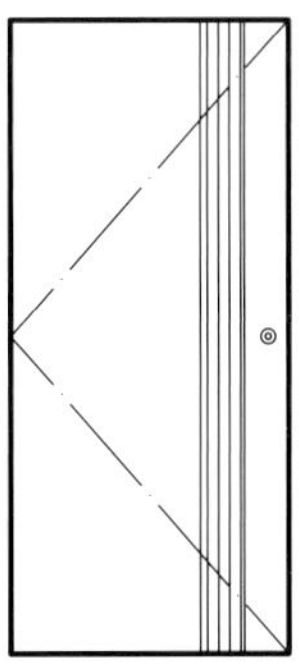

D-12
W950 H2100
BED ROOM 3
1 no
dwg no:

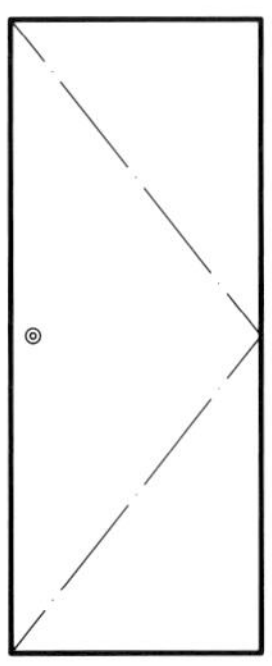

D-13
W850 H2100
BATH ROOM
1 no
dwg no:

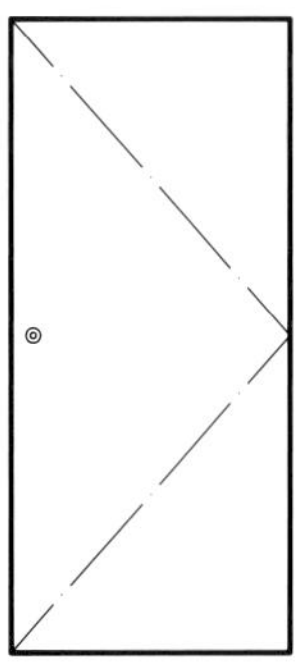

D-14
W950 H2100
BATH ROOM
1 no
dwg no:

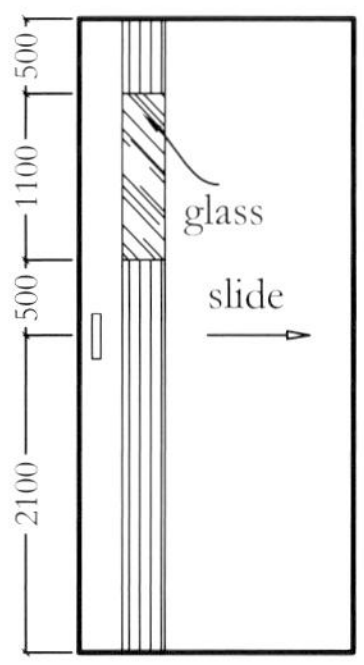

D-15
W950 H2100
KITCHEN
1 no
dwg no:

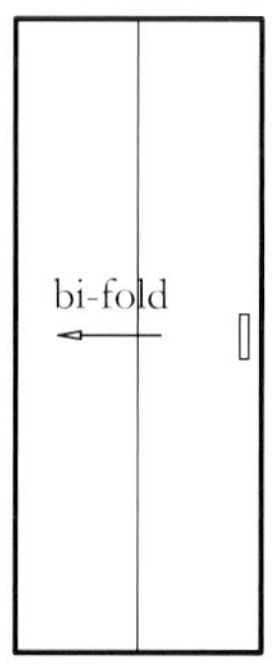

D-16
W850 H2100
MAID's BATH
1 no
dwg no:

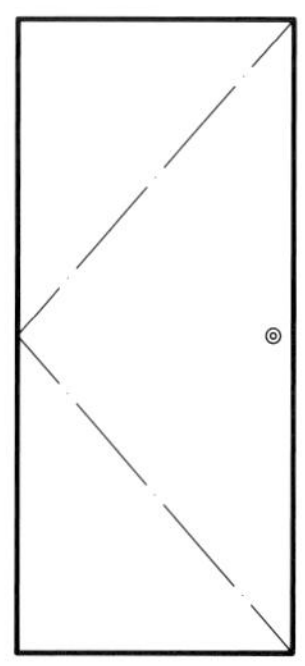

D-17
W950 H2100
MAID's ROOM
1 no
dwg no:

PROJECT TITLE:	DRAWN BY	CHECKED	DATE	address 1 address 2 address 3 postal code email address
	PROJECT NO		SCALE	
DRAWING TITLE: DOOR ELEVATIONS & VARIOUS TYPES OF DOORS	DRAWING NO		REVISION △	Interior Designers

DATA SHEET	DESCRIPTION DOOR SCHEDULE & DETAILS	D-01	SHEET NO 1 OF 3 TOTAL QTY:

ILLUSTRATION:

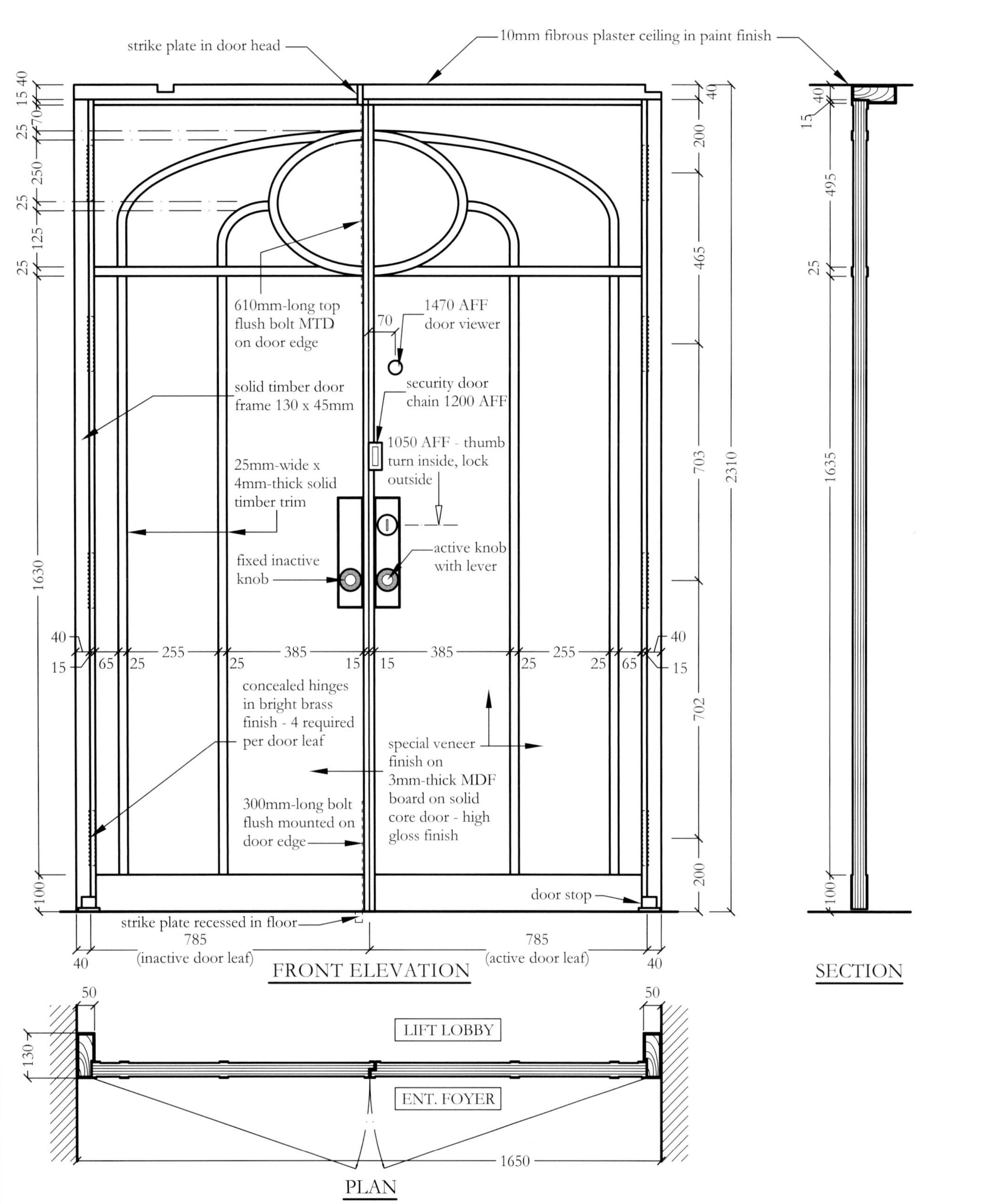

PROJECT TITLE:	DRAWN BY	CHECKED	DATE	address 1 address 2 address 3 postal code email address
	PROJECT NO		SCALE	
DRAWING TITLE: DOOR D-01 - PLAN, ELEVATION, AND SECTION	DRAWING NO		REVISION △	Interior Designers

DATA SHEET	DESCRIPTION DOOR SCHEDULE & DETAILS	D	SHEET NO 2 OF 3 TOTAL QTY:

ILLUSTRATION:

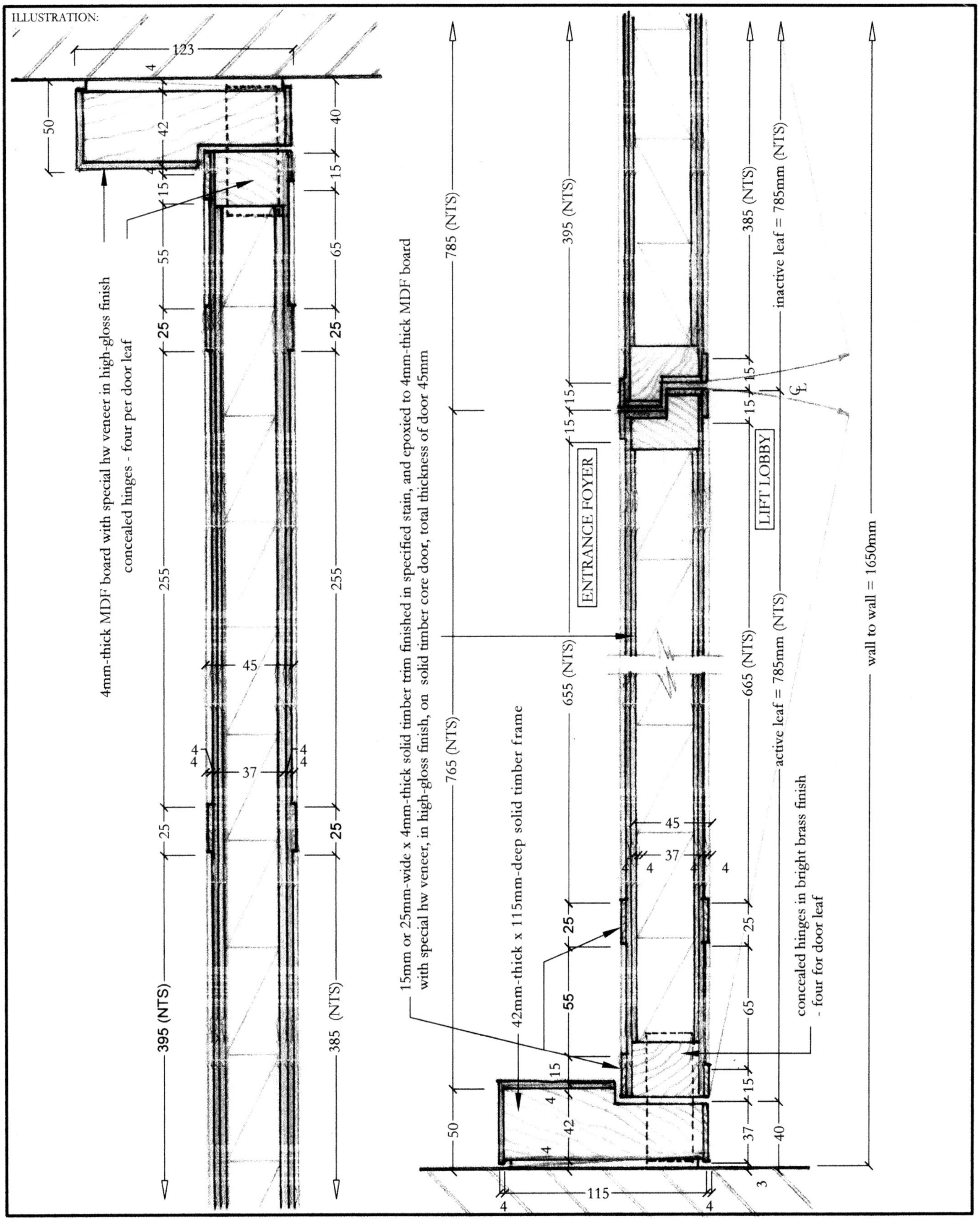

PROJECT TITLE:	DRAWN BY	CHECKED	DATE	address 1 address 2 address 3 postal code email address
	PROJECT NO		SCALE	
DRAWING TITLE: DETAIL PLAN OF DOOR D-01	DRAWING NO		REVISION △	Interior Designers

DATA SHEET	DESCRIPTION DOOR SCHEDULE & DETAILS	D	SHEET NO 3 OF 3 TOTAL QTY:

ILLUSTRATION:

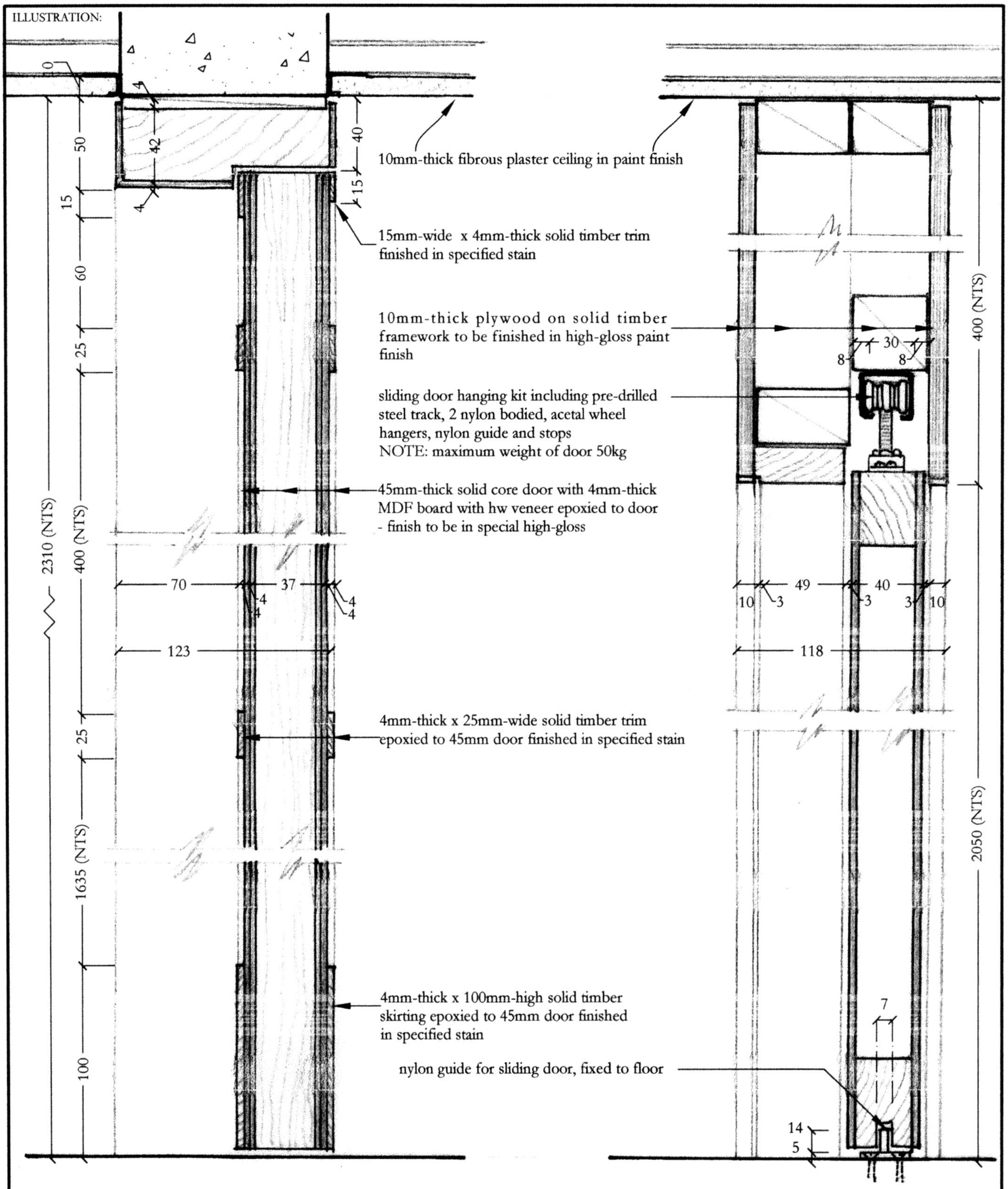

DETAIL SECTION OF DOOR D-01

DETAIL SECTION OF SLIDING DOOR

PROJECT TITLE:	DRAWN BY	CHECKED	DATE	address 1 address 2 address 3 postal code email address
	PROJECT NO		SCALE	
DRAWING TITLE: DETAIL SECTION OF ENTRANCE AND SLIDING DOOR	DRAWING NO		REVISION △	Interior Designers

DATA SHEET	DESCRIPTION DOOR SCHEDULE & DETAILS	D	SHEET NO 2 OF 3 TOTAL QTY:

ILLUSTRATION:

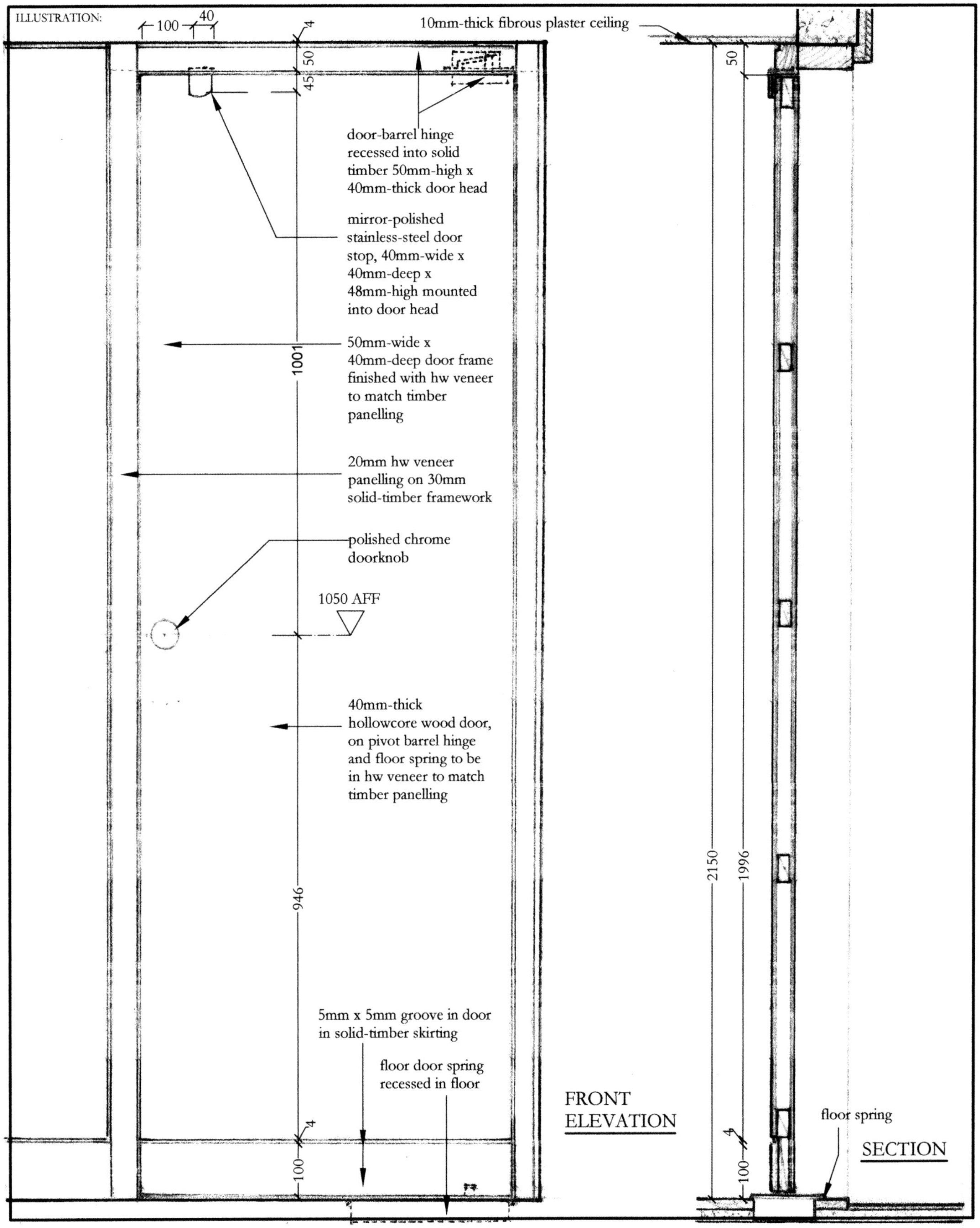

PROJECT TITLE:	DRAWN BY	CHECKED	DATE	address 1 address 2 address 3 postal code email address
	PROJECT NO		SCALE	
DRAWING TITLE: CONCEALED DOOR WITH TIMBER PANELLING - FRONT ELEVATION AND SECTION	DRAWING NO		REVISION △	Interior Designers

DATA SHEET	DESCRIPTION DOOR SCHEDULE & DETAILS	D	SHEET NO 3 OF 3 TOTAL QTY:

ILLUSTRATION:

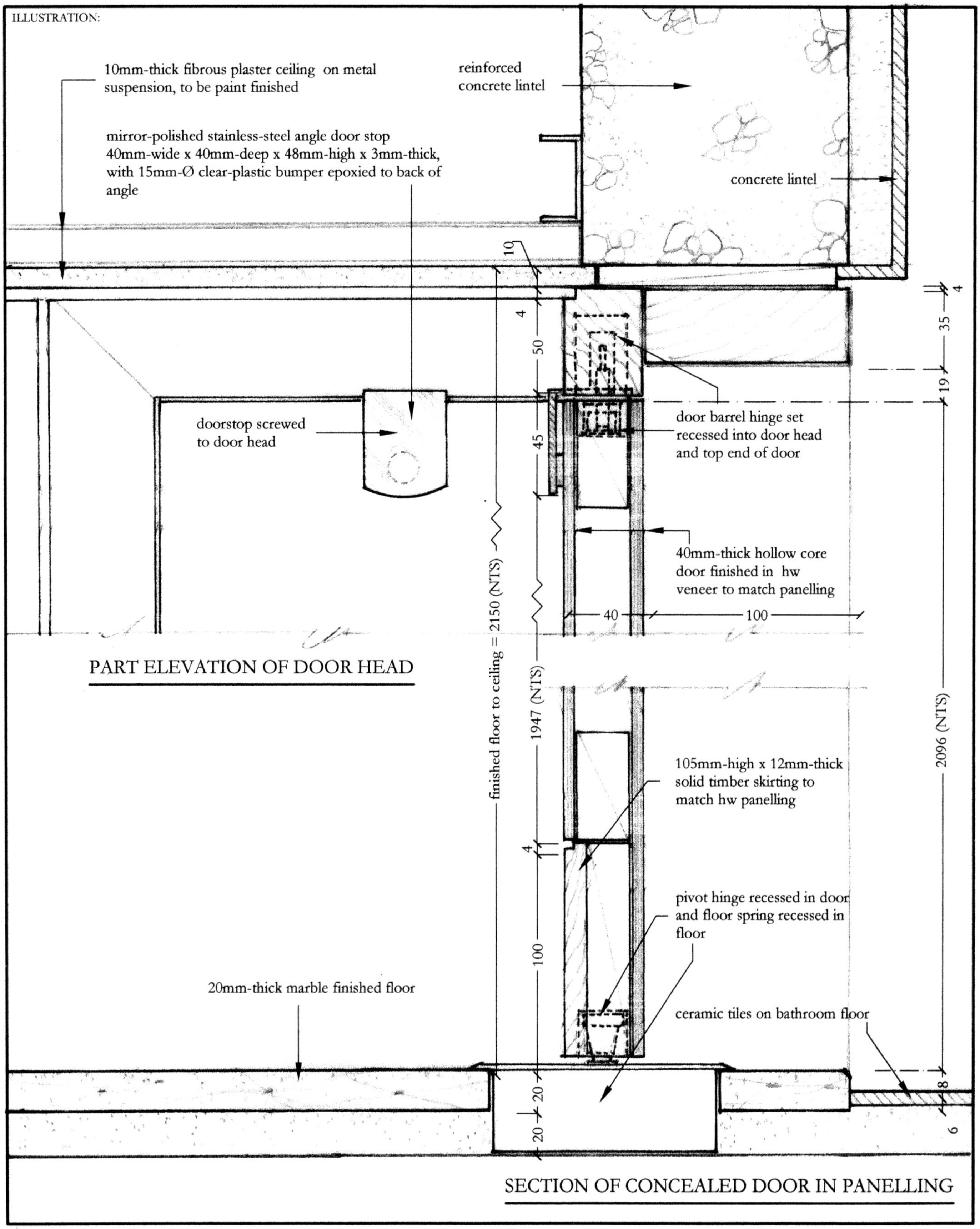

PROJECT TITLE:	DRAWN BY	CHECKED	DATE	address 1 address 2 address 3 postal code email address Interior Designers
	PROJECT NO		SCALE	
DRAWING TITLE: CONCEALED DOOR WITH TIMBER PANELLING - DETAIL ELEVATION AND DETAIL SECTION	DRAWING NO		REVISION △	

DATA SHEET	DESCRIPTION DOOR SCHEDULE & DETAILS	D	SHEET NO 1 OF 3 TOTAL QTY:

ILLUSTRATION:

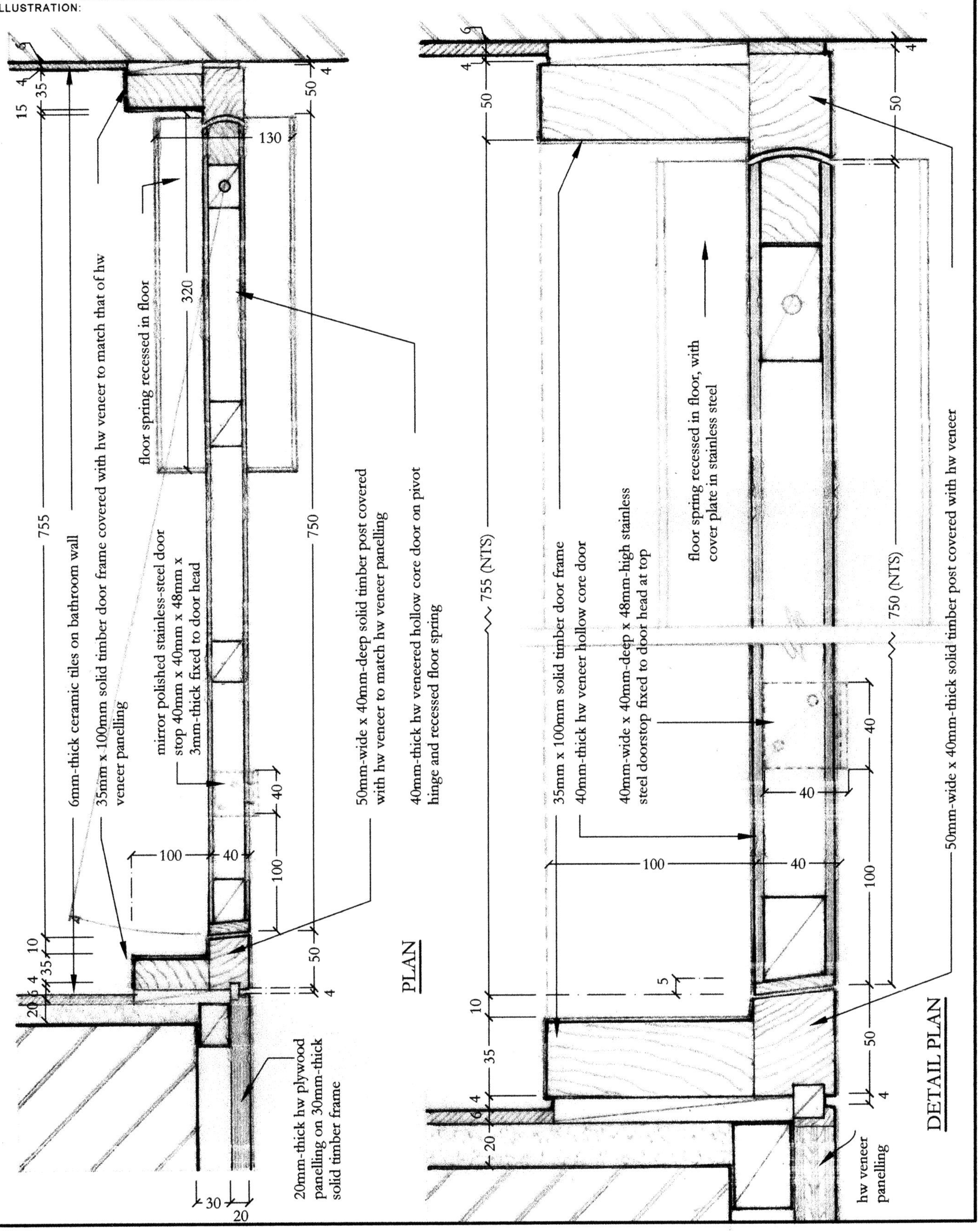

PROJECT TITLE:	DRAWN BY	CHECKED	DATE	address 1 address 2 address 3 postal code email address
DRAWING TITLE: CONCEALED DOOR WITH TIMBER PANELLING - MAIN PLAN AND DETAILED PLAN	PROJECT NO		SCALE	
	DRAWING NO		REVISION △	Interior Designers

DATA SHEET	DESCRIPTION DOOR SCHEDULE & DETAILS	D	SHEET NO 1 OF 3 TOTAL QTY:

ILLUSTRATION:

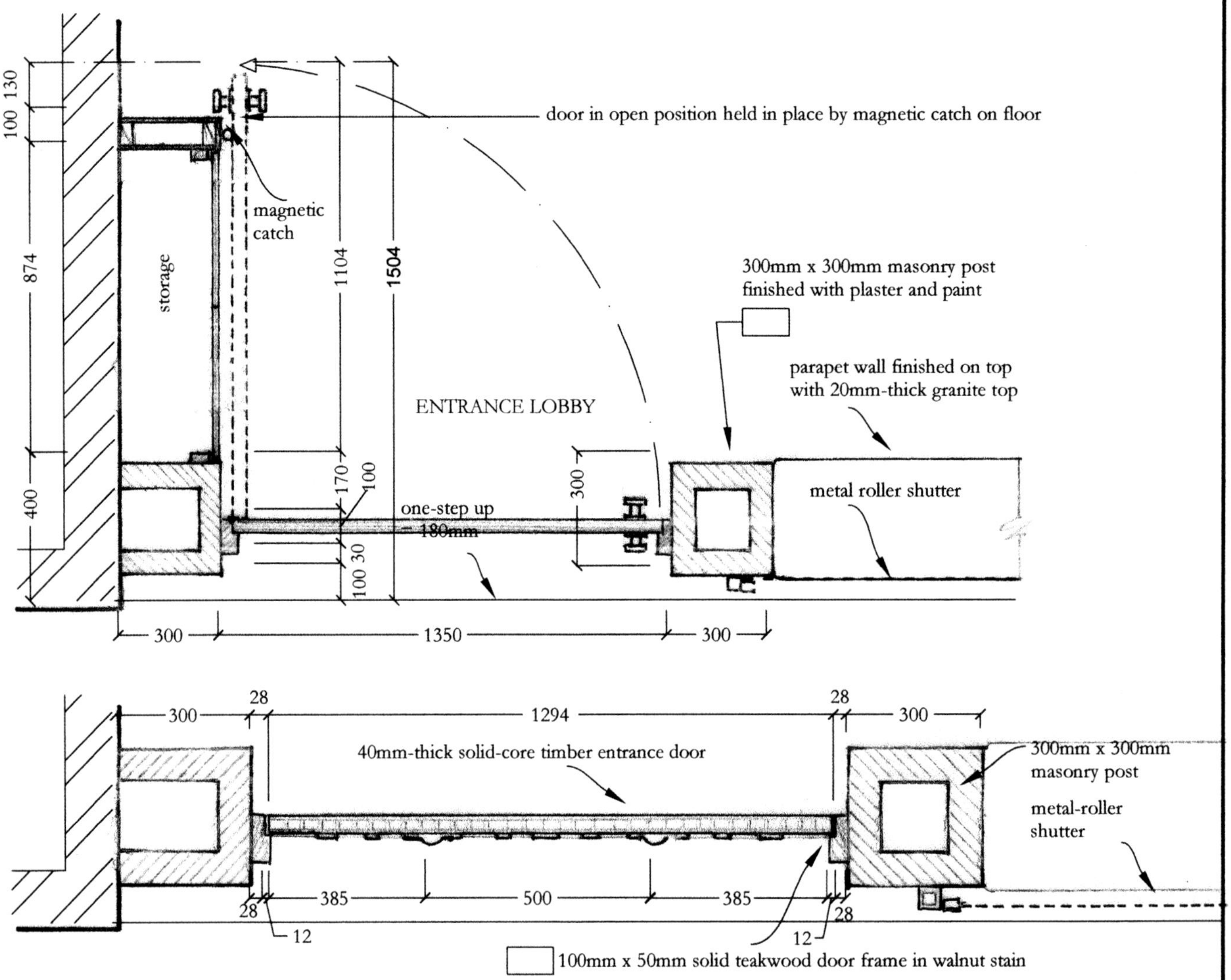

SPECIFICATION / DESCRIPTION:

SUPPLIER / MANUFACTURER: NAME/FIRM OF FURNITURE CONTRACTOR	Furniture Supplier code	Finishes Supplier & Code

MODEL NO: custom design	DIMENSIONS (mm): 1350mm-wide x 40mm-thick x 2250mm-high	ROOM TYPE:	QUANTITY:
OTHER FINISHES CODE: - - - -	AREA LOCATION:	1	
		2	
		3	
COSTINGS: ☐ BUDGET : \$ ☐ QUOTATION : \$ ☐ FINAL PRICE : \$	TOTAL: TOTAL QUANTITY: TOTAL PRICE: \$	4	
		5	
		TOTAL QTY:	

REMARKS/NOTES /SPECIAL INSTRUCTIONS:

PROJECT TITLE:	DRAWN BY	CHECKED	DATE	address 1 address 2 address 3 postal code email address Interior Designers
	PROJECT NO		SCALE	
DRAWING TITLE: ENTRANCE DOOR WITH ARABESQUE DESIGN - PLAN AND DETAIL	DRAWING NO		REVISION △	

DATA SHEET	DESCRIPTION DOOR SCHEDULE & DETAILS	D	SHEET NO 2 OF 3 TOTAL QTY:

ILLUSTRATION:

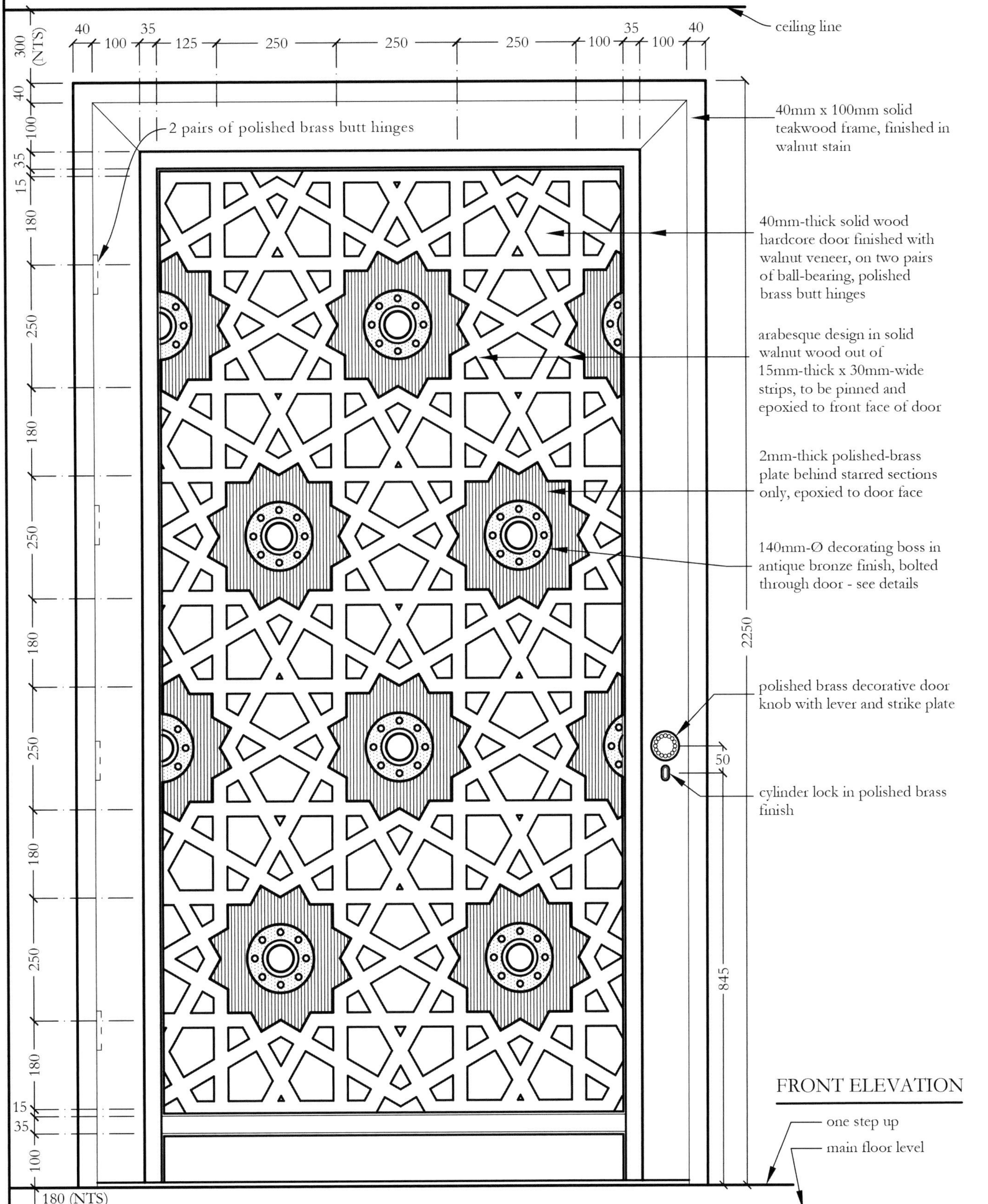

PROJECT TITLE:	DRAWN BY	CHECKED	DATE	address 1 address 2 address 3 postal code email address Interior Designers
	PROJECT NO		SCALE	
DRAWING TITLE: ENTRANCE DOOR WITH ARABESQUE DESIGN - FRONT ELEVATION	DRAWING NO		REVISION △	

DATA SHEET	DESCRIPTION DOOR SCHEDULE & DETAILS	D	SHEET NO 3 OF 3 TOTAL QTY:

ILLUSTRATION:

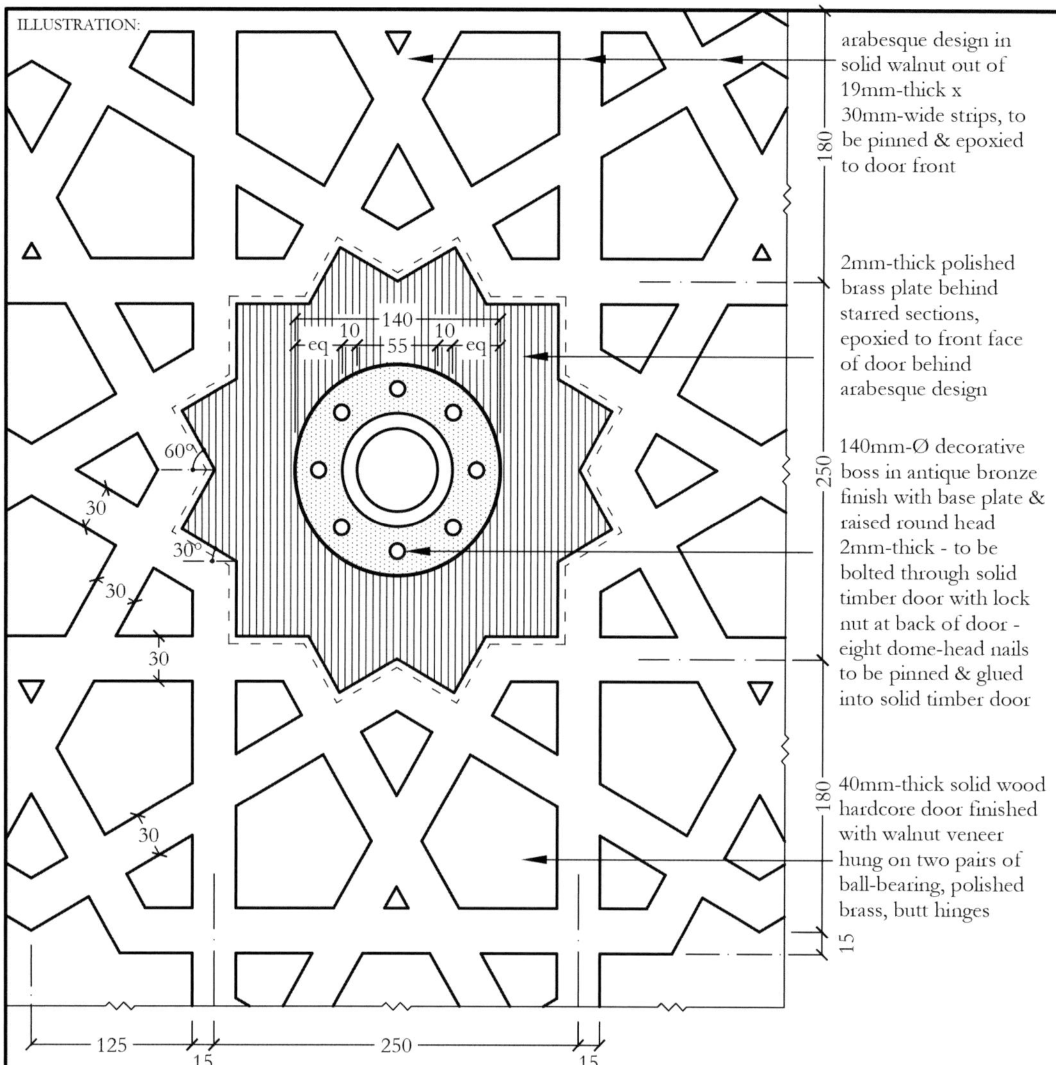

DETAIL OF STARRED PANEL - ELEVATION

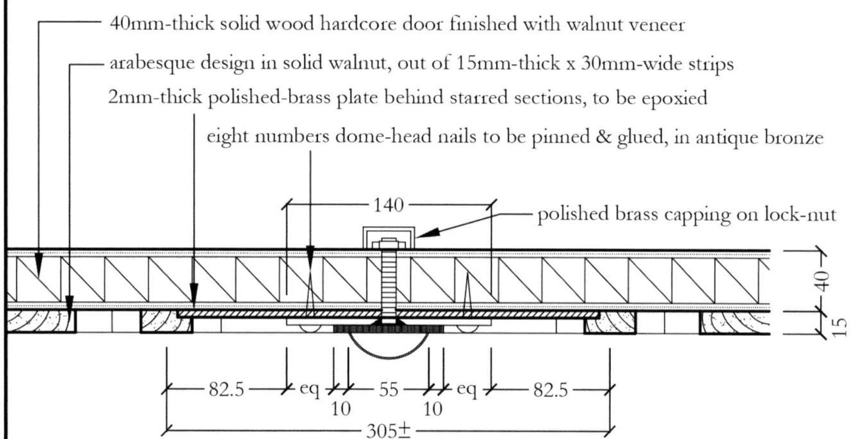

DETAIL OF STARRED PANEL - PLAN

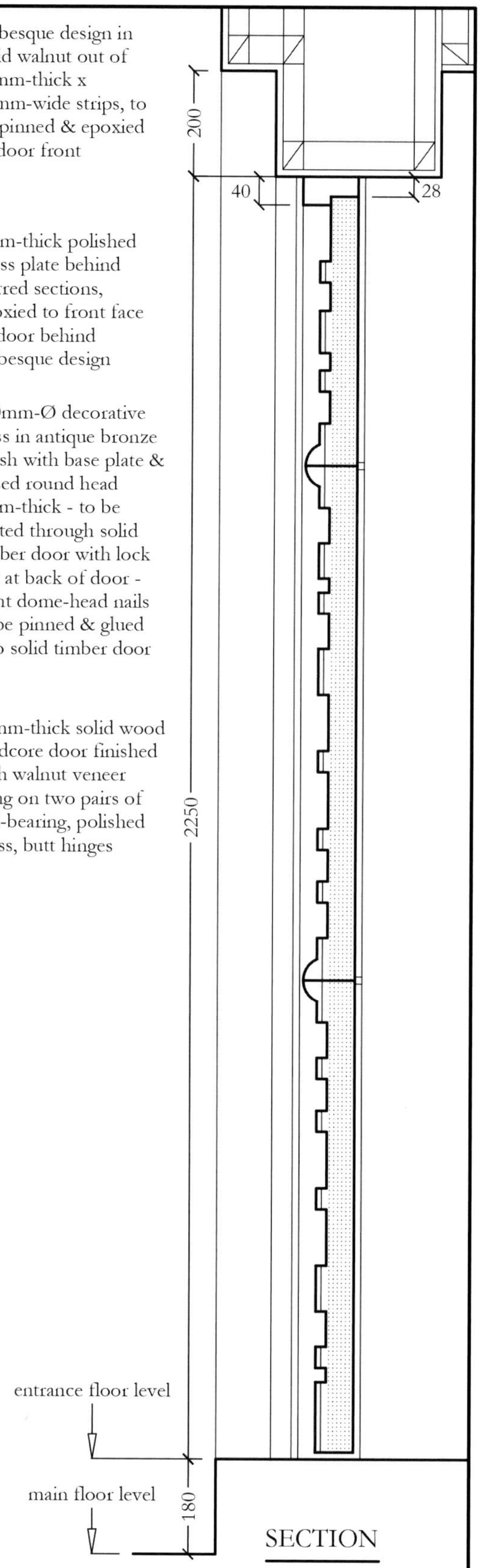

SECTION

PROJECT TITLE:	DRAWN BY	CHECKED	DATE	address 1 address 2 address 3 postal code email address
	PROJECT NO		SCALE	
DRAWING TITLE: ENTRANCE DOOR WITH ARABESQUE DESIGN - PLAN, DETAIL ELEVATION AND SECTION	DRAWING NO		REVISION △	Interior Designers

Restaurant entrance door (Thai theme).

DATA SHEET	DESCRIPTION DOOR SCHEDULE HARDWARE SPECIFICATIONS	SHEET NO 1 OF 1 TOTAL QTY:

DOOR NO	LOCATION	SERIAL NO	HARDWARE SPECIFICATION	DOOR THK	QUANTITY		LIST PRICE	TOTAL PRICE	REMARKS
D-01	Main Entrance	1-a	Manufacturer: HOUSTON 6506.003 KCIS/KTIS + K003-003 knob, complete with mortice lock key/thumb-turn cylinder (key outside, thumb-turn inside) in polished brass, inclusive of dummy set.	45mm	1	set			Finish to be in lifetime (PVD) polished brass, anti-tarnish
D-01	Main Entrance	1-b	Manufacturer: Rebated edge plate	-	1	no.			Finish in polished brass
D-01	Main Entrance	1-c	Manufacturer: 0600.030; 24" x 12" flush, bolt + dust proof strike	-	1	no.			Finish in polished brass
D-01	Main Entrance	1-d	Manufacturer: 218 concealed hinges	-	8	nos.			Finish in bright brass
D-01	Main Entrance	1-e	Manufacturer: 0155.030 door viewer	-		no.			Finish in polished brass
D-01	Main Entrance	1-f	Manufacturer: L193 Oro Lucido magnetic floor stopper	-	2	nos.			Finish in polished brass
D-02	Lift Lobby	2-a	Manufacturer: 5025.003 pass knobset, with both sides free	45mm	1	set			Finish to be in lifetime (PVD) polished brass, anti-tarnish
D-02	Lift Lobby	2-b	Manufacturer: 8231.003, single cylinder dead bolt with key outside, & thumb turn inside	-	1	set			Finish to be in lifetime (PVD) polished brass, anti-tarnish
D-02	Lift Lobby	2-c	Manufacturer: hinges, 4" x 3" with ball bearings	-	2	pairs			Finish in polished brass
D-02	Lift Lobby	2-d	Manufacturer: magnetic door stopper	-	1	no.			Finish in polished brass
D-07 + D-13	Master Bathroom	07-a + 13-d	Manufacturer: Serie ORFEIDE Design SCRIGNO K1211 Oro-privacy sliding with coin slot outside and thumb turn inside	42mm	2	sets			Finish in polished brass, sliding door
D-11+ D-15+ D-16+ D-22	Bathrooms	11-a+ 15-a+ 16-a+ 22-a	Manufacturer: 5025.003 PRIV knobset with emergency hole outside & press button inside	42mm	2	sets			Finish to be in lifetime (PVD) polished brass, anti-tarnish
D-11+ D-15+ D-16+ D-22	Bathrooms	11-b+ 15-b+ 16-b+ 22-b	Manufacturer: hinges, 4" x 3" with ball bearings	-	6	pairs			Finish in polished brass
D-11+ D-15+ D-16+ D-22	Bathrooms	11-c+ 15-c+ 16-c+ 22-c	Manufacturer: L198 ORO LUCIDO magnetic floor stopper	-	4	nos.			Finish in polished brass
D-09+ D-10+ D-14	Bedrooms	09-a+ 10-a+ 14-a	Manufacturer: 5228.003 ENTR knobset with key outside and thumb turn piece inside	-	3	sets			Finish to be in lifetime (PVD) polished brass, anti-tarnish
D-09+ D-10+ D-14	Bedrooms	09-b+ 10-b+ 14-b	Manufacturer: hinges, 4" x 3" with ball bearings	-	4.5	pairs			Finish in polished brass
D-09+ D-10+ D-14	Bedrooms	09-c+ 10-c+ 14-c	Manufacturer: L193 ORO LUCIDO magnetic floor stopper	-	3	nos.			Finish in polished brass

PROJECT TITLE:	DRAWN BY	CHECKED	DATE	
	PROJECT NO		SCALE	*address 1* *address 2* *address 3* *postal code* *email address*
DRAWING TITLE: TYPICAL DOOR HARDWARE SCHEDULE CHART	DRAWING NO		REVISION △	Interior Designers

CHAPTER 8

BATHROOMS, POWDER ROOMS, AND BATHROOM LAYOUTS - DETAILS

1. Data sheet - four-fixture bathroom layouts (economical)
2. Data sheet - three-fixture bathroom layouts (economical)
3. Data sheet - four-fixture bathroom layouts Ouxurious)
4. Data sheet - bathroom elevations A & B
5. Data sheet - bathroom elevations C, D & E
6. Data sheet - plan of wash basin and counter
7. Data sheet - washroom area, elevation of wash basin and counter
8. Data sheet - washroom area, sectional detail and wash basin
9. Photograph of outdoor Jacuzzi with water feature

DATA SHEET	DESCRIPTION BATHROOM LAYOUT	SHEET NO 1 OF 1 TOTAL QTY:

ILLUSTRATION:

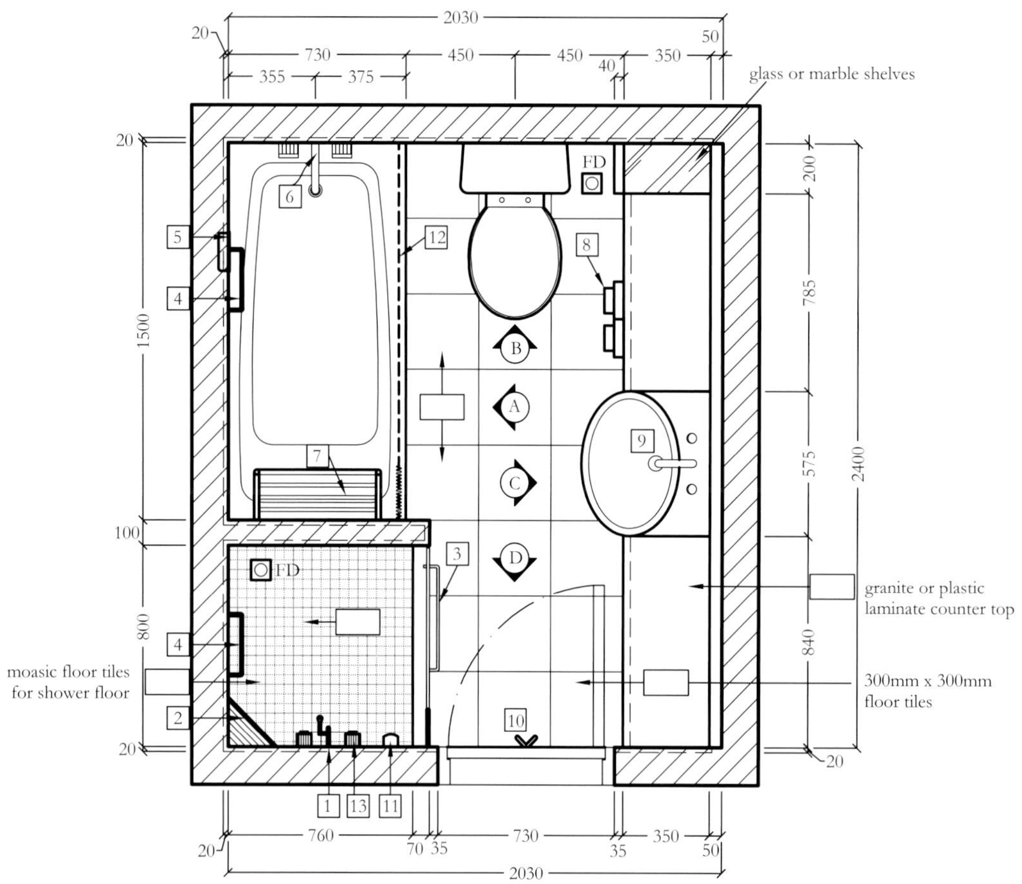

LEGEND:

1	Shower head/rail set
2	Triangular soap dish
3	Shower door towel bar & door handle
4	Grab bar x 2
5	Built-in soap dish
6	Bathtub tap fittings
7	Towel shelf
8	Double toilet-paper holder
9	Lavatory tap fittings
10	Double robe hook
11	Water inlet
12	Rail for shower curtain
13	Shower tap fittings
FD	Floor drain

TIP:

* For shower floor use small mosaic tiles. They will give a better grip and will help avoid slipping due to more joints. Marble floor tiles to be honed finish.
* Bathroom floor area to be fully waterproofed.
* Bathroom walls to be waterproofed to a height of 300mm and shower walls for a height of 1800mm.

PROJECT TITLE:	DRAWN BY	CHECKED	DATE	*address 1* *address 2* *address 3* *postal code* *email address* Interior Designers
	PROJECT NO		SCALE	
DRAWING TITLE: FOUR-FIXTURE BATHROOM (ECONOMICAL LAYOUT)	DRAWING NO		REVISION △	

DATA SHEET	DESCRIPTION BATHROOM LAYOUT	SHEET NO 1 OF 1 TOTAL QTY:

ILLUSTRATION:

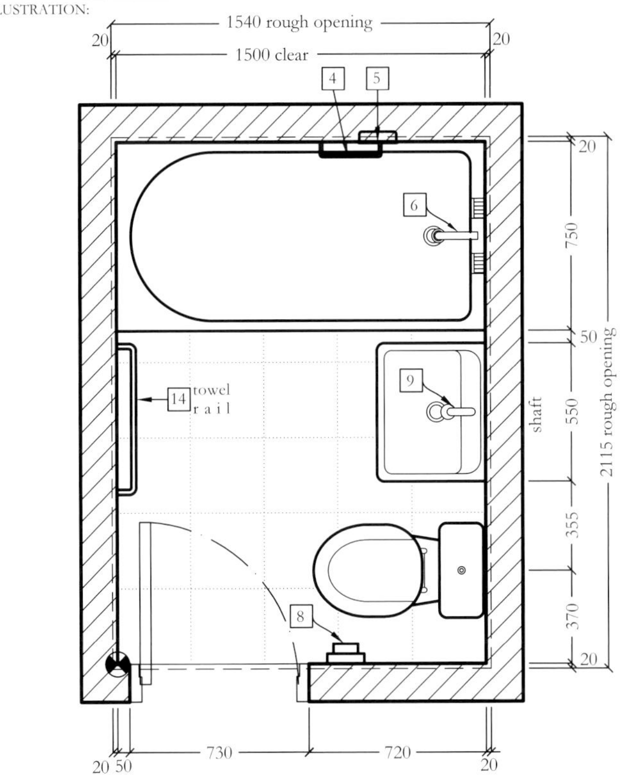

IDEAL/ECONOMICAL LAYOUT

This layout has a shorter run of waste pipe.

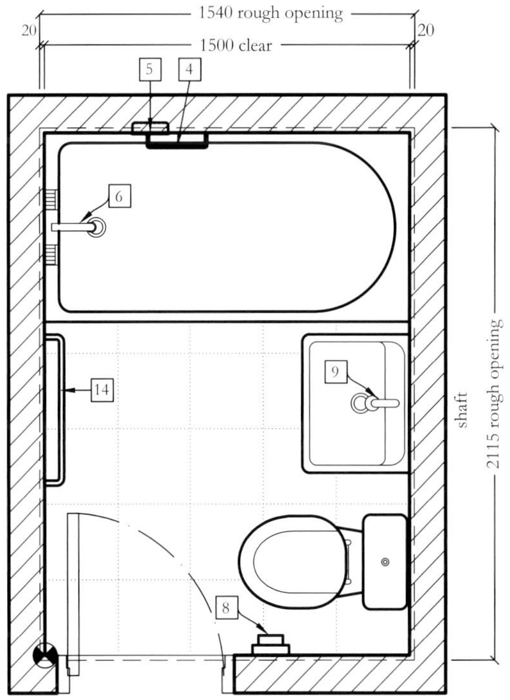

UNECONOMICAL LAYOUT

This layout will require cut-out in concrete floor slab and creating a dropped ceiling in floor below to conceal waste pipe; longer run of waste pipe.

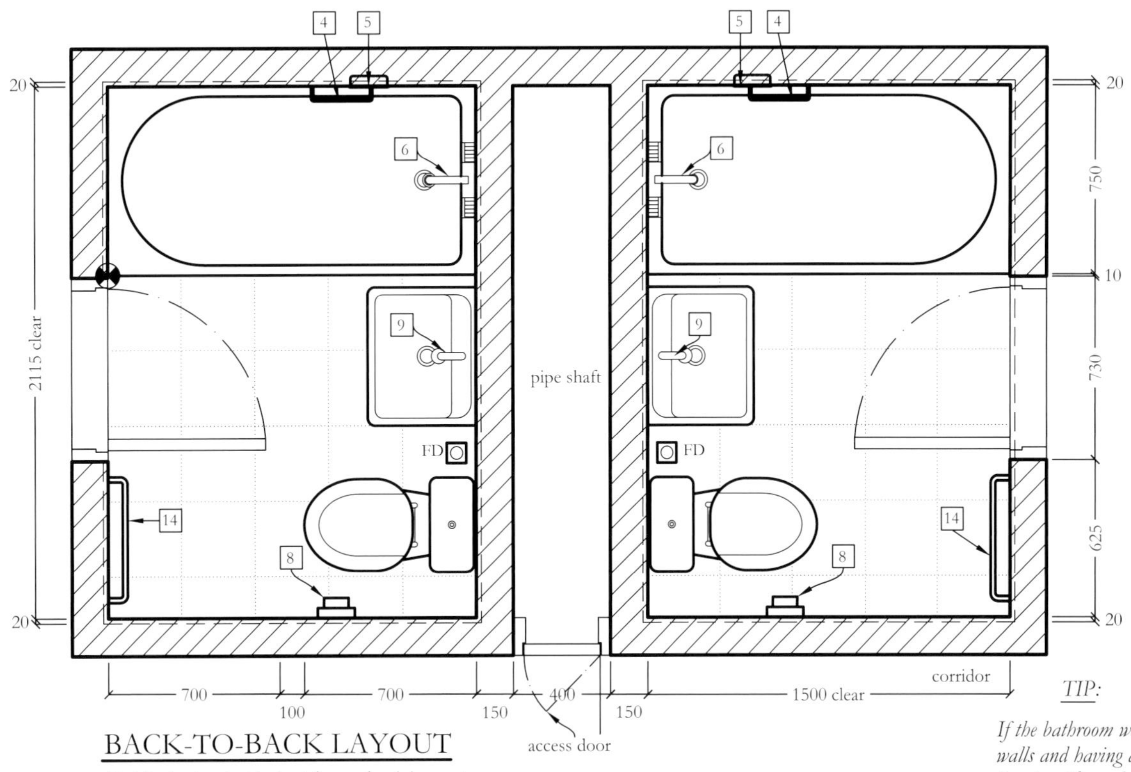

BACK-TO-BACK LAYOUT

ideal for budget hotels, hostels, condominiums, etc.

TIP:

If the bathroom walls are not exterior walls and having a window is not possible then provide mechanical ventilation.

PROJECT TITLE:	DRAWN BY	CHECKED	DATE	address 1 address 2 address 3 postal code email address
	PROJECT NO		SCALE	
DRAWING TITLE: ECONOMICAL BATHROOM LAYOUTS (3-FIXTURES)	DRAWING NO		REVISION △	Interior Designers

DATA SHEET	DESCRIPTION BATHROOM LAYOUT	SHEET NO 1 OF 3 TOTAL QTY:

ILLUSTRATION:

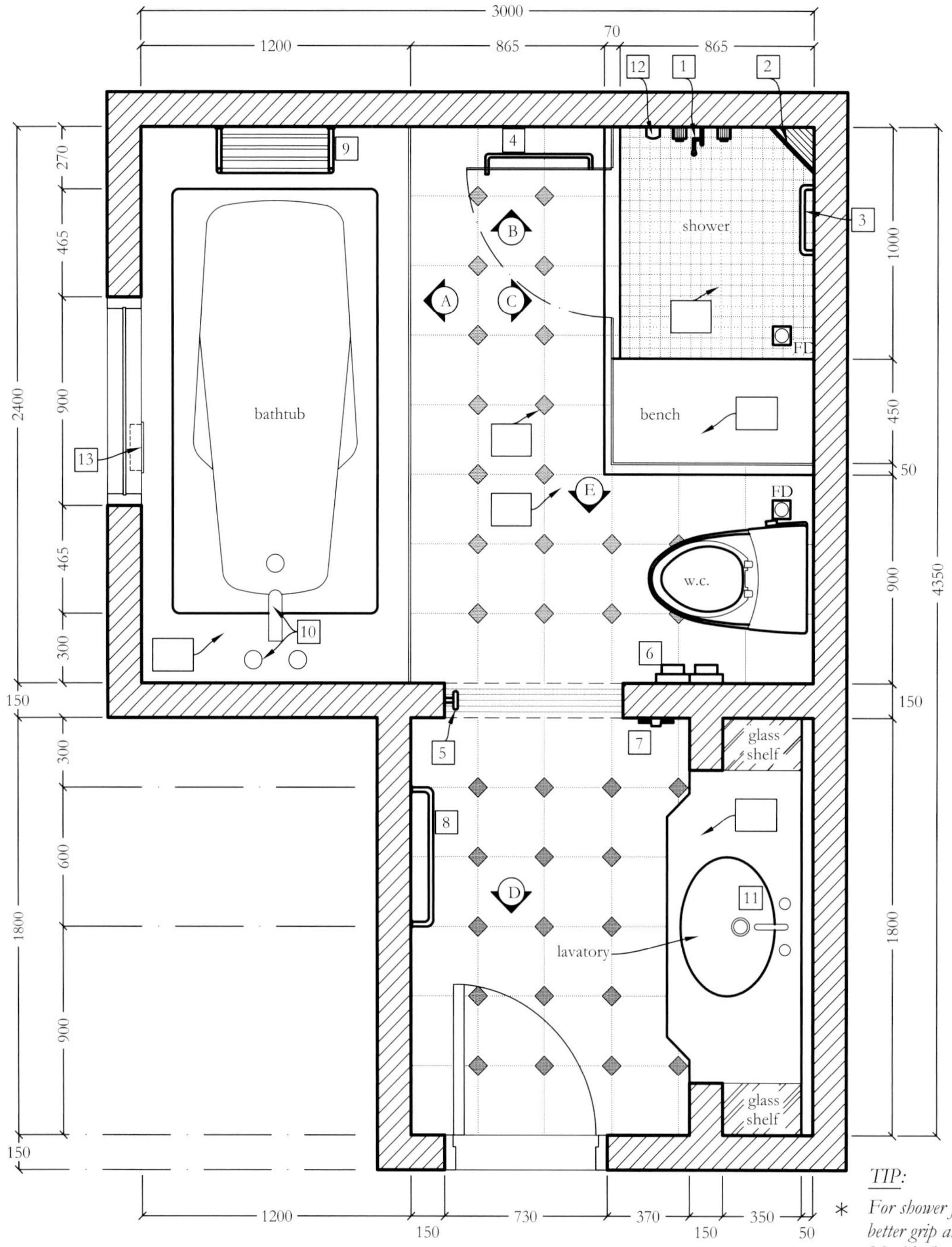

LEGEND:

1	Shower head/rail set
2	Triangular soap dish
3	Grab bar
4	Shower door towel bar & door handle
5	Robe hook
6	Toilet-paper holder (2)
7	Towel ring
8	Towel bar
9	Towel shelf
10	Bath tap fittings
11	Lavatory tap fittings
12	Water inlet
13	Built-in soap dish
FD	Floor drain
*	Marble or ceramic floor tiles 300mm x 300mm
*	Insert tiles 60mm x 60mm

TIP:

* *For shower floor use mosaic tiles. They will give a better grip and help avoid slipping due to more joints. Marble floor tiles to be honed finish.*
* *Bathroom floor area to be fully waterproofed.*
* *Bathroom walls to be waterproofed to a height of 300mm and shower walls for a height of 1800mm.*
* *In a toilet cubicle or a urinal layout (public toilet), do not put a light point in the center of the cubicle as you will cast a shadow on the toilet or urinal. Put the source of light at the center of the toilet/urinal or against the wall like a cove light.*

PROJECT TITLE:	DRAWN BY	CHECKED	DATE	*address 1* *address 2* *address 3* *postal code* *email address*
	PROJECT NO		SCALE	
DRAWING TITLE: FOUR-FIXTURE BATHROOM (LUXURIOUS)	DRAWING NO		REVISION △	Interior Designers

DATA SHEET	DESCRIPTION BATHROOM ELEVATIONS	SHEET NO 2 OF 3 TOTAL QTY:

ILLUSTRATION:

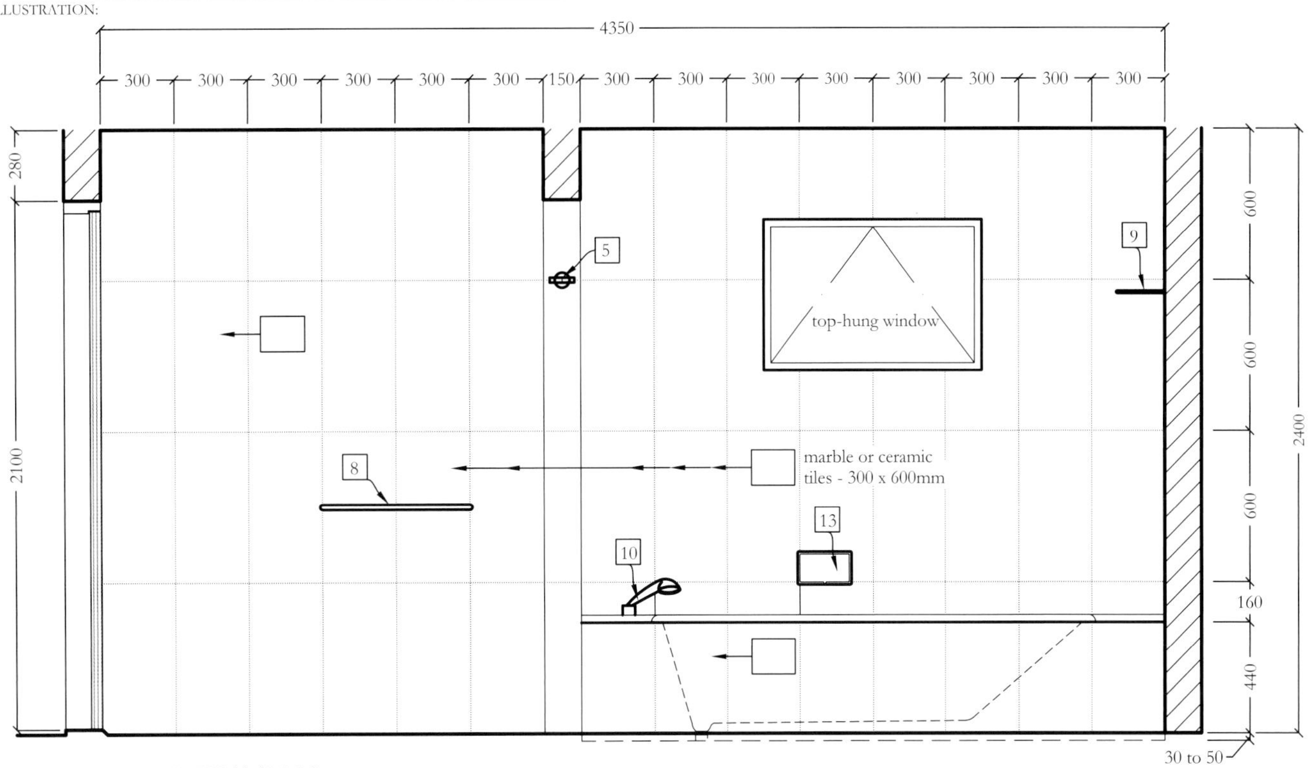

A ELEVATION

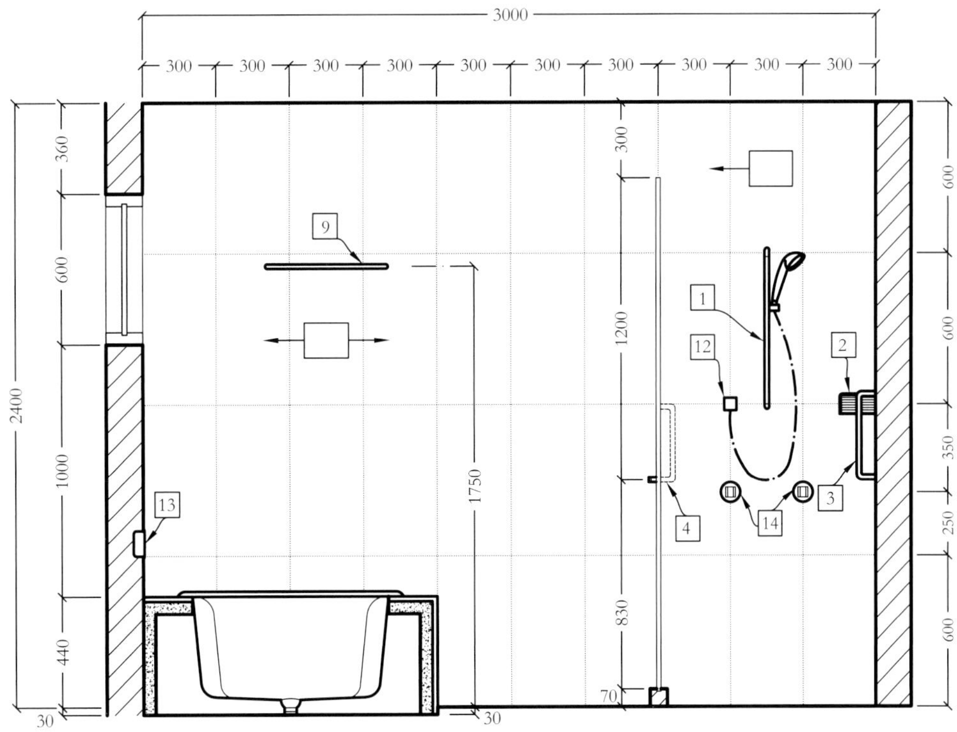

B ELEVATION

LEGEND:

1	Shower head/rail set
2	Triangular soap dish
3	Grab bar
4	Shower door towel bar & door handle
5	Robe hook
6	Toilet-paper holder (2)
7	Towel ring
8	Towel bar
9	Towel shelf
10	Bath tap fittings
11	Lavatory tap fittings
12	Water inlet
13	Built-in soap dish
14	Shower tap fittings
FD	Floor drain

PROJECT TITLE:	DRAWN BY	CHECKED	DATE	address 1 address 2 address 3 postal code email address Interior Designers
DRAWING TITLE: BATHROOM ELEVATIONS A AND B	PROJECT NO		SCALE	
	DRAWING NO		REVISION △	

DATA SHEET	DESCRIPTION BATHROOM ELEVATIONS	SHEET NO 3 OF 3 TOTAL QTY:

ILLUSTRATION:

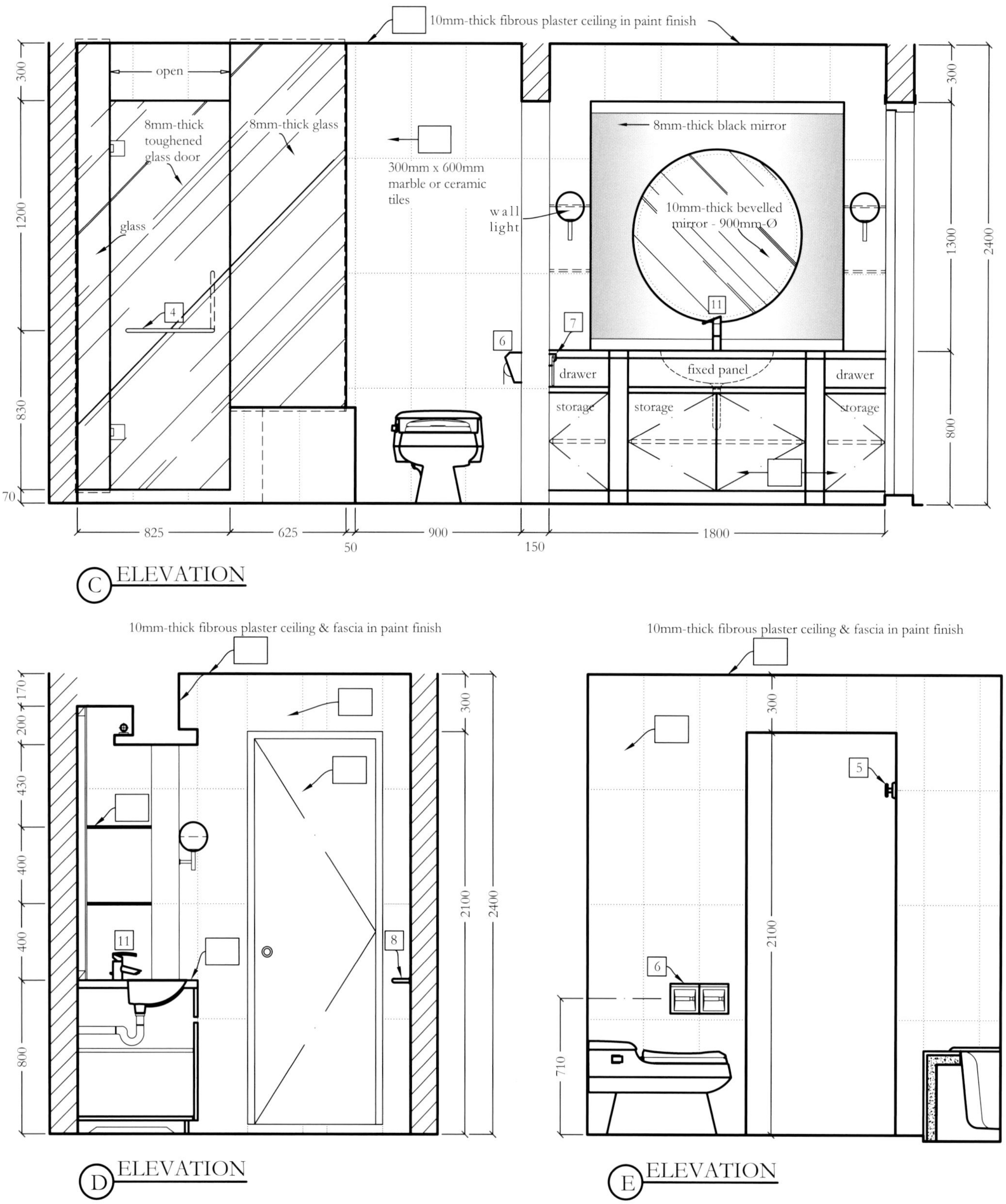

PROJECT TITLE:	DRAWN BY	CHECKED	DATE	address 1 address 2 address 3 postal code email address
	PROJECT NO		SCALE	
DRAWING TITLE: BATHROOM ELEVATIONS C, D & E	DRAWING NO		REVISION △	Interior Designers

DATA SHEET	DESCRIPTION WASHROOM AREA		SHEET NO 1 OF 3 TOTAL QTY:

ILLUSTRATION:

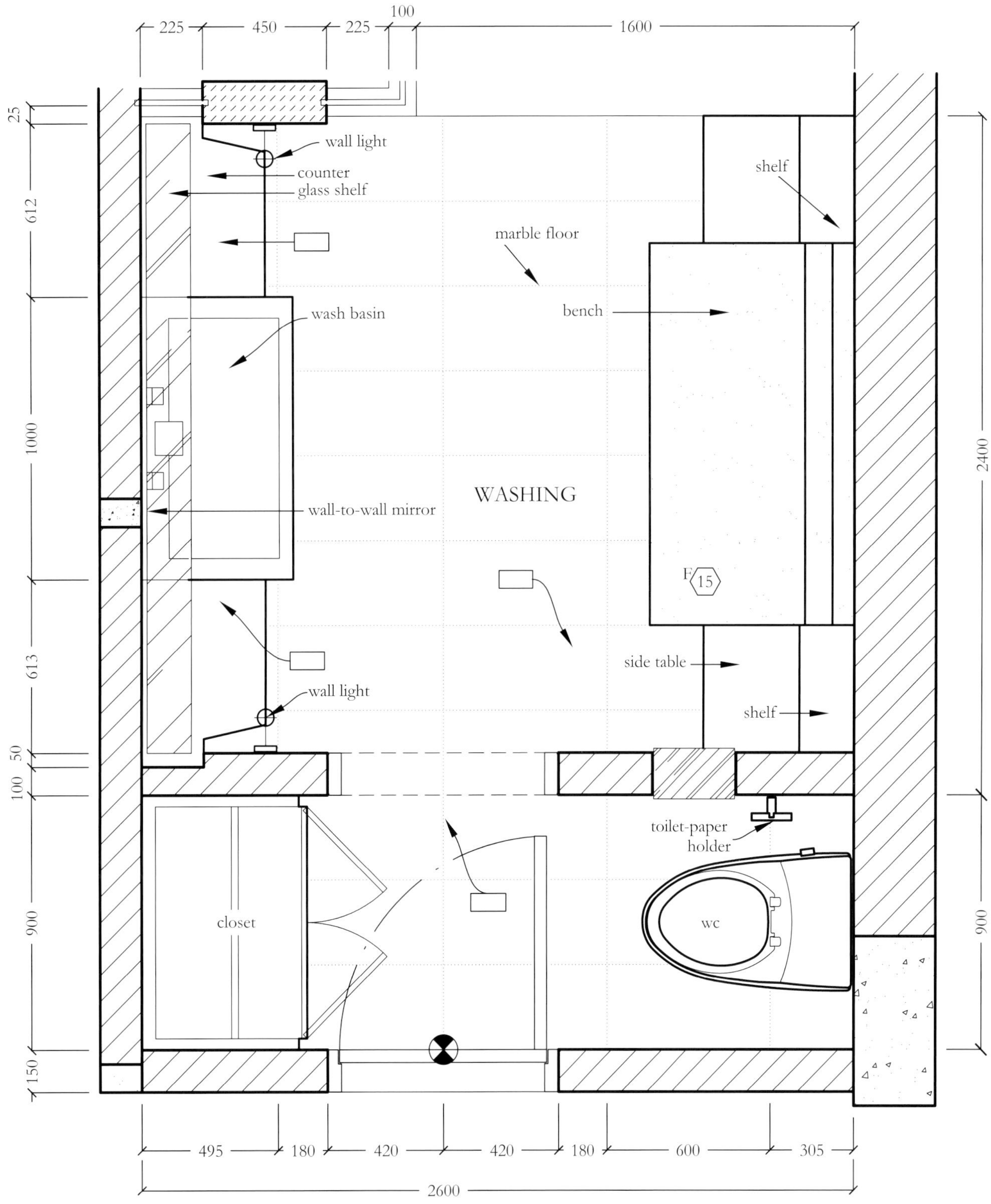

Fill in the finishes numbers

PROJECT TITLE:	DRAWN BY	CHECKED	DATE	address 1 address 2 address 3 postal code email address
	PROJECT NO		SCALE	
DRAWING TITLE: PLAN OF WASH BASIN AND COUNTER	DRAWING NO		REVISION △	Interior Designers

DATA SHEET	DESCRIPTION WASHROOM AREA	SHEET NO 2 OF 3 TOTAL QTY:

ILLUSTRATION:

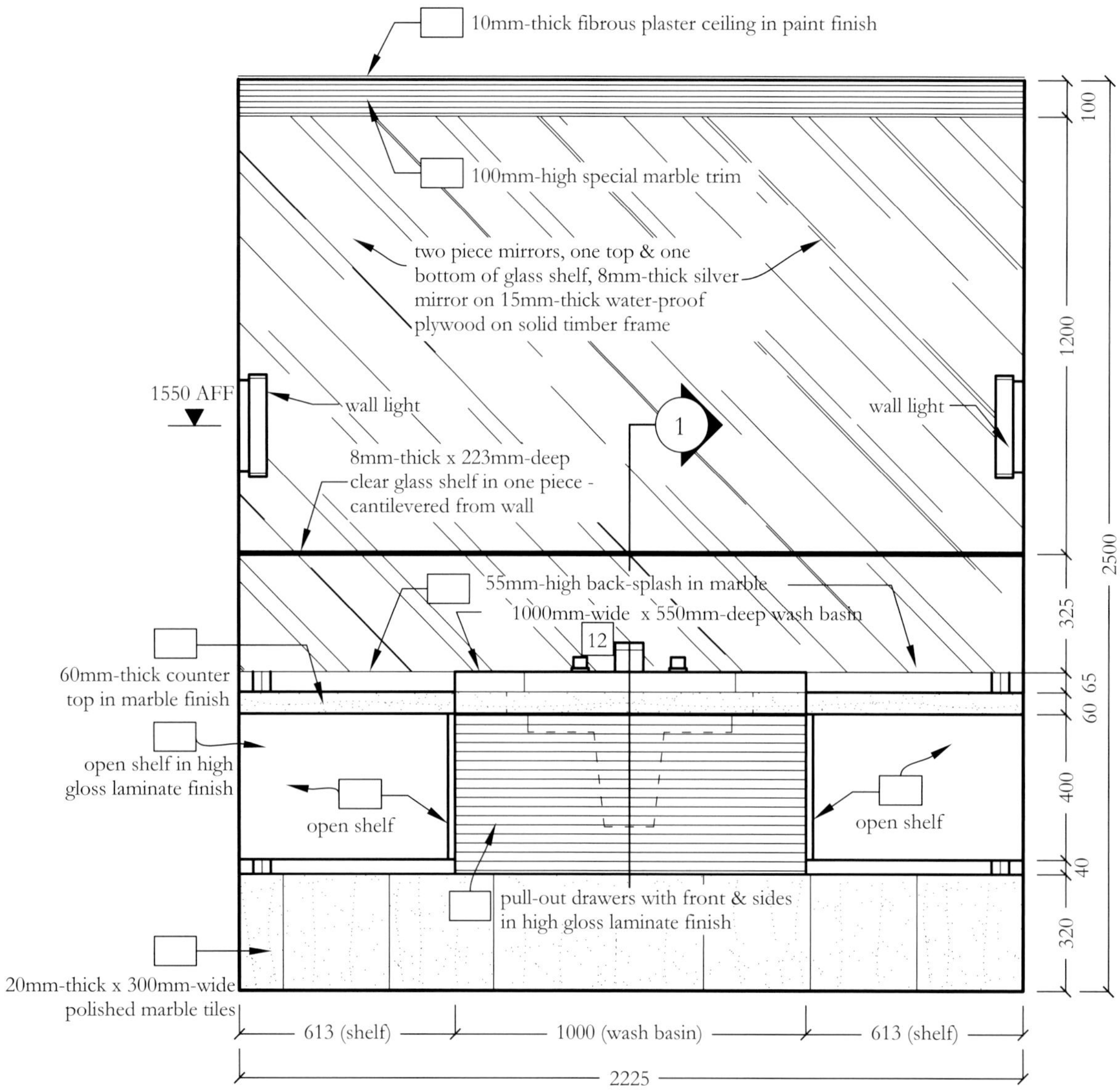

PROJECT TITLE:	DRAWN BY	CHECKED	DATE	address 1 address 2 address 3 postal code email address
	PROJECT NO		SCALE	
DRAWING TITLE: ELEVATION OF WASH BASIN & COUNTER	DRAWING NO		REVISION △	Interior Designers

DATA SHEET	DESCRIPTION WASHROOM AREA		SHEET NO 2 OF 2 TOTAL QTY:

ILLUSTRATION:

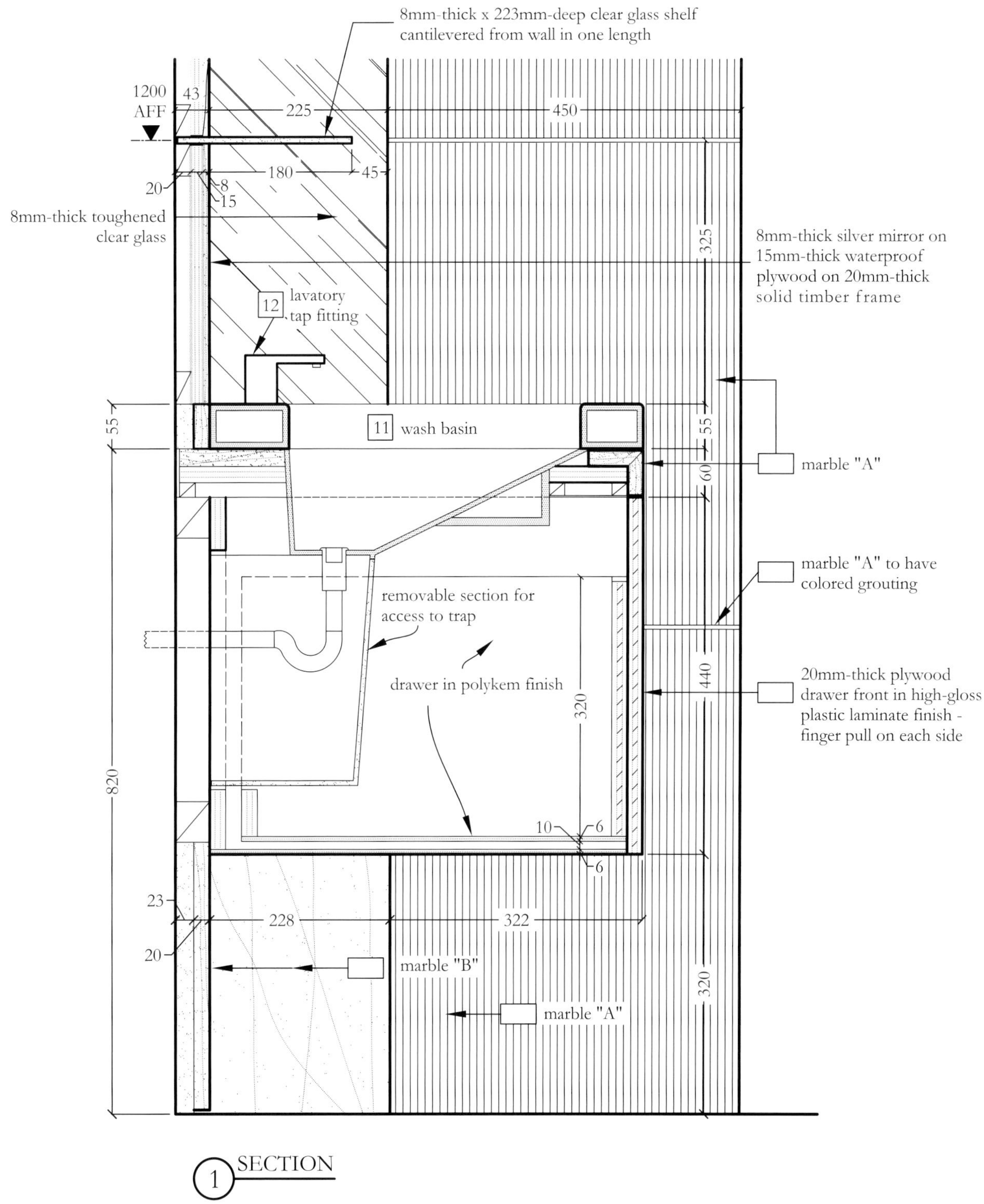

1 SECTION

PROJECT TITLE:	DRAWN BY	CHECKED	DATE	address 1 address 2 address 3 postal code email address
	PROJECT NO		SCALE	
DRAWING TITLE: SECTIONAL DETAIL @ WASH BASIN	DRAWING NO		REVISION △	Interior Designers

Outdoor Jacuzzi with water feature for a house in Jakarta, Indonesia.

CHAPTER 9

DRESSING AREAS ~ WARDROBES, DRESSING TABLES, DRESSING STOOLS, HEADBOARDS, AND NIGHT TABLES

1. Data sheet - plan of wardrobes and detail
2. Data sheet - elevation of wardrobes (with doors)
3. Data sheet - elevation of wardrobes (without doors)
4. Data sheet - section 1 of wardrobes
5. Data sheet - section 2 of wardrobes
6. Data sheet - plan of dressing table and dressing stool
7. Data sheet - plan of dressing table (top removed) and side elevation of stool and dressing table
8. Data sheet - elevation of dressing table, dressing stool and mirror
9. Data sheet - section through dressing table and stool plus detail of framed mirror
10. Data sheet - plan and side elevation of dressing stool/ottoman
11. Data sheet - front elevation, section and details of dressing stool/ ottoman
12. Data sheet - elevation of headboard and night table
13. Data sheet - section and side elevation of headboard
14. Data sheet - elevations and details of night table

DATA SHEET	DESCRIPTION WARDROBES	SHEET NO 1 OF 5 TOTAL QTY:

ILLUSTRATION:

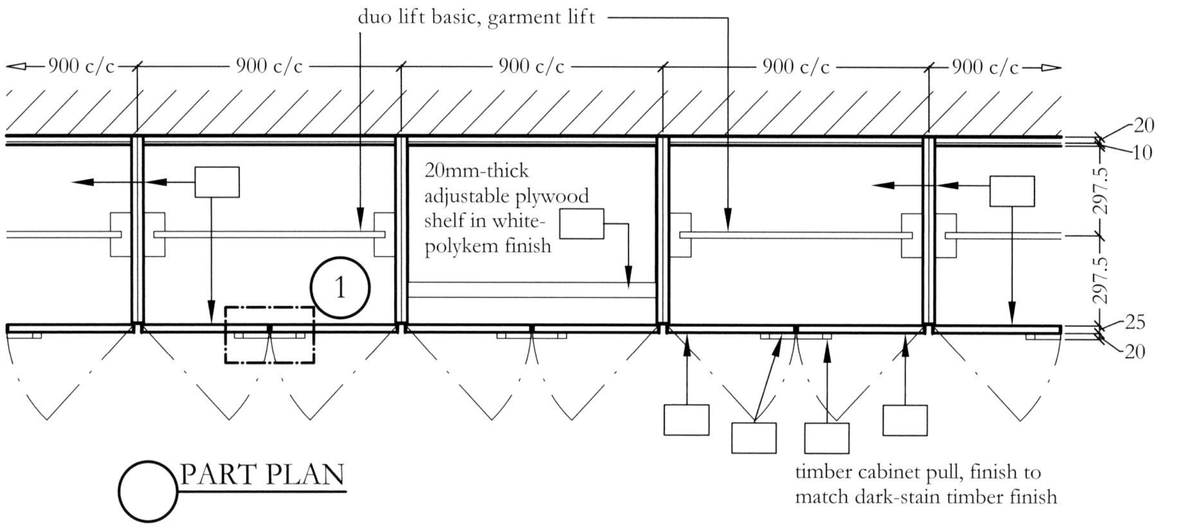

PART PLAN

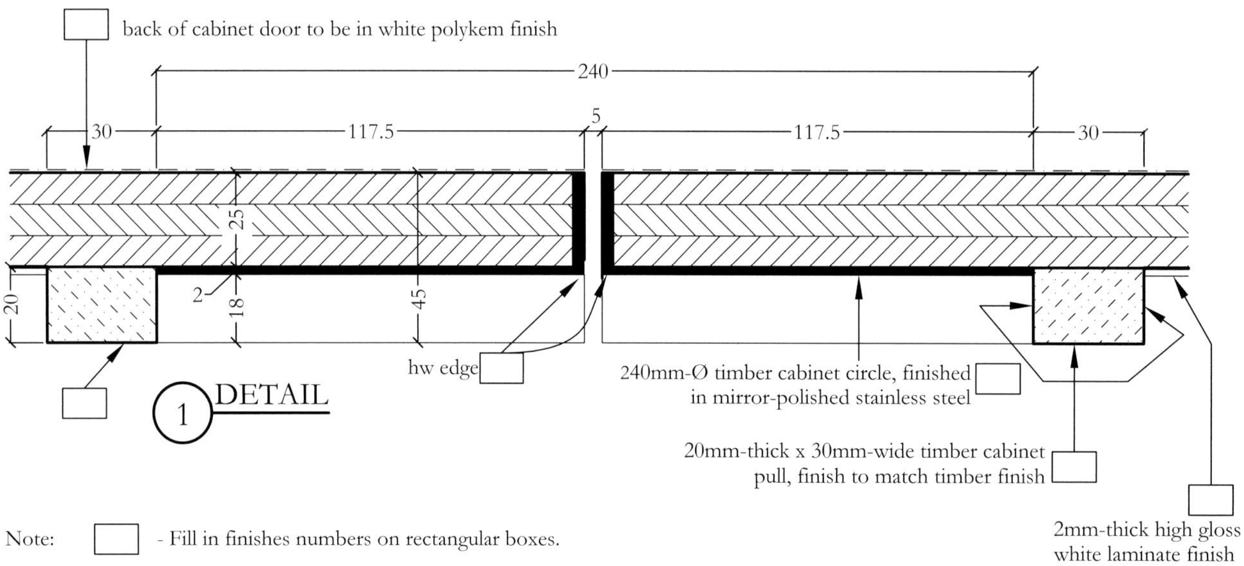

1 DETAIL

Note: ☐ - Fill in finishes numbers on rectangular boxes.

PROJECT TITLE:	DRAWN BY	CHECKED	DATE	address 1 address 2 address 3 postal code email address Interior Designers
	PROJECT NO		SCALE	
DRAWING TITLE: PLAN OF WARDROBE AND DETAIL	DRAWING NO		REVISION △	

DATA SHEET	DESCRIPTION WARDROBES	SHEET NO 2 OF 5 TOTAL QTY:

ILLUSTRATION:

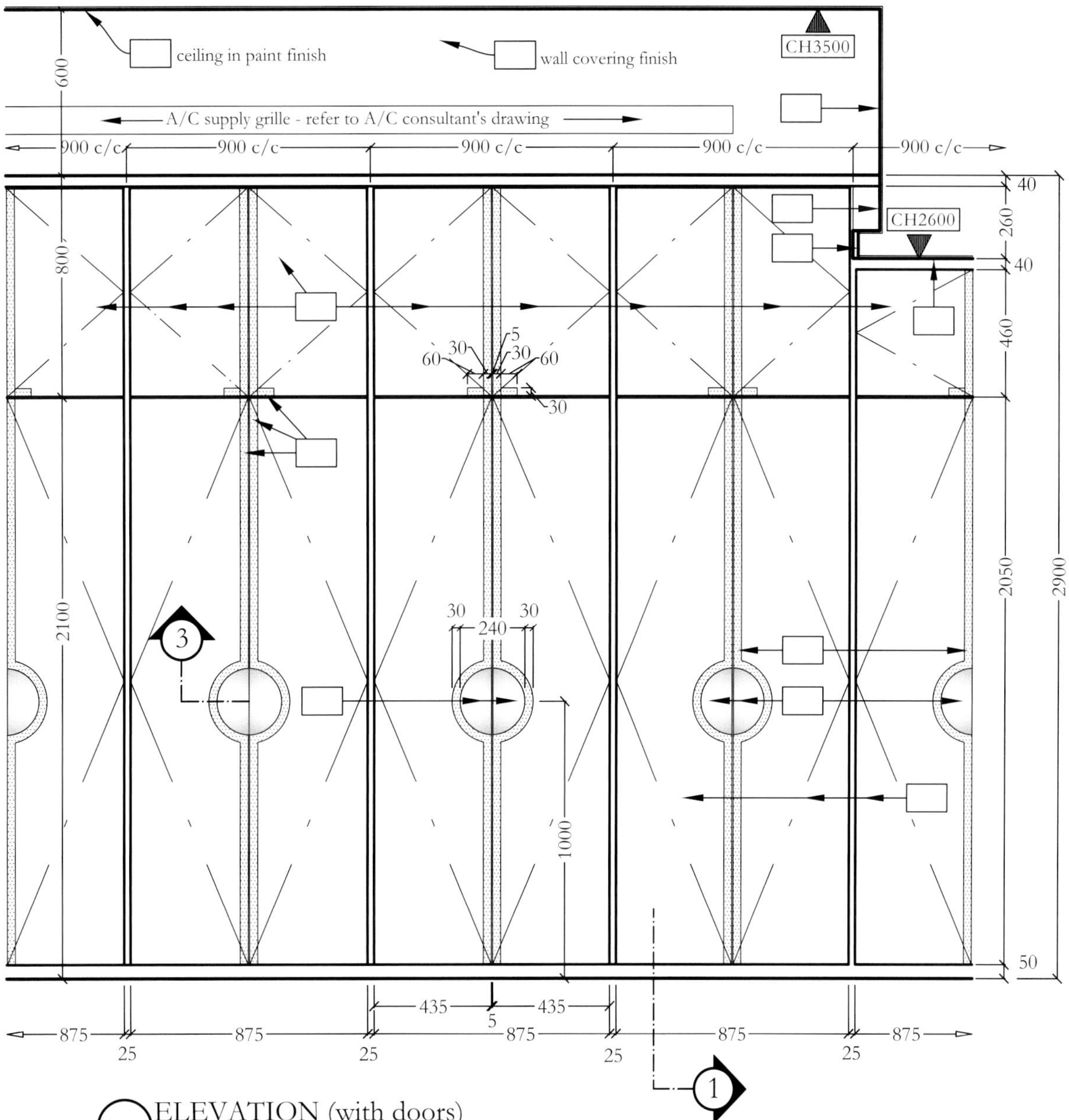

ELEVATION (with doors)

Note: ☐ Fill in finishes numbers on rectangular boxes.

PROJECT TITLE:	DRAWN BY	CHECKED	DATE	*address 1* *address 2* *address 3* *postal code* *email address*
	PROJECT NO		SCALE	
DRAWING TITLE: ELEVATION OF WARDROBE (with doors)	DRAWING NO		REVISION △	Interior Designers

DATA SHEET	DESCRIPTION WARDROBES	SHEET NO 3 OF 5 TOTAL QTY:

ILLUSTRATION:

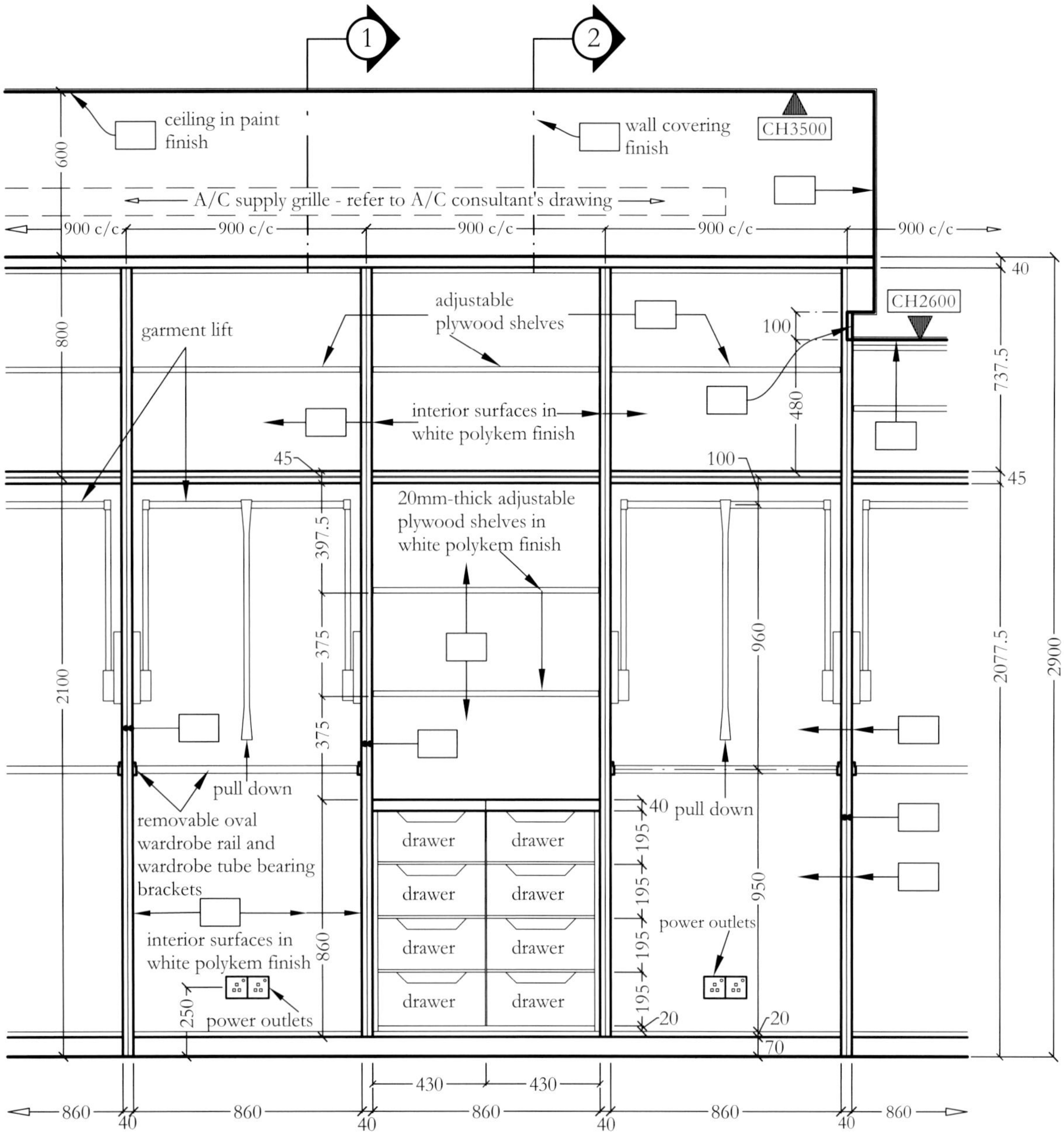

ELEVATION (without doors)

Note: 1. Garment lift can be electrically controlled, up and down, by remote control pad, so central pull-bar will not be required.

2. ☐ Fill in finishes numbers on rectangular boxes.

PROJECT TITLE:	DRAWN BY	CHECKED	DATE	address 1 address 2 address 3 postal code email address Interior Designers
	PROJECT NO		SCALE	
DRAWING TITLE: ELEVATION OF WARDROBE (without doors)	DRAWING NO		REVISION △	

DATA SHEET	DESCRIPTION WARDROBES	SHEET NO 4 OF 5 TOTAL QTY:

ILLUSTRATION:

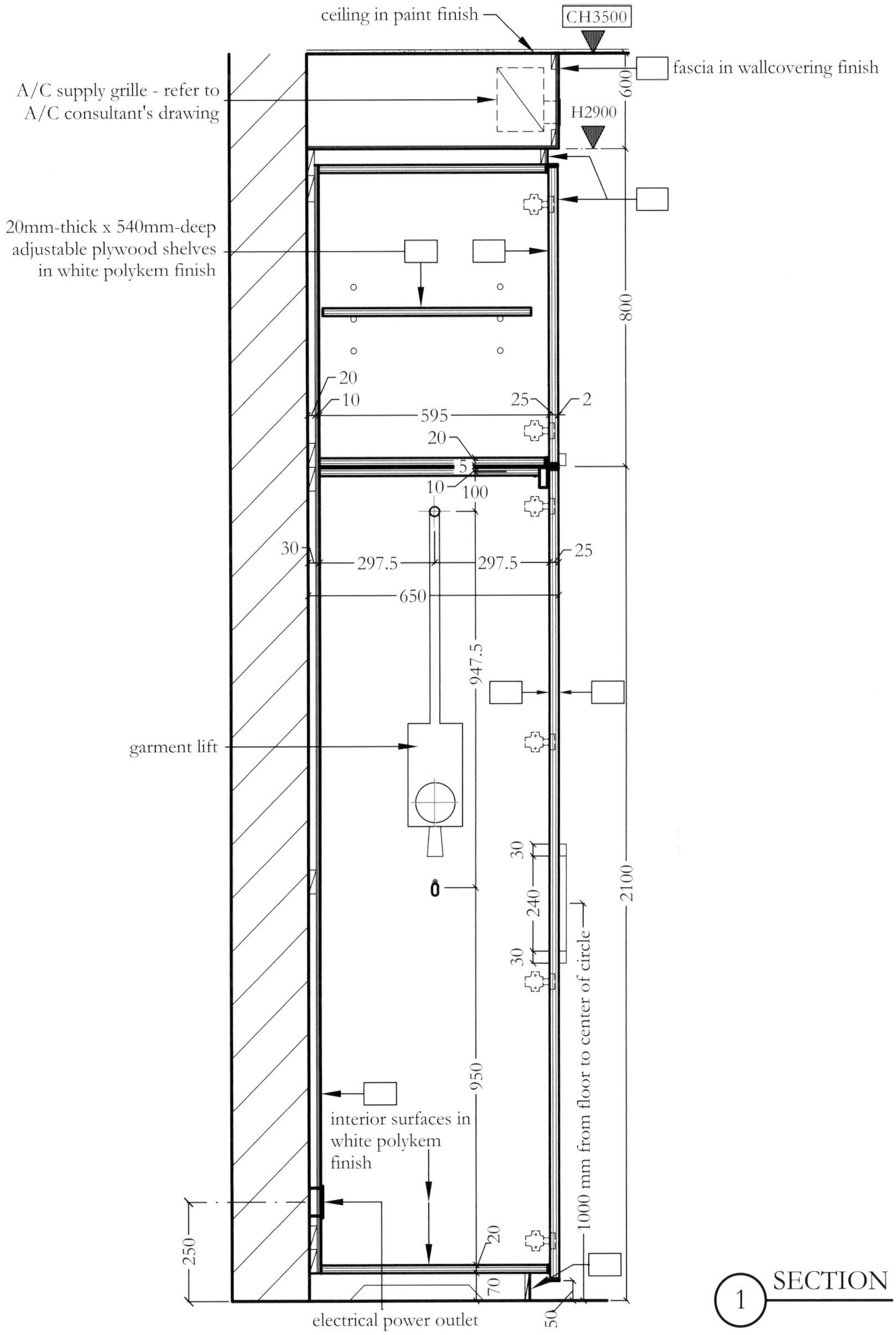

PROJECT TITLE:	DRAWN BY	CHECKED	DATE	address 1 address 2 address 3 postal code email address
	PROJECT NO		SCALE	
DRAWING TITLE: SECTION 1 OF WARDROBE	DRAWING NO		REVISION △	Interior Designers

DATA SHEET	DESCRIPTION WARDROBES	SHEET NO 5 OF 5 TOTAL QTY:

ILLUSTRATION:

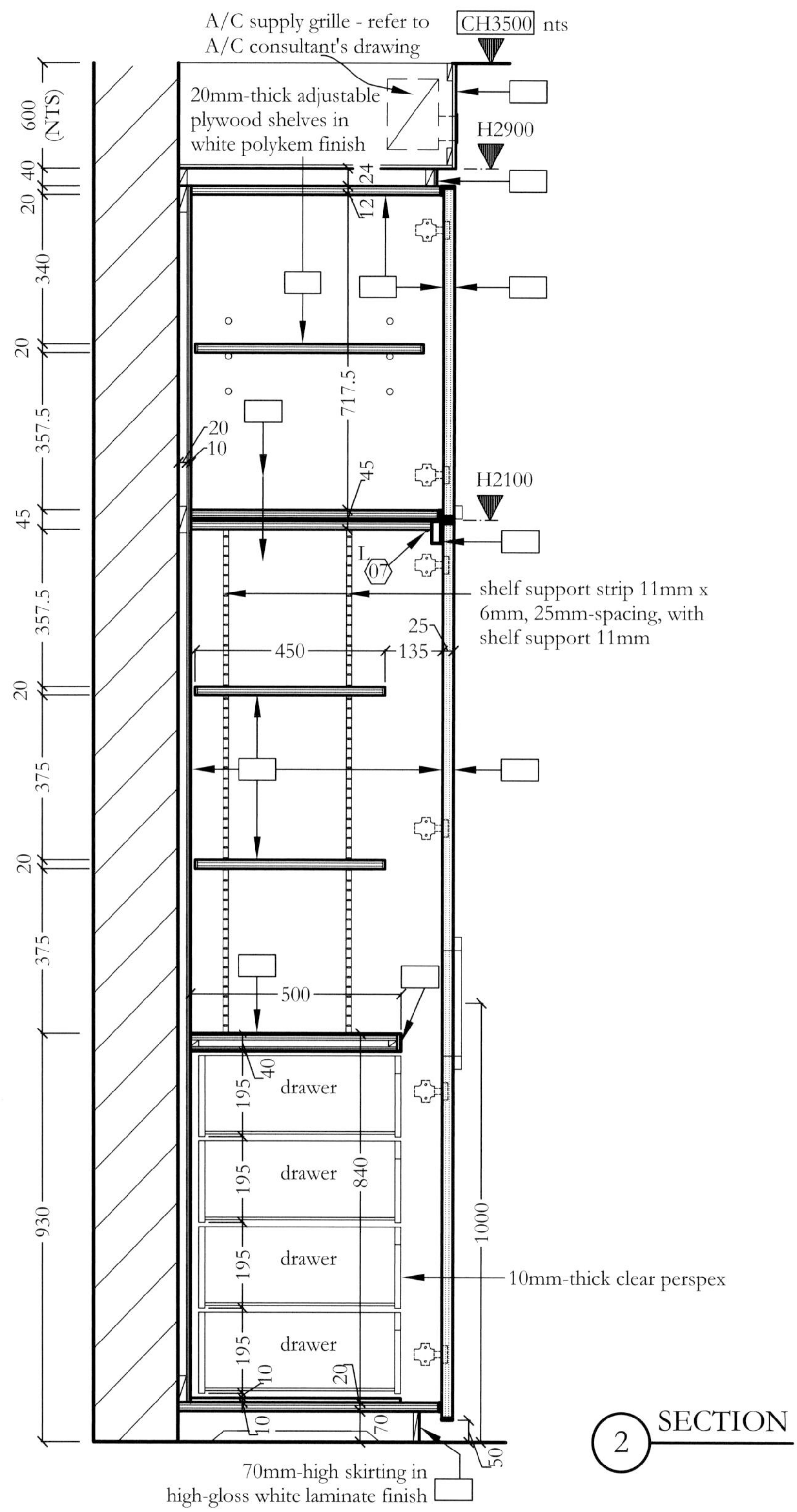

PROJECT TITLE:	DRAWN BY	CHECKED	DATE	address 1 address 2 address 3 postal code email address
	PROJECT NO		SCALE	
DRAWING TITLE: SECTION 2 OF WARDROBE	DRAWING NO		REVISION △	Interior Designers

DATA SHEET	DESCRIPTION: DRESSING TABLE AND STOOL	F	SHEET NO 1 OF 4 / TOTAL QTY:

ILLUSTRATION:

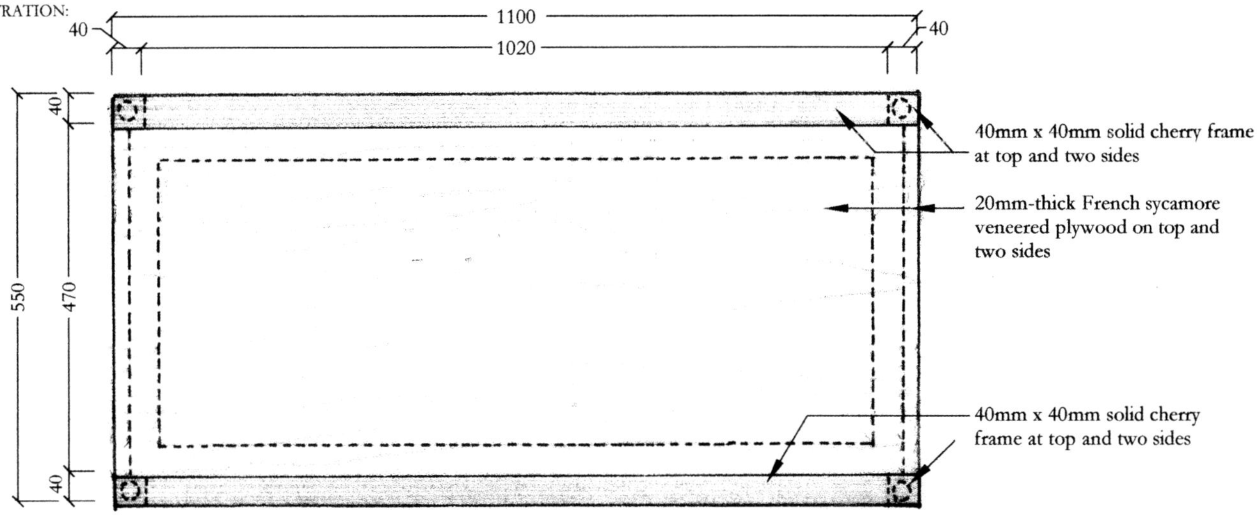

PLAN - DRESSING TABLE

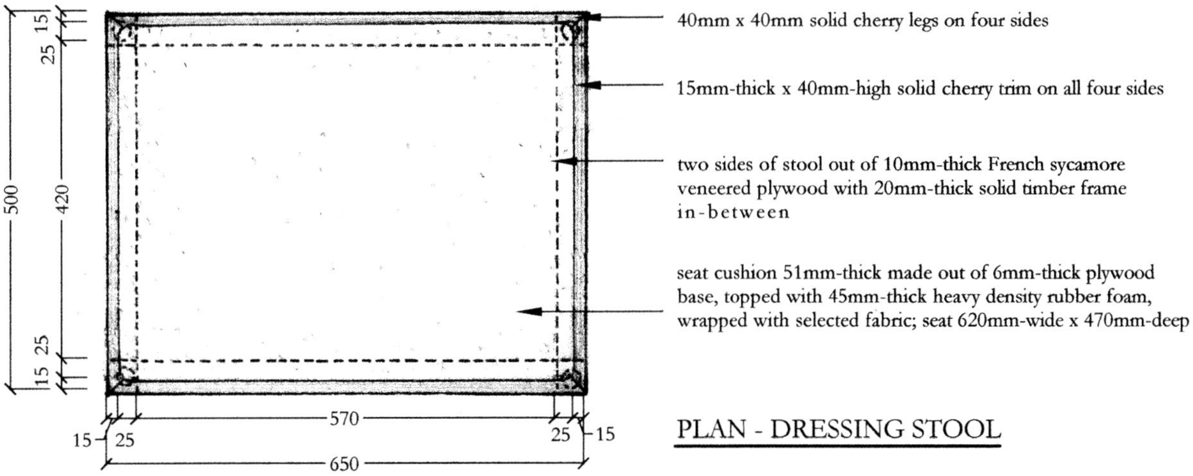

PLAN - DRESSING STOOL

SPECIFICATION / DESCRIPTION:

SUPPLIER / MANUFACTURER: NAME/FIRM OF FURNITURE CONTRACTOR	Furniture Supplier code	Finishes Supplier & Code

MODEL NO:	DIMENSIONS (mm):	ROOM TYPE:	QUANTITY:
custom-made	dressing table - W1100 D550 H750 dressing stool - W650 D500 H450	1	
OTHER FINISHES CODE:	AREA LOCATION:	2	
		3	
COSTINGS: ☐ BUDGET : \$ ☐ QUOTATION : \$ ☐ FINAL PRICE : \$	TOTAL: TOTAL QUANTITY: TOTAL PRICE: \$	4	
		5	
		TOTAL QTY:	

REMARKS/NOTES /SPECIAL INSTRUCTIONS:

PROJECT TITLE:	DRAWN BY	CHECKED	DATE	*address 1* *address 2* *address 3* *postal code* *email address*
	PROJECT NO		SCALE	
DRAWING TITLE: DRESSING TABLE AND DRESSING STOOL - PLANS	DRAWING NO		REVISION △	Interior Designers

DATA SHEET	DESCRIPTION: DRESSING TABLE AND STOOL	SHEET NO 2 OF 4 / TOTAL QTY:

ILLUSTRATION:

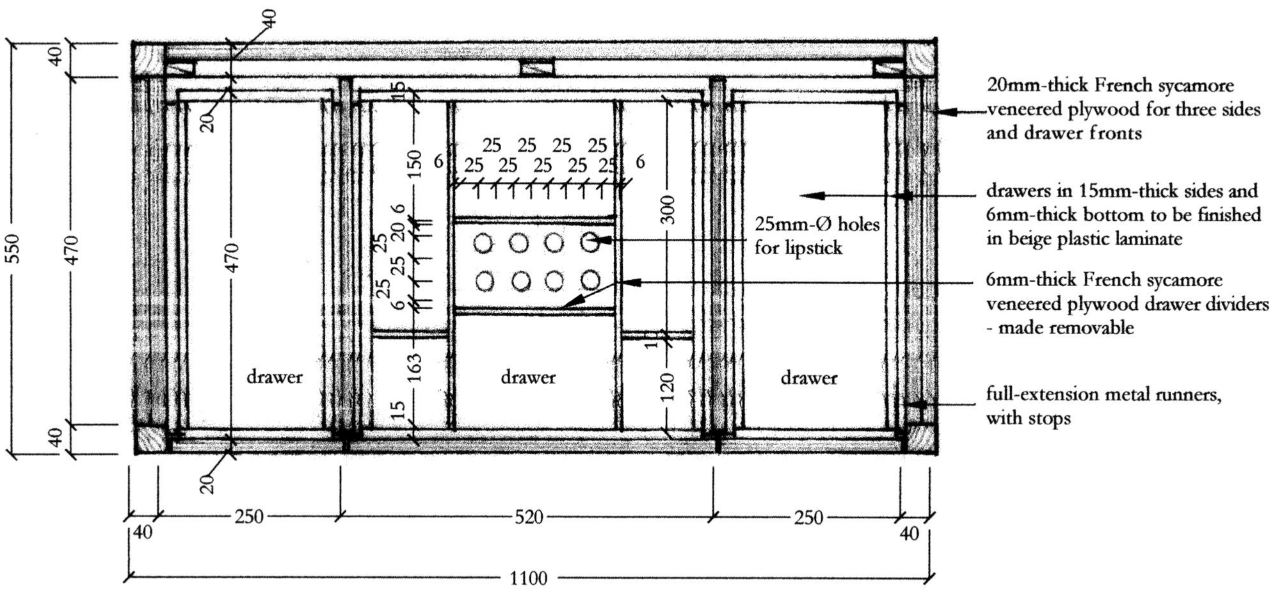

PLAN OF DRESSING TABLE WITH TOP REMOVED

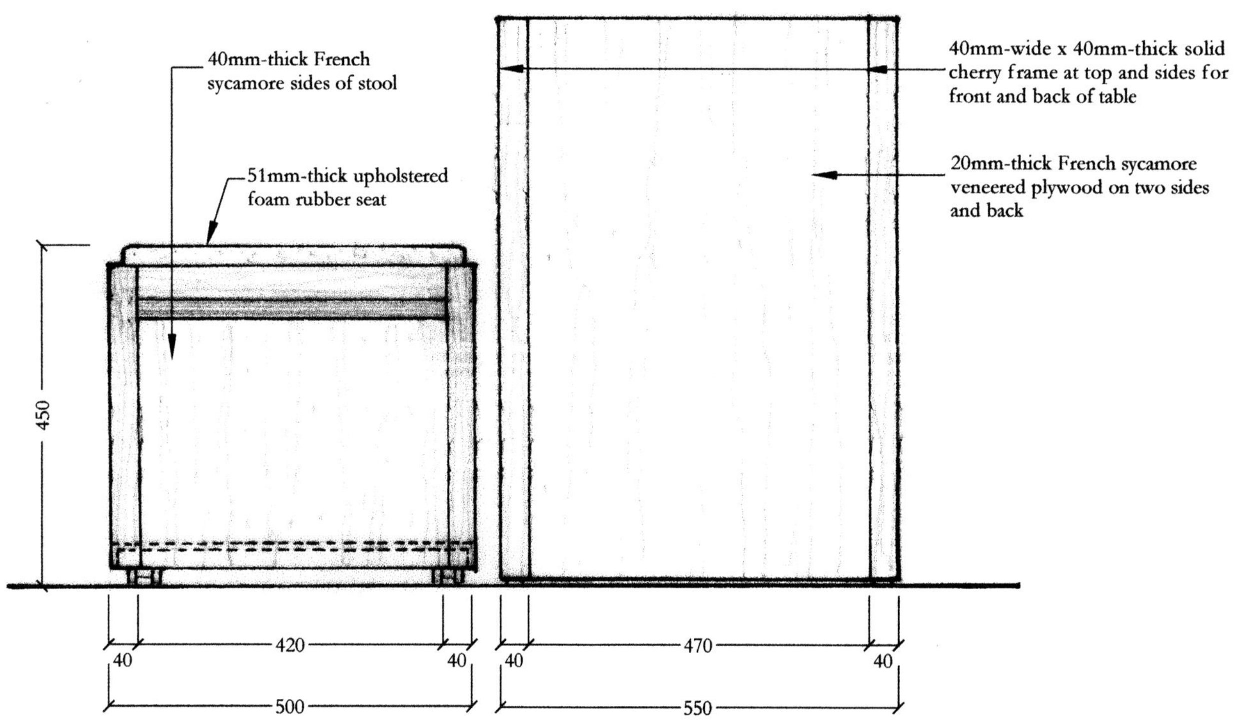

SIDE ELEVATION OF STOOL AND DRESSING TABLE

PROJECT TITLE:	DRAWN BY	CHECKED	DATE	*address 1* *address 2* *address 3* *postal code* *email address* Interior Designers
DRAWING TITLE: PLAN AND SIDE ELEVATION OF STOOL AND DRESSING TABLE	PROJECT NO		SCALE	
	DRAWING NO		REVISION △	

DATA SHEET	DESCRIPTION: DRESSING TABLE AND STOOL	F	SHEET NO 3 OF 4 / TOTAL QTY:

ILLUSTRATION:

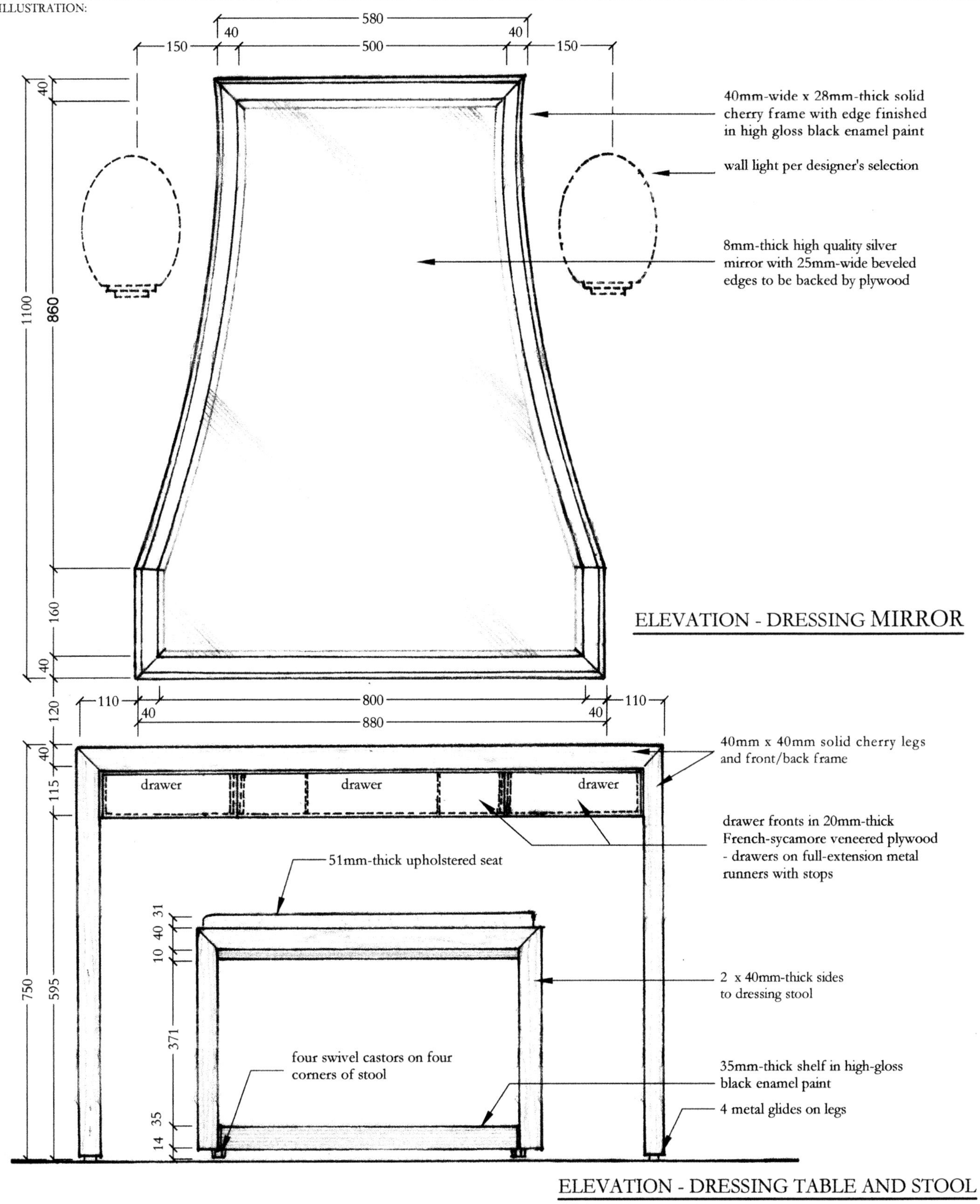

PROJECT TITLE:	DRAWN BY	CHECKED	DATE	address 1 address 2 address 3 postal code email address Interior Designers
	PROJECT NO		SCALE	
DRAWING TITLE: ELEVATIONS - DRESSING TABLE, STOOL, AND DRESSING MIRROR	DRAWING NO		REVISION △	

DATA SHEET	DESCRIPTION: DRESSING TABLE AND STOOL		SHEET NO 4 OF 4 TOTAL QTY:

ILLUSTRATION:

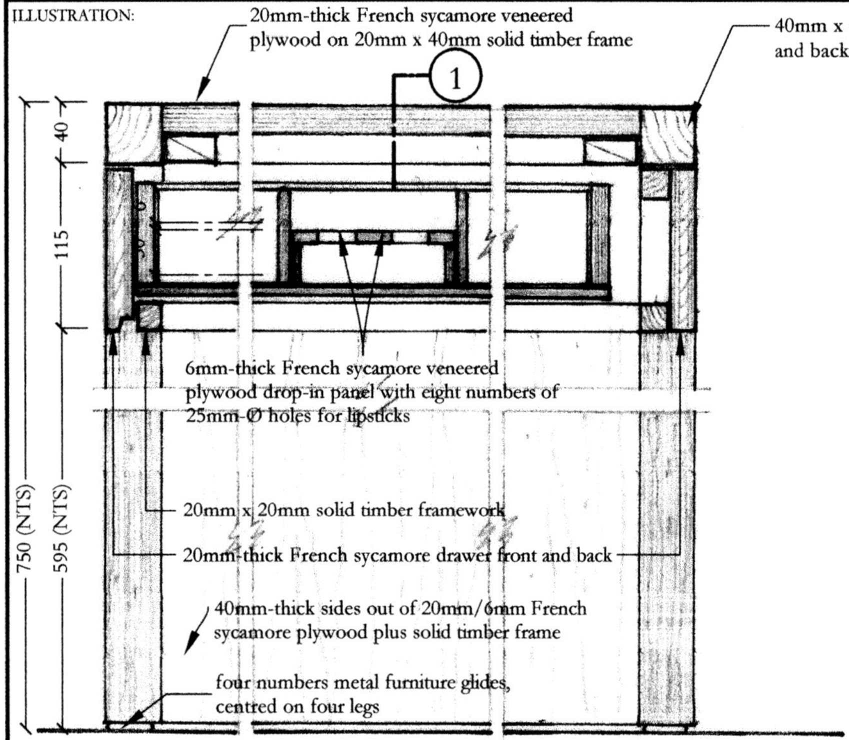

SECTION THROUGH DRESSING TABLE
(INDICATING SOLID TOP)

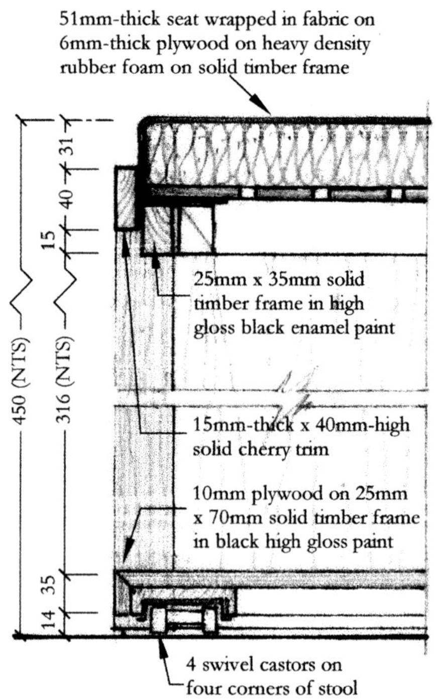

SECTION THROUGH STOOL

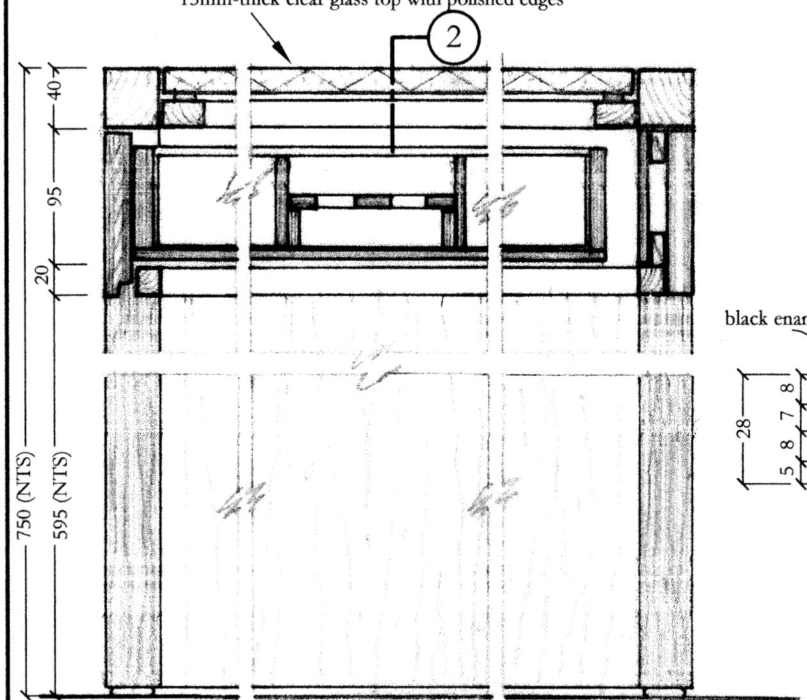

SECTION THROUGH DRESSING TABLE
(INDICATING CLEAR GLASS TOP)

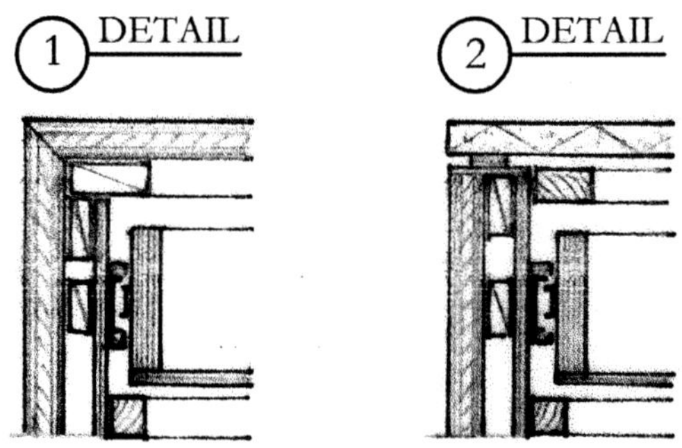

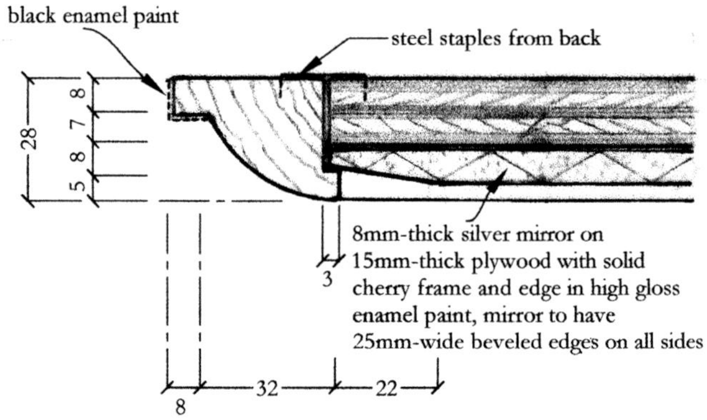

DETAIL OF FRAMED MIRROR

PROJECT TITLE:	DRAWN BY	CHECKED	DATE	address 1 address 2 address 3 postal code email address Interior Designers
	PROJECT NO		SCALE	
DRAWING TITLE: DRESSING TABLE, STOOL, AND MIRROR - SECTIONS AND DETAILS	DRAWING NO		REVISION △	

DATA SHEET	LOCATION DRESSING AREA	F	SHEET NO 1 OF 2 TOTAL QTY:

ILLUSTRATION:

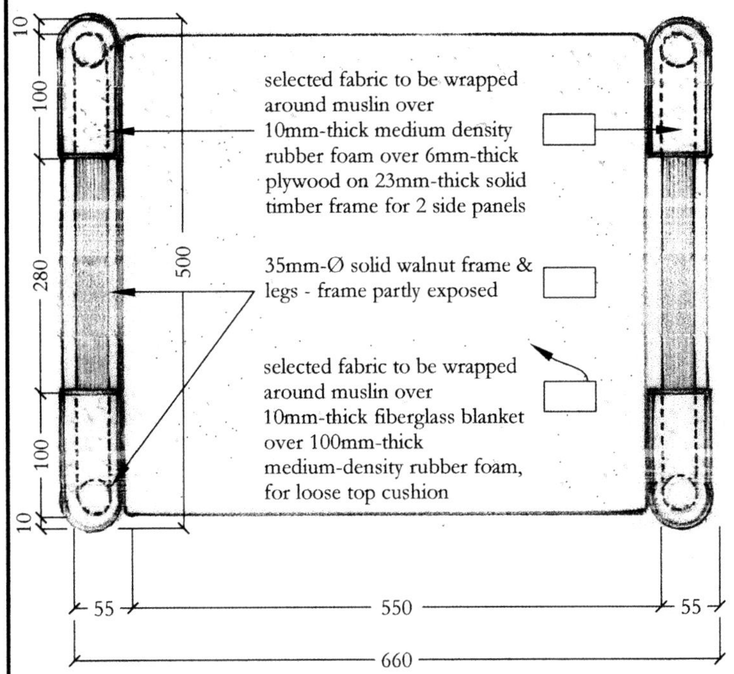

PLAN

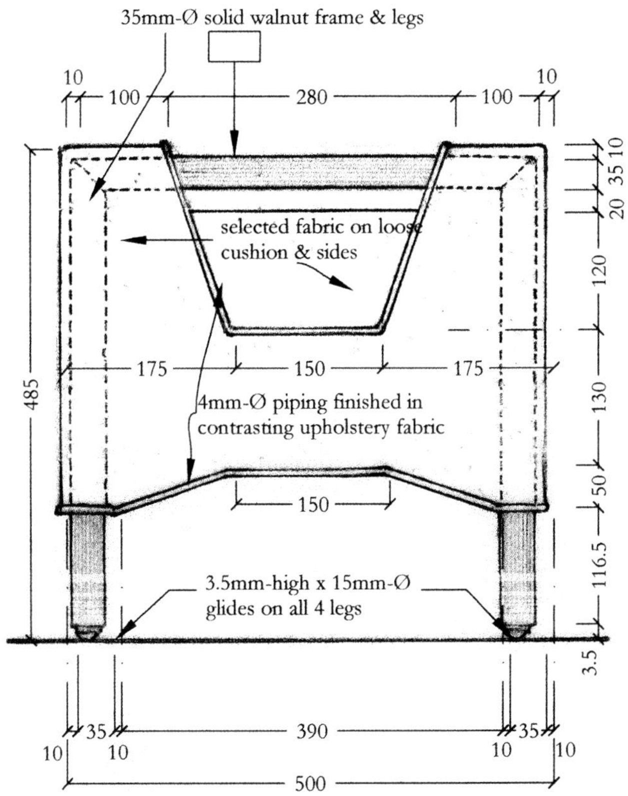

SIDE ELEVATION

SPECIFICATION / DESCRIPTION:

SUPPLIER / MANUFACTURER:	Furniture Supplier code	Finishes Supplier & Code	
NAME/FIRM OF FURNITURE CONTRACTOR			
MODEL NO: custom design	DIMENSIONS (mm): 660mm-wide x 500mm-deep x 485mm-high	ROOM TYPE:	QUANTITY:
OTHER FINISHES CODE:	AREA LOCATION:	1	
		2	
		3	
COSTINGS: ☐ BUDGET : \$ ☐ QUOTATION : \$ ☐ FINAL PRICE : \$	TOTAL: TOTAL QUANTITY: TOTAL PRICE: \$	4	
		5	
		TOTAL QTY:	

REMARKS/NOTES /SPECIAL INSTRUCTIONS:

PROJECT TITLE:	DRAWN BY	CHECKED	DATE	address 1 address 2 address 3 postal code email address
	PROJECT NO		SCALE	
DRAWING TITLE: DRESSING STOOL/OTTOMAN - PLAN & SIDE ELEVATION	DRAWING NO		REVISION △	Interior Designers

DATA SHEET	LOCATION DRESSING AREA	F	SHEET NO 2 OF 2 TOTAL QTY:

ILLUSTRATION:

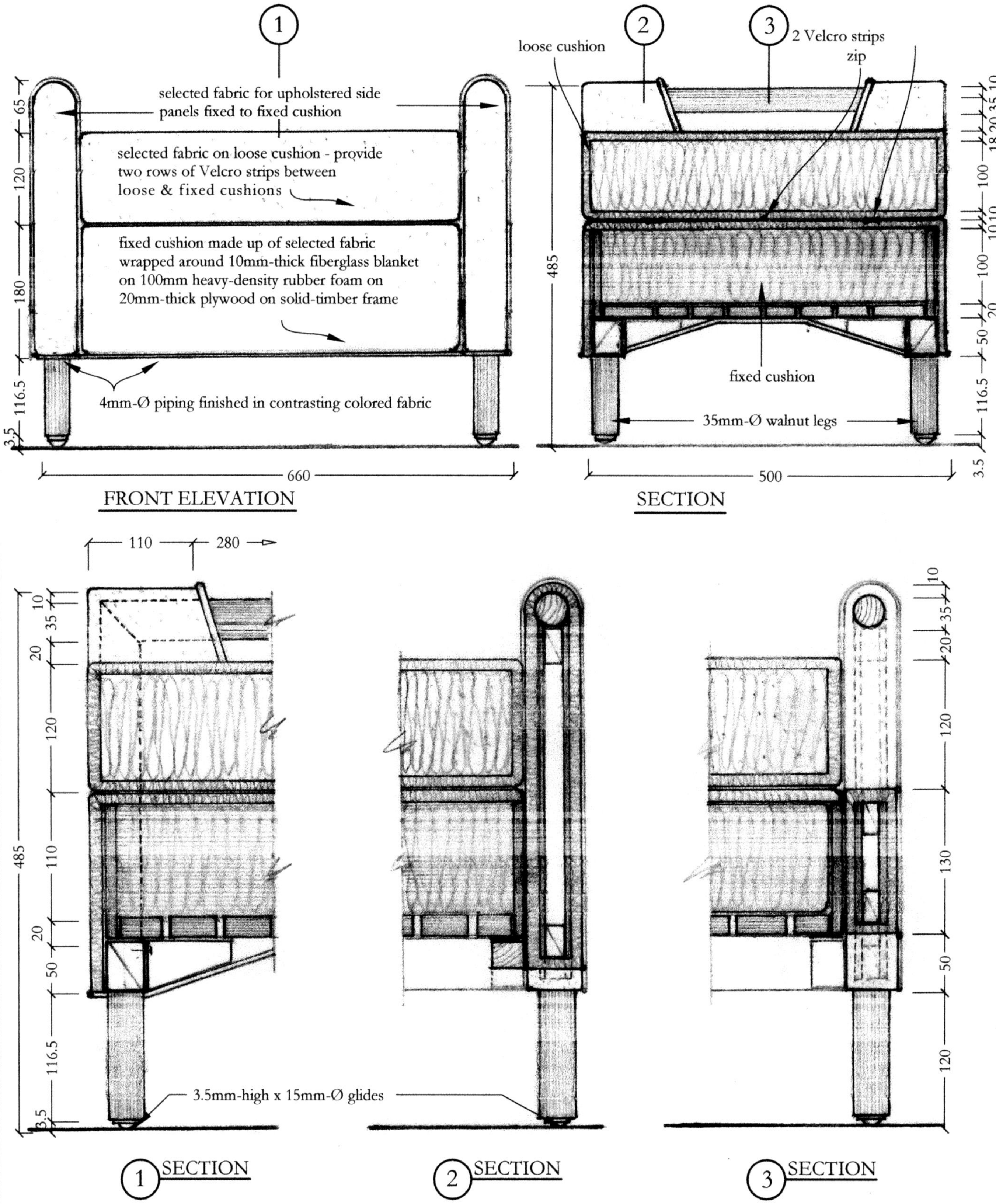

FRONT ELEVATION

SECTION

1 SECTION

2 SECTION

3 SECTION

PROJECT TITLE:	DRAWN BY	CHECKED	DATE
	PROJECT NO		SCALE
DRAWING TITLE: DRESSING STOOL/OTTOMAN - FRONT ELEVATION, SECTION, AND DETAILS	DRAWING NO		REVISION △

address 1
address 2
address 3
postal code
email address

Interior Designers

DATA SHEET	DESCRIPTION HEADBOARD + NIGHT TABLE	F	SHEET NO 1 OF 3 TOTAL QTY:

ILLUSTRATION:

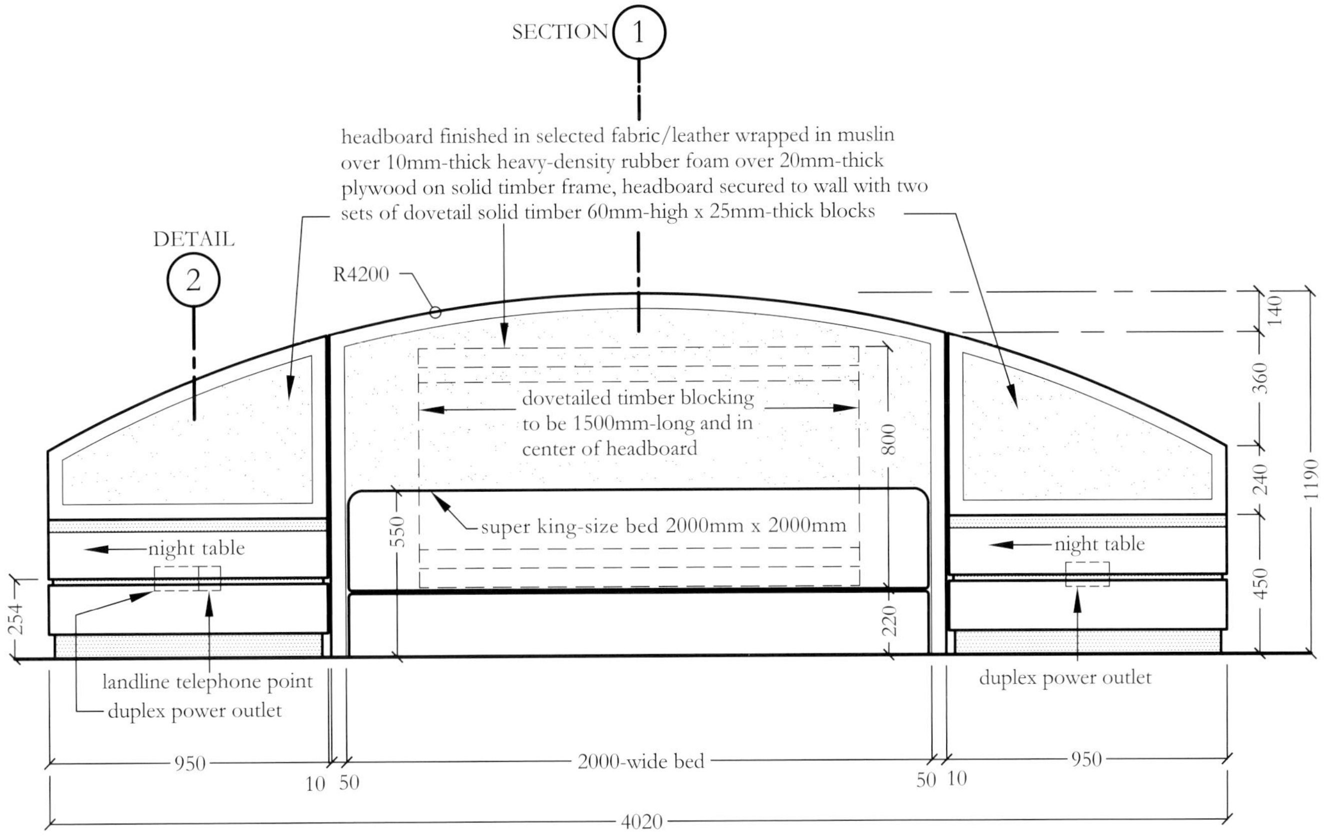

FRONT ELEVATION (KING BED + NIGHT TABLES)

SPECIFICATION / DESCRIPTION:

SUPPLIER / MANUFACTURER:		Furniture Supplier code	Finishes Supplier & Code	
MODEL NO:	DIMENSIONS (mm):		ROOM TYPE:	QUANTITY:
			1	
OTHER FINISHES CODE:	AREA LOCATION:		2	
			3	
COSTINGS: ☐ BUDGET : $ ☐ QUOTATION : $ ☐ FINAL PRICE : $	TOTAL: TOTAL QUANTITY: TOTAL PRICE: $		4	
			5	
			TOTAL QTY:	

REMARKS/NOTES /SPECIAL INSTRUCTIONS:

PROJECT TITLE:	DRAWN BY	CHECKED	DATE	address 1 address 2 address 3 postal code email address
	PROJECT NO		SCALE	
DRAWING TITLE: HEADBOARD AND NIGHT TABLE - ELEVATION	DRAWING NO		REVISION △	Interior Designers

DATA SHEET

DESCRIPTION
HEADBOARD + NIGHT TABLE

F

SHEET NO 2 OF 3

TOTAL QTY:

ILLUSTRATION:

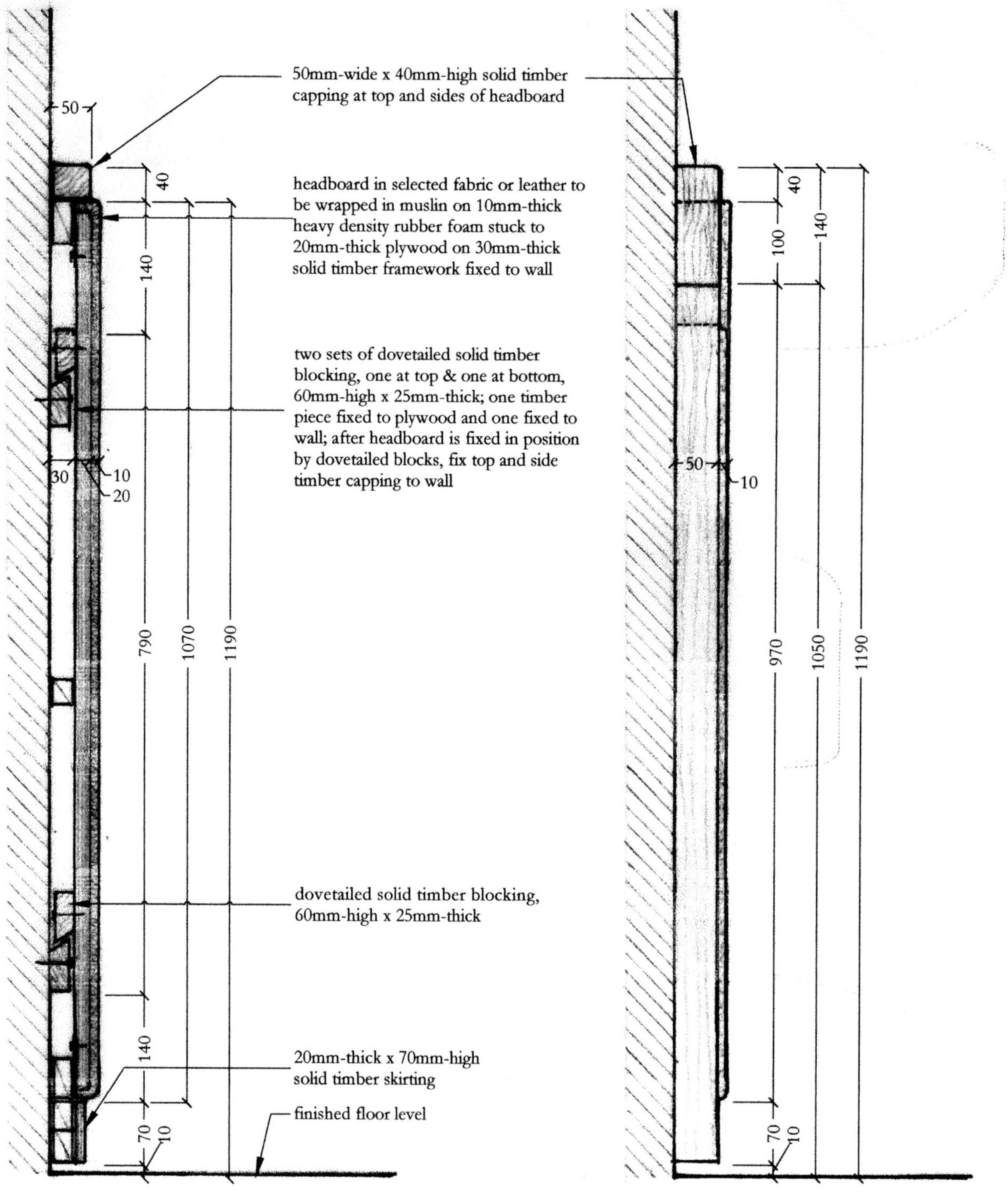

1 SECTION

SIDE ELEVATION

PROJECT TITLE:

DRAWING TITLE:
HEADBOARD - SECTION AND SIDE ELEVATION

DRAWN BY | CHECKED | DATE

PROJECT NO | SCALE

DRAWING NO | REVISION △

address 1
address 2
address 3
postal code
email address

Interior Designers

DATA SHEET	DESCRIPTION HEADBOARD + NIGHT TABLE	F	SHEET NO 3 OF 3 TOTAL QTY:

ILLUSTRATION:

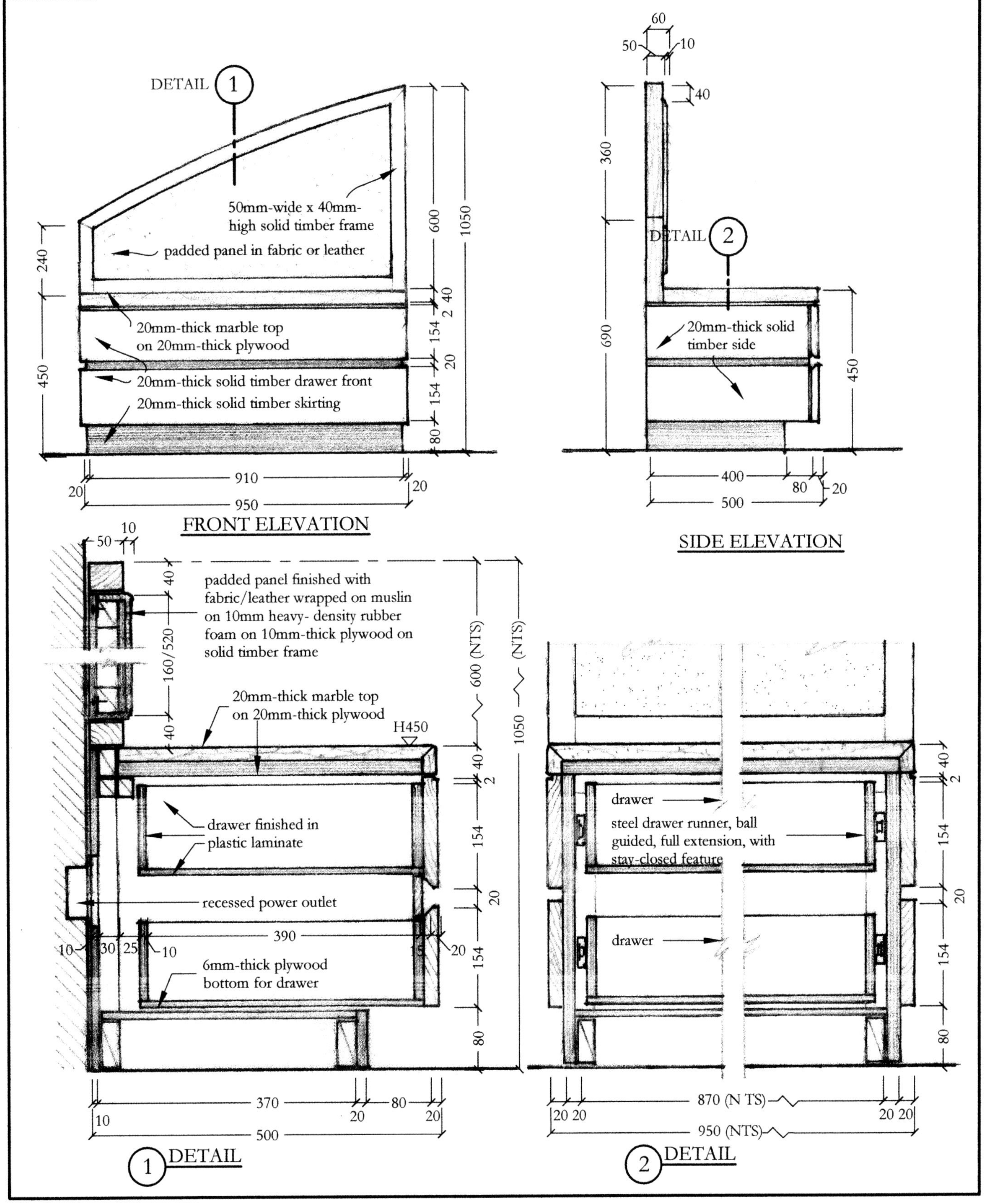

PROJECT TITLE:	DRAWN BY	CHECKED	DATE	address 1 address 2 address 3 postal code email address
DRAWING TITLE: NIGHT TABLE - ELEVATIONS + DETAILS 2 AND 3	PROJECT NO		SCALE	
	DRAWING NO		REVISION △	Interior Designers

Master bedroom looking towards outdoor Jacuzzi in a house in Indonesia (artist's rendering).

DATA SHEET	DESCRIPTION BED HEARDBOARD ~ KING-SIZE BED	F	SHEET NO 1 OF 3 TOTAL QTY:

ILLUSTRATION:

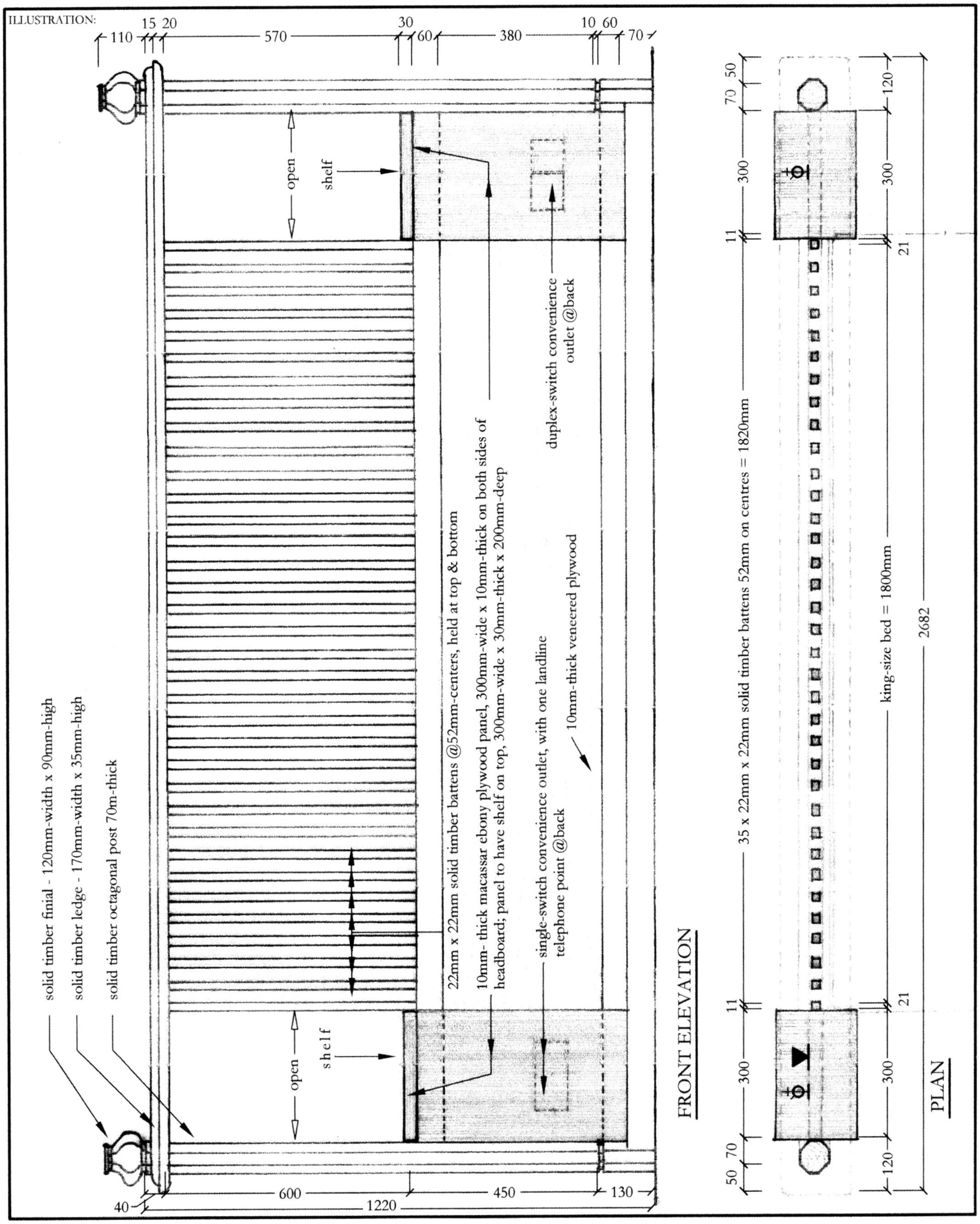

PROJECT TITLE:	DRAWN BY	CHECKED	DATE	address 1 address 2 address 3 postal code email address Interior Designers
DRAWING TITLE: FREE-STANDING KING-SIZE HEADBOARD (bolted to finished floor) - PLAN AND FRONT ELEVATION	PROJECT NO		SCALE	
	DRAWING NO		REVISION △	

DATA SHEET	DESCRIPTION BED HEARDBOARD ~ KING-SIZE BED	F	SHEET NO 2 OF 3 TOTAL QTY:

ILLUSTRATION:

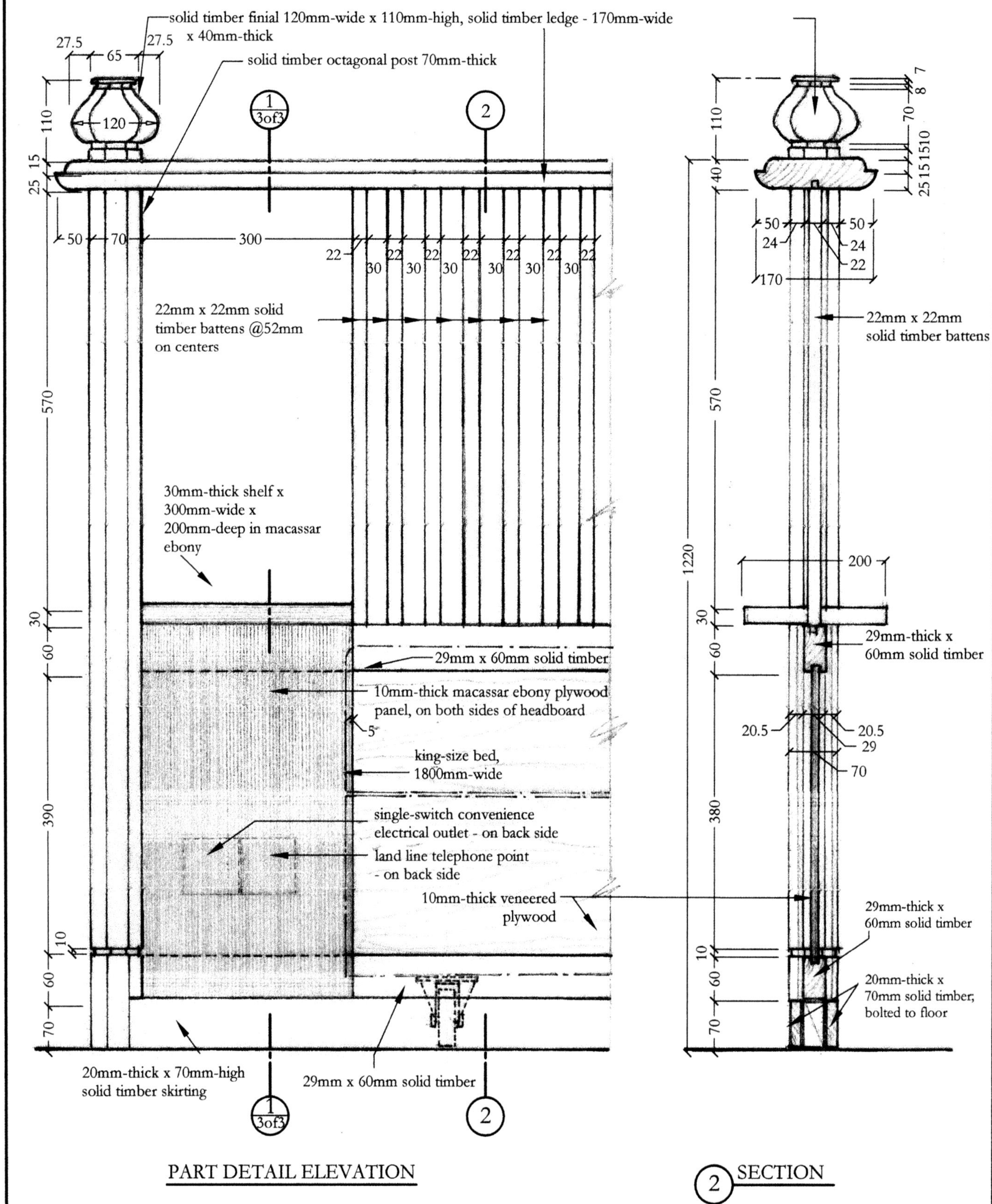

PROJECT TITLE:	DRAWN BY	CHECKED	DATE	address 1 address 2 address 3 postal code email address Interior Designers
	PROJECT NO		SCALE	
DRAWING TITLE: FREE-STANDING KING-SIZE HEADBOARD (bolted to finished floor) - PART DETAIL ELEVATION AND SECTION 2	DRAWING NO		REVISION △	

DATA SHEET	DESCRIPTION BED HEARDBOARD ~ KING-SIZE BED	F	SHEET NO 3 OF 3 TOTAL QTY:

ILLUSTRATION:

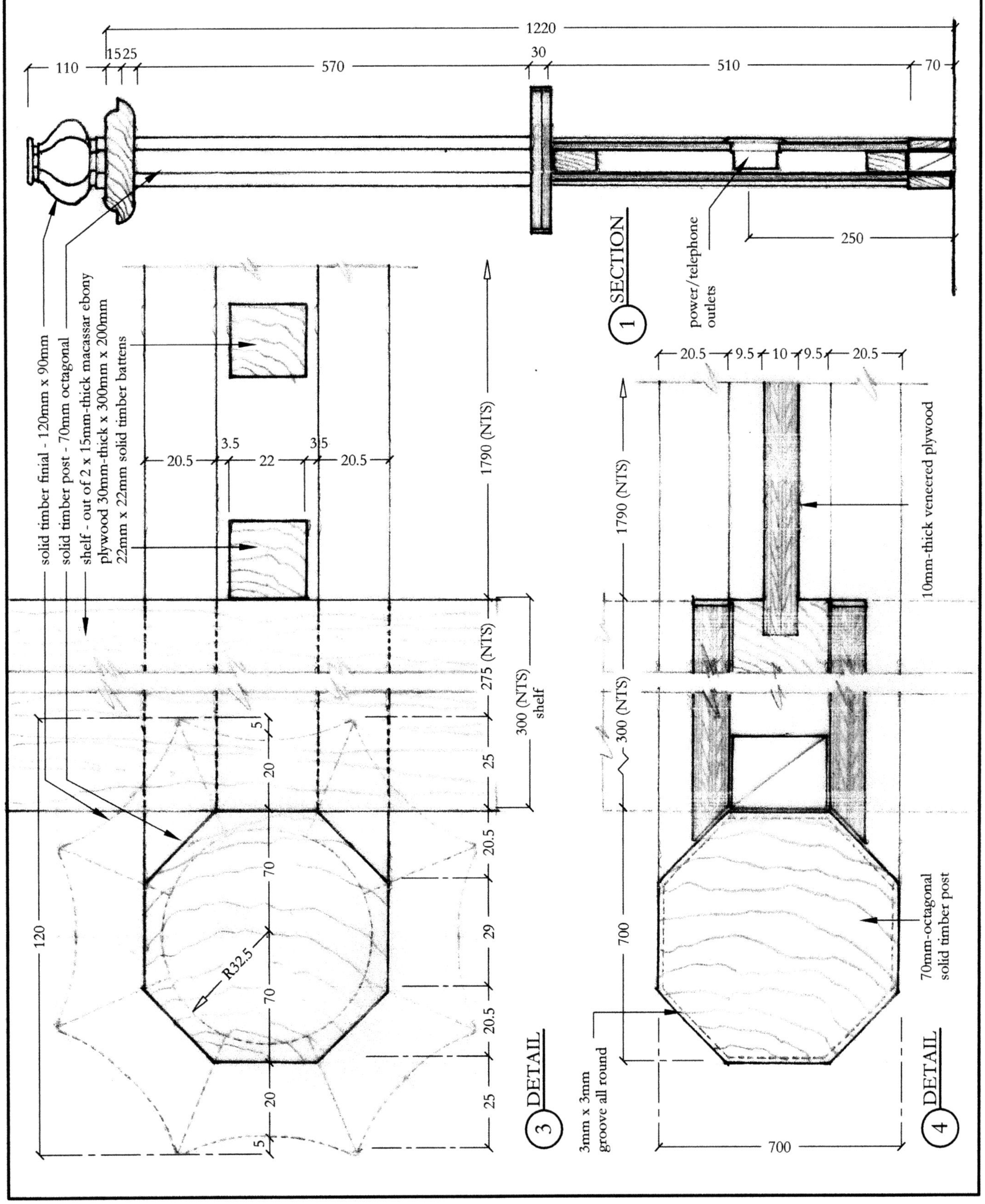

PROJECT TITLE:	DRAWN BY	CHECKED	DATE	address 1 address 2 address 3 postal code email address
	PROJECT NO		SCALE	
DRAWING TITLE: FREE-STANDING KING-SIZE HEADBOARD (bolted to finished floor) - DETAILS 3 AND 4	DRAWING NO		REVISION △	Interior Designers

DATA SHEET	DESCRIPTION FULL-HEIGHT HEADBOARD	F	SHEET NO 1 OF 2 TOTAL QTY:

ILLUSTRATION:

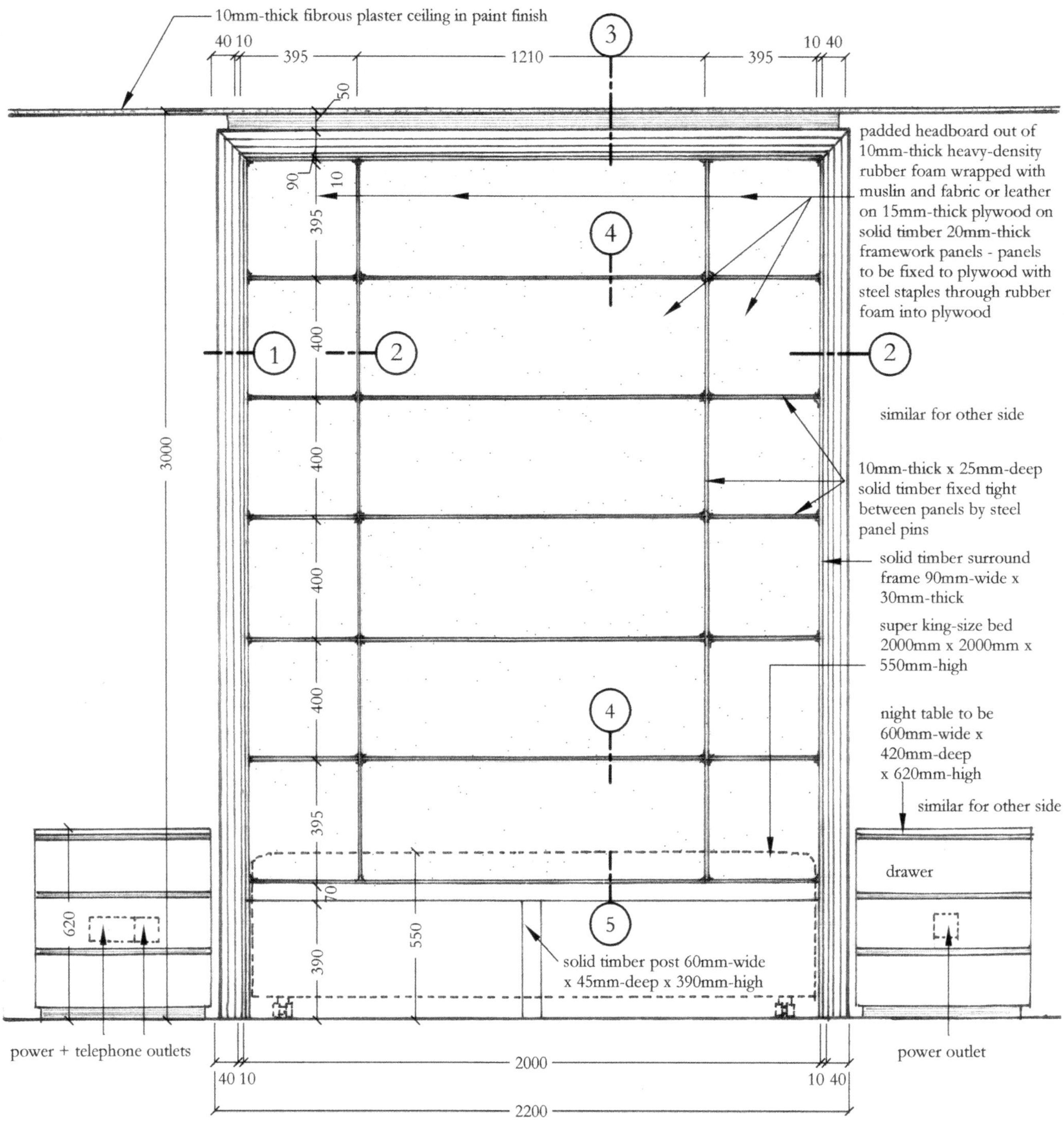

ELEVATION

PROJECT TITLE:	DRAWN BY	CHECKED	DATE	address 1 address 2 address 3 postal code email address Interior Designers
	PROJECT NO		SCALE	
DRAWING TITLE: FULL-HEIGHT HEADBOARD - FRONT ELEVATION	DRAWING NO		REVISION △	

Master bedroom of an apartment in Singapore (artist's rendering).

DATA SHEET	DESCRIPTION FULL-HEIGHT HEADBOARD	F	SHEET NO 2 OF 2 TOTAL QTY:

ILLUSTRATION:

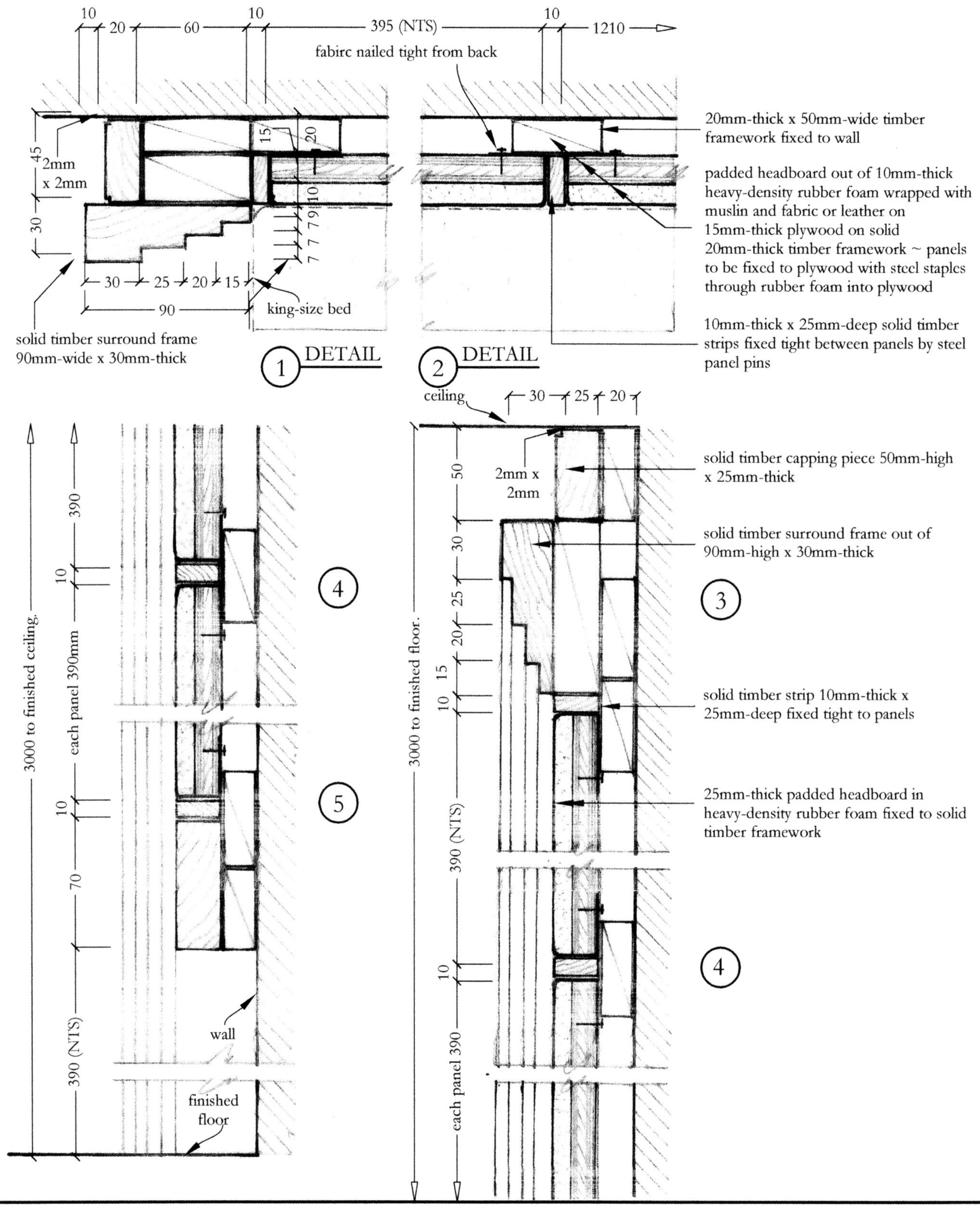

PROJECT TITLE:	DRAWN BY	CHECKED	DATE	address 1 address 2 address 3 postal code email address
	PROJECT NO		SCALE	
DRAWING TITLE: FULL-HEIGHT HEADBOARD -DETAILS	DRAWING NO		REVISION △	Interior Designers

CHAPTER 10

RESTAURANT SEATINGS (BANQUETTES)

1. Data sheet - various permutations of seating
2. Data sheet - central configuration of banquettes
3. Data sheet - details of banquette (ledge may be omitted)
4. Data sheet - details of banquette (with storage below & light above)
5. Data sheet - details of banquette (for circular or back to back)

<u>Note</u>: Also see Chapter 18.

DATA SHEET	DESCRIPTION BANQUETTES	F	SHEET NO: 1 OF 5 TOTAL QTY:

ILLUSTRATION:

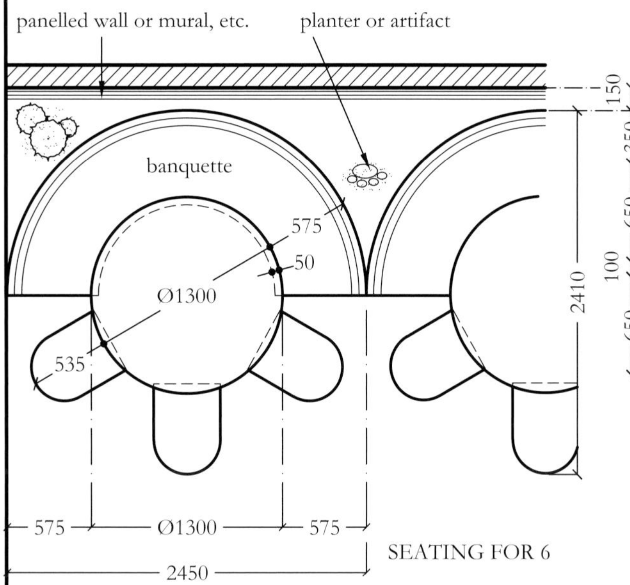

CIRCULAR SEATING

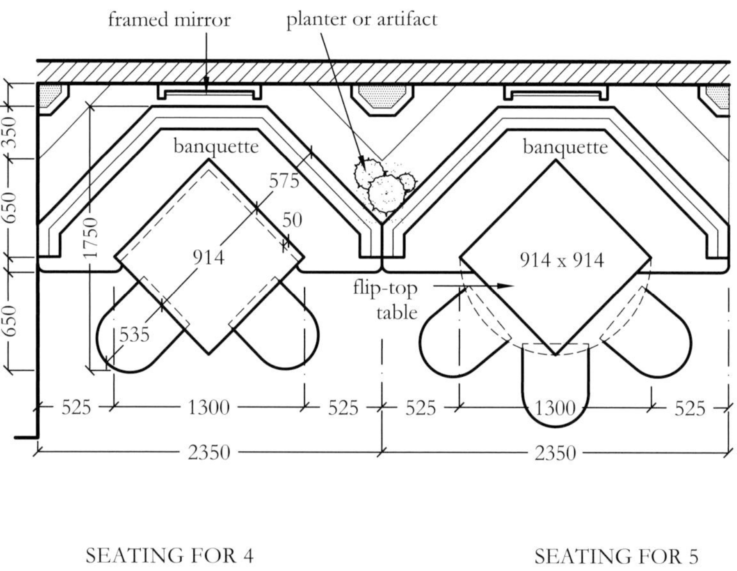

DIAGONAL SEATING

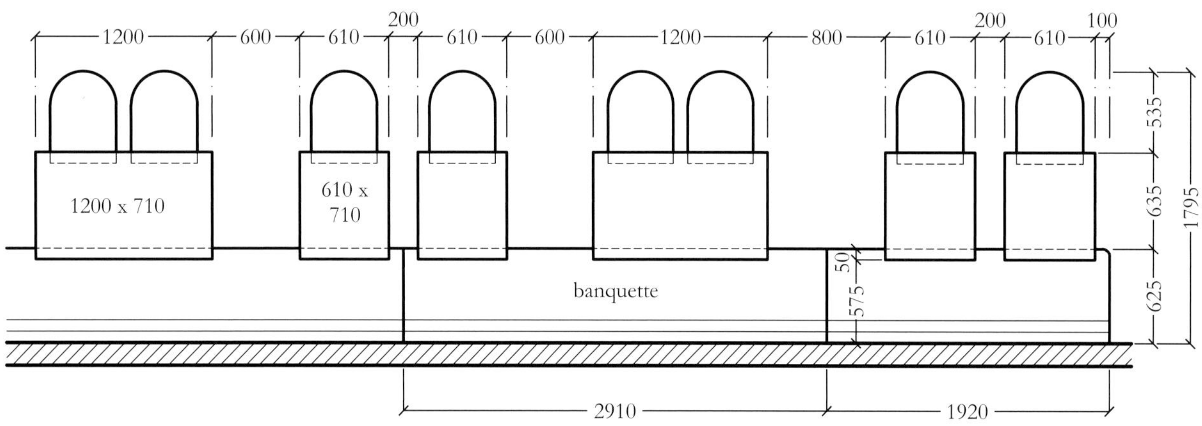

LINEAR SEATING

PROJECT TITLE:	DRAWN BY	CHECKED	DATE	address 1 address 2 address 3 postal code email address
	PROJECT NO		SCALE	
DRAWING TITLE: VARIOUS PERMUTATIONS OF SEATING	DRAWING NO		REVISION △	Interior Designers

DATA SHEET	DESCRIPTION BANQUETTES	F	SHEET NO: 2 OF 5 TOTAL QTY:

ILLUSTRATION:

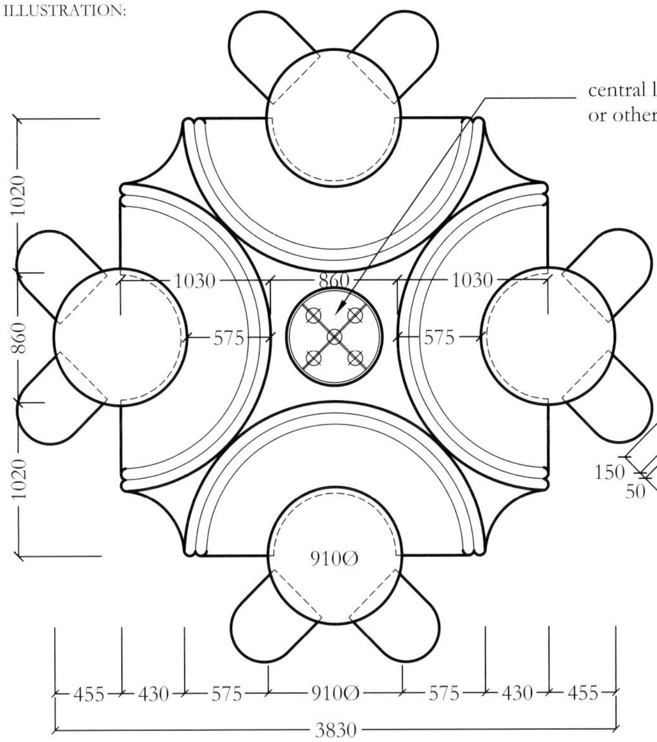

CIRCULAR

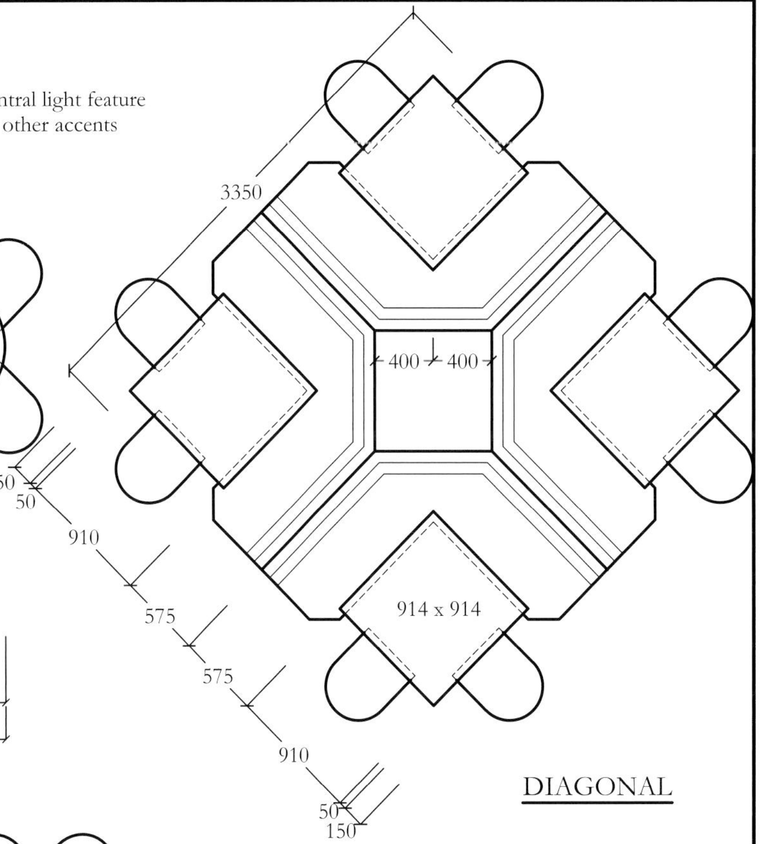

DIAGONAL

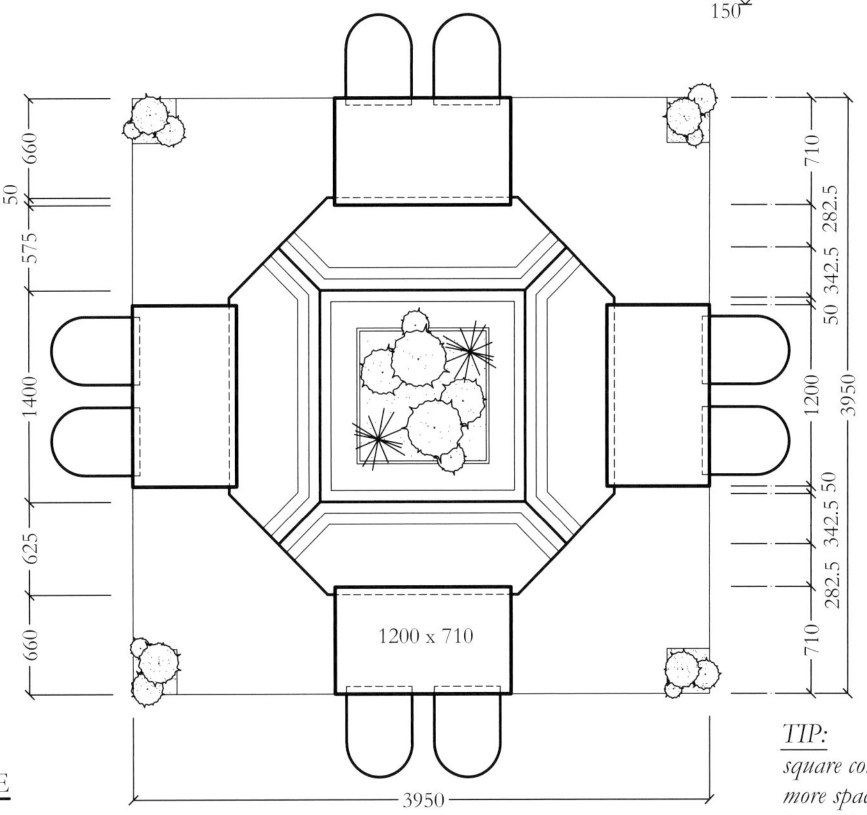

SQUARE

TIP:
square configuration will take up more space, so use when you have a larger floor space, and a higher ceiling, it will create a grandiose effect.

PROJECT TITLE:	DRAWN BY	CHECKED	DATE	address 1 address 2 address 3 postal code email address
	PROJECT NO		SCALE	
DRAWING TITLE: CENTRAL CONFIGURATION OF BANQUETTES	DRAWING NO		REVISION △	Interior Designers

DATA SHEET	DESCRIPTION BANQUETTE - SECTION	F	SHEET NO 3 OF 5 TOTAL QTY:

ILLUSTRATION:

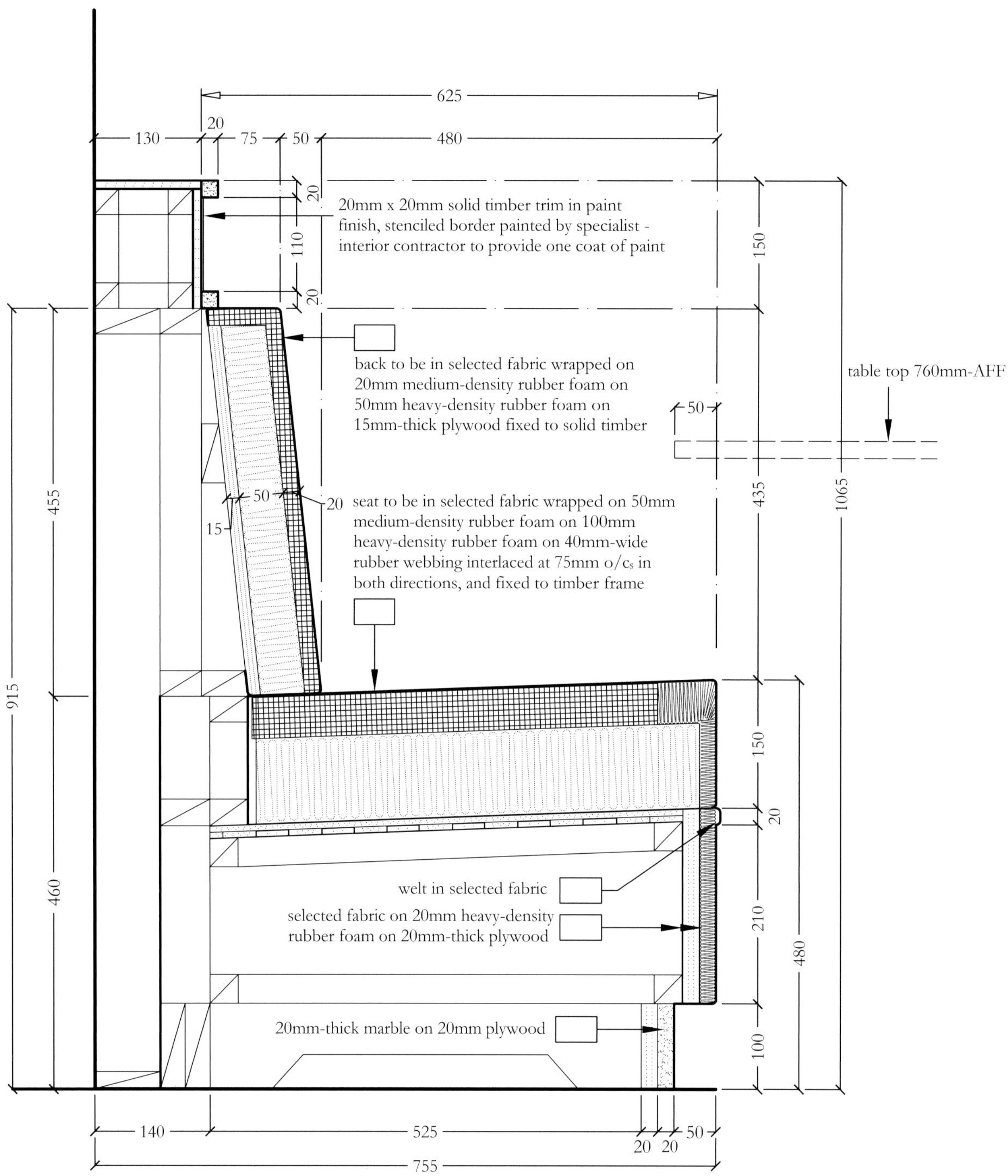

TYPICAL SECTION (for linear and diagonal)

TIP:

Ledge could be created for display of artifacts, etc.

PROJECT TITLE:	DRAWN BY	CHECKED	DATE	address 1 address 2 address 3 postal code email address
	PROJECT NO		SCALE	
DRAWING TITLE: DETAILS OF BANQUETTE (ledge may be omitted)	DRAWING NO		REVISION △	Interior Designers

DATA SHEET	DESCRIPTION BANQUETTE - SECTION	F	SHEET NO 4 OF 5 TOTAL QTY:

ILLUSTRATION:

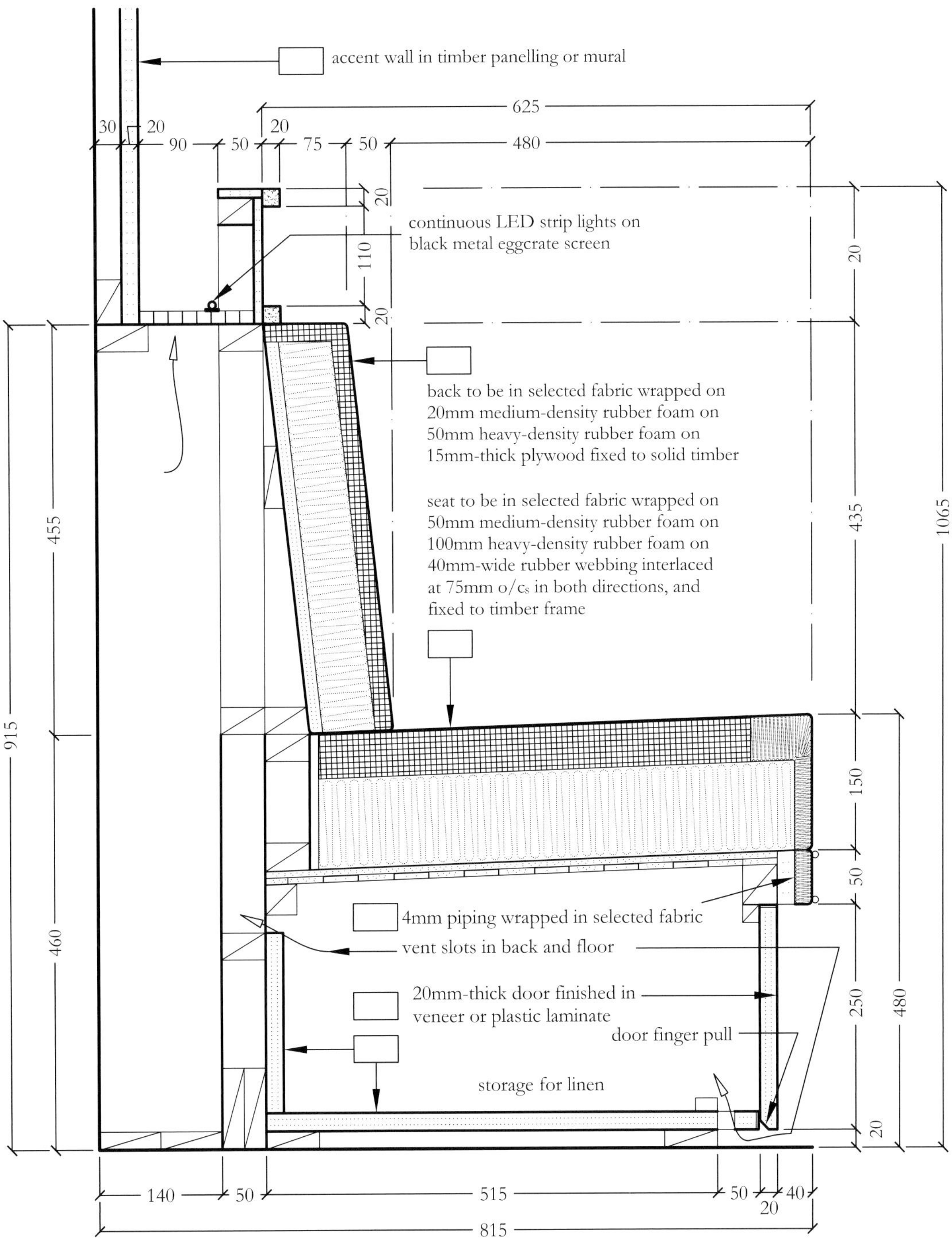

TYPICAL SECTION (for linear and diagonal)

TIP:

Provide vent slots at bottom and back of storage space plus at top of ledge.

PROJECT TITLE:	DRAWN BY	CHECKED	DATE	address 1 address 2 address 3 postal code email address
	PROJECT NO		SCALE	
DRAWING TITLE: DETAILS OF BANQUETTE (with storage below and light above)	DRAWING NO		REVISION △	Interior Designers

DATA SHEET	DESCRIPTION BANQUETTE - SECTION	F	SHEET NO 4 OF 5 TOTAL QTY:

ILLUSTRATION:

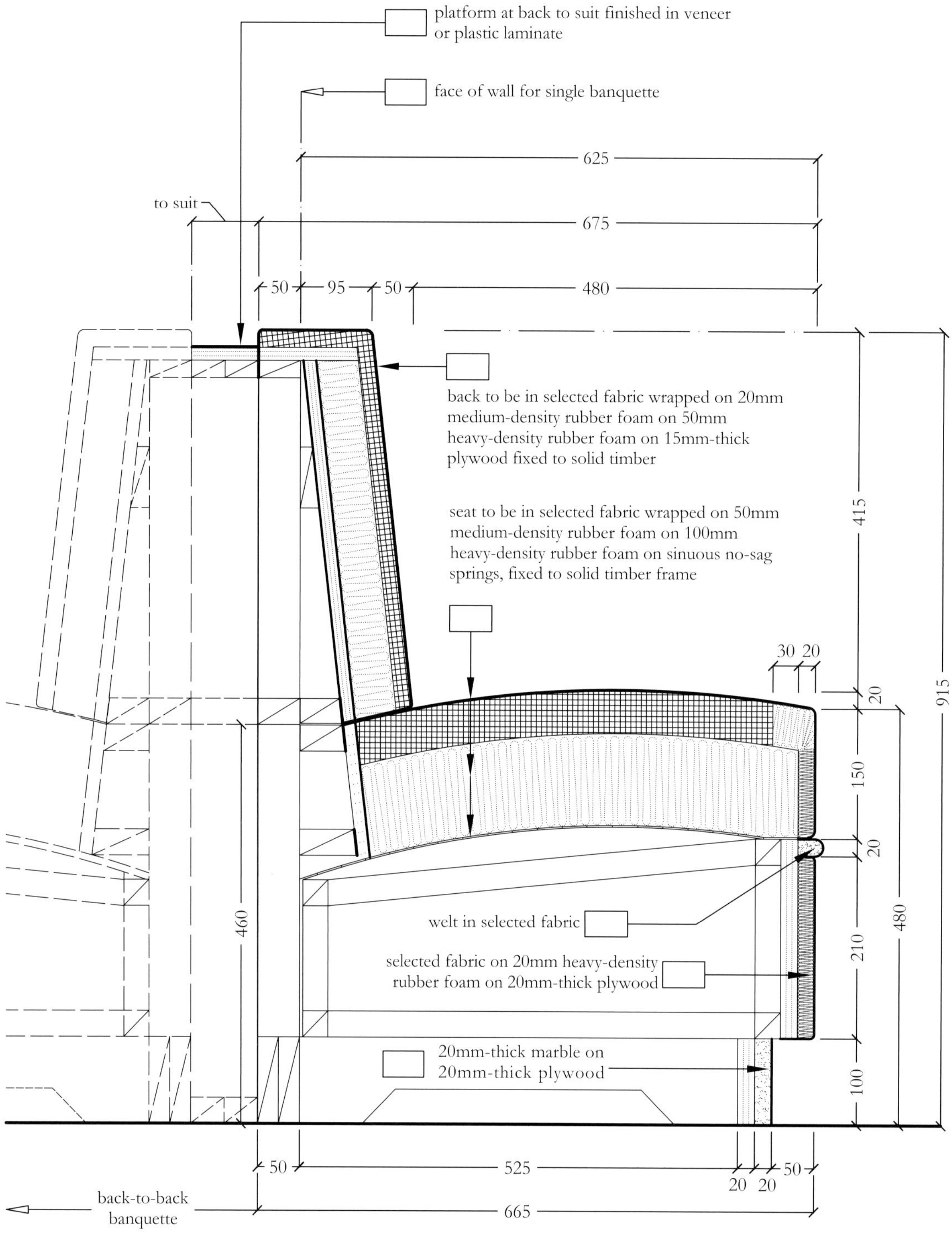

TYPICAL SECTION (for circular banquette)

PROJECT TITLE:	DRAWN BY	CHECKED	DATE	address 1 address 2 address 3 postal code email address
	PROJECT NO		SCALE	
DRAWING TITLE: DETAILS OF BANQUETTE (for circular or back-to-back)	DRAWING NO		REVISION	Interior Designers

CHAPTER 11

DOMESTIC KITCHENS

1. General information
2. Data sheet - domestic kitchen; plan and front elevation
3. Data sheet - domestic kitchen; sections 1 and 4
4. Data sheet - domestic kitchen; sections 2 and 3
5. Data sheet - domestic kitchen; furniture layout plan (apartment)
6. Data sheet - domestic kitchen; reflected ceiling plus lighting plan (apartment)
7. Data sheet - domestic kitchen; floor finishes layout plan (apartment)
8. Data sheet - domestic kitchen; elevations A and C plus section 1 of island table (apartment)
9. Data sheet - domestic kitchen; elevations Band D plus plan & elevations of island table (apartment)
10. Data sheet - domestic kitchen; elevations E and F (apartment)
11. Data sheet - domestic kitchen; sections 2 and 3 (apartment)
12. Data sheet - domestic kitchen; sections 4 and 5 (apartment)

Today's kitchen is becoming the heart and soul of a home. For the person doing the cooking in the family, this space needs to be clean, airy, bright, cheerful, functional, and free from clutter. It needs to be well organized with plenty of storage space. Key to a well-organized kitchen is the location of the stove, in relation to the kitchen door. To create a good circulation pattern and smooth traffic flow, the refrigerator, sink, and stove, should form a triangle. The refrigerator should be closest to the kitchen door, so food brought into the house can be quickly stored in the fridge or freezer. Then, when ready to cook, it can be easily brought out from the fridge, cleaned at the sink, and then cooked, as required. If you believe in feng shui the stove should face east, and if the stove is next to the sink, you should introduce a tree element like a wooden chopping block, or wooden plate-rack, to balance the fire and water energy. If the cook is standing in front of the stove, with his or her back to the door, provide a shiny surface on the wall above the stove, to alert the cook if anyone is coming into the kitchen.

The modern kitchen is more than a work area for cooking. With the addition of a television set and a dining corner, it becomes an entertainment area, where family and friends can get together. Today, fitted kitchens can either be bought off the rack or can be custom-designed. Fitted kitchen cabinets have doors and drawer fronts in various sizes, doors from 300mm to 600mm and drawers up to 1,000mm widths. They come in plain, flat surfaces or in traditional timber molded surfaces. They are made out of 16mm chipboard or 18mm plywood. The back panel is in 3mm thick hardboard. Cabinets come in various finishes such as painted lacquered, natural wood, plastic laminate, or multi-layered high-gloss lacquer. Plinths or skirting comes in various heights and construction types. Ready-made fitted kitchens have feet in impact-resistant plastic, in heights of 100mm, 150mm, or 200mm, to which plinths are fixed by clips. Plinths are made out of plywood and moisture sealed; they are 100mm, 150mm, or 200mm-high and 18mm thick. They are finished in lacquer, plastic laminate, wood, or stainless steel cemented to plywood.

Hoods for extracting greasy air and smells, form an integral part of a modern kitchen. They come in various sizes and finishes, mostly in stainless steel, although the hood can also be hidden in the same finish as the wall cabinet. The hood can be vented or of a recirculated type.

Cooking is gaining in prestige and there are various cooking appliances to choose from, including electric stoves, gas stoves, appliances that combine both electric and gas, solid hot plates heated by induction, and ceramic glass plates.

No modern kitchen should be without a microwave oven. For one, it saves an enormous amount of energy and time. Frozen items that would normally take over an hour to thaw, can be thawed and cooked in minutes. Bear in mind that when built into the cabinet, microwave ovens, should ideally be installed at eye level - around 1,200mm above the finished floor. Refrigeration, in the form of a fridge and freezer, for food and wine, is a must in a modern kitchen. There are various sizes of refrigerators and wine coolers available on the market so one cannot fail to find an ideal model to fit.

Washing up is chore not appreciated by many, but is a necessity. There are two washing requirements: one for dirty dishes and the other for washing vegetables, fruits, etc. before cooking. This requires a sink, built into the counter, or a dish-washer, below the counter. There is a wide range of built-in sinks in the market, in various sizes, shapes, and finishes: stainless steel, ceramic, or colored enamel.

DATA SHEET	DESCRIPTION DOMESTIC KITCHENS	SHEET NO 1 OF 3 TOTAL QTY:

ILLUSTRATION:

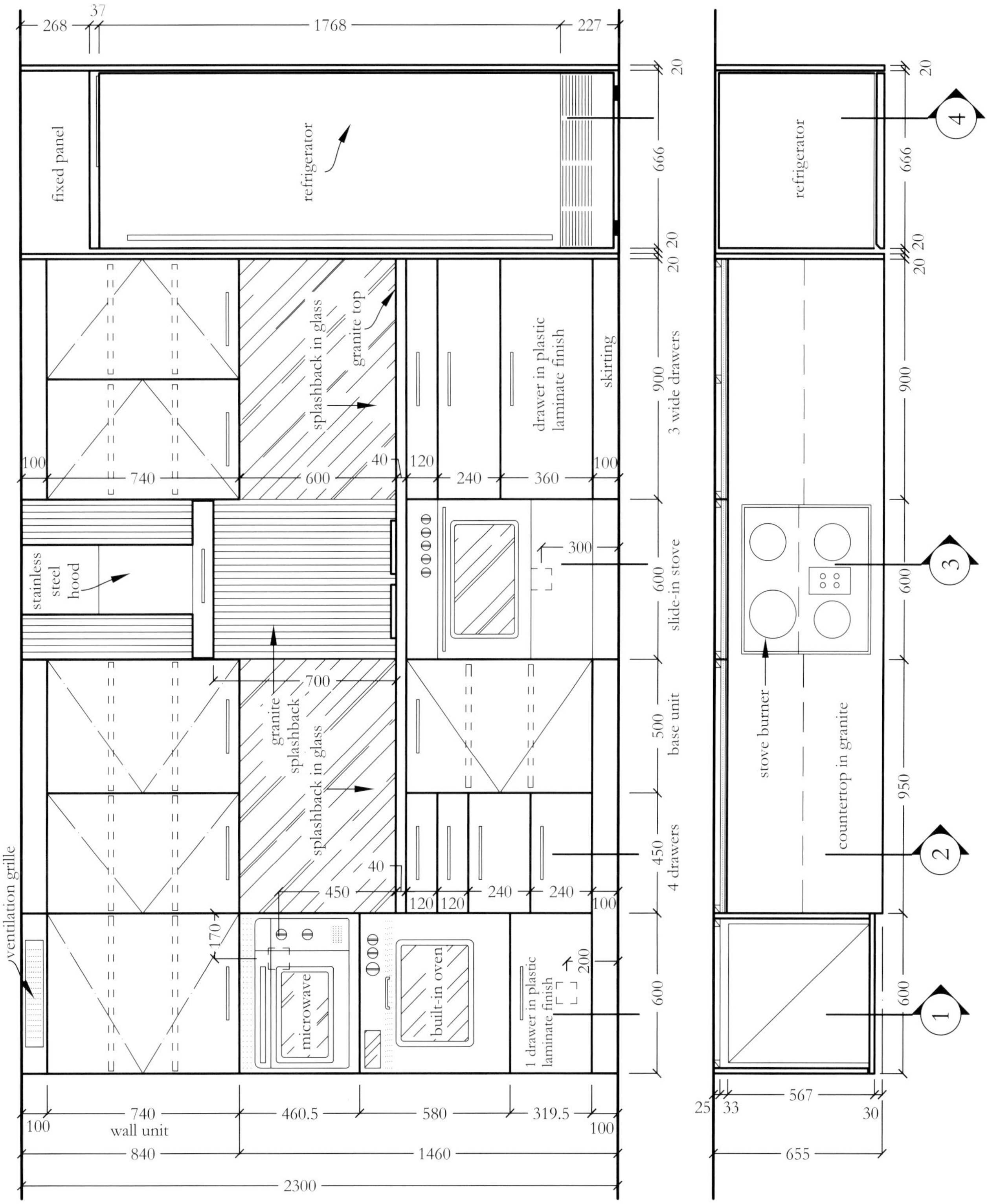

PROJECT TITLE:	DRAWN BY	CHECKED	DATE	address 1 address 2 address 3 postal code email address
	PROJECT NO		SCALE	
DRAWING TITLE: DOMESTIC KITCHEN - PLAN AND FRONT ELEVATION	DRAWING NO		REVISION △	Interior Designers

DATA SHEET	DESCRIPTION DOMESTIC KITCHENS		SHEET NO 2 OF 3 TOTAL QTY:

ILLUSTRATION:

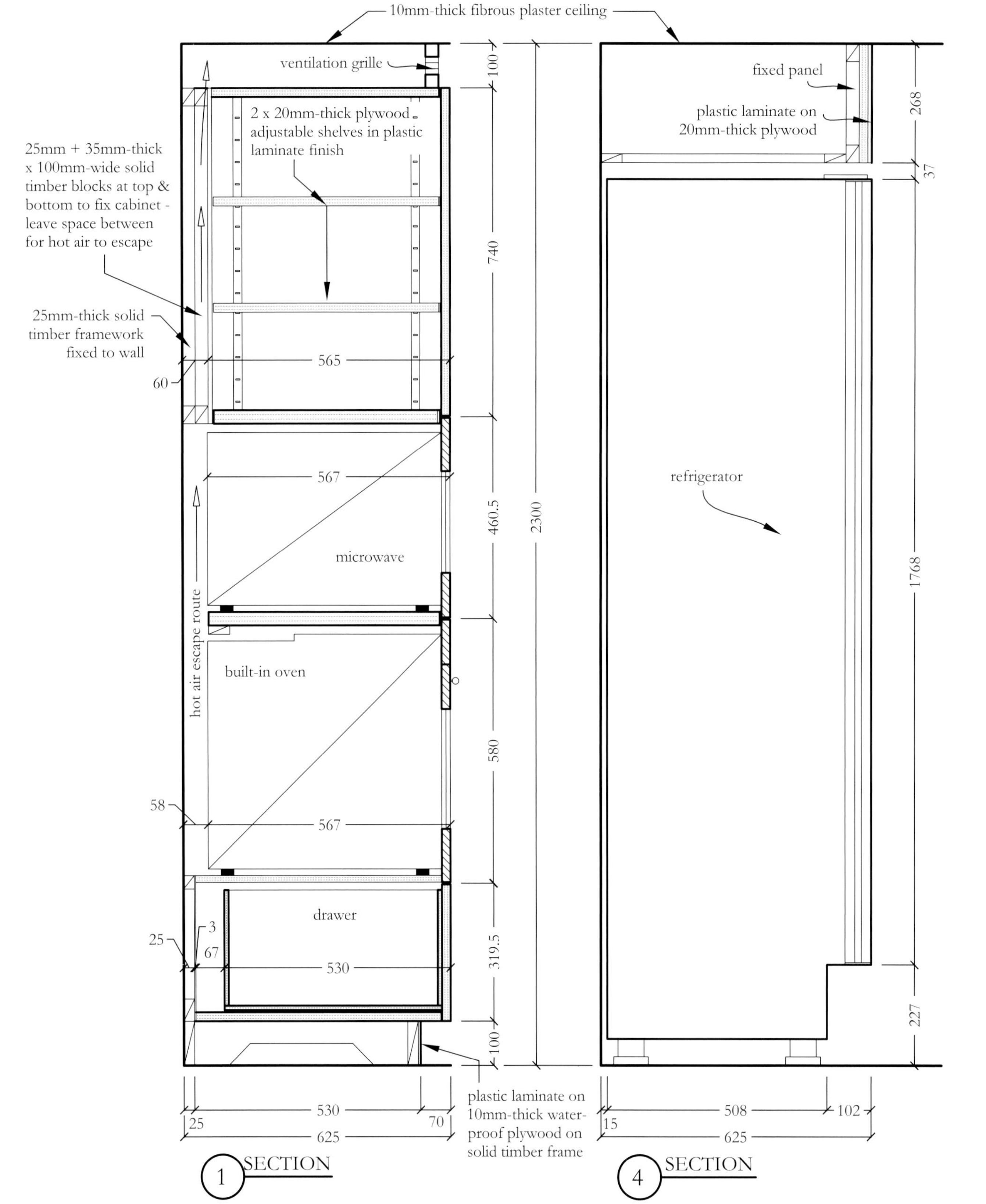

PROJECT TITLE:	DRAWN BY	CHECKED	DATE	address 1 address 2 address 3 postal code email address
	PROJECT NO		SCALE	
DRAWING TITLE: DOMESTIC KITCHENS - SECTIONS 1 AND 4	DRAWING NO		REVISION △	Interior Designers

DATA SHEET	DESCRIPTION DOMESTIC KITCHENS	SHEET NO 3 OF 3 TOTAL QTY:

ILLUSTRATION:

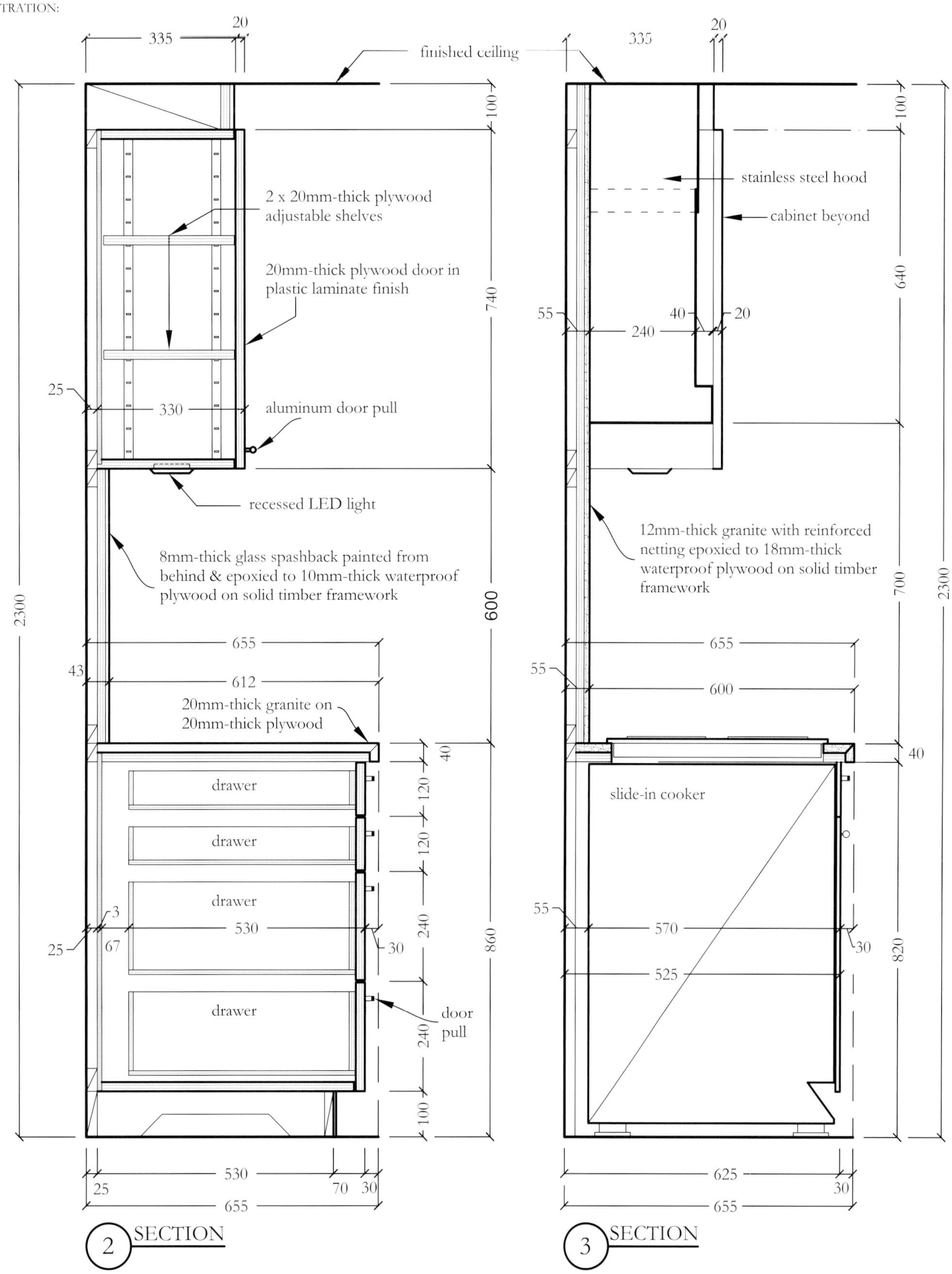

PROJECT TITLE:	DRAWN BY	CHECKED	DATE	address 1 address 2 address 3 postal code email address
	PROJECT NO		SCALE	
DRAWING TITLE: DOMESTIC KITCHENS - SECTIONS 2 AND 3	DRAWING NO		REVISION	Interior Designers

DATA SHEET	DESCRIPTION DOMESTIC KITCHENS	⬡	SHEET NO 1 OF 7 TOTAL QTY:

ILLUSTRATION:

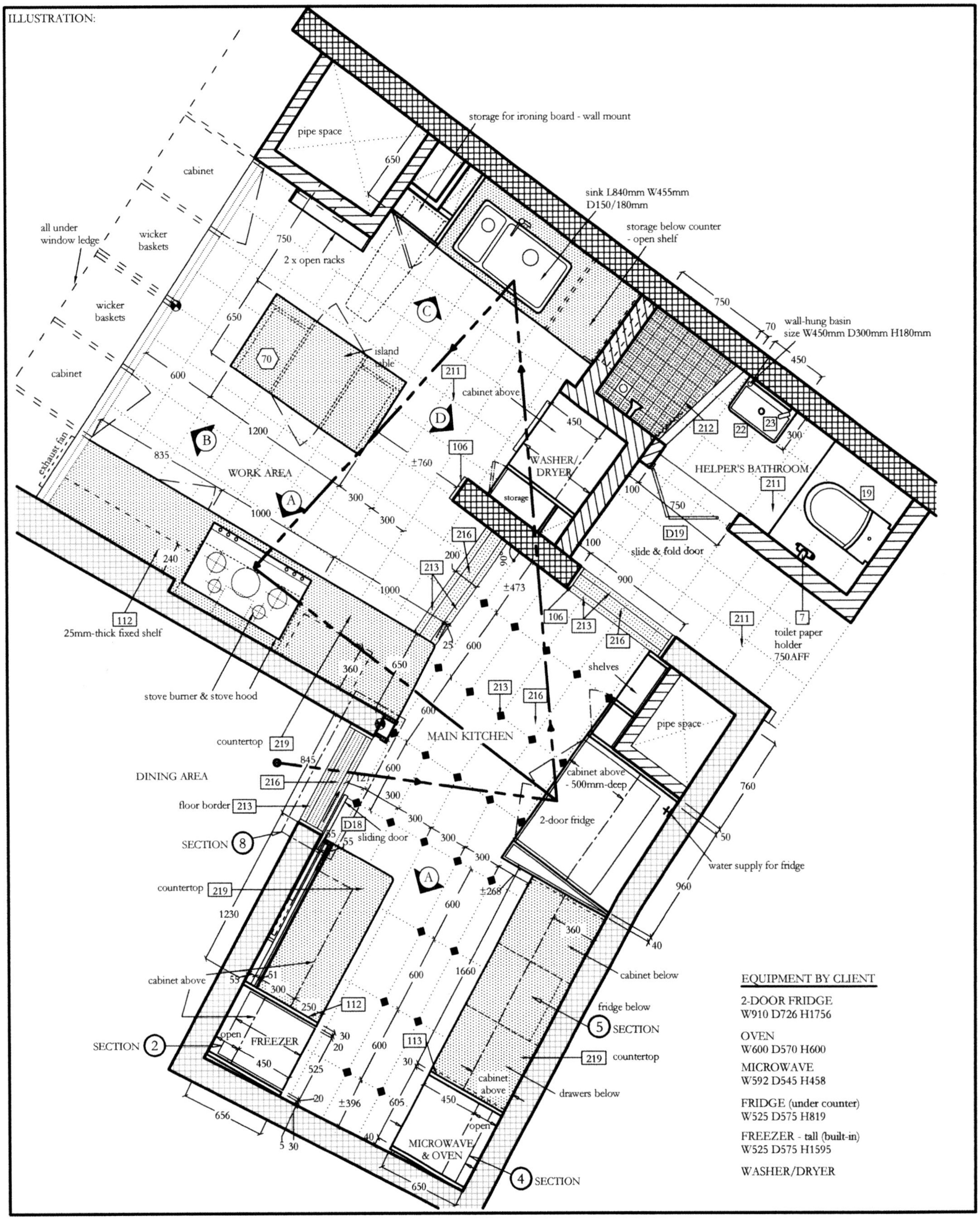

EQUIPMENT BY CLIENT

2-DOOR FRIDGE
W910 D726 H1756

OVEN
W600 D570 H600

MICROWAVE
W592 D545 H458

FRIDGE (under counter)
W525 D575 H819

FREEZER - tall (built-in)
W525 D575 H1595

WASHER/DRYER

PROJECT TITLE: APARTMENT	DRAWN BY	CHECKED	DATE	*address 1* *address 2* *address 3* *postal code* *email address*
	PROJECT NO		SCALE	
DRAWING TITLE: DOMESTIC KITCHENS - EQUIPMENT LAYOUT PLAN	DRAWING NO		REVISION △	Interior Designers

DATA SHEET	DESCRIPTION DOMESTIC KITCHENS	⬡	SHEET NO 2 OF 7 TOTAL QTY:

ILLUSTRATION:

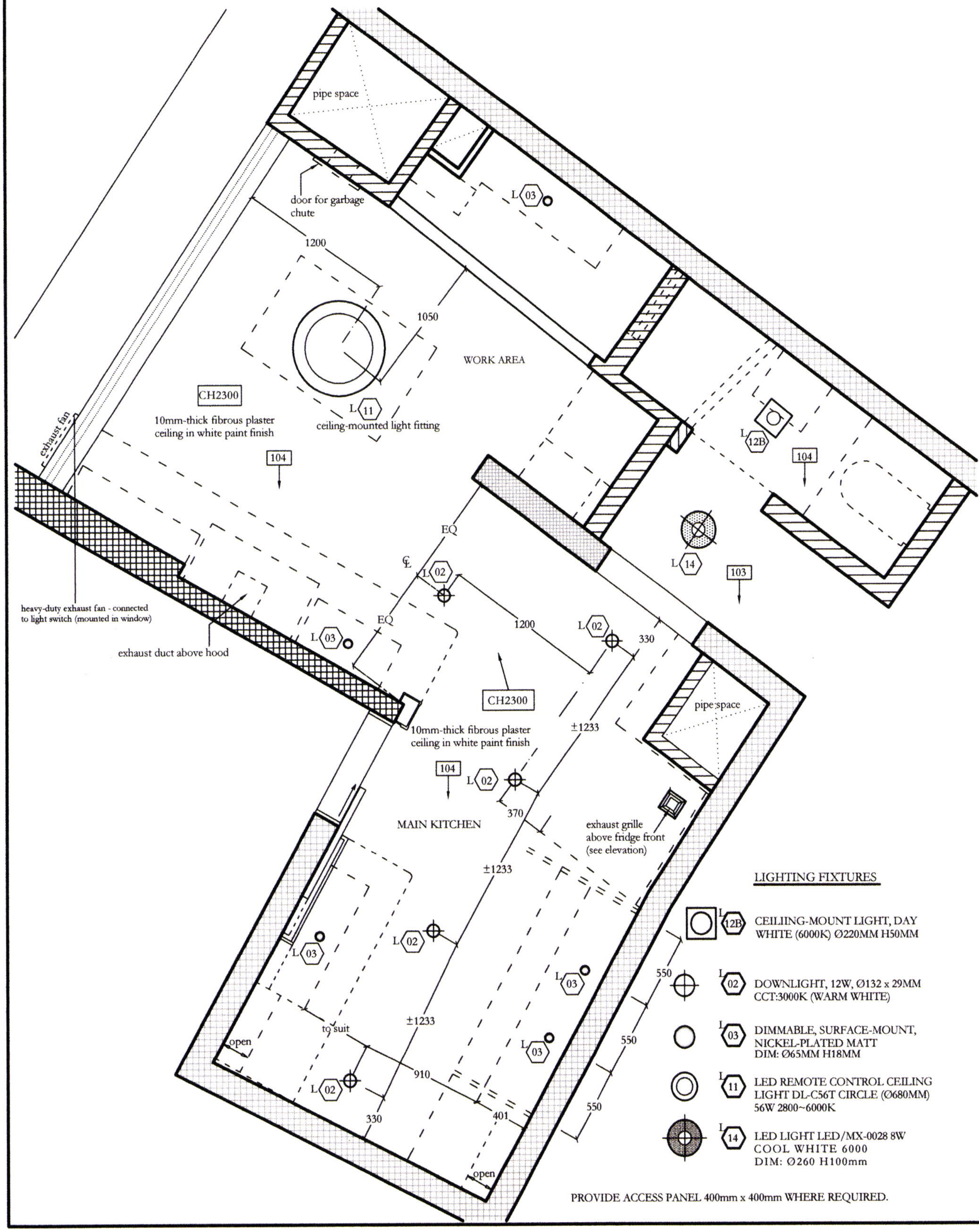

LIGHTING FIXTURES

- L 12B — CEILING-MOUNT LIGHT, DAY WHITE (6000K) Ø220MM H50MM
- L 02 — DOWNLIGHT, 12W, Ø132 x 29MM CCT:3000K (WARM WHITE)
- L 03 — DIMMABLE, SURFACE-MOUNT, NICKEL-PLATED MATT DIM: Ø65MM H18MM
- L 11 — LED REMOTE CONTROL CEILING LIGHT DL-C56T CIRCLE (Ø680MM) 56W 2800~6000K
- L 14 — LED LIGHT LED/MX-0028 8W COOL WHITE 6000 DIM: Ø260 H100mm

PROVIDE ACCESS PANEL 400mm x 400mm WHERE REQUIRED.

PROJECT TITLE: APARTMENT	DRAWN BY	CHECKED	DATE	address 1 address 2 address 3 postal code email address
	PROJECT NO		SCALE	
DRAWING TITLE: DOMESTIC KITCHENS - REFLECTED CEILING & LIGHTING PLAN	DRAWING NO		REVISION △	Interior Designers

DATA SHEET	DESCRIPTION DOMESTIC KITCHENS		SHEET NO 3 OF 7 TOTAL QTY:

ILLUSTRATION:

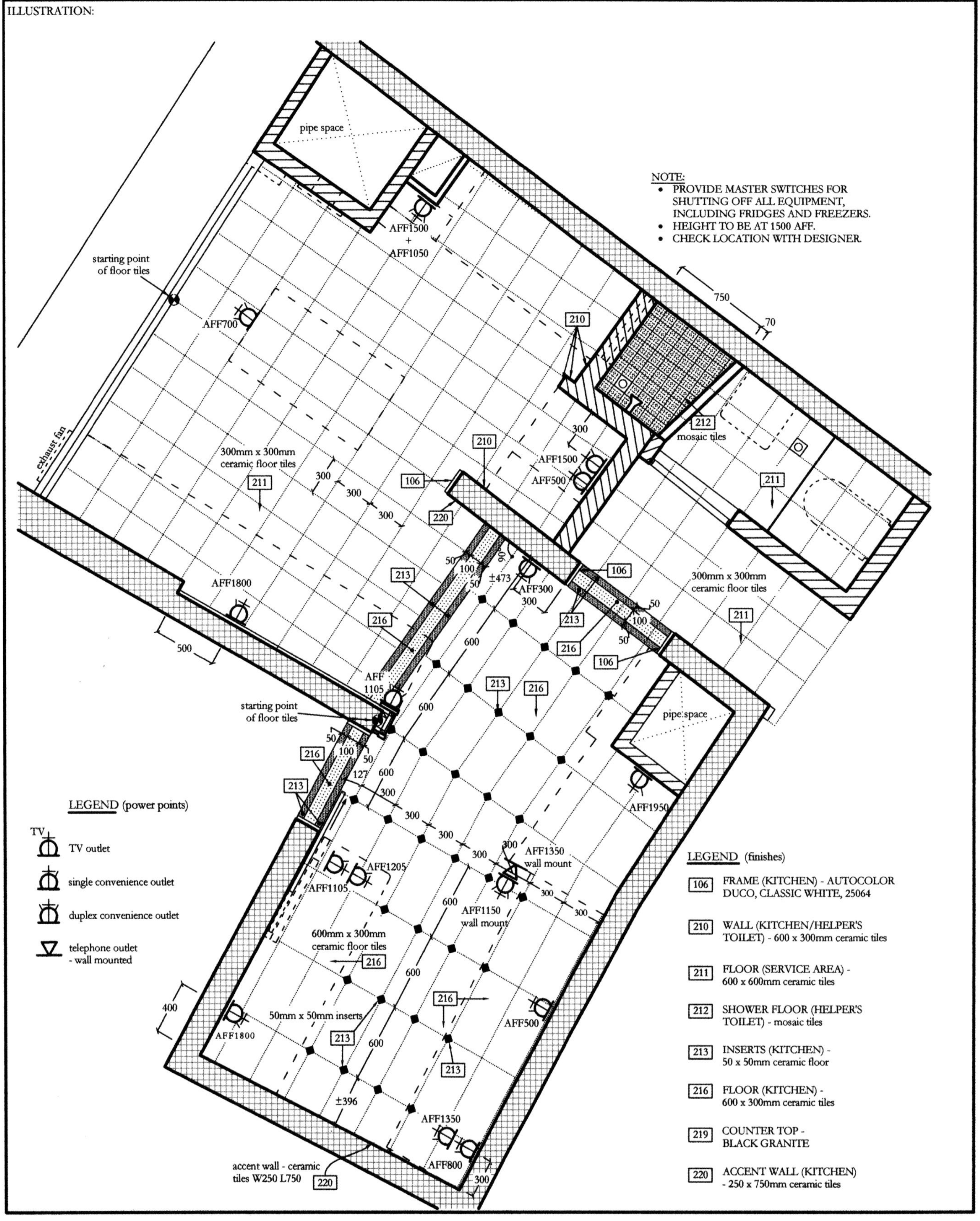

PROJECT TITLE: APARTMENT	DRAWN BY	CHECKED	DATE	address 1 address 2 address 3 postal code email address
DRAWING TITLE: DOMESTIC KITCHENS - FLOOR LAYOUT PLAN	PROJECT NO		SCALE	
	DRAWING NO		REVISION △	Interior Designers

DATA SHEET	DESCRIPTION DOMESTIC KITCHENS		SHEET NO 4 OF 7 TOTAL QTY:

ILLUSTRATION:

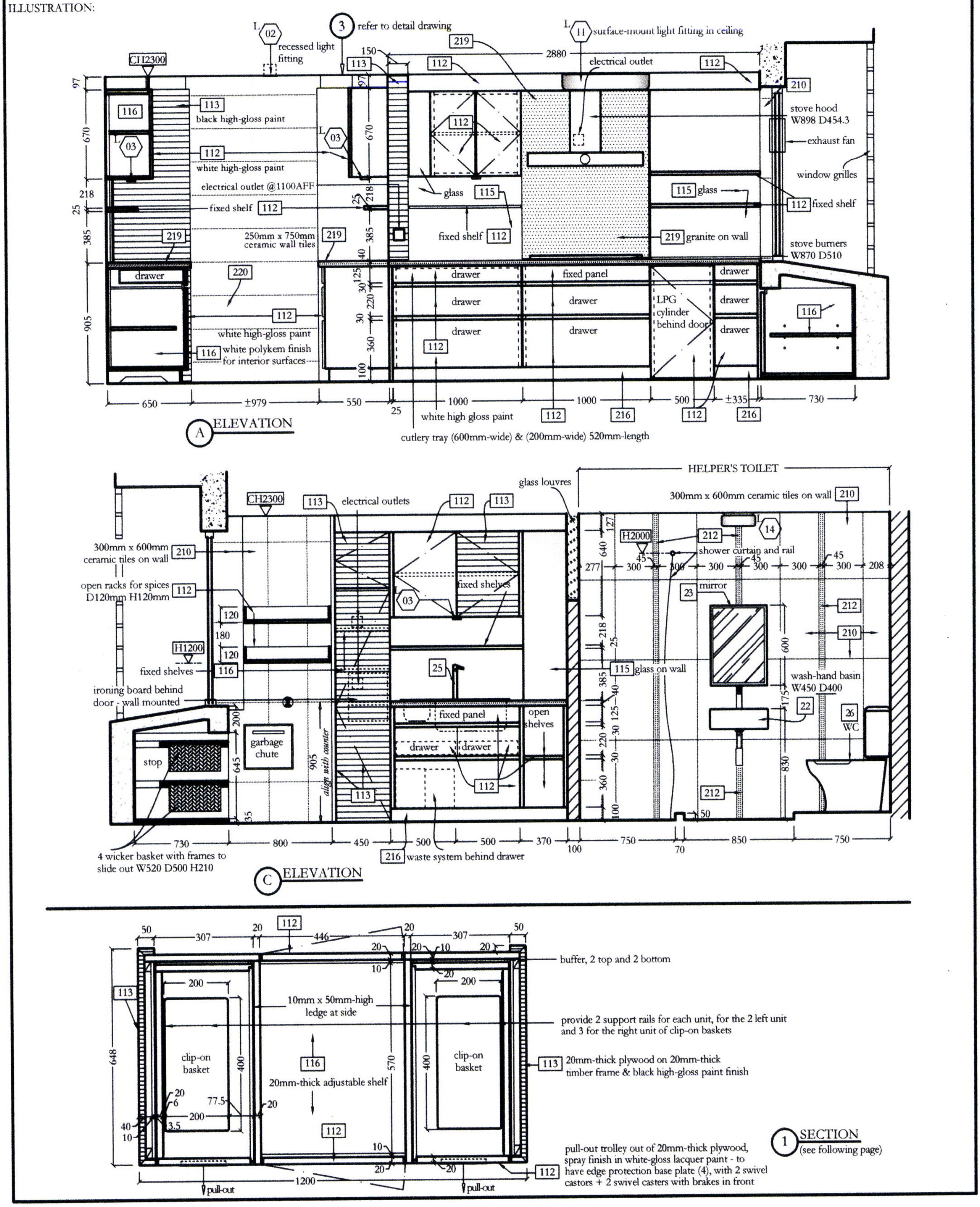

PROJECT TITLE: APARTMENT	DRAWN BY	CHECKED	DATE	address 1 address 2 address 3 postal code email address Interior Designers
	PROJECT NO		SCALE	
DRAWING TITLE: DOMESTIC KITCHENS - ELEVATIONS AND SECTION 1	DRAWING NO		REVISION △	

DATA SHEET	DESCRIPTION DOMESTIC KITCHENS		SHEET NO 5 OF 7 TOTAL QTY:

ILLUSTRATION:

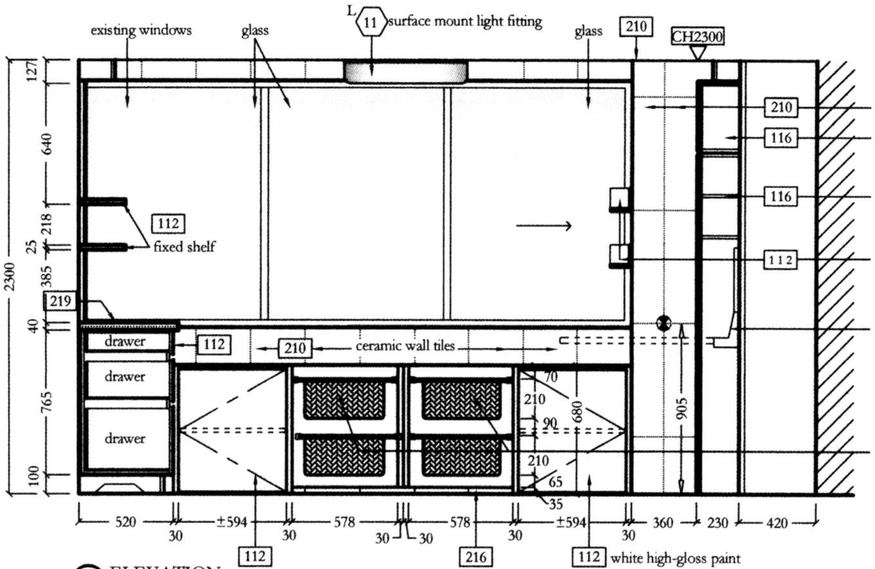

B ELEVATION

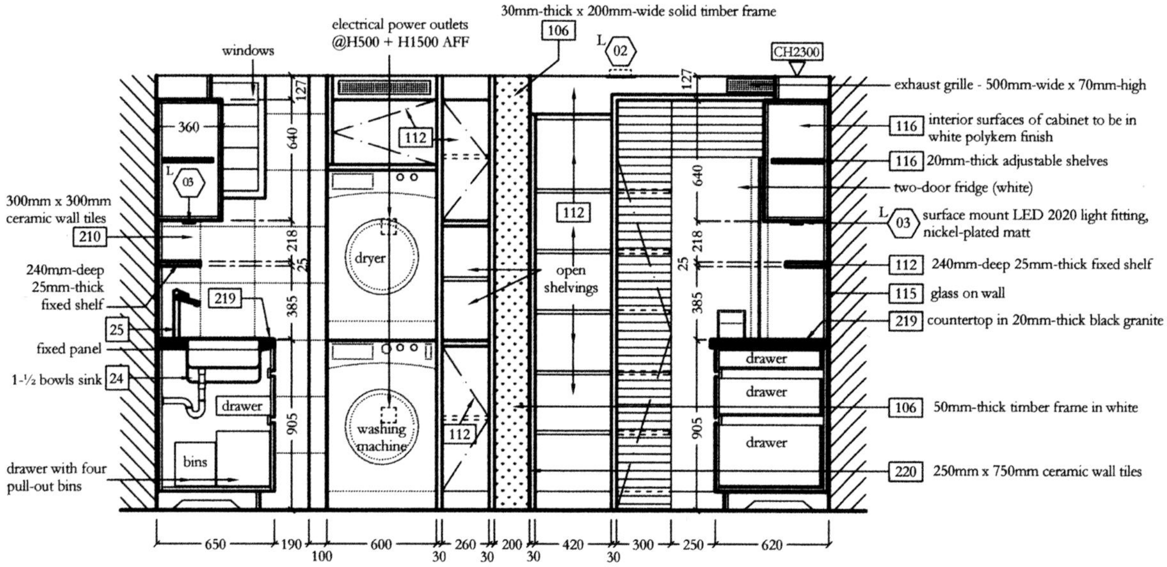

D ELEVATION

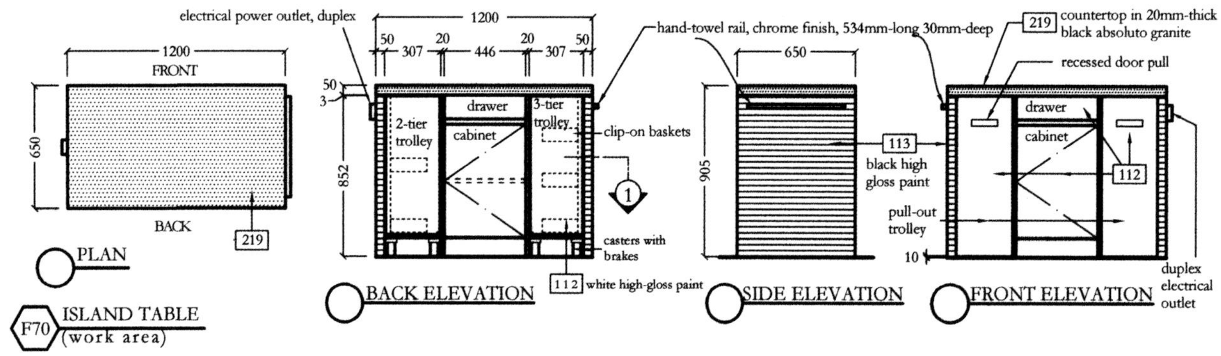

F70 ISLAND TABLE (work area)

PROJECT TITLE: APARTMENT	DRAWN BY	CHECKED	DATE	address 1 address 2 address 3 postal code email address Interior Designers
	PROJECT NO		SCALE	
DRAWING TITLE: DOMESTIC KITCHENS - ELEVATIONS AND ISLAND TABLE	DRAWING NO		REVISION △	

DATA SHEET	DESCRIPTION DOMESTIC KITCHENS		SHEET NO 6 OF 7
			TOTAL QTY:

ILLUSTRATION:

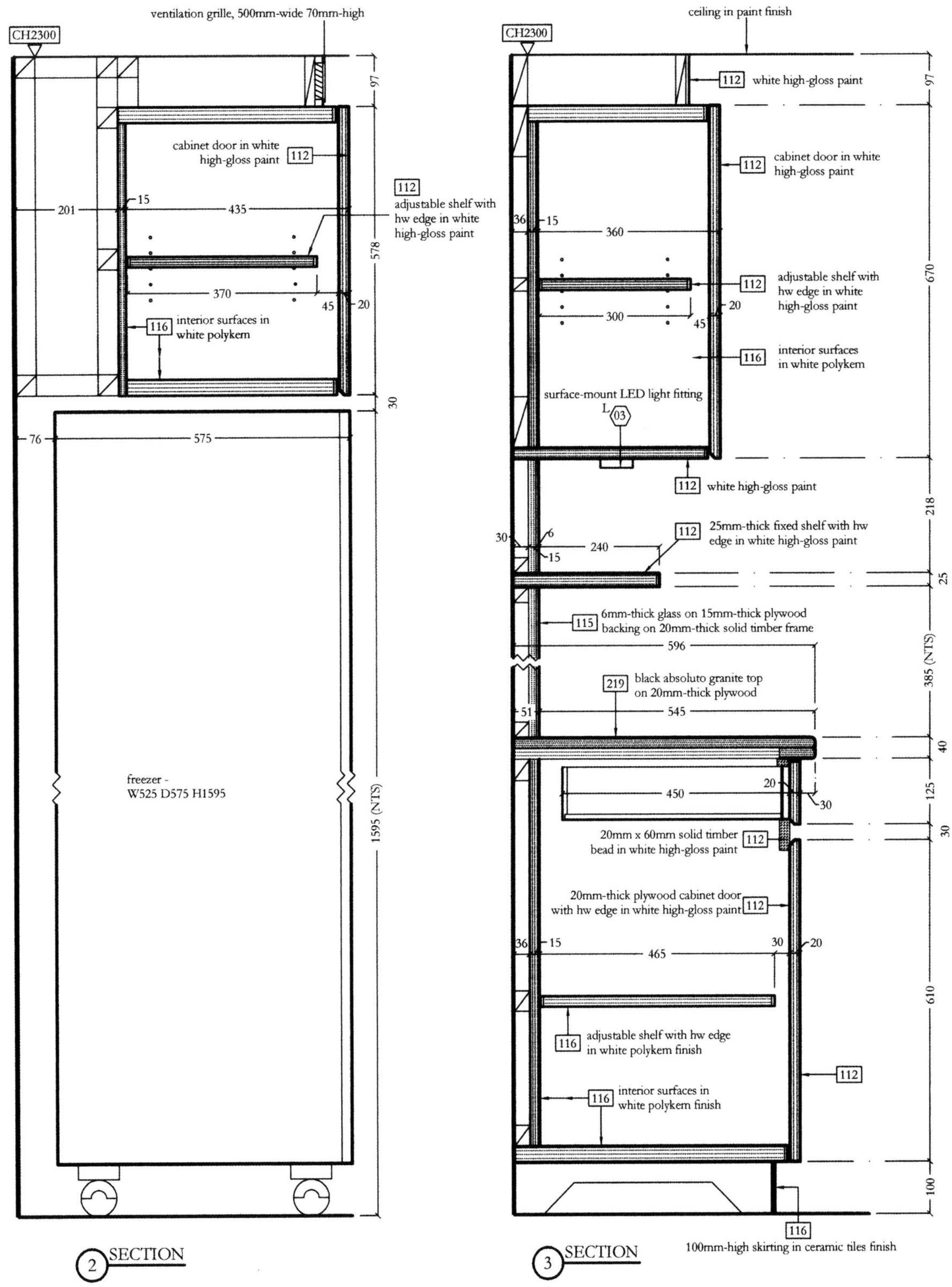

PROJECT TITLE: APARTMENT	DRAWN BY	CHECKED	DATE	address 1 address 2 address 3 postal code email address
	PROJECT NO		SCALE	
DRAWING TITLE: DOMESTIC KITCHENS - SECTION 2 AND 3	DRAWING NO		REVISION △	Interior Designers

DATA SHEET	DESCRIPTION DOMESTIC KITCHENS	SHEET NO 7 OF 7 TOTAL QTY:

ILLUSTRATION:

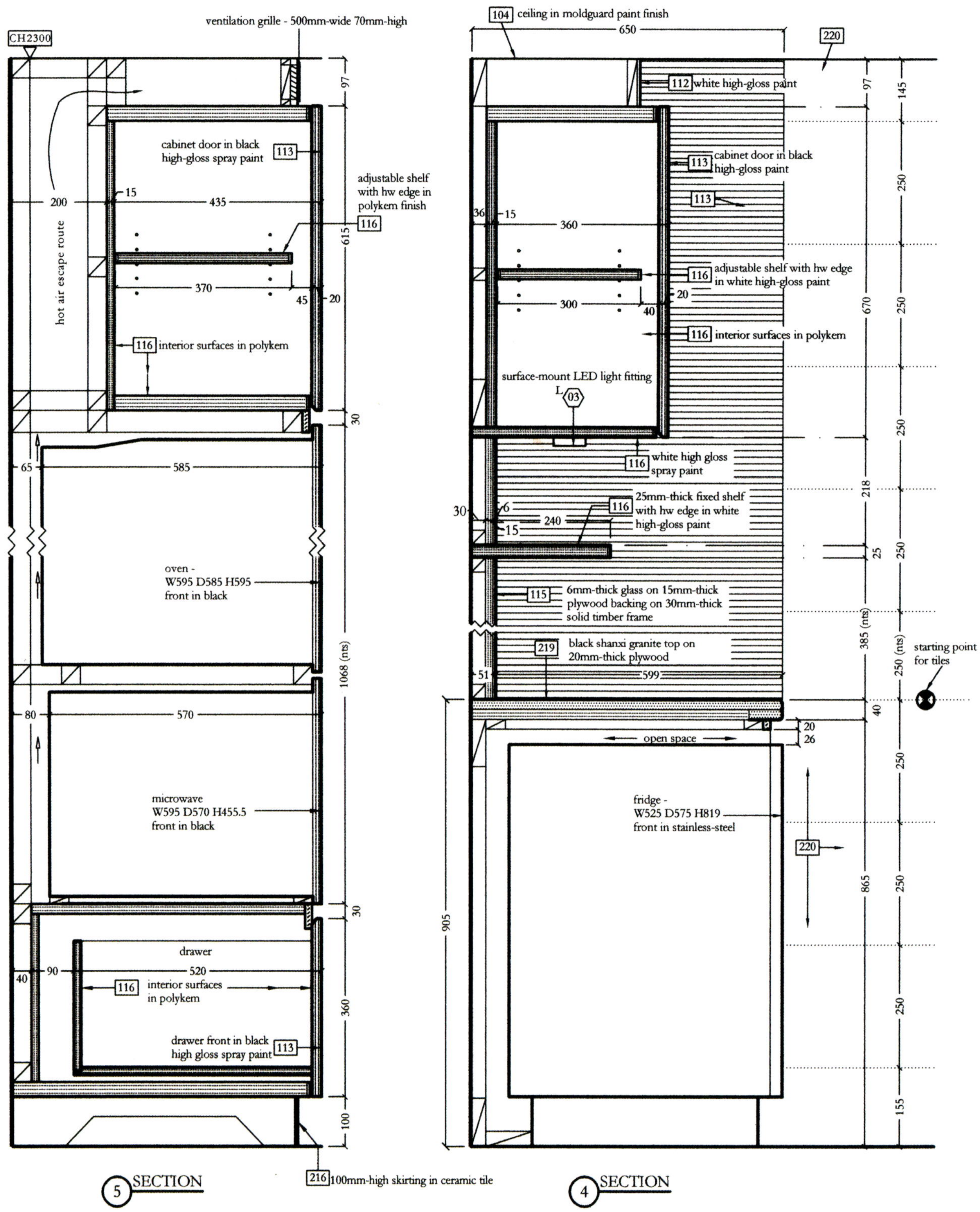

PROJECT TITLE: APARTMENT	DRAWN BY	CHECKED	DATE	address 1 address 2 address 3 postal code email address Interior Designers
DRAWING TITLE: DOMESTIC KITCHENS - SECTION 4 AND 5	PROJECT NO		SCALE	
	DRAWING NO		REVISION △	

CHAPTER 12

STAIRCASES

1. Main ornamental staircase - house in Indonesia
2. Plan - circular, ornamental staircase
3. Detail - elevation of staircase balustrade
4. Section - through wrought-iron balustrade
5. Section - through cantilevered steps

Main ornamental staircase for a house in Indonesia.

DATA SHEET	DESCRIPTION STAIRCASE		SHEET NO 1 OF 3 TOTAL QTY

ILLUSTRATION:

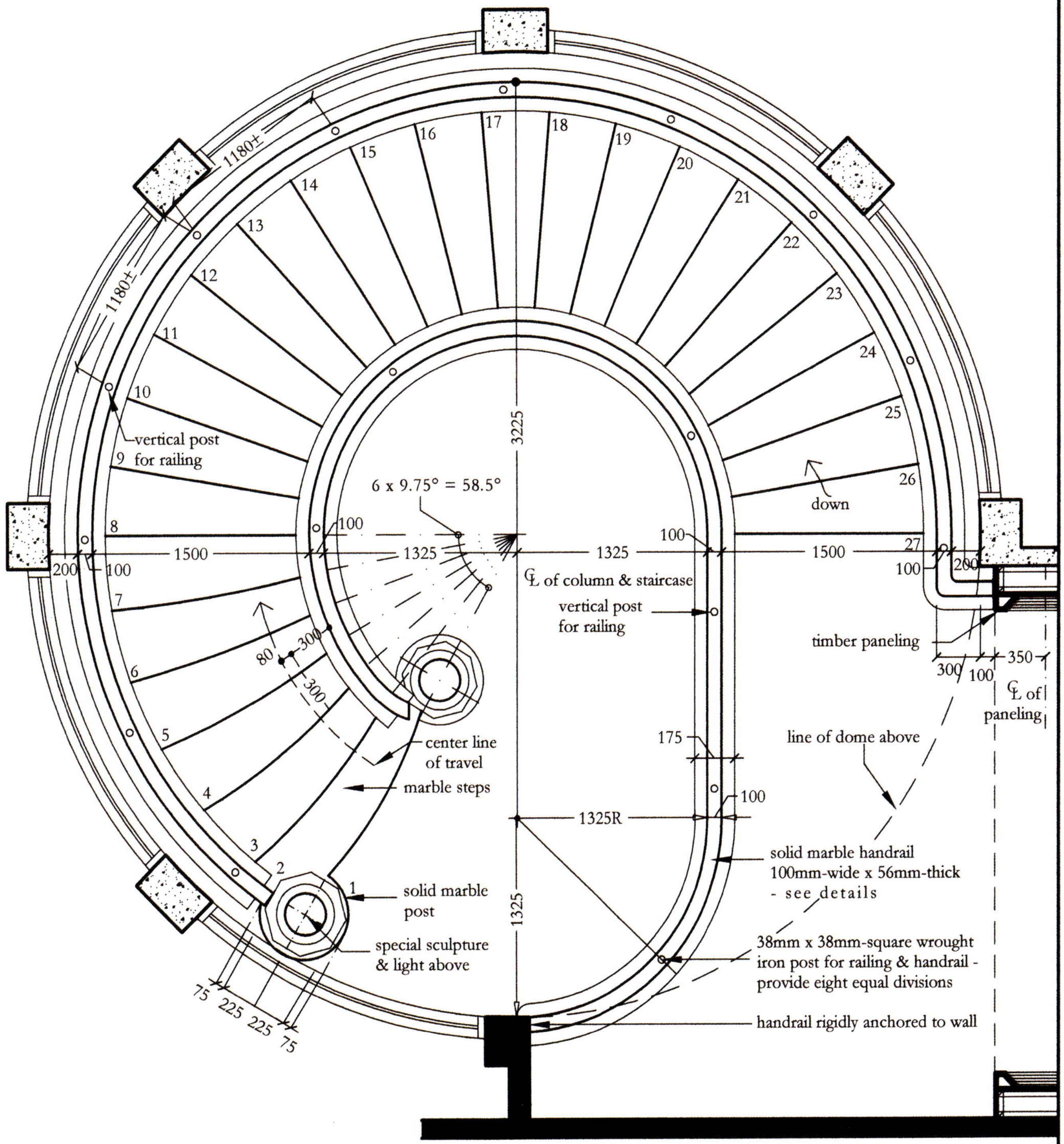

PROJECT TITLE:	DRAWN BY	CHECKED	DATE	address 1 address 2 address 3 postal code email address Interior Designers
DRAWING TITLE: STAIRCASE - PLAN	PROJECT NO		SCALE	
	DRAWING NO		REVISION △	

DATA SHEET	DESCRIPTION STAIRCASE	SHEET NO 2 OF 3 TOTAL QTY:

ILLUSTRATION:

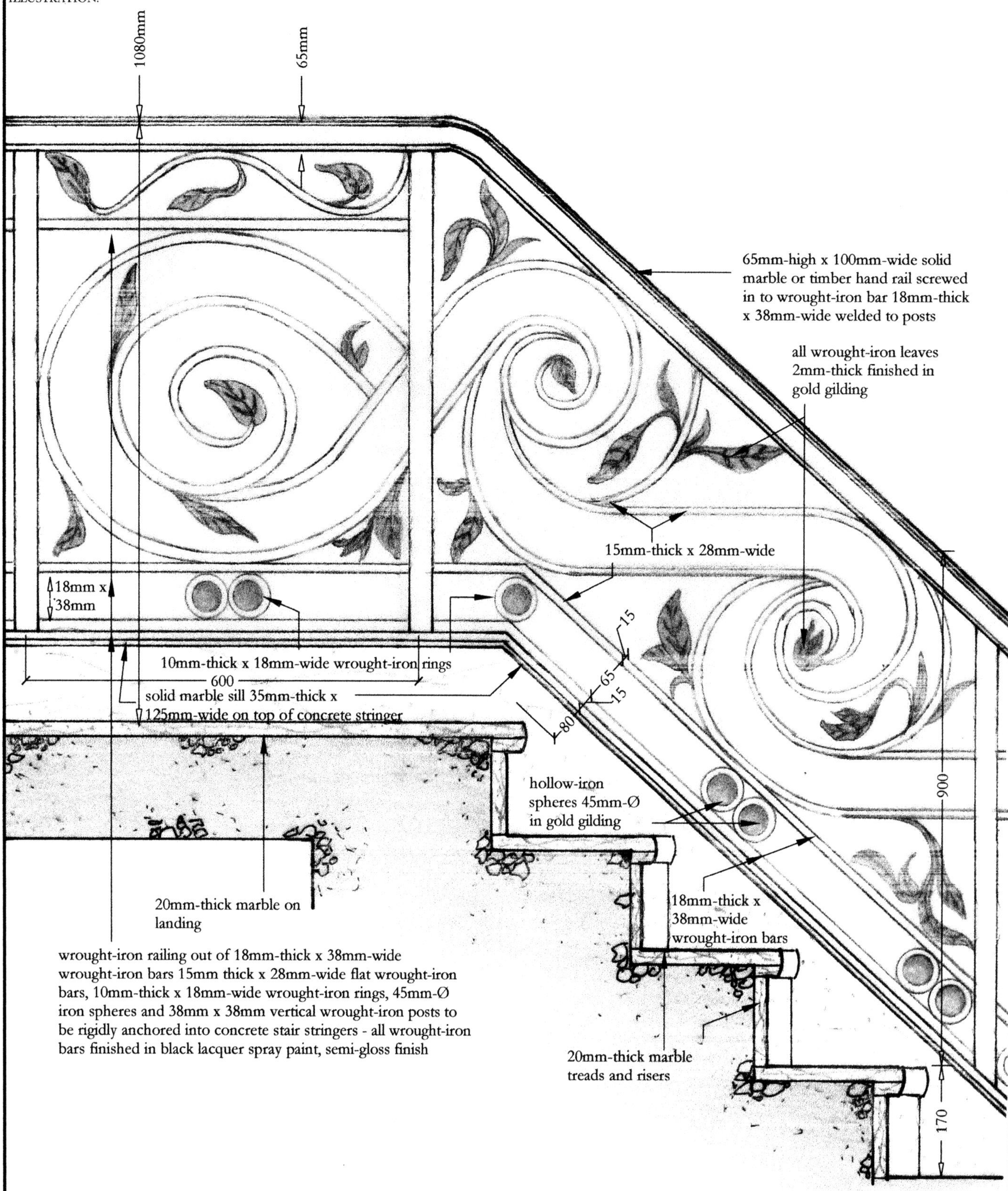

PROJECT TITLE:	DRAWN BY	CHECKED	DATE	*address 1* *address 2* *address 3* *postal code* *email address*
	PROJECT NO		SCALE	
DRAWING TITLE: STAIRCASE - DETAIL ELEVATION OF BALUSTRADE	DRAWING NO		REVISION △	Interior Designers

DATA SHEET	DESCRIPTION STAIRCASE	SHEET No 3 OF 3 TOTAL QTY:

ILLUSTRATION:

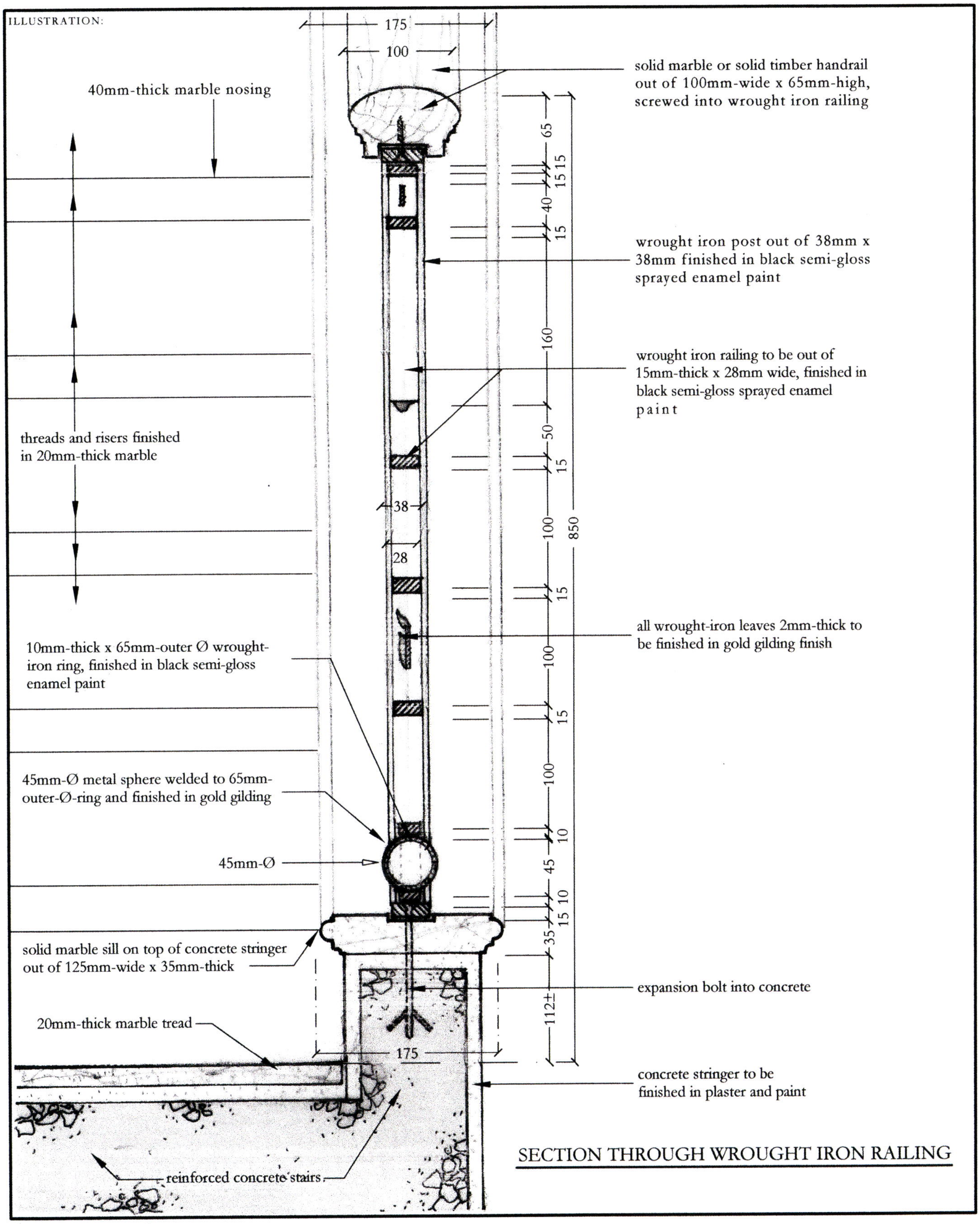

SECTION THROUGH WROUGHT IRON RAILING

PROJECT TITLE:	DRAWN BY	CHECKED	DATE	address 1 address 2 address 3 postal code email address Interior Designers
DRAWING TITLE: STAIRCASE - SECTION THROUGH W. I. BALUSTRADE	PROJECT NO		SCALE	
	DRAWING NO		REVISION	

DATA SHEET	DESCRIPTION STAIRCASE	SHEET NO 1 OF 1 TOTAL QTY:

ILLUSTRATION:

DATA FOR DESIGNING STAIRCASE

- Tread multiply by riser should be a product of 72 to 75± (example 12" x 6" x 72" imperial or 450 for metric, 30cm x 15cm)
- Tread plus riser should be 18± (imperial in inches or 45± metric in centimeters)
- Minimum width of tread (nosing to riser) should be 11" or 280mm and maximum should be 1'-3" or 380mm
- Minimum height of riser should be 6" or 150mm and maximum should be 7-1/2" or 190mm
- Each riser should be the same to avoid tripping hazard.
- For circular stairs line of travel should be a minimum of 380mm from handrail

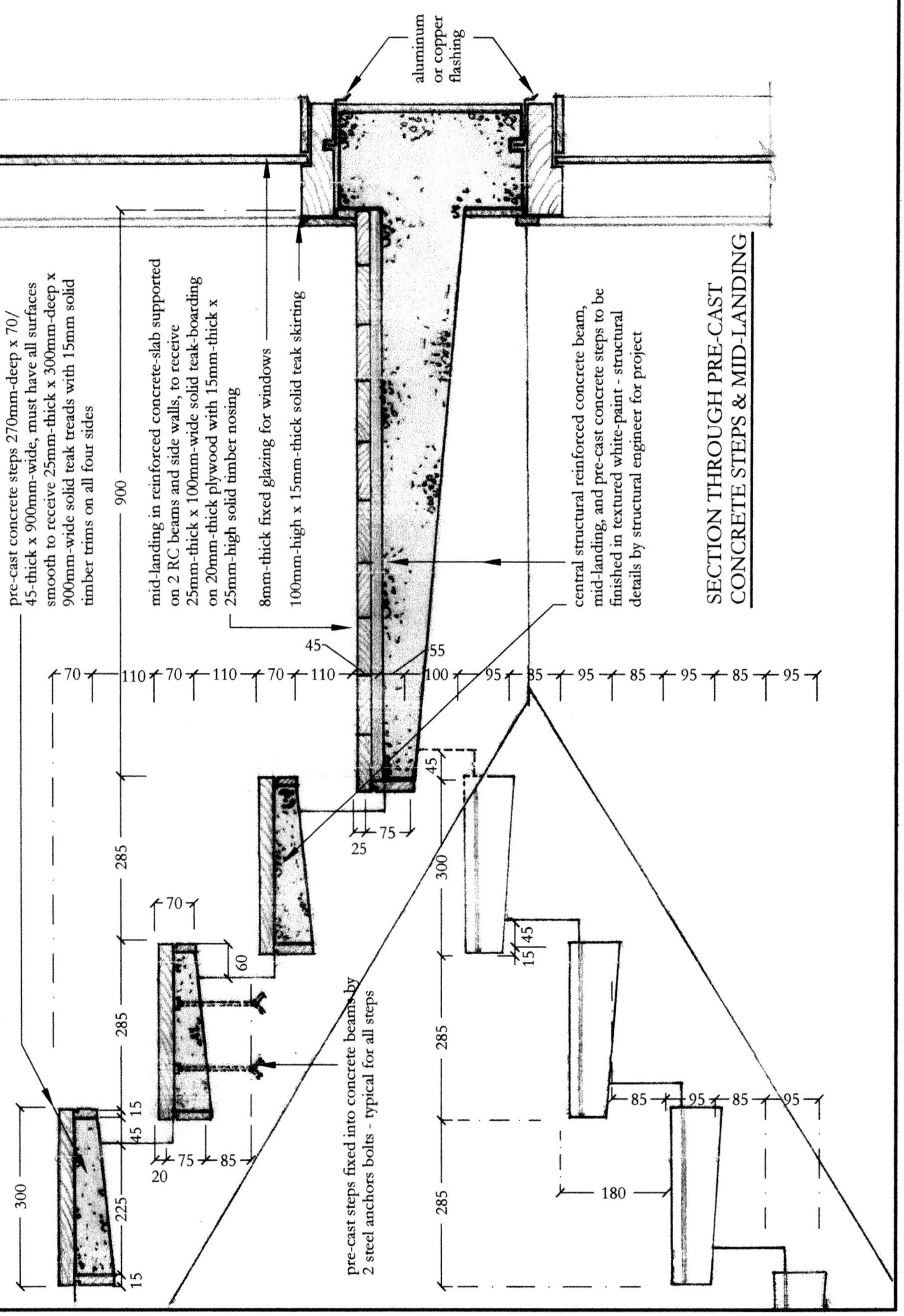

PROJECT TITLE:	DRAWN BY	CHECKED	DATE	address 1 address 2 address 3 postal code email address
	PROJECT NO		SCALE	
DRAWING TITLE: CONCRETE/TIMBER OPEN RISER STAIRS - WITH CANTILEVERED STEPS ON CENTRAL STRINGER	DRAWING NO		REVISION △	Interior Designers

CHAPTER 13

WALL TREATMENTS

1. Write-up on the preparation for a Balinese sculptured wall
2. Photograph of Balinese sculptured wall - house in Indonesia
3. Data sheet - plan, elevation of timber paneling with recessed TV unit
4. Data sheet - detail plan of timber paneling
5. Data sheet - detail plan 4 of timber paneling with recessed TV unit
6. Data sheet - detail section 5, 6, and 7 of timber paneling with recessed TV unit
7. Data sheet - plan & elevation of mirrored paneling
8. Data sheet - detail plan of mirrored wall paneling

Bas-relief sculpted wall in sandstone in the entrance lobby with inlay marble in floor for a house in Indonesia.

PREPARATION OF A BALINESE SCULPTURED WALL

From time to time, you may be called upon to commission a custom design, such as a sculpture wall. This example is an assignment that I undertook, which shows the procedure for the commission of a Balinese sculptor to create a wall scene.

This example is the procedure for the commission of a Balinese sculptor to create a scene or design on a wall.

- A Balinese sculptor is commissioned to create a scene or design on a wall.
- The sculptor goes to the site and measures the exact size of the wall to be sculpted.
- The sculptor then provides the designer and client with a few sketches of the images/designs of the art he envisages, bearing in mind the interior space and the subject matter that has been discussed with the designer/client.
- Once the sculptor has drawn up his sketches and the selection has been made by the designer/client, the sculptor will proceed to sculpt the images onto the stones.
- The stone to be used, for most stone carvings, is a volcanic ash sandstone, generally, ivory colored, and 10cm to 15cm thick (4" to 6"). It is called paras stone.
- Before starting sculpting in his studio from the approved sketch, the sculptor will cut the stone in various sizes to suit the site measurements that have previously been taken to suit the site conditions.
- After the stone pieces have been sculpted, the sculptor will spray the stone with a clear coat of anti-fungus application.
- The sculpted stones will then be brought to the site, and the slabs applied to the wall, and the joints and cracks filled in.
- Once the slabs have been stuck to the wall, and the adhesion has taken effect, the sculptor will spray the whole sculpted wall with one more coat of anti-fungus treatment.

DATA SHEET	DESCRIPTION WALL TREATMENT		SHEET NO 1 OF 4 TOTAL QTY:

ILLUSTRATION:

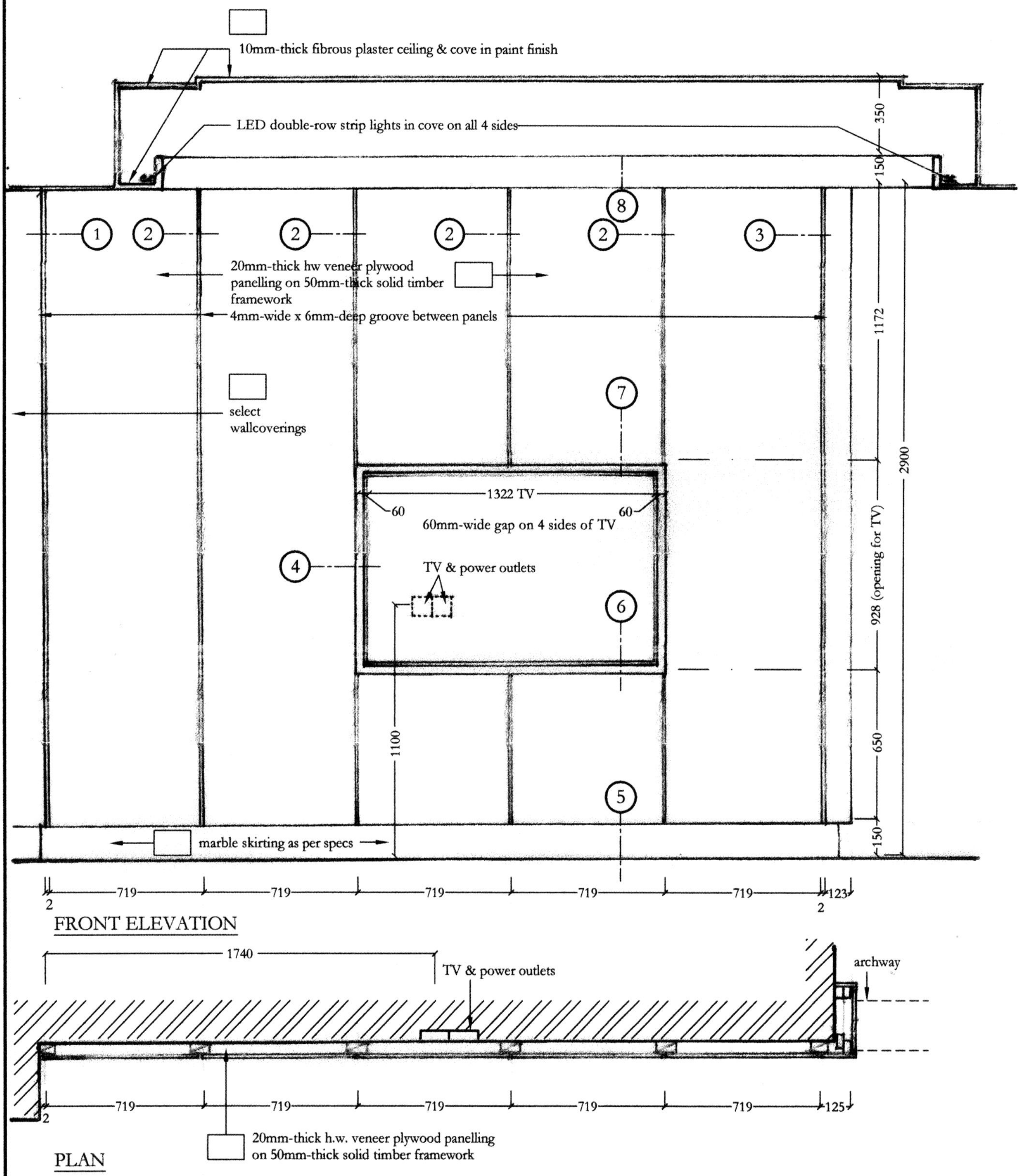

PROJECT TITLE:	DRAWN BY	CHECKED	DATE	address 1 address 2 address 3 postal code email address
	PROJECT NO		SCALE	
DRAWING TITLE: PLAN, ELEVATION of TIMBER PANELING with RECESSED TV	DRAWING NO		REVISION △	Interior Designers

DATA SHEET	DESCRIPTION: WALL TREATMENT		SHEET NO 2 OF 4 TOTAL QTY:

ILLUSTRATION:

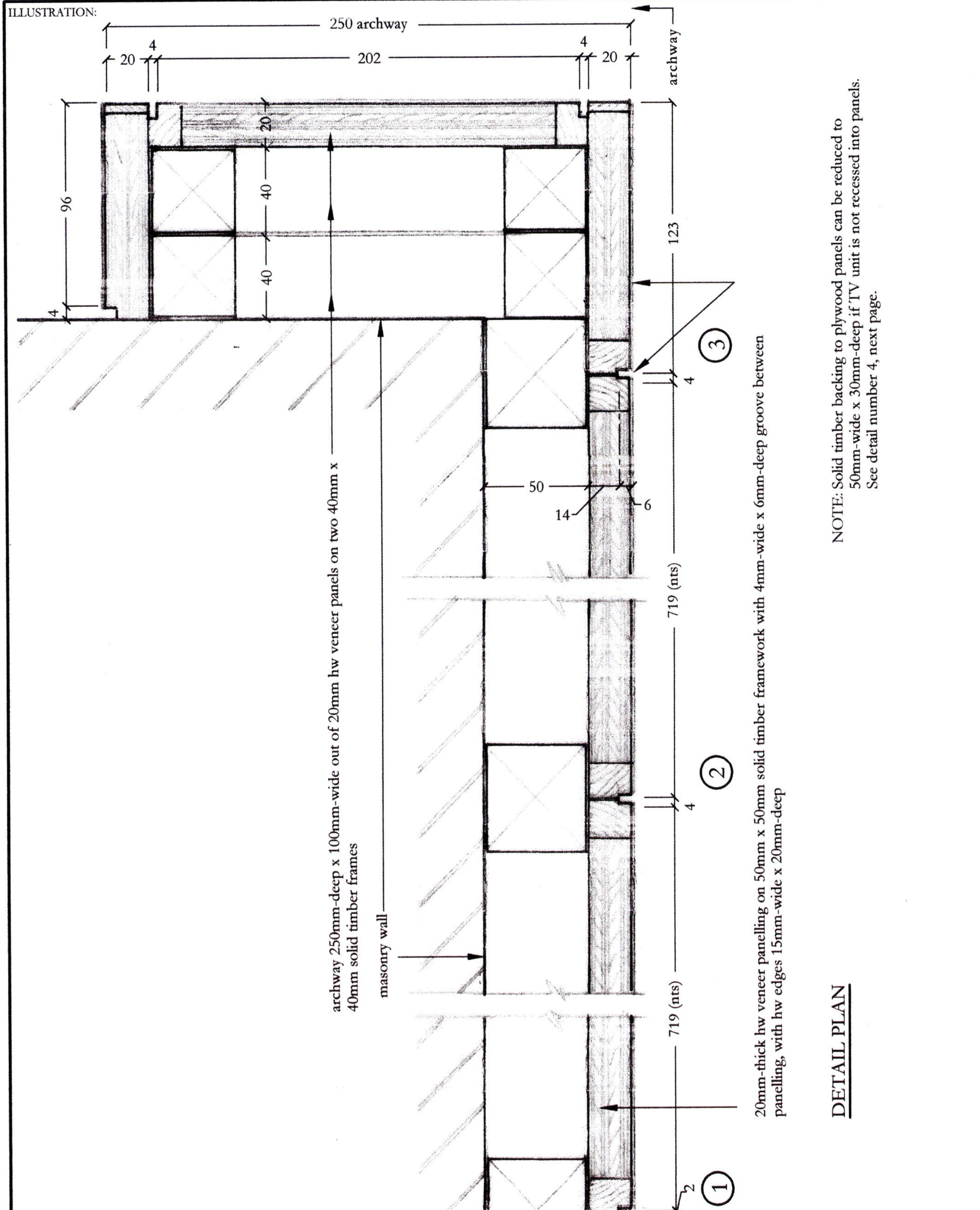

PROJECT TITLE:	DRAWN BY	CHECKED	DATE	address 1 address 2 address 3 postal code email address Interior Designers
	PROJECT NO		SCALE	
DRAWING TITLE: DETAIL PLAN of TIMBER PANELING	DRAWING NO		REVISION △	

DATA SHEET	DESCRIPTION WALL TREATMENT	SHEET NO 3 OF 4 TOTAL QTY:

ILLUSTRATION:

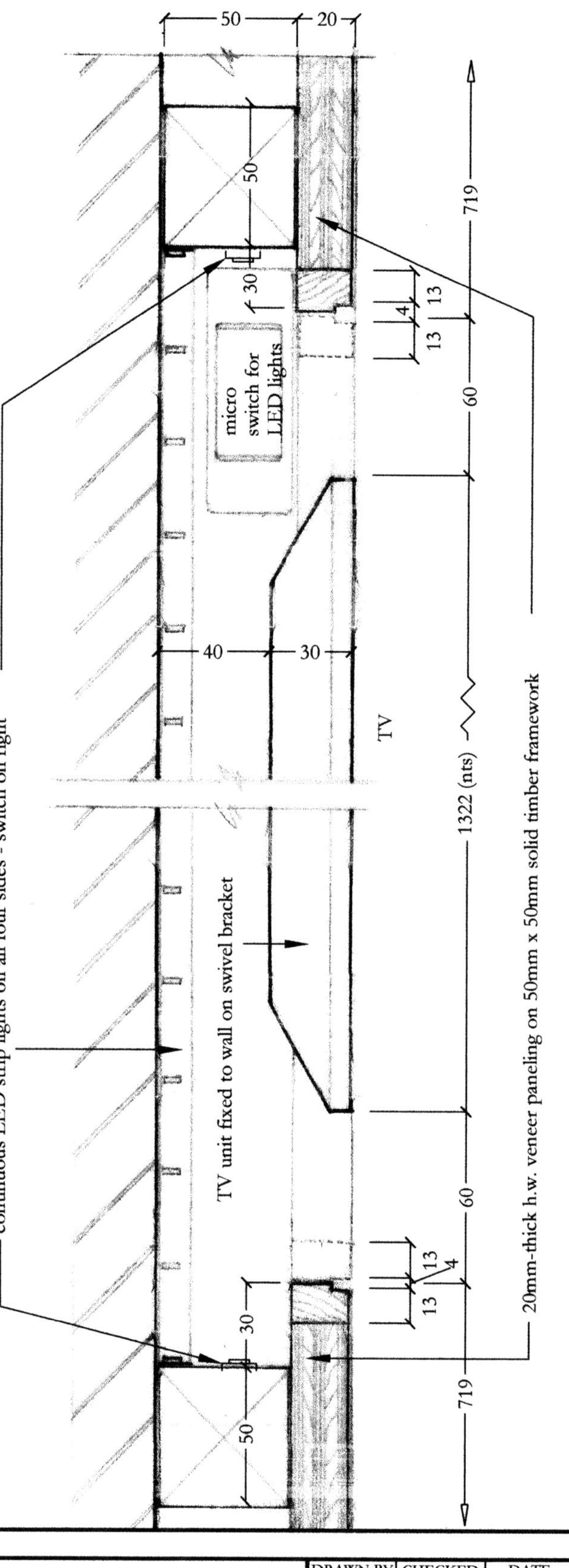

4 DETAIL PLAN OF TIMBER PANELLING WITH RECESSED T.V. UNIT

PROJECT TITLE: TIMBER PANELED WALL	DRAWN BY	CHECKED	DATE	address 1 address 2 address 3 postal code email address Interior Designers
	PROJECT NO		SCALE	
DRAWING TITLE: DETAIL PLAN 4 of WALL PANELING with RECESSED TV UNIT	DRAWING NO		REVISION △	

DATA SHEET	DESCRIPTION WALL TREATMENT		SHEET NO 4 OF 4 TOTAL QTY:

ILLUSTRATION:

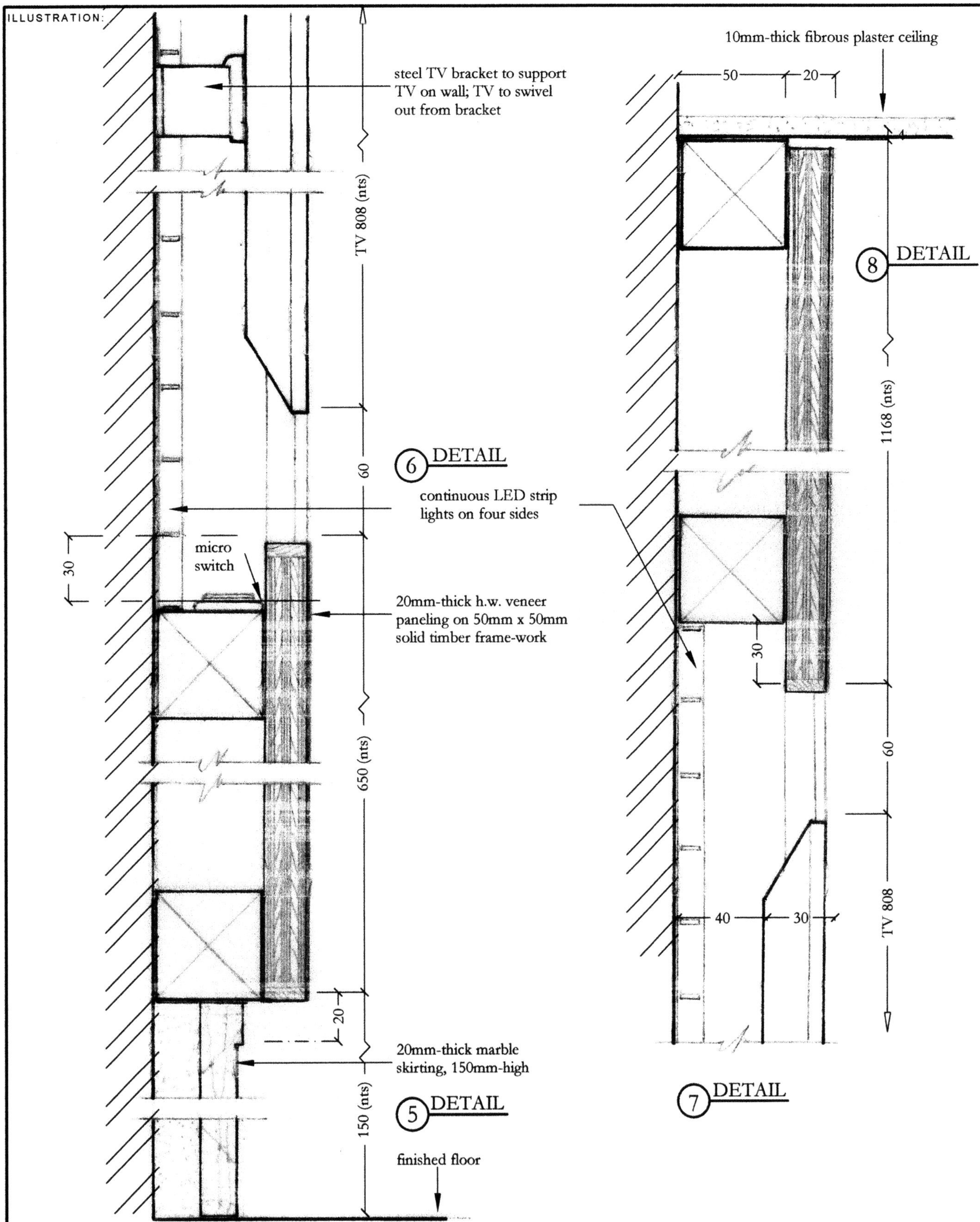

PROJECT TITLE: TIMBER PANELED WALL	DRAWN BY	CHECKED	DATE	address 1 address 2 address 3 postal code email address
	PROJECT NO		SCALE	
DRAWING TITLE: DETAIL SECTION of WALL PANELING with RECESSED TV UNIT	DRAWING NO		REVISION △	Interior Designers

DATA SHEET	DESCRIPTION WALL TREATMENT		SHEET NO 1 OF 3 TOTAL QTY:

ILLUSTRATION:

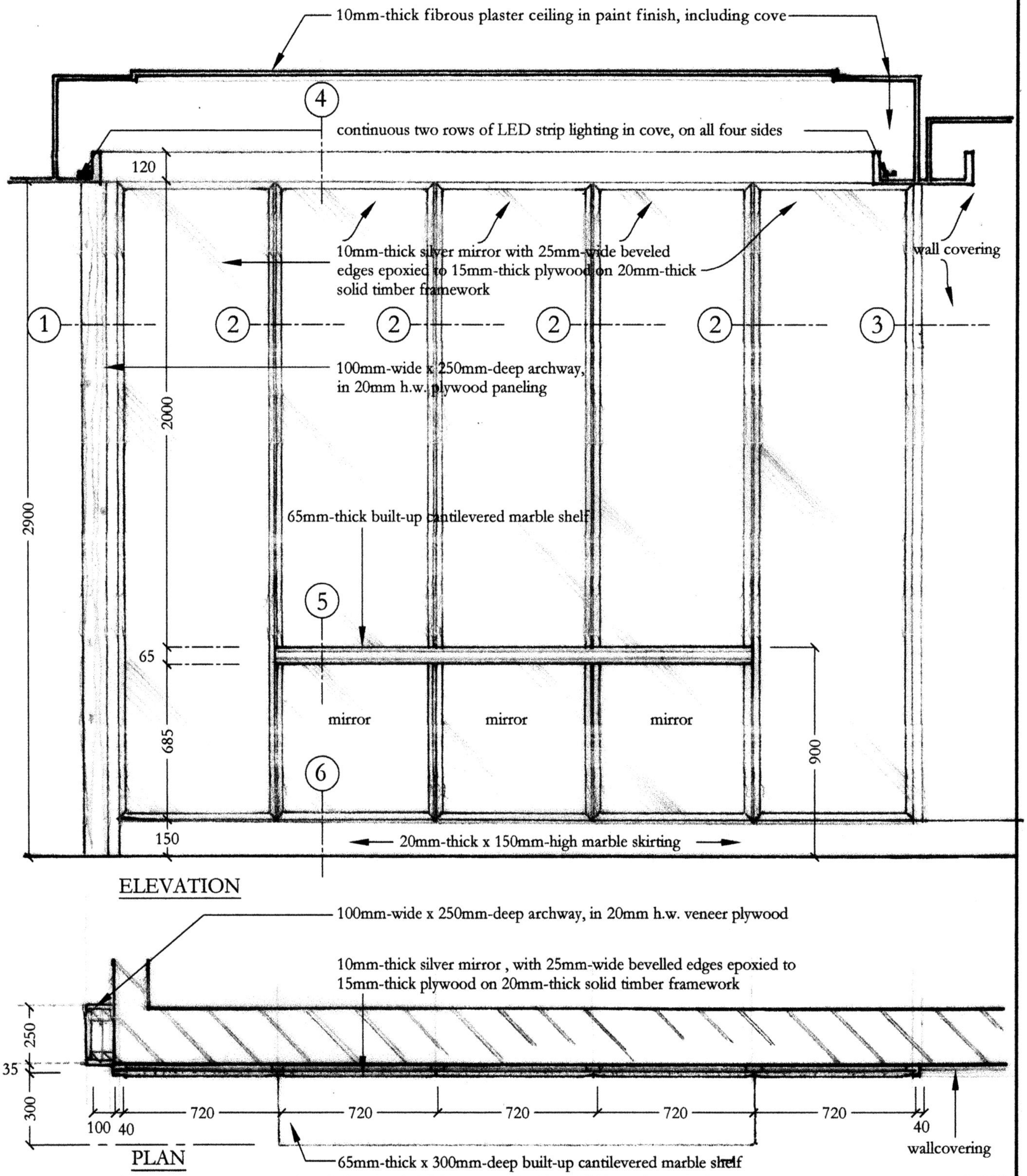

PROJECT TITLE: MIRROR PANELED WALL	DRAWN BY	CHECKED	DATE	address 1 address 2 address 3 postal code email address Interior Designers
	PROJECT NO		SCALE	
DRAWING TITLE: PLAN & ELEVATION of MIRROR PANELING with CANTILEVERED SHELF	DRAWING NO		REVISION △	

DATA SHEET	DESCRIPTION WALL TREATMENT		SHEET NO 2 OF 3 TOTAL QTY:

ILLUSTRATION:

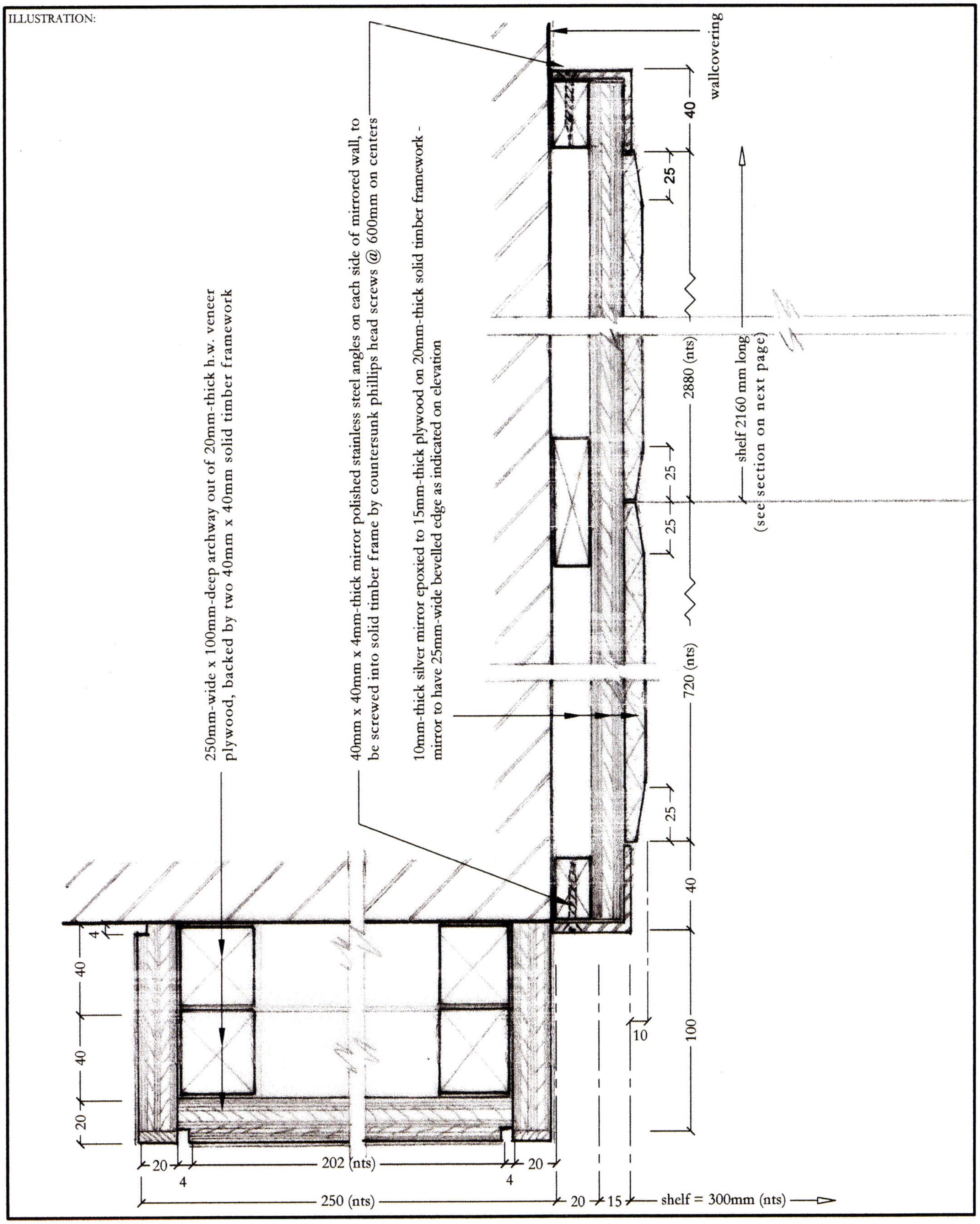

PROJECT TITLE: MIRROR PANELED WALL	DRAWN BY	CHECKED	DATE	address 1 address 2 address 3 postal code email address
	PROJECT NO		SCALE	
DRAWING TITLE: DETAIL PLAN of MIRRORED WALL PANELING	DRAWING NO		REVISION △	Interior Designers

DATA SHEET	DESCRIPTION WALL TREATMENT	SHEET NO 3 OF 3 TOTAL QTY:

ILLUSTRATION:

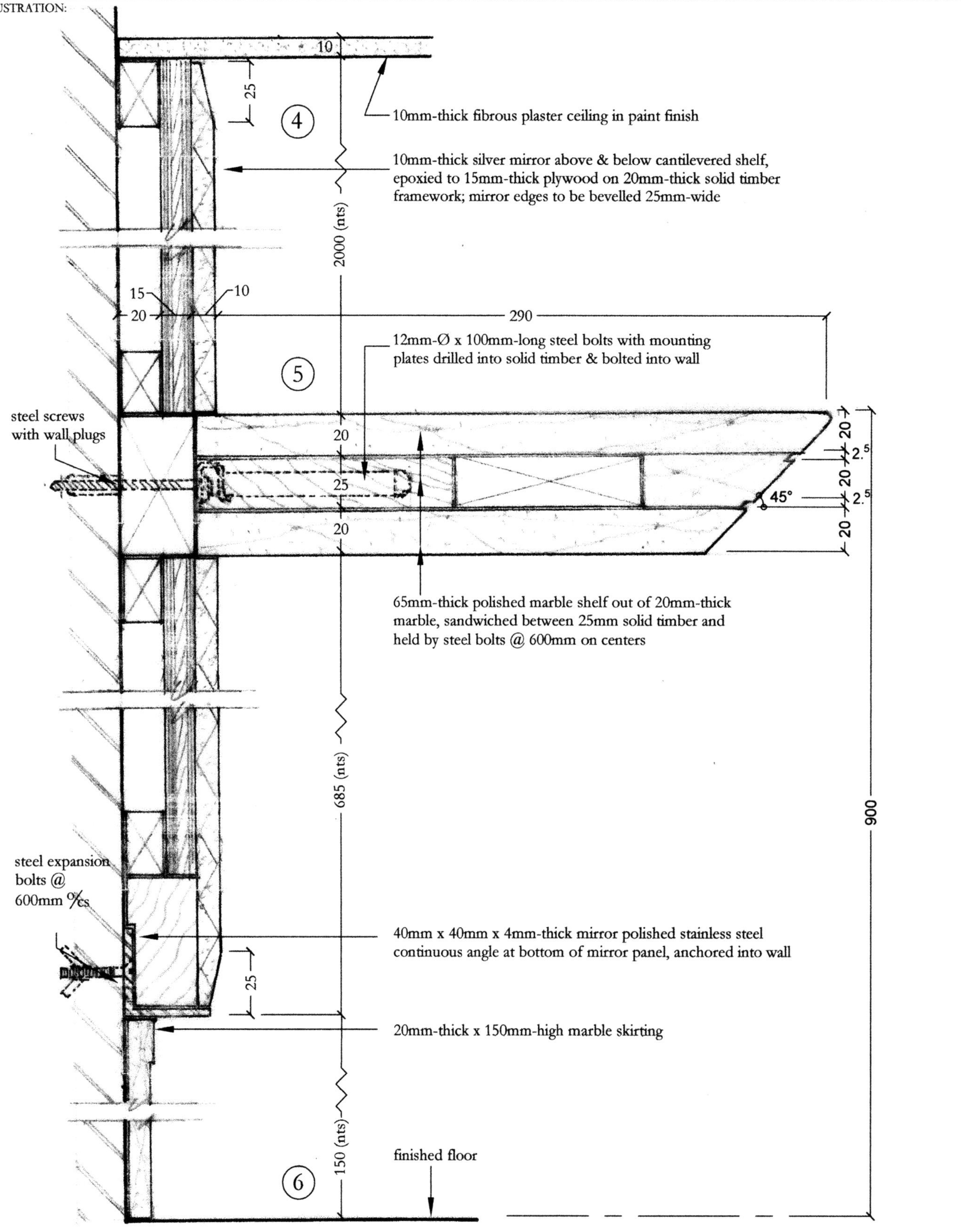

PROJECT TITLE: MIRROR PANELED WALL	DRAWN BY	CHECKED	DATE	address 1 address 2 address 3 postal code email address Interior Designers
DRAWING TITLE: PLAN & ELEVATION of MIRROR PANELING with CANTILEVERED MARBLE SHELF	PROJECT NO		SCALE	
	DRAWING NO		REVISION △	

CHAPTER 14

PATTERNS (FOR AREA RUGS, FLOORS, AND TABLE TOPS)

1. For floors - in marble or ceramic tiles
2. For floors - in timber/marble or marble/ceramic tiles
3. For floors - in marble or ceramic tiles
4. Photographs
   a. Border pattern in a ceramic tile floor for a house in Indonesia
   b. Inlaid marble panel with colored marble border in a bathroom marble floor for a house in Indonesia
5. For floors - in marble or ceramic tiles and area rugs

DATA SHEET	DESCRIPTION PATTERNS	⬡	SHEET NO OF TOTAL QTY:

ILLUSTRATION:

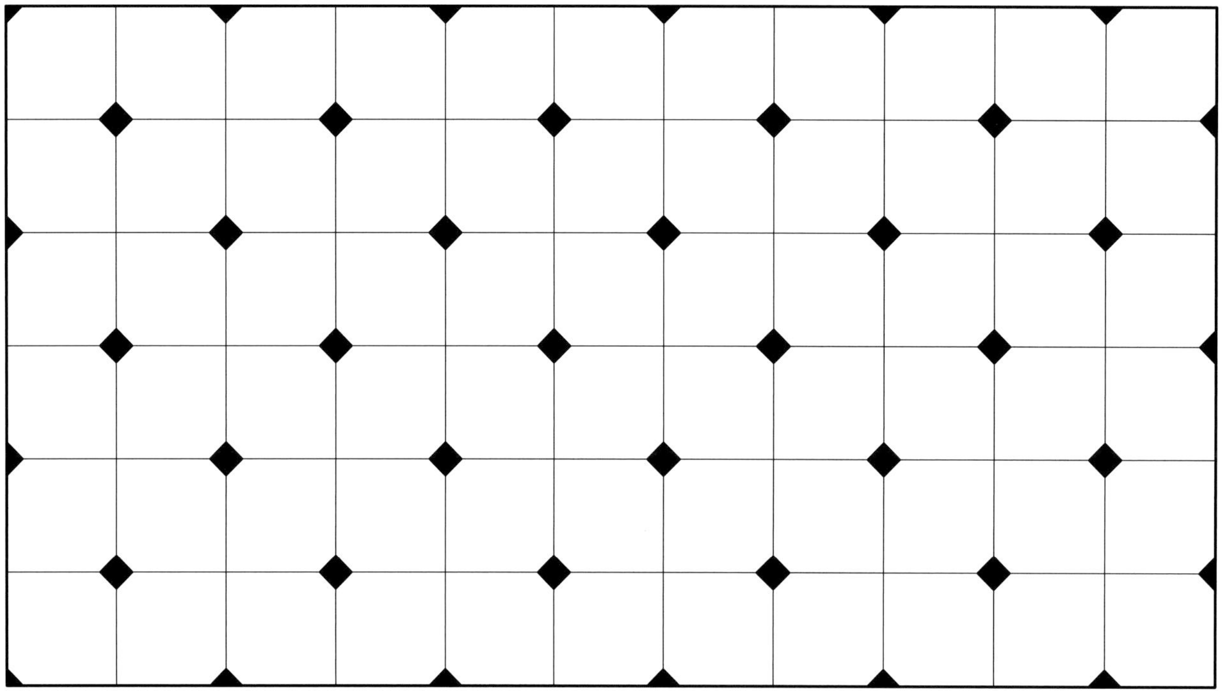

IN MARBLE OR CERAMIC TILES

IN MARBLE

PROJECT TITLE:	DRAWN BY	CHECKED	DATE	*address 1* *address 2* *address 3* *postal code* *email address*
	PROJECT NO		SCALE	
DRAWING TITLE: FOR FLOORS - (IN MARBLE OR CERAMIC TILES)	DRAWING N˚O		REVISION △	Interor Designers

DATA SHEET	DESCRIPTION PATTERNS		SHEET NO OF
			TOTAL QTY:

ILLUSTRATION:

IN TIMBER OR MARBLE

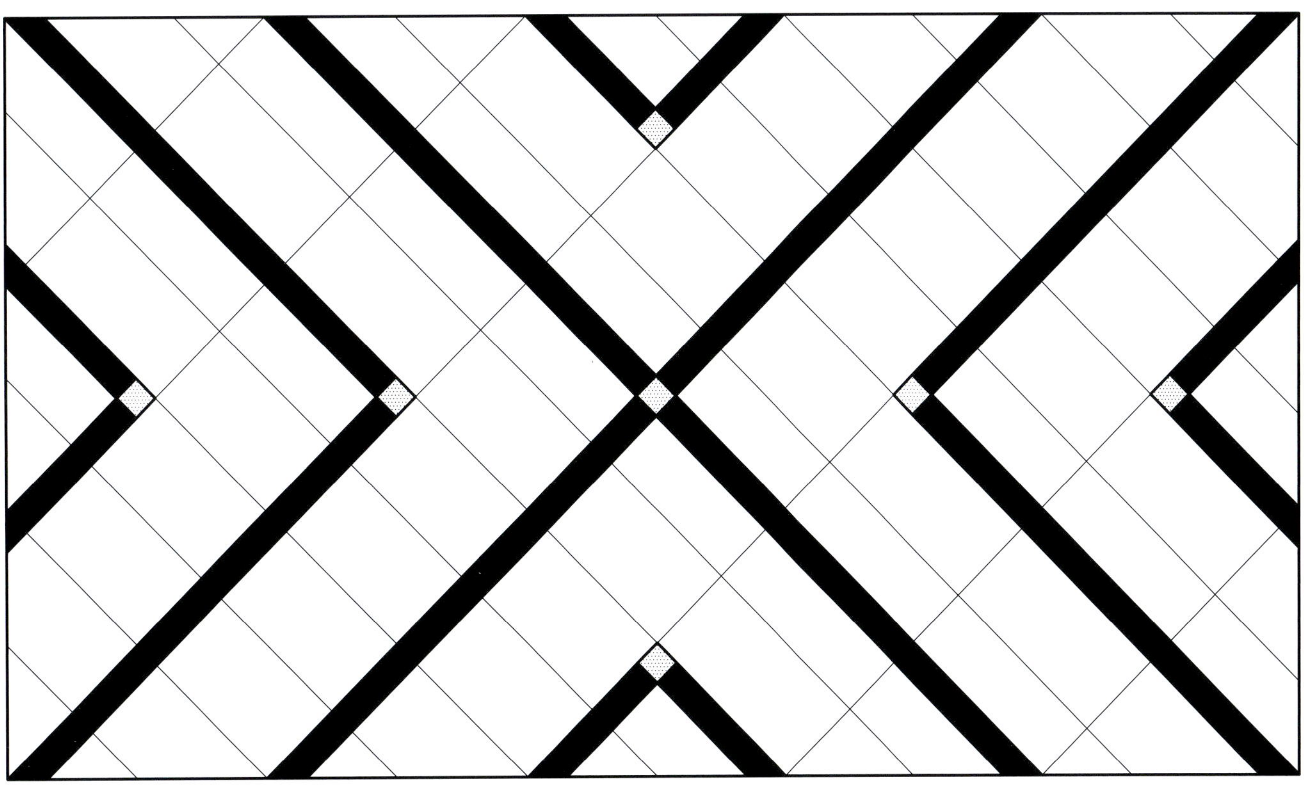

IN MARBLE OR CERAMIC TILES

PROJECT TITLE:	DRAWN BY	CHECKED	DATE	address 1 address 2 address 3 postal code email address
	PROJECT NO		SCALE	
DRAWING TITLE: FOR FLOORS - (TIMBER/MARBLE) AND MARBLE/ CERAMIC TILES)	DRAWING NO		REVISION △	Interior Designers

DATA SHEET	DESCRIPTION PATTERNS	⬡	SHEET NO OF TOTAL QTY

ILLUSTRATION:

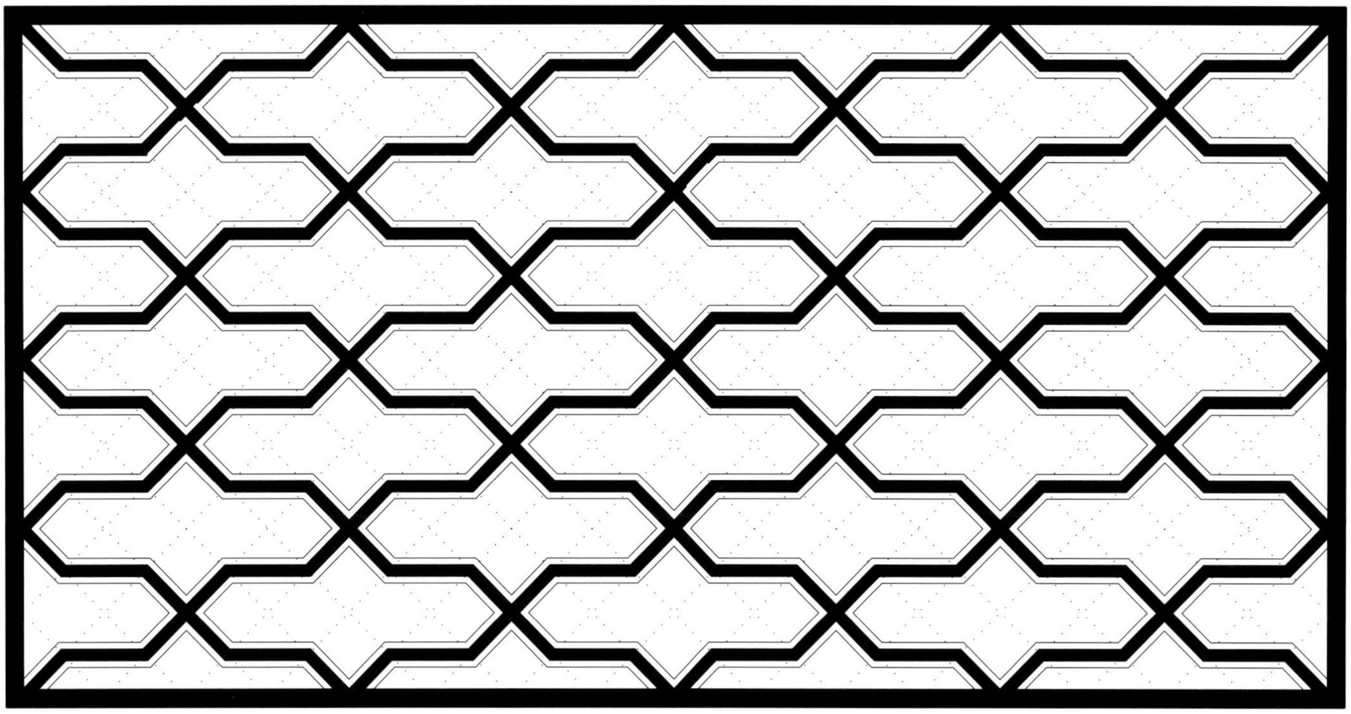

IN MARBLE

IN MARBLE, CERAMIC, OR MOSAIC TILES

PROJECT TITLE:	DRAWN BY	CHECKED	DATE	*address 1* *address 2* *address 3* *postal code* *email address*
	PROJECT NO		SCALE	
DRAWING TITLE: FOR FLOORS - (IN MARBLE OR CERAMIC TILES)	DRAWING NO		REVISION △	Interor Designers

Border pattern in a ceramic floor tile for a house in Indonesia.

Inlaid marble with colored marble border in a bathroom floor for a house in Indonesia.

DATA SHEET	DESCRIPTION PATTERNS		SHEET NO OF TOTAL QTY:

ILLUSTRATION:

IN MARBLE OR CERAMIC TILES - DIFFERENT COLORS OF TILES/MARBLE TO BE SELECTED BY DESIGNER

ROSE - PATTERNED AREA RUG - COLORS TO BE SELECTED BY DESIGNER

PROJECT TITLE:	DRAWN BY	CHECKED	DATE	address 1 address 2 address 3 postal code email address
	PROJECT NO		SCALE	
DRAWING TITLE: FOR FLOORS - (IN MARBLE OR CERAMIC TILES AND AREA RUGS)	DRAWING NO		REVISION △	Interior Designers

CHAPTER 15

SHELVING

1. Modular shelving unit - section and details
2. Various permutations of a single modular shelving unit
3. Cabinet with adjustable shelves - plan, elevation and section
4. Cabinet with adjustable shelves - details, sheet 1
5. Cabinet with adjustable shelves - details, sheet 2
6. Open bookcase with shelving on timber strips
7. Slim-line bookcase - fixed shelving

DATA SHEET	DESCRIPTION SHELVING	F ⬡	SHEET NO 1 OF 2 TOTAL QTY:

ILLUSTRATION:

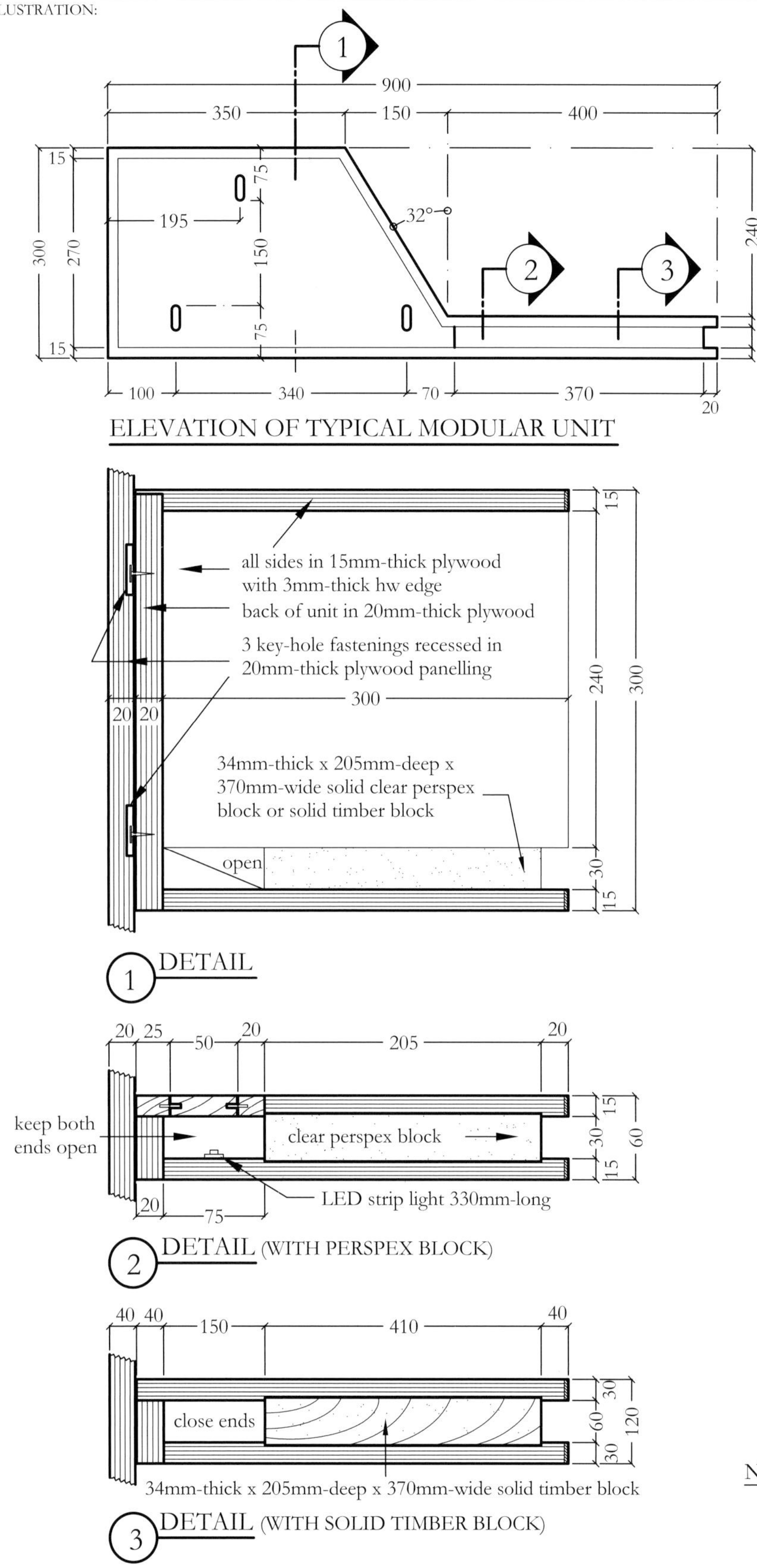

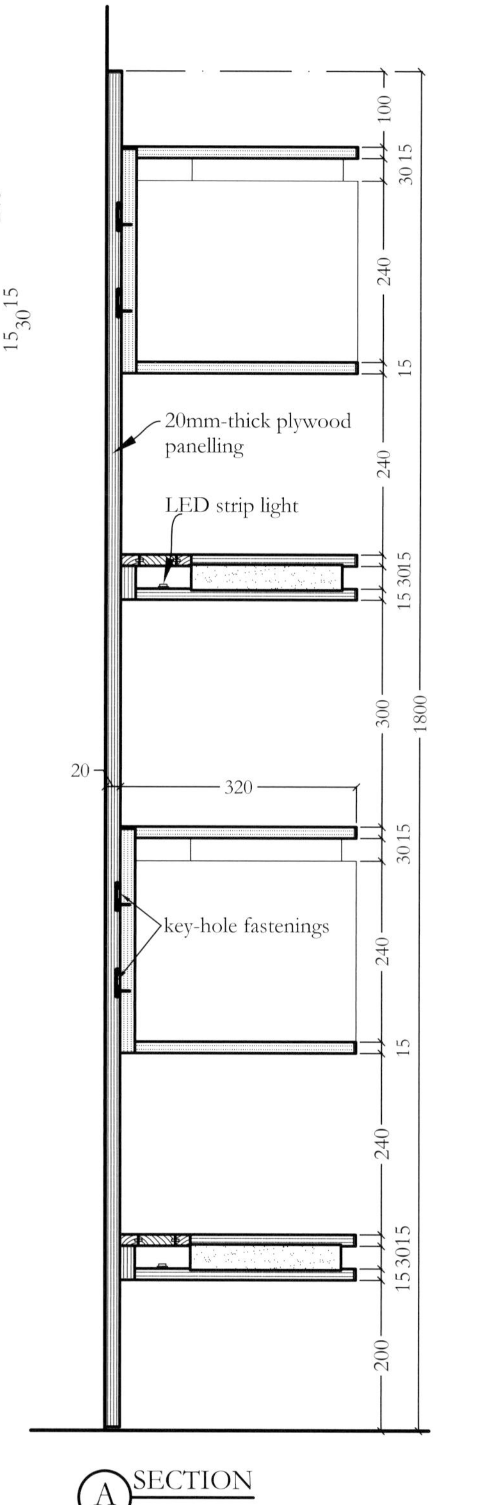

NOTE: Plywood could be finished in h.w. veneer or plastic laminate or spray paint. For LED lighting, use clear perspex block, otherwise use solid timber block.

PROJECT TITLE:	DRAWN BY	CHECKED	DATE	address 1 address 2 address 3 postal code email address
	PROJECT NO		SCALE	
DRAWING TITLE: SECTION & DETAILS OF MODULAR SHELVING UNIT	DRAWING NO		REVISION △	Interior Designers

DATA SHEET	DESCRIPTION SHELVING	F	SHEET NO 2 OF 2 TOTAL QTY:

ILLUSTRATION:

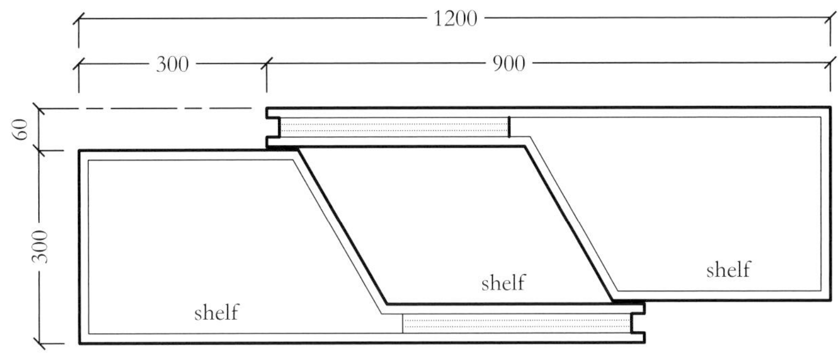

TWO-UNIT COMBINATION

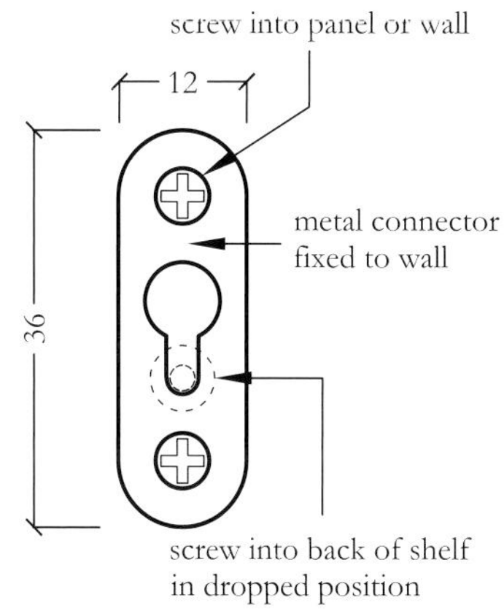

KEYHOLE
FASTENING CONNECTOR

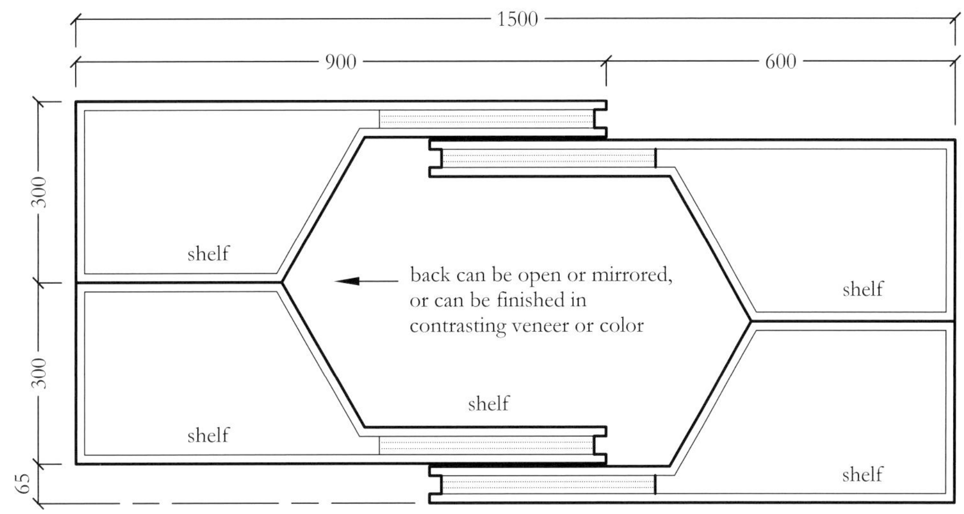

FOUR-UNIT COMBINATION

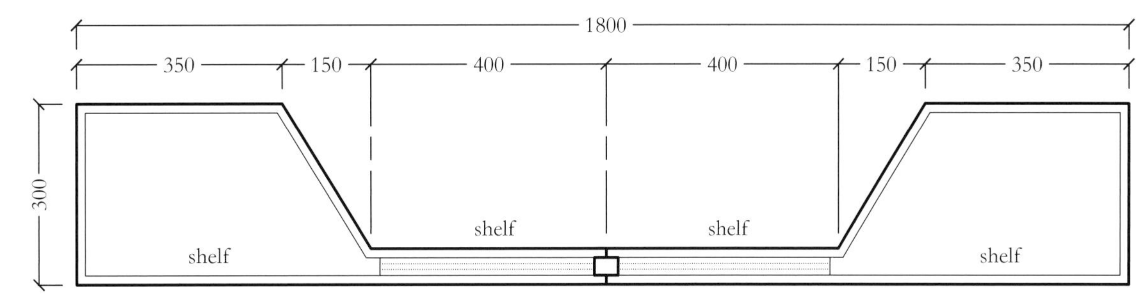

TWO-UNIT COMBINATION

PROJECT TITLE:	DRAWN BY	CHECKED	DATE	address 1 address 2 address 3 postal code email address
	PROJECT NO		SCALE	
DRAWING TITLE: VARIOUS PERMUTATIONS OF SINGLE, MODULAR SHELVING UNIT	DRAWING NO		REVISION △	Interior Designers

DATA SHEET	DESCRIPTION: SHELVING	F	SHEET NO 1 OF 3
			TOTAL QTY:

ILLUSTRATION:

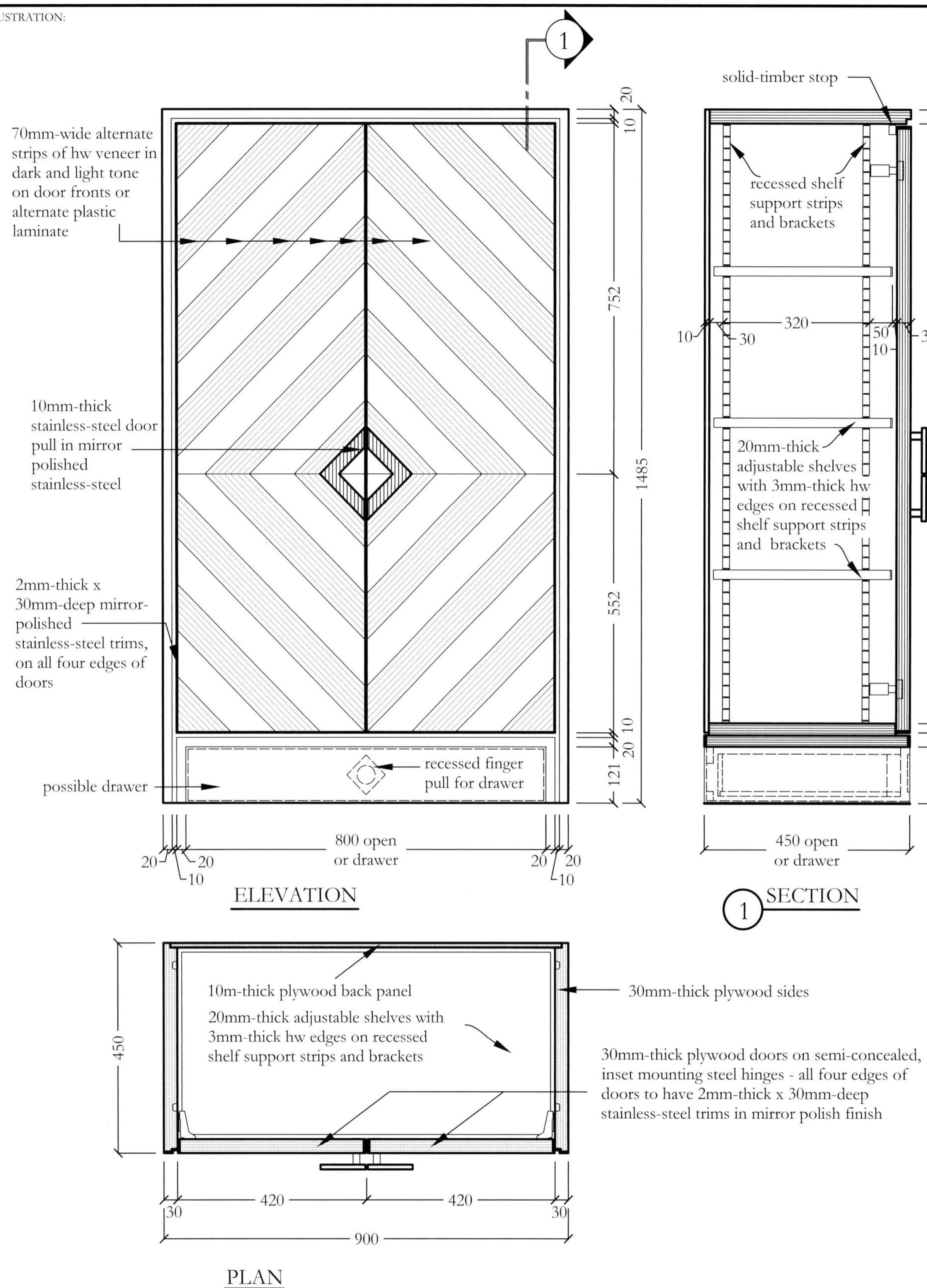

PROJECT TITLE:	DRAWN BY	CHECKED	DATE	address 1 address 2 address 3 postal code email address
	PROJECT NO		SCALE	
DRAWING TITLE: CABINET WITH ADJUSTABLE SHELVES - PLAN, ELEVATION, AND SECTION	DRAWING NO		REVISION △	Interior Designers

DATA SHEET	DESCRIPTION SHELVING	F	SHEET NO 2 OF 3 TOTAL QTY:

ILLUSTRATION:

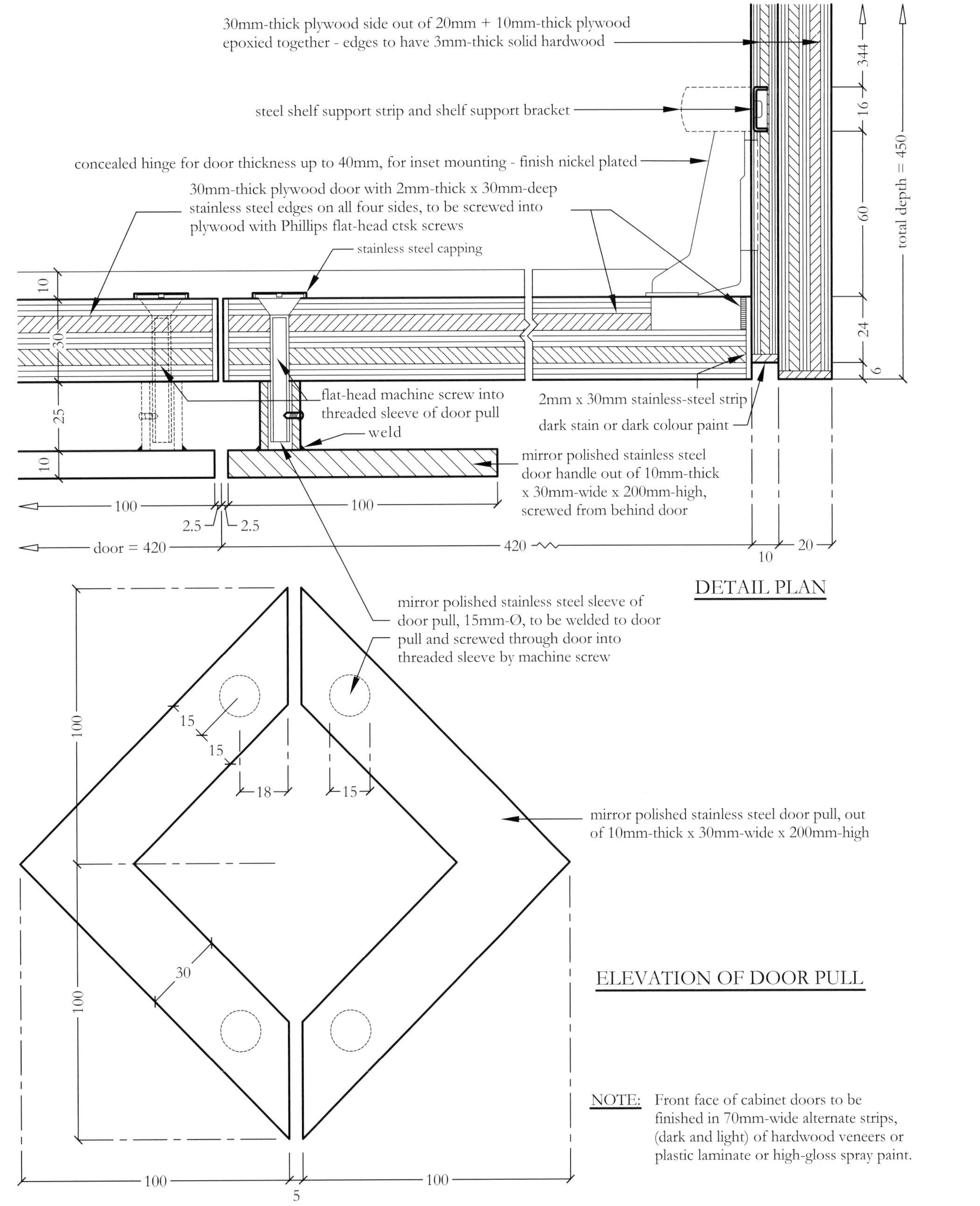

PROJECT TITLE:	DRAWN BY	CHECKED	DATE	address 1 address 2 address 3 postal code email address
	PROJECT NO		SCALE	
DRAWING TITLE: CABINET WITH ADJUSTABLE SHELVES - DETAILS	DRAWING NO		REVISION △	Interior Designers

DATA SHEET	DESCRIPTION SHELVING	F	SHEET NO 3 OF 3 TOTAL QTY:

ILLUSTRATION:

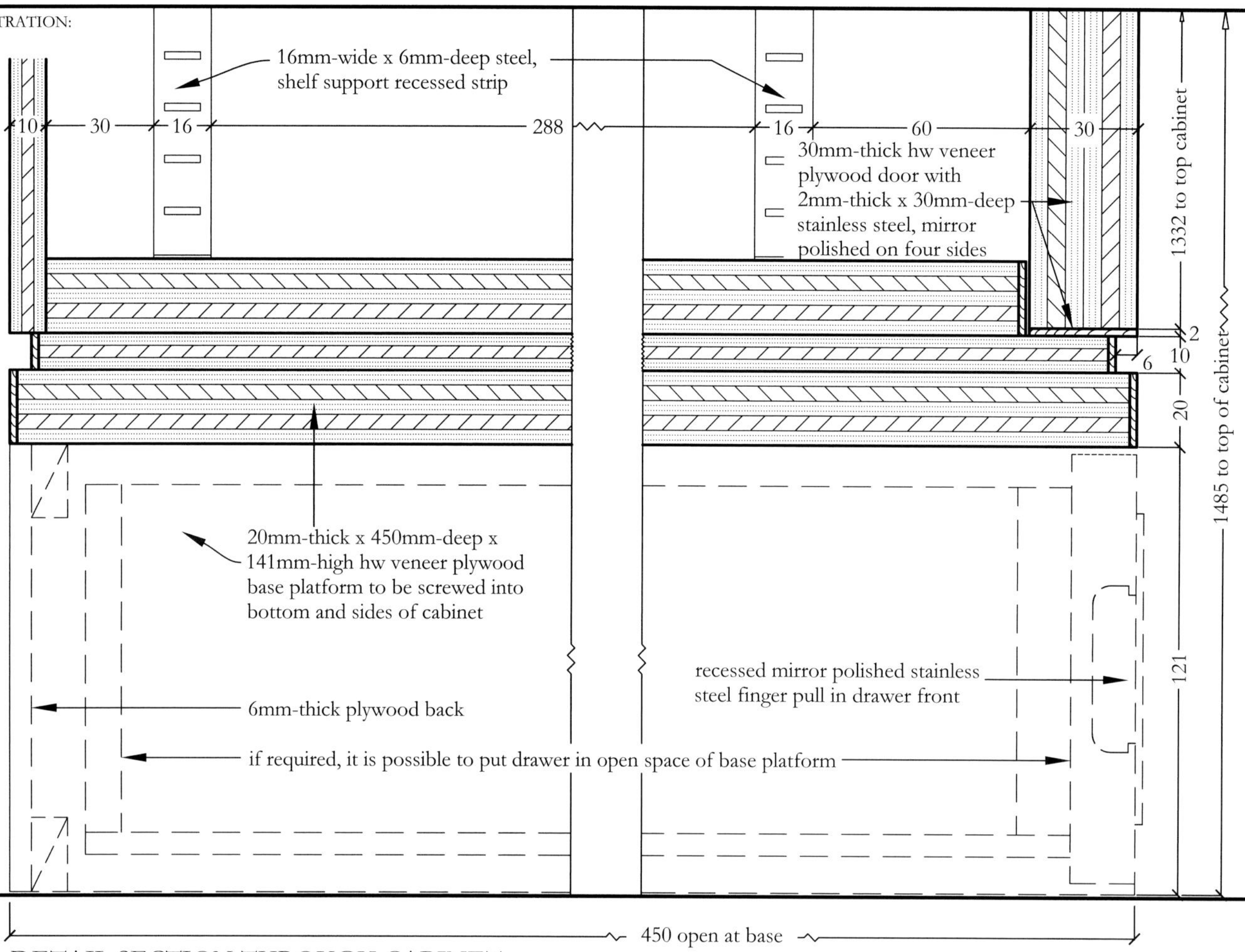

DETAIL SECTION THROUGH CABINET

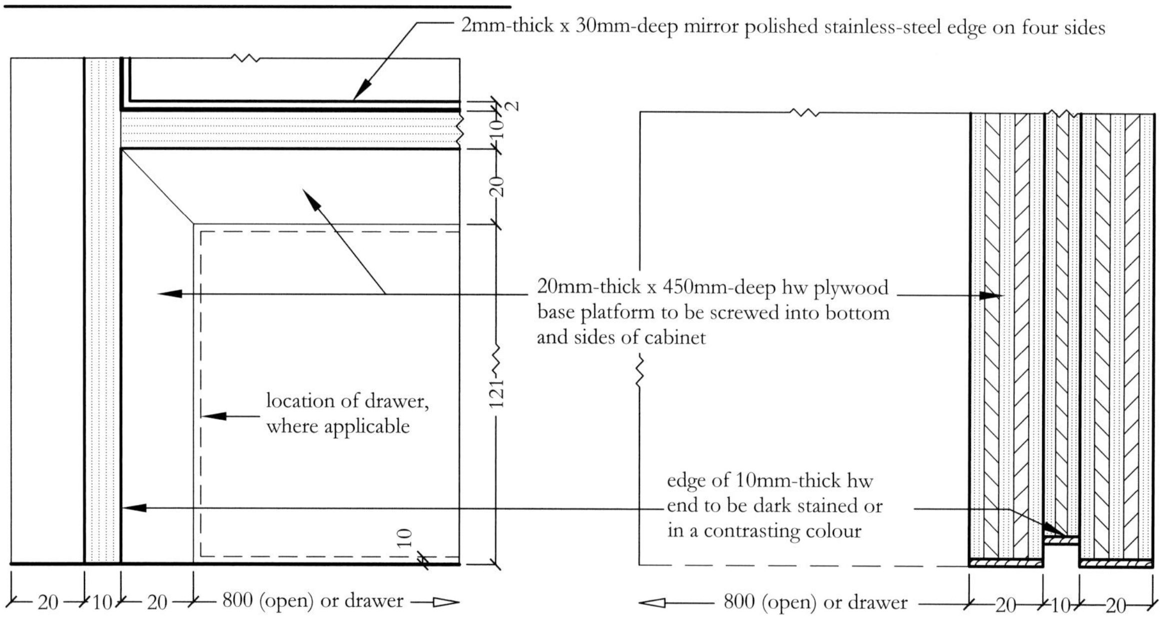

DETAIL ELEVATION OF BASE

DETAIL SECTION OF BASE

PROJECT TITLE:	DRAWN BY	CHECKED	DATE	*address 1* *address 2* *address 3* *postal code* *email address*
	PROJECT NO		SCALE	
DRAWING TITLE: CABINET WITH ADJUSTABLE SHELVES - DETAILS	DRAWING NO		REVISION △	Interior Designers

DATA SHEET	DESCRIPTION SHELVING	F	SHEET NO 1 OF 1 TOTAL QTY:

ILLUSTRATION:

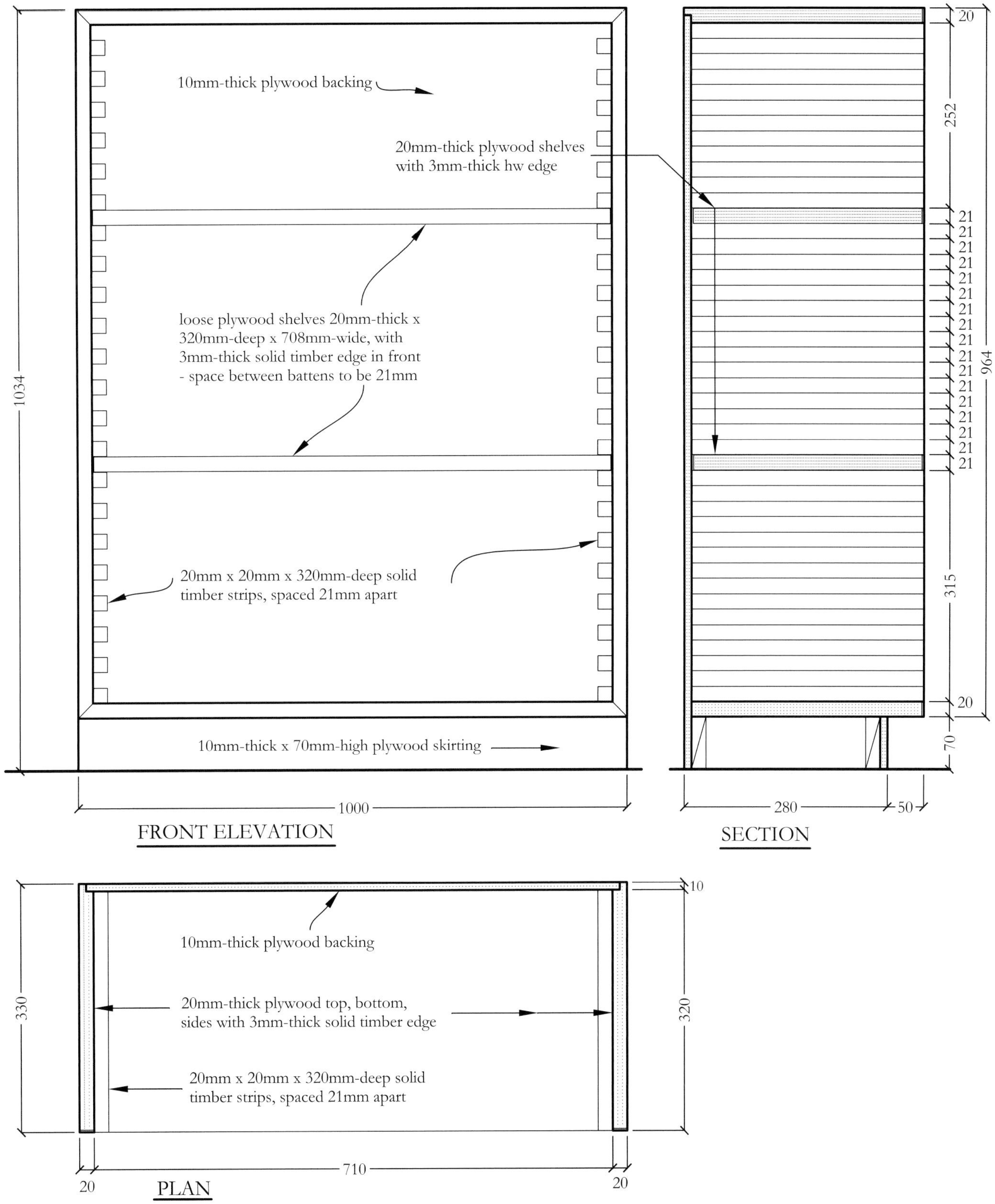

PROJECT TITLE:	DRAWN BY	CHECKED	DATE	address 1 address 2 address 3 postal code email address
	PROJECT NO		SCALE	
DRAWING TITLE: OPEN BOOKCASE WITH SHELVING ON TIMBER STRIPS	DRAWING NO		REVISION △	Interior Designers

DATA SHEET	DESCRIPTION SHELVING	F	SHEET NO 1 OF 1 TOTAL QTY:

ILLUSTRATION:

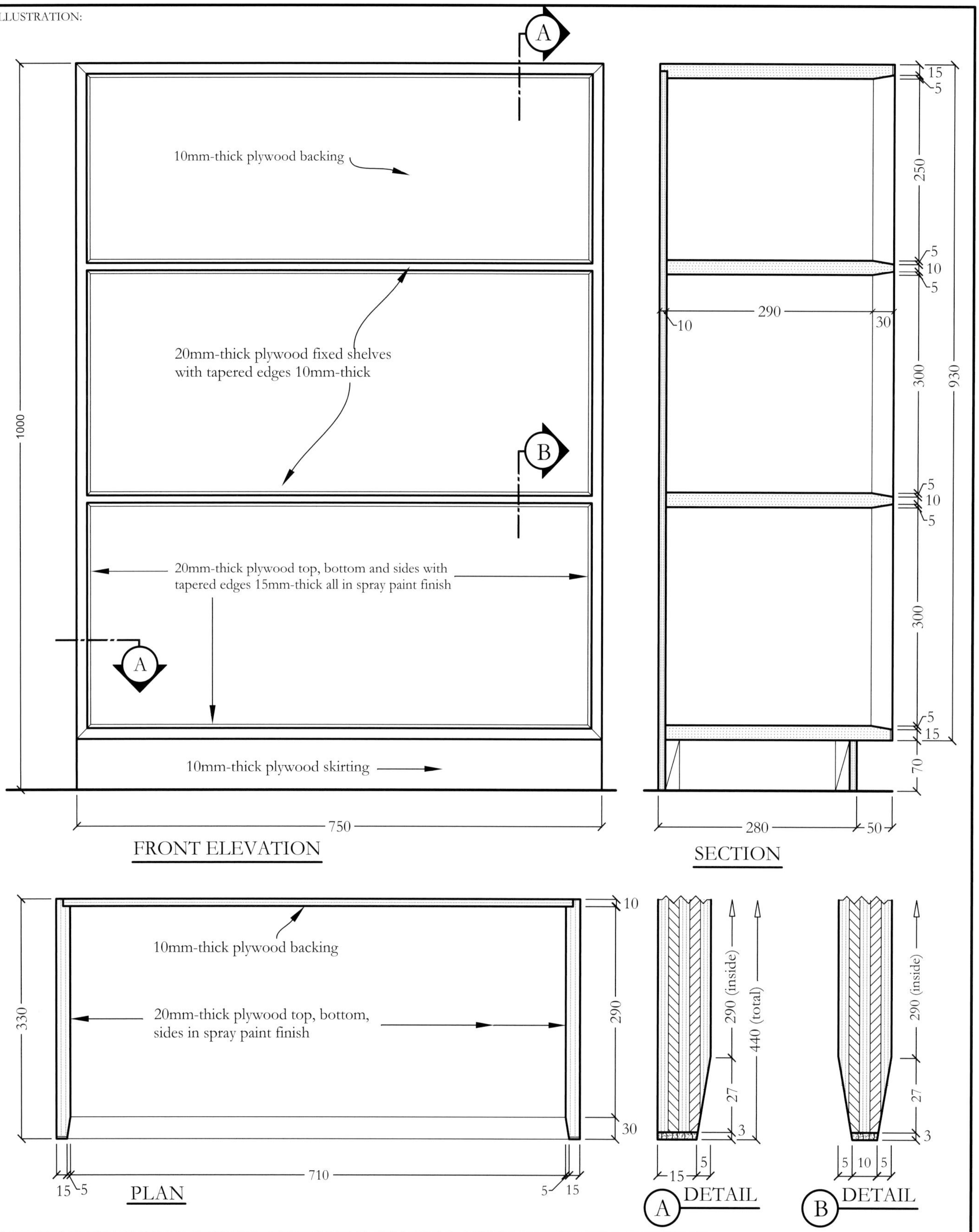

PROJECT TITLE:	DRAWN BY	CHECKED	DATE	address 1 address 2 address 3 postal code email address Interior Designers
	PROJECT NO		SCALE	
DRAWING TITLE: SLIM-LINE BOOKCASE - FIXED SHELVING	DRAWING NO		REVISION △	

CHAPTER 16

FURNITURE AND CASE GOODS

1. Arm chair - side elevation and section
2. Arm chair - front elevation and perspective
3. Lounge chair - plan and front elevation
4. Lounge chair - section and side elevation
5. Three-seater sofa - plan
6. Three-seater sofa - section and elevation
7. Shoe cabinet - front elevation and top plan
8. Shoe cabinet - front elevation (without door) and top plan (without top)
9. Shoe cabinet - section, side elevation, details and variation of shoe rack installation
10. TV console for video/CD cassette and equipment storage - plan, sections and details
11. TV console for video/ CD cassette and equipment storage - front elevations
12. TV console for video/CD cassette and equipment storage - sections A and B
13. Coffee table for living room or public areas - plan (looking from top)
14. Coffee table for living room or public areas - elevations
15. Coffee table for living room or public areas - details 1 and 2

DATA SHEET	DESCRIPTION FURNITURE & CASE GOODS	F	SHEET NO 1 OF 2 TOTAL QTY:

ILLUSTRATION:

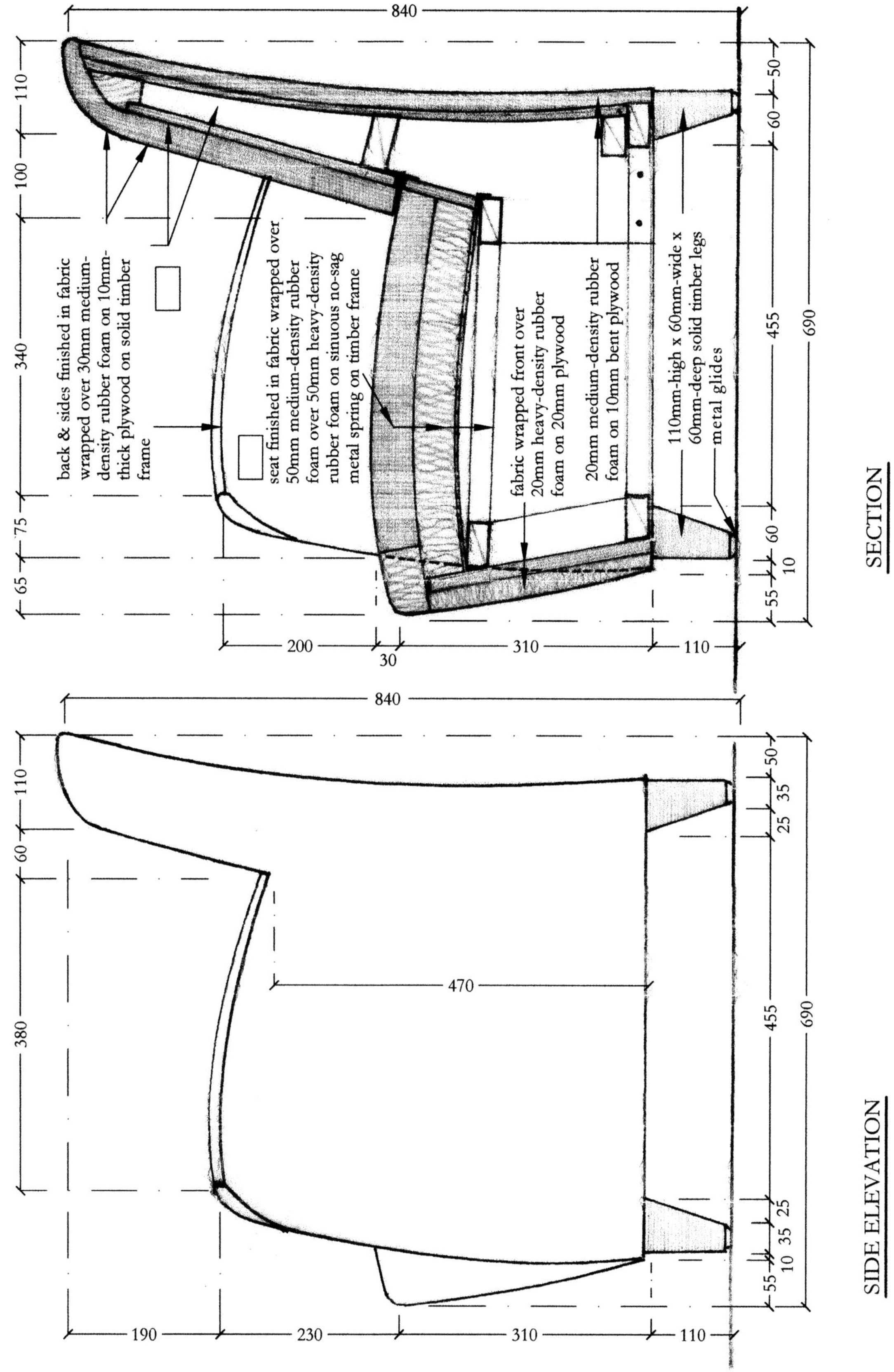

PROJECT TITLE:	DRAWN BY	CHECKED	DATE	address 1 address 2 address 3 postal code email address
	PROJECT NO		SCALE	
DRAWING TITLE: ARM CHAIR - SIDE ELEVATION AND SECTION	DRAWING NO		REVISION △	Interior Designers

DATA SHEET	DESCRIPTION FURNITURE & CASE GOODS	F	SHEET NO 2 OF 2 TOTAL QTY:

ILLUSTRATION:

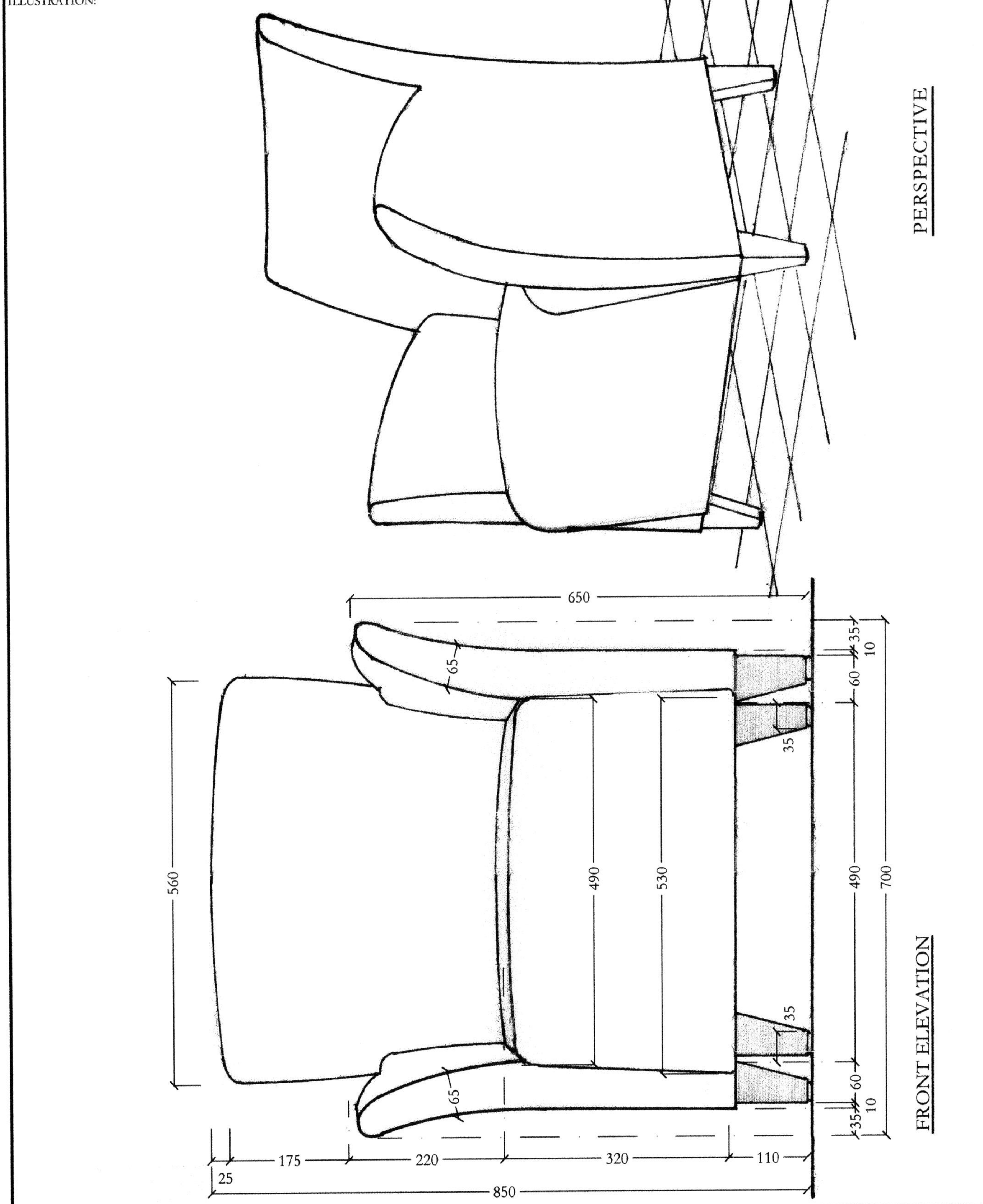

PROJECT TITLE:	DRAWN BY	CHECKED	DATE	address 1 address 2 address 3 postal code email address
	PROJECT NO		SCALE	
DRAWING TITLE: ARM CHAIR - FRONT ELEVATION AND PERSPECTIVE	DRAWING NO		REVISION △	Interior Designers

DATA SHEET	DESCRIPTION FURNITURE & CASE GOODS	F	SHEET NO 1 OF 2 TOTAL QTY:

ILLUSTRATION:

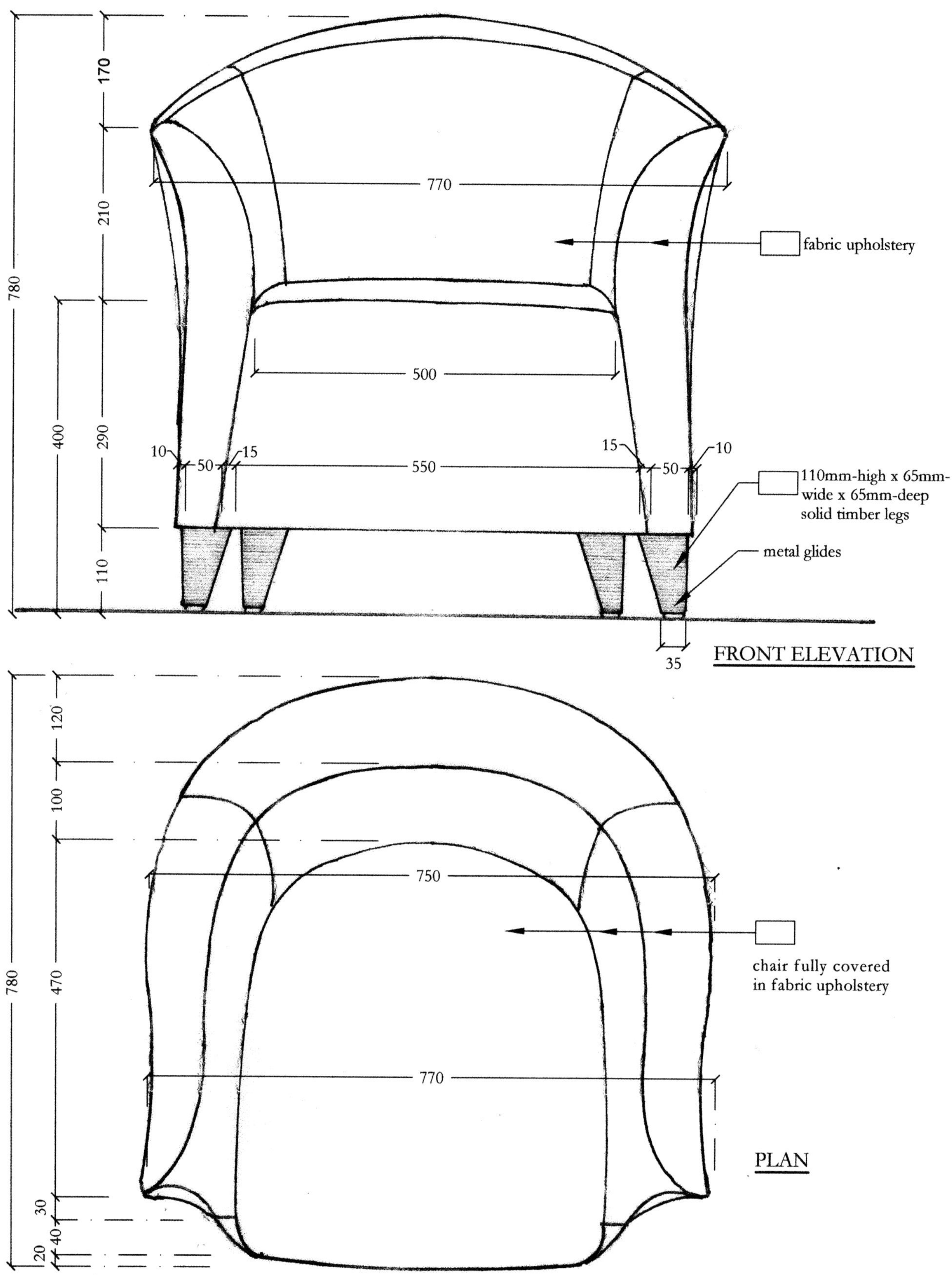

PROJECT TITLE:	DRAWN BY	CHECKED	DATE	address 1 address 2 address 3 postal code email address
	PROJECT NO		SCALE	
DRAWING TITLE: LOUNGE CHAIR - PLAN AND FRONT ELEVATION	DRAWING NO		REVISION △	Interior Designers

DATA SHEET	DESCRIPTION FURNITURE & CASE GOODS	F	SHEET NO 2 OF 2 TOTAL QTY:

ILLUSTRATION:

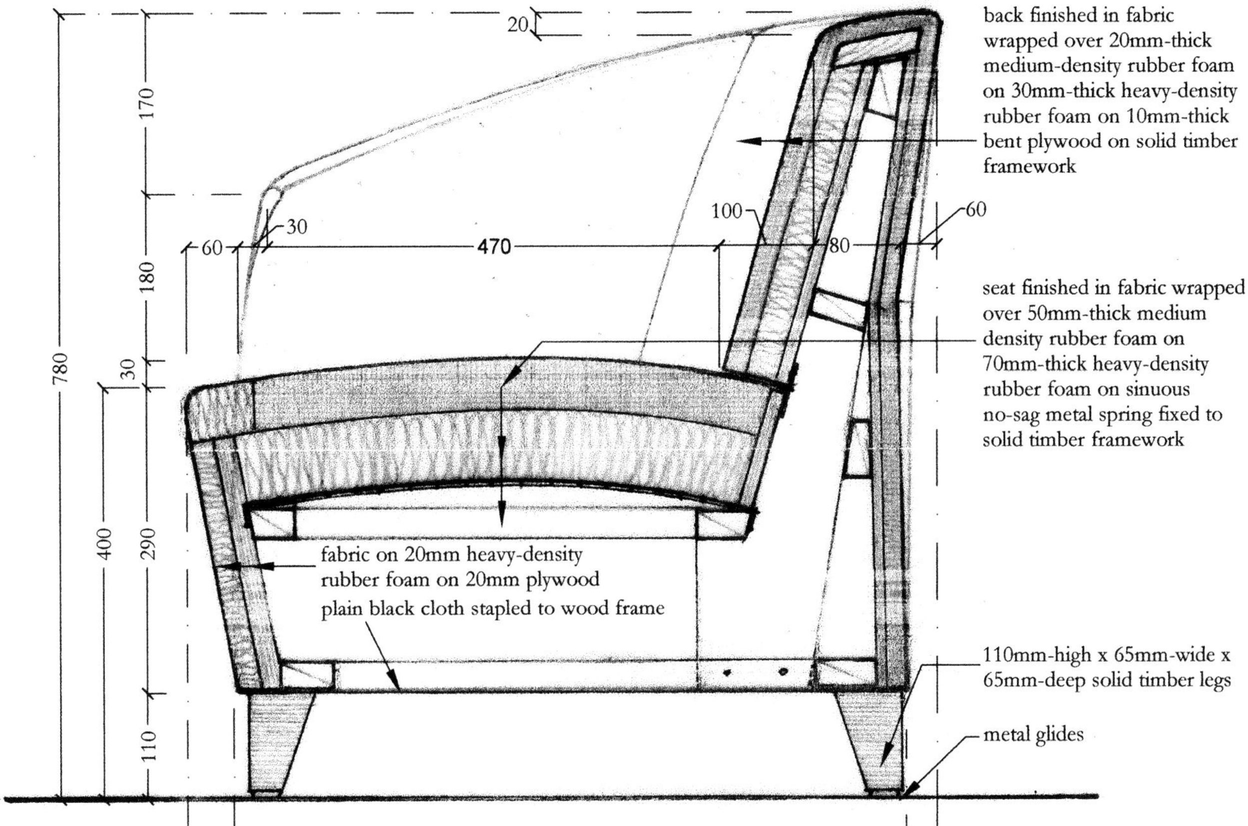

SECTION

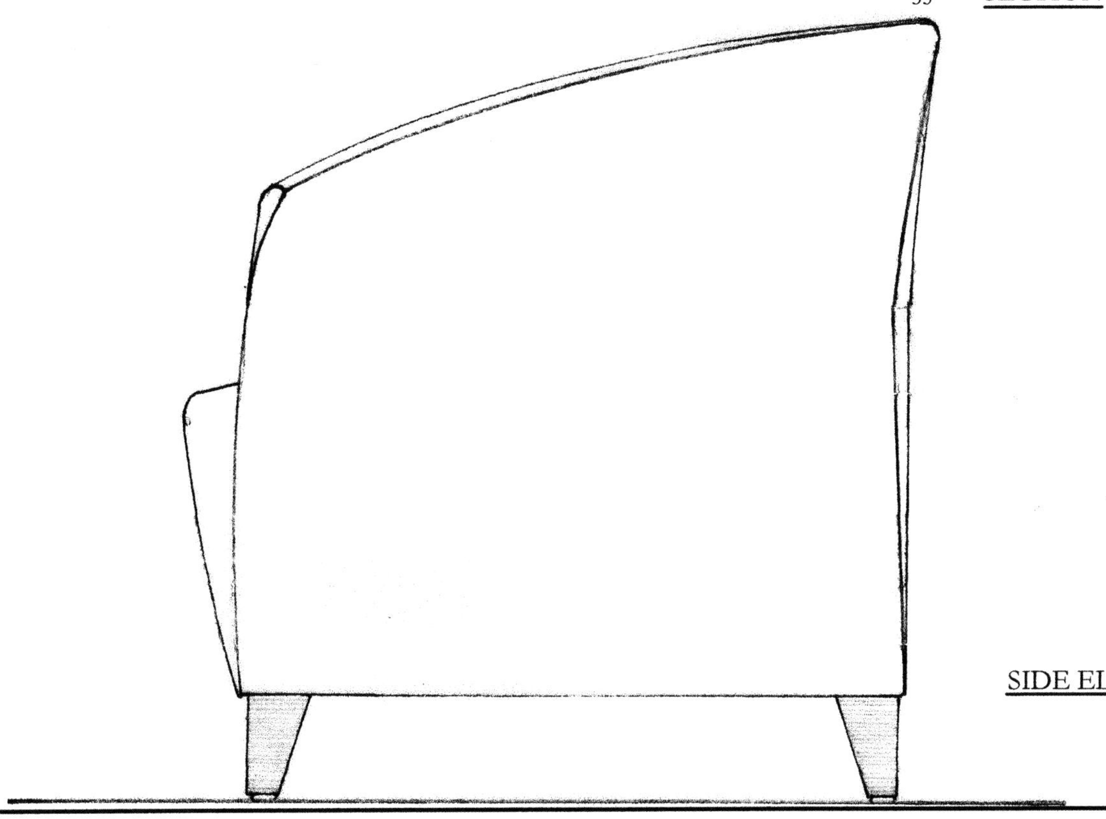

SIDE ELEVATION

PROJECT TITLE:	DRAWN BY	CHECKED	DATE	address 1 address 2 address 3 postal code email address
	PROJECT NO		SCALE	
DRAWING TITLE: LOUNGE CHAIR - SECTION AND SIDE ELEVATION	DRAWING NO		REVISION △	Interior Designers

DATA SHEET	DESCRIPTION FURNITURE & CASE GOODS	F	SHEET NO 1 OF 2 TOTAL QTY:

ILLUSTRATION:

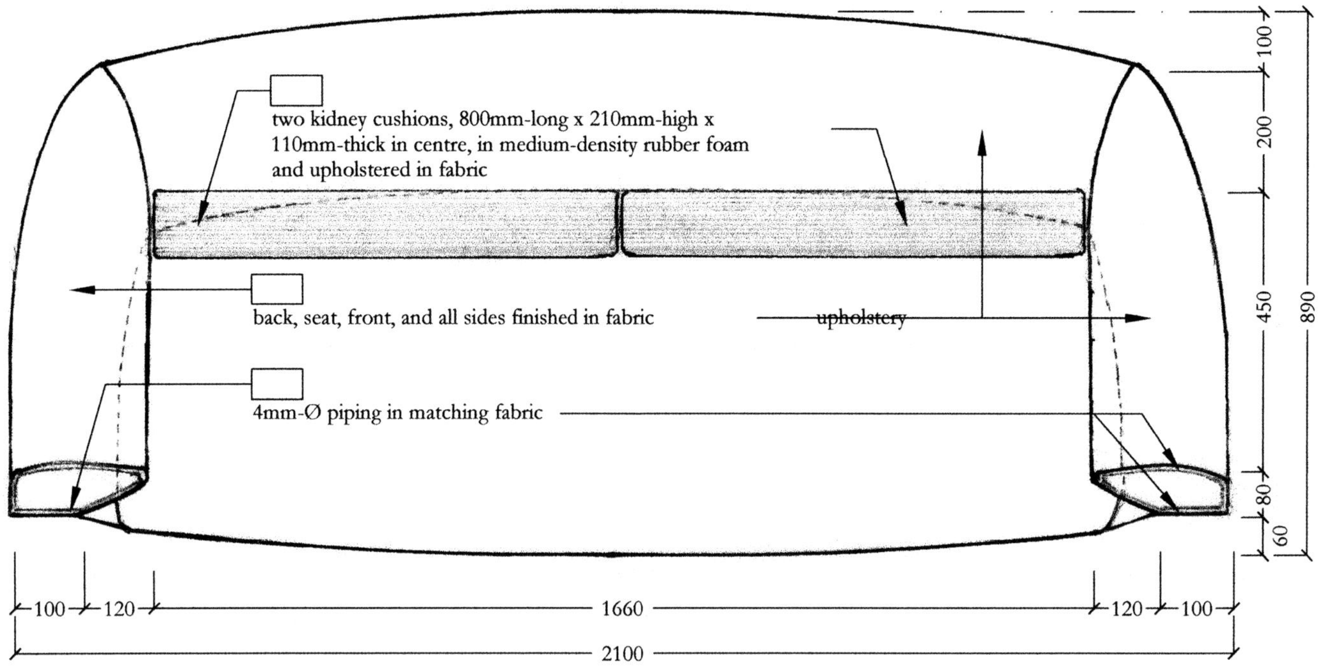

SPECIFICATION / DESCRIPTION:

SUPPLIER / MANUFACTURER: NAME/FIRM OF FURNITURE CONTRACTOR	Furniture supplier code	Finishes supplier & code	
MODEL NO: custom design	DIMENSIONS (mm): 2100mm-long x 890mm-deep x 830mm-high *(420mm-seat height)*	ROOM TYPE:	QUANTITY:
		1	
OTHER FINISHES CODE: - - - -	AREA LOCATION:	2	
		3	
COSTINGS: ☐ BUDGET : $ ☐ QUOTATION : $ ☐ FINAL PRICE : $	TOTAL: TOTAL QUANTITY: TOTAL PRICE: $	4	
		5	
		TOTAL QTY:	

REMARKS/NOTES /SPECIAL INSTRUCTIONS:

PROJECT TITLE:	DRAWN BY	CHECKED	DATE	*address 1* *address 2* *address 3* *postal code* *email address*
	PROJECT NO		SCALE	
DRAWING TITLE: THREE-SEAT SOFA - PLAN	DRAWING NO		REVISION △	Interior Designers

DATA SHEET	DESCRIPTION FURNITURE & CASE GOODS	F	SHEET NO 2 OF 2 TOTAL QTY:

ILLUSTRATION:

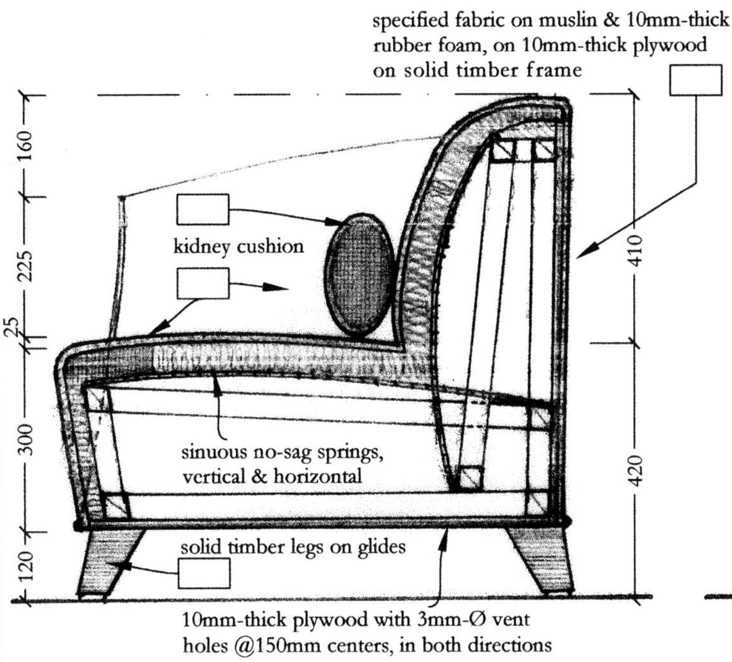

SECTION

NOTE:
Seat, back, front, and sides in 50mm-thick medium-density rubber foam, with seat edge in 50mm-thick x 150mm-wide heavy-density rubber foam covered with 10mm-thick fiberglass floss + muslin and selected fabric. Seat & back on sinuous zig-zag springs on solid timber frame.

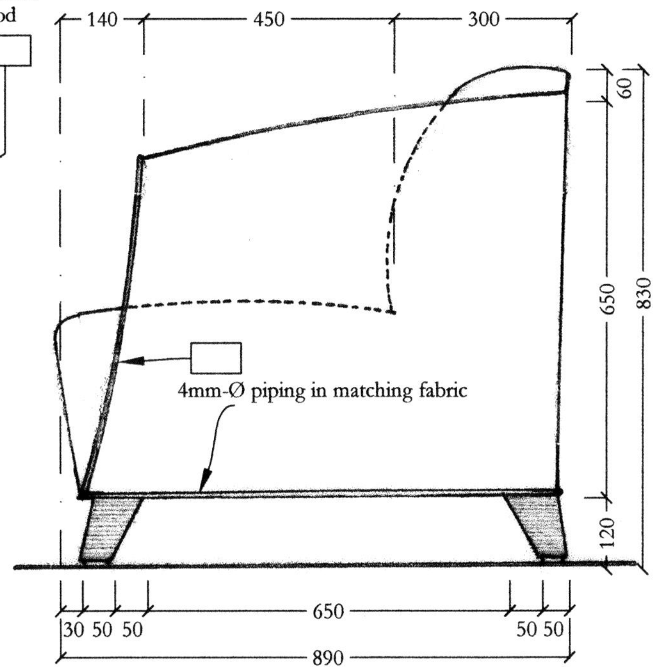

SIDE ELEVATION

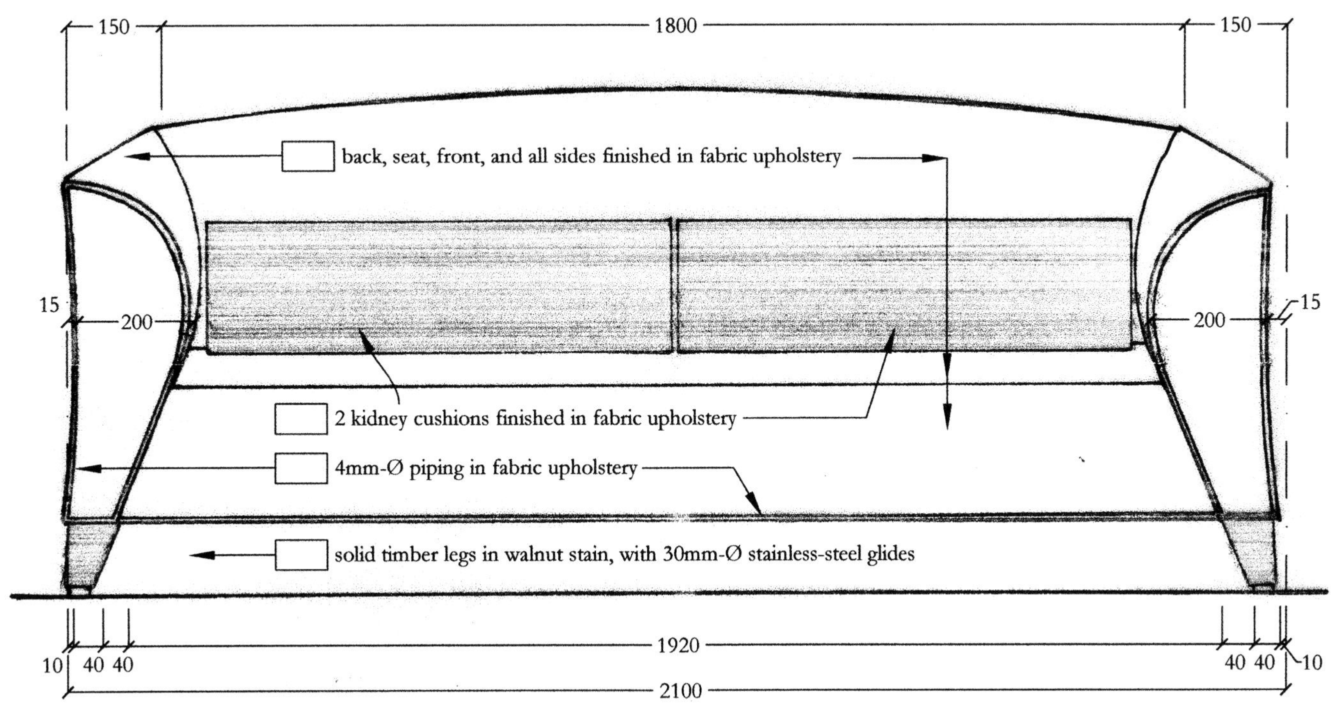

FRONT ELEVATION

NOTE: Fill in finish numbers in rectangular boxes.

PROJECT TITLE:	DRAWN BY	CHECKED	DATE	*address 1* *address 2* *address 3* *postal code* *email address*
	PROJECT NO		SCALE	
DRAWING TITLE: THREE-SEAT SOFA - SECTION AND ELEVATION	DRAWING NO		REVISION △	Interior Designers

DATA SHEET	DESCRIPTION: FURNITURE & CASE GOODS	F	SHEET NO 1 OF 3 TOTAL QTY:

ILLUSTRATION:

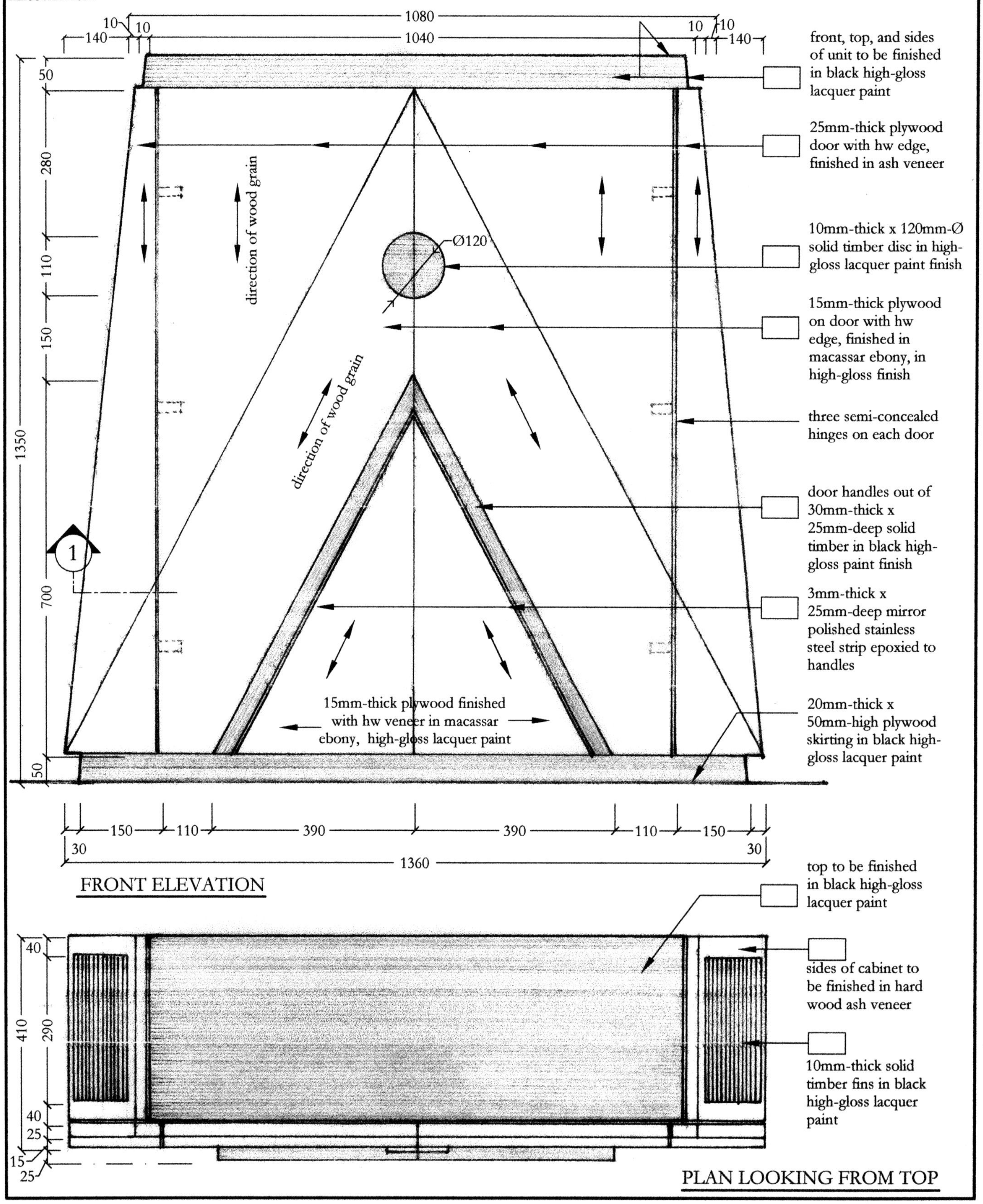

PROJECT TITLE:	DRAWN BY	CHECKED	DATE	*address 1* *address 2* *address 3* *postal code* *email address*
	PROJECT NO		SCALE	
DRAWING TITLE: SHOE CABINET - FRONT ELEVATION AND TOP PLAN	DRAWING NO		REVISION △	Interior Designers

DATA SHEET	DESCRIPTION: FURNITURE & CASE GOODS	F	SHEET NO 2 OF 3
			TOTAL QTY:

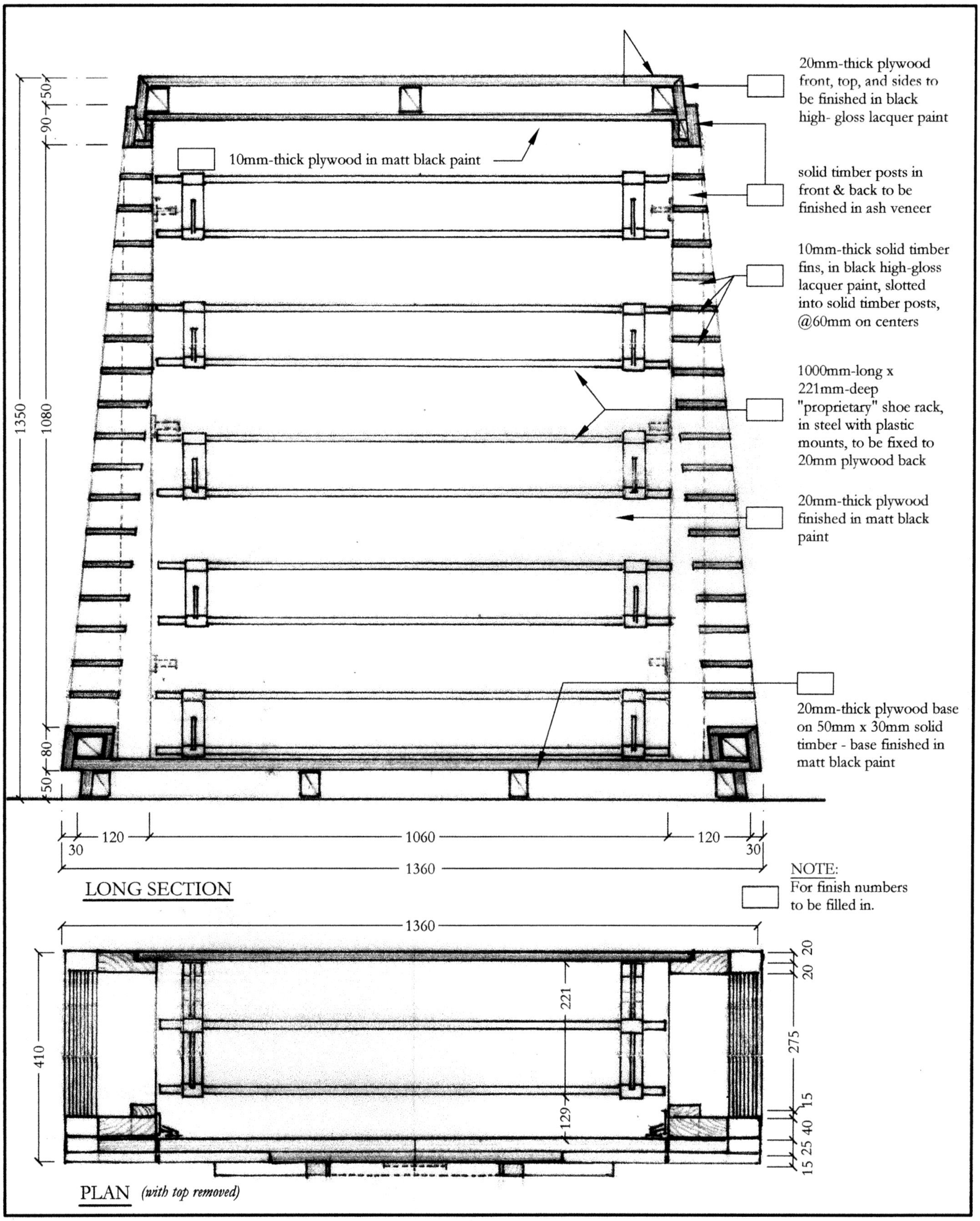

PROJECT TITLE:	DRAWN BY	CHECKED	DATE	address 1 address 2 address 3 postal code email address Interior Designers
	PROJECT NO		SCALE	
DRAWING TITLE: SHOE CABINET - LONG SECTION AND PLAN WITH TOP REMOVED	DRAWING NO		REVISION △	

DATA SHEET	DESCRIPTION: FURNITURE & CASE GOODS	F	SHEET NO 3 OF 3 / TOTAL QTY:

ILLUSTRATION:

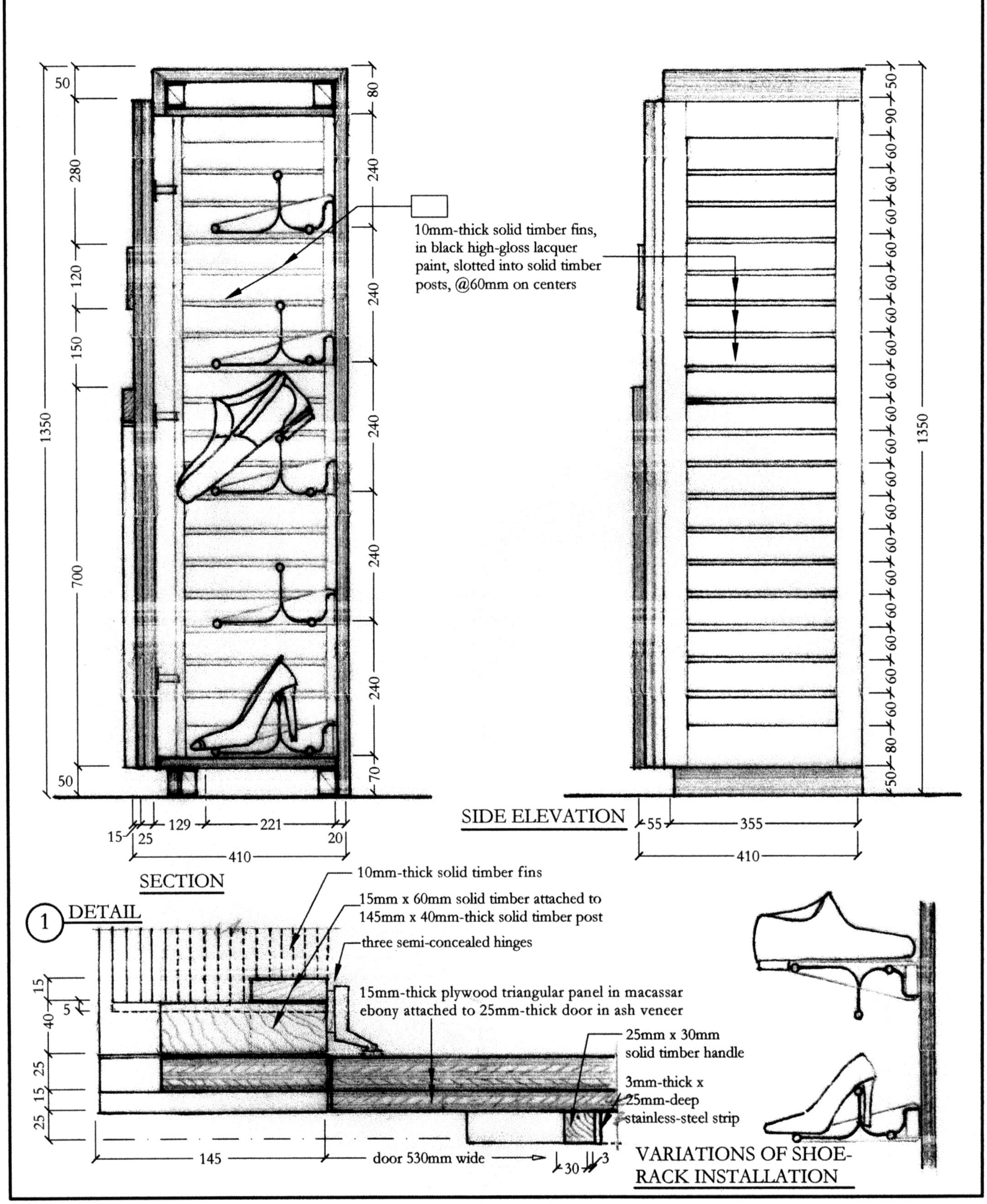

PROJECT TITLE:	DRAWN BY	CHECKED	DATE	address 1 address 2 address 3 postal code email address
	PROJECT NO		SCALE	
DRAWING TITLE: SHOE CABINET - SECTION, SIDE ELEVATION, DETAIL, AND VARIATIONS OF SHOE-RACK INSTALLATION	DRAWING NO		REVISION △	Interior Designers

DATA SHEET	DESCRIPTION FURNITURE & CASE GOODS	F	SHEET NO 1 OF 3 TOTAL QTY:

ILLUSTRATION:

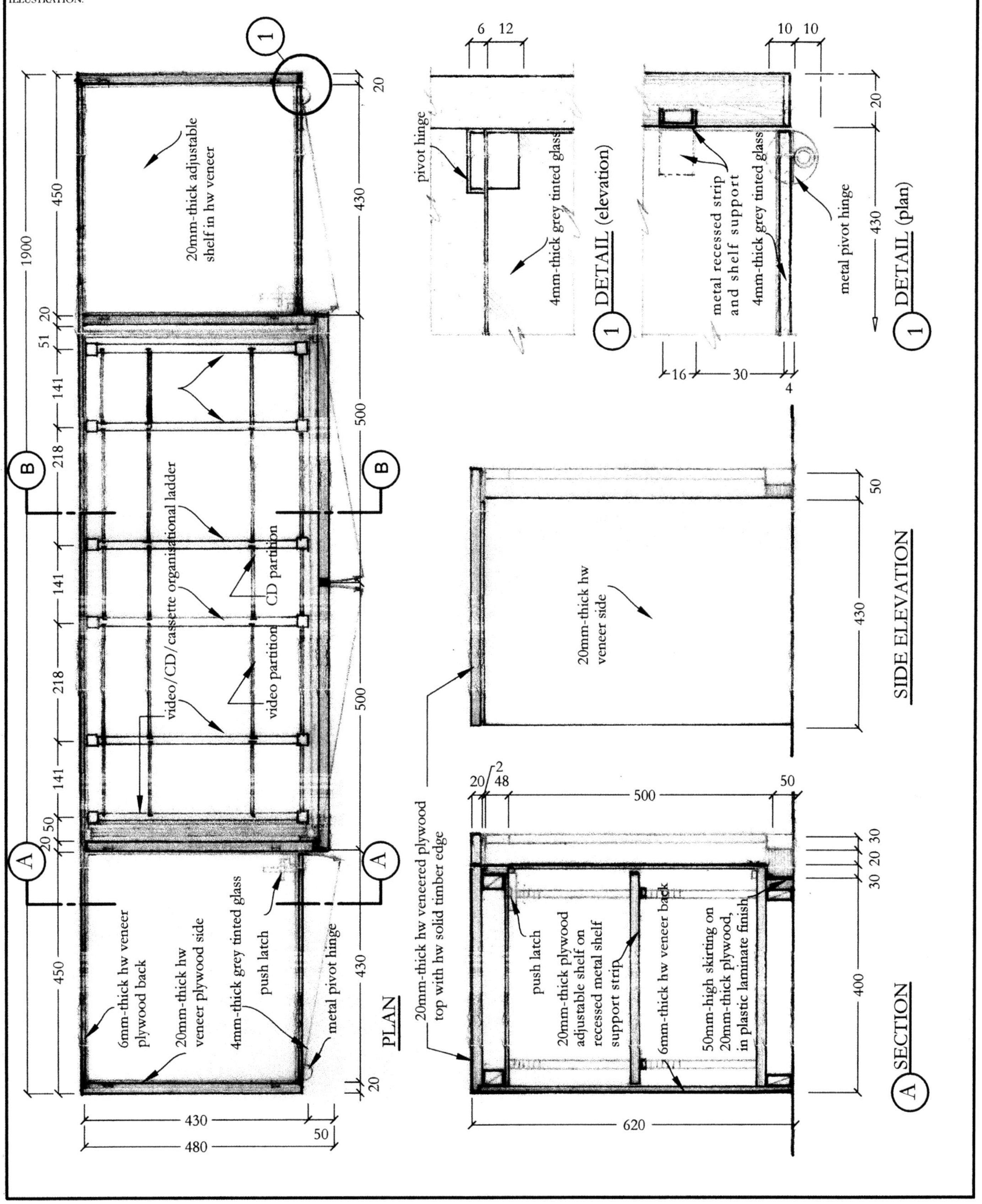

PROJECT TITLE:	DRAWN BY	CHECKED	DATE	
	PROJECT NO		SCALE	address 1 address 2 address 3 postal code email address
DRAWING TITLE: TV CONSOLE FOR VIDEO/CD CASSETTE AND EQUIPMENT STORAGE - PLAN, SECTIONS AND DETAILS	DRAWING NO		REVISION △	Interior Designers

DATA SHEET	DESCRIPTION FURNITURE & CASE GOODS	F	SHEET NO 2 OF 3 TOTAL QTY:

ILLUSTRATION:

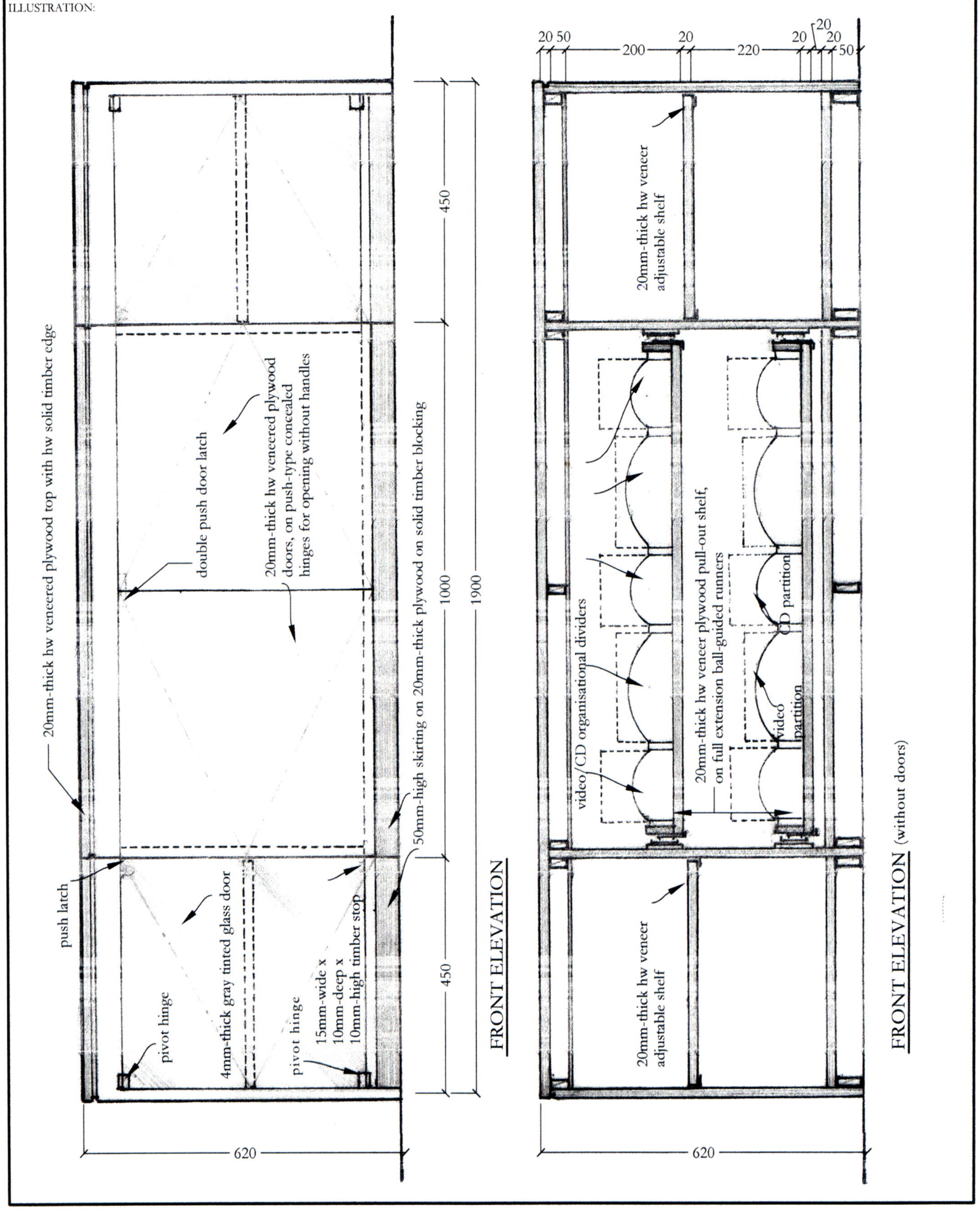

PROJECT TITLE:	DRAWN BY	CHECKED	DATE	address 1 address 2 address 3 postal code email address Interior Designers
	PROJECT NO		SCALE	
DRAWING TITLE: TV CONSOLE FOR VIDEO/CD AND EQUIPMENT STORAGE - FRONT ELEVATIONS	DRAWING NO		REVISION △	

DATA SHEET	DESCRIPTION FURNITURE & CASE GOODS	F	SHEET NO 3 OF 3 TOTAL QTY:

ILLUSTRATION:

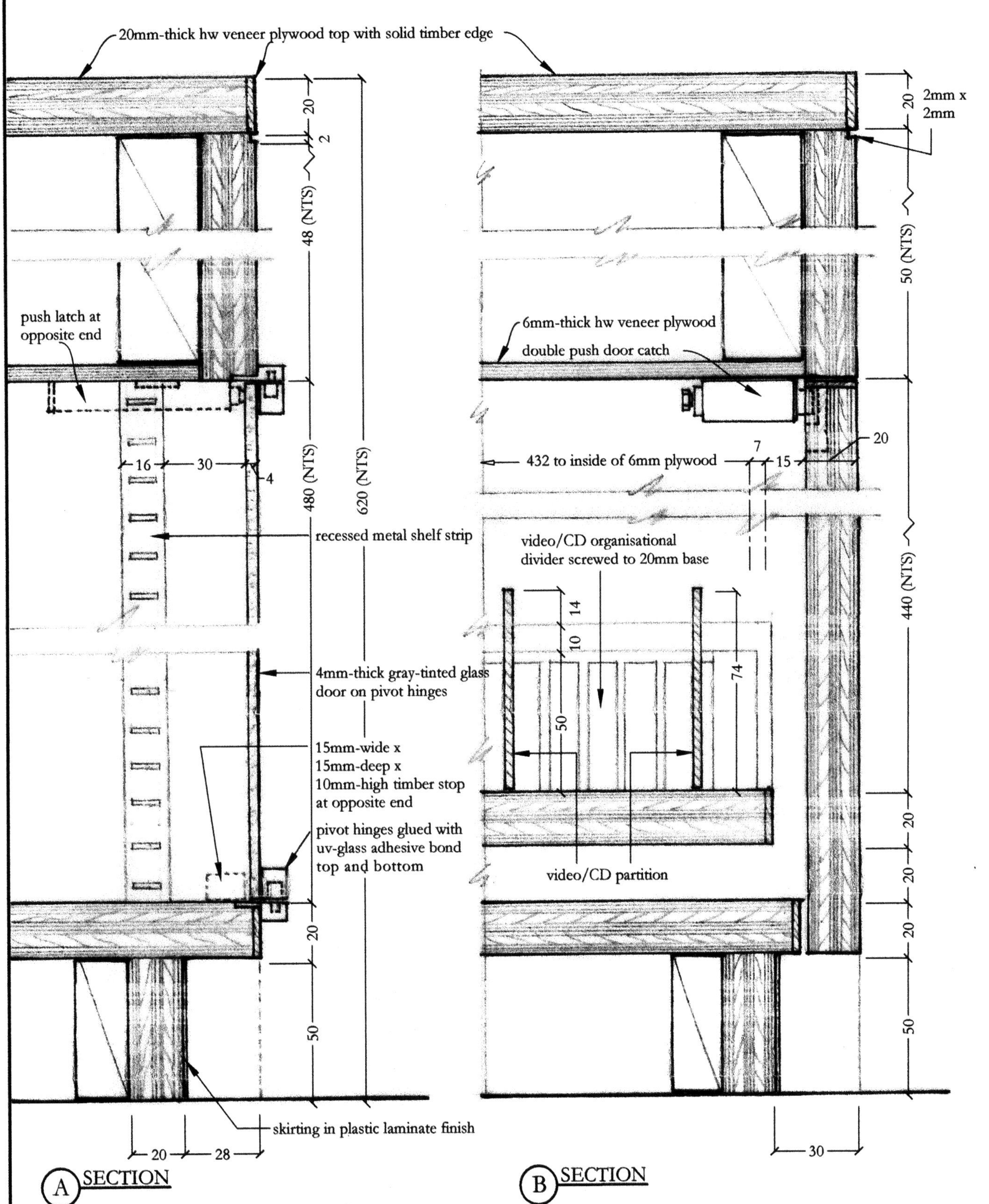

PROJECT TITLE:	DRAWN BY	CHECKED	DATE	address 1 address 2 address 3 postal code email address
	PROJECT NO		SCALE	
DRAWING TITLE: TV CONSOLE FOR VIDEO/CD AND EQUIPMENT STORAGE - SECTIONS A AND B	DRAWING NO		REVISION △	Interior Designers

DATA SHEET	DESCRIPTION FURNITURE & CASE GOODS	F	SHEET NO 1 OF 3 TOTAL QTY

ILLUSTRATION:

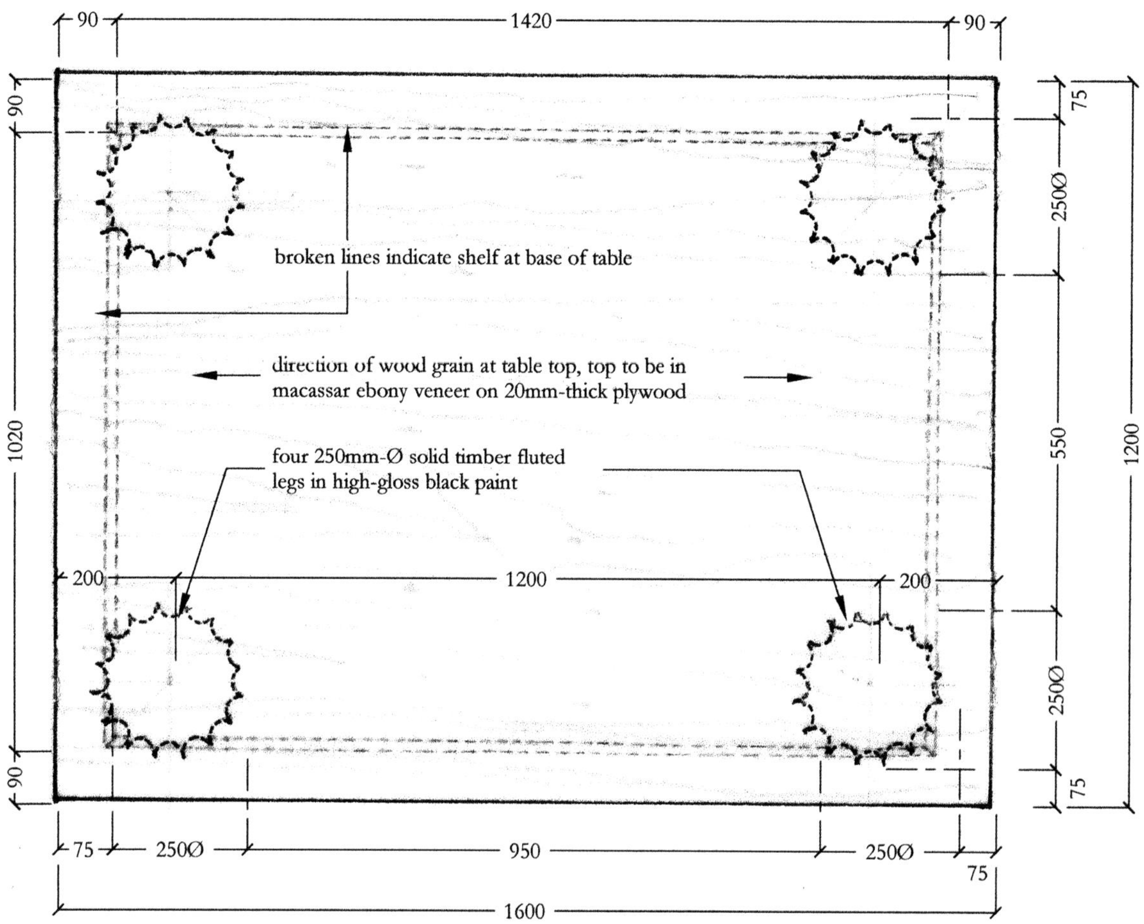

PLAN (looking from top)

SPECIFICATION / DESCRIPTION:

SUPPLIER / MANUFACTURER:	Furniture Supplier code	Finishes Supplier & Code
NAME/FIRM OF FURNITURE CONTRACTOR		

MODEL NO:	DIMENSIONS (mm):	ROOM TYPE:	QUANTITY:
custom made	L1600 D1200 H480	1	
OTHER FINISHES CODE:	AREA LOCATION:	2	
		3	
COSTINGS:	TOTAL:	4	
☐ BUDGET : $ ☐ QUOTATION : $ ☐ FINAL PRICE : $	TOTAL QUANTITY:	5	
	TOTAL PRICE: $	TOTAL QTY:	

REMARKS/NOTES /SPECIAL INSTRUCTIONS:

PROJECT TITLE:	DRAWN BY	CHECKED	DATE	*address 1* *address 2* *address 3* *postal code* *email address*
	PROJECT NO		SCALE	
DRAWING TITLE: COFFEE TABLE FOR LIVING ROOM OR PUBLIC AREAS - PLAN (LOOKING FROM TOP)	DRAWING NO		REVISION △	Interior Designers

DATA SHEET	DESCRIPTION FURNITURE & CASE GOODS		SHEET NO 2 OF 3 TOTAL QTY

ILLUSTRATION:

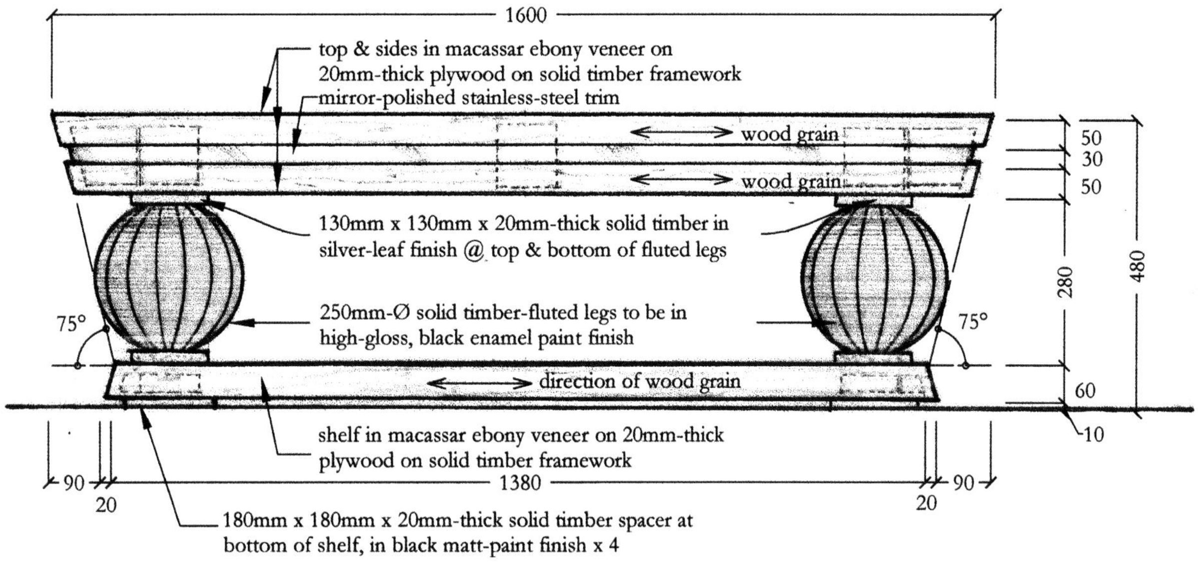

FRONT ELEVATION

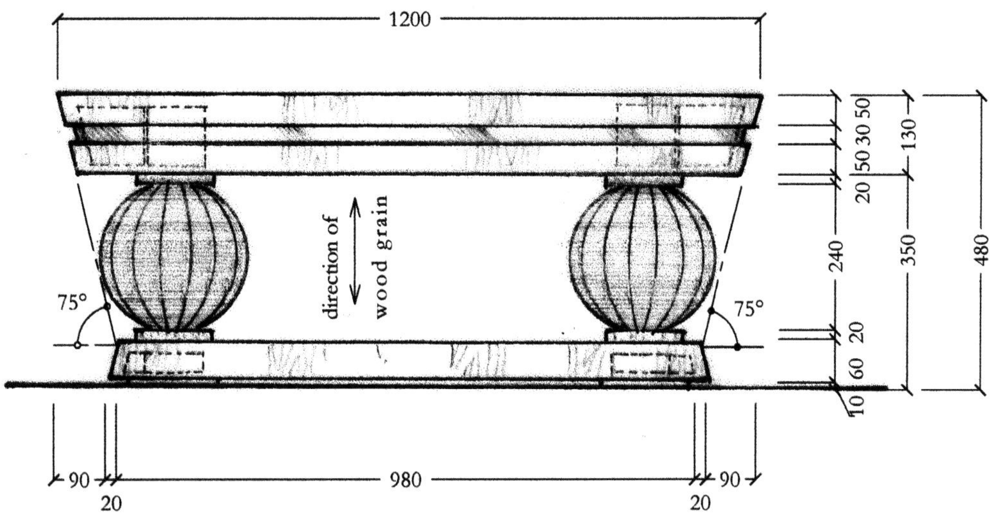

SIDE ELEVATION

PROJECT TITLE:	DRAWN BY	CHECKED	DATE	address 1 address 2 address 3 postal code email address Interior Designers
	PROJECT NO		SCALE	
DRAWING TITLE: COFFEE TABLE FOR LIVING ROOM OR PUBLIC AREAS - ELEVATIONS	DRAWING NO		REVISION △	

DATA SHEET	DESCRIPTION FURNITURE & CASE GOODS	F	SHEET NO 3 OF 3 TOTAL QTY

ILLUSTRATION:

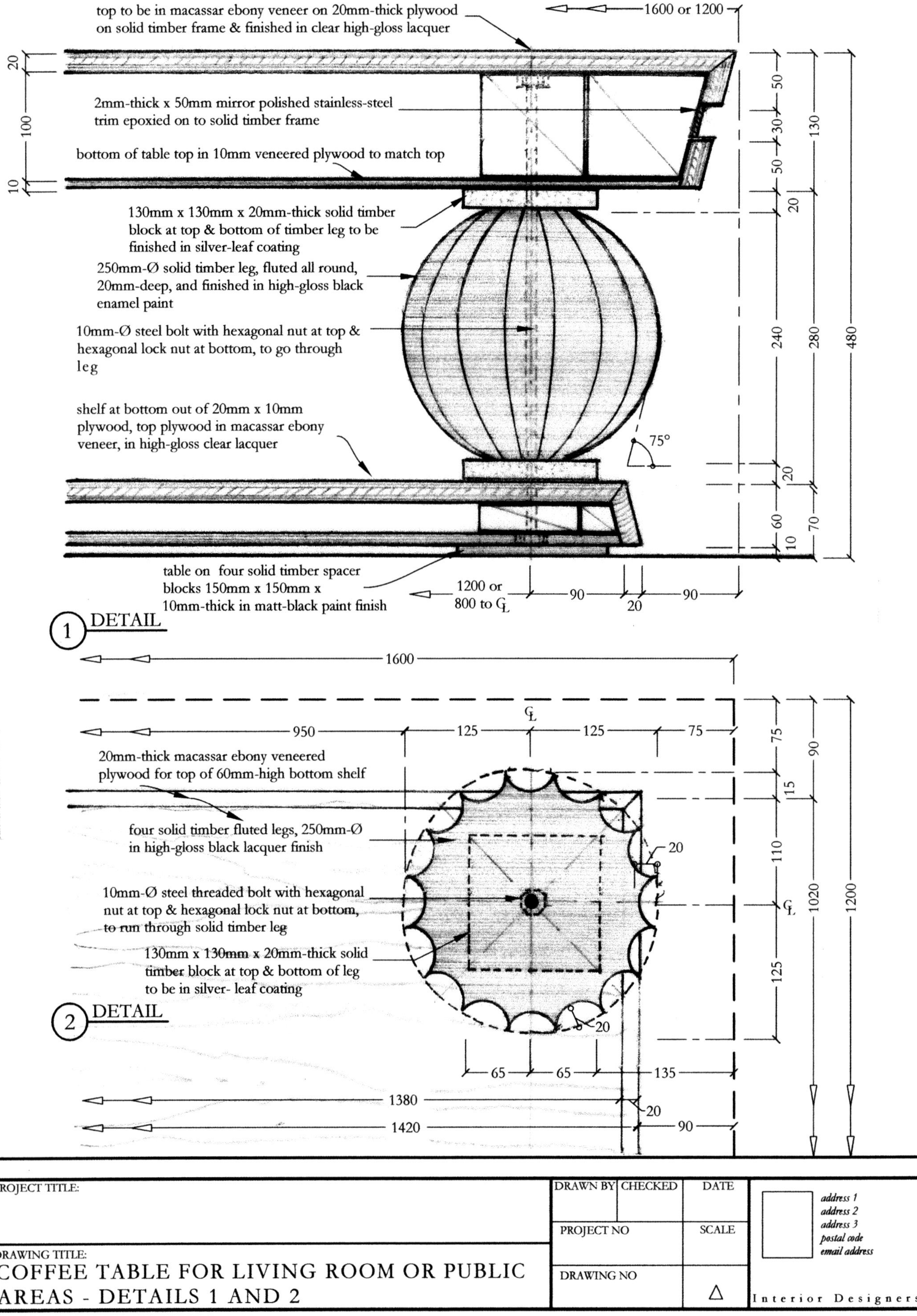

PROJECT TITLE:	DRAWN BY	CHECKED	DATE	address 1 address 2 address 3 postal code email address Interior Designers
DRAWING TITLE: COFFEE TABLE FOR LIVING ROOM OR PUBLIC AREAS - DETAILS 1 AND 2	PROJECT NO DRAWING NO		SCALE △	

CHAPTER 17

FRAMING OF ARTWORK AND PHOTOGRAPHS

1. Introduction by Angie Mui, owner of Framing Angie
2. Photographs and types of framing
3. Photographs and types of framing
4. General information by Jimmy F. Doctor

Follow Your Heart

by Angie Mui, owner of Framing Angie

Many people have asked me where I learned the art of framing and whether there is a school for framing. There isn't one. While I have had the benefit of being in the industry for over 20 years, the principle of what works still stands.

I am known to be bossy; I will not frame in a style that I know will not work. However, I will also not insist on framing it my way, but will consider the customers' interior decor and personalities. Each frame is personalized based on what they like, and then I add my creativity to it. The result is a frame that exceeds my customers' expectation.

Framers and interior designers move on from projects to projects, but customers are the ones who have to live with the framed pieces, so it is important that they really love what they see for many years to come.

Don't Listen to Your Framers

I always tell my customers, "Do not listen to me or any other framer or your interior designer. Follow your heart. When you get up in the morning with a cup of tea in your hand, what you see on the wall should put a smile on your face."

Most of the times when customers bring their art pieces to me it is not easy for them to picture them framed. They may seem comfortable with my recommendations, but if I detect a hint of uncertainty, I will immediately do a digital mock-up on my computer, to show them my recommended frame and style for their art piece. It is easier to decide with a strong visual than by looking at corner samples of the frames. This exercise helps tremendously, especially when I want to prove or reverse a decision. My customers know exactly what they will be expecting.

Don't Follow the Rules

While there is definite need to adhere to preservation methods in framing, there are no fixed rules in creativity. I always raise an eyebrow when customers start to vigorously scroll through their phones to show me what the galleries where they bought their artworks recommended for framing. They are usually display pieces. After getting a better knowledge of the customers' interiors and background, I either readily agree to do as the galleries recommend or I propose alternative designs. Many customers were pleasantly surprised to learn of options they never thought of and are truly pleased with the final outcome.

In my 20 years in framing I have had only one customer who walked out on me because I disagreed with her and refused to do what she wanted. I have produced over 120,000 frames and served over 20,000 customers and not one is wrong for the piece framed.

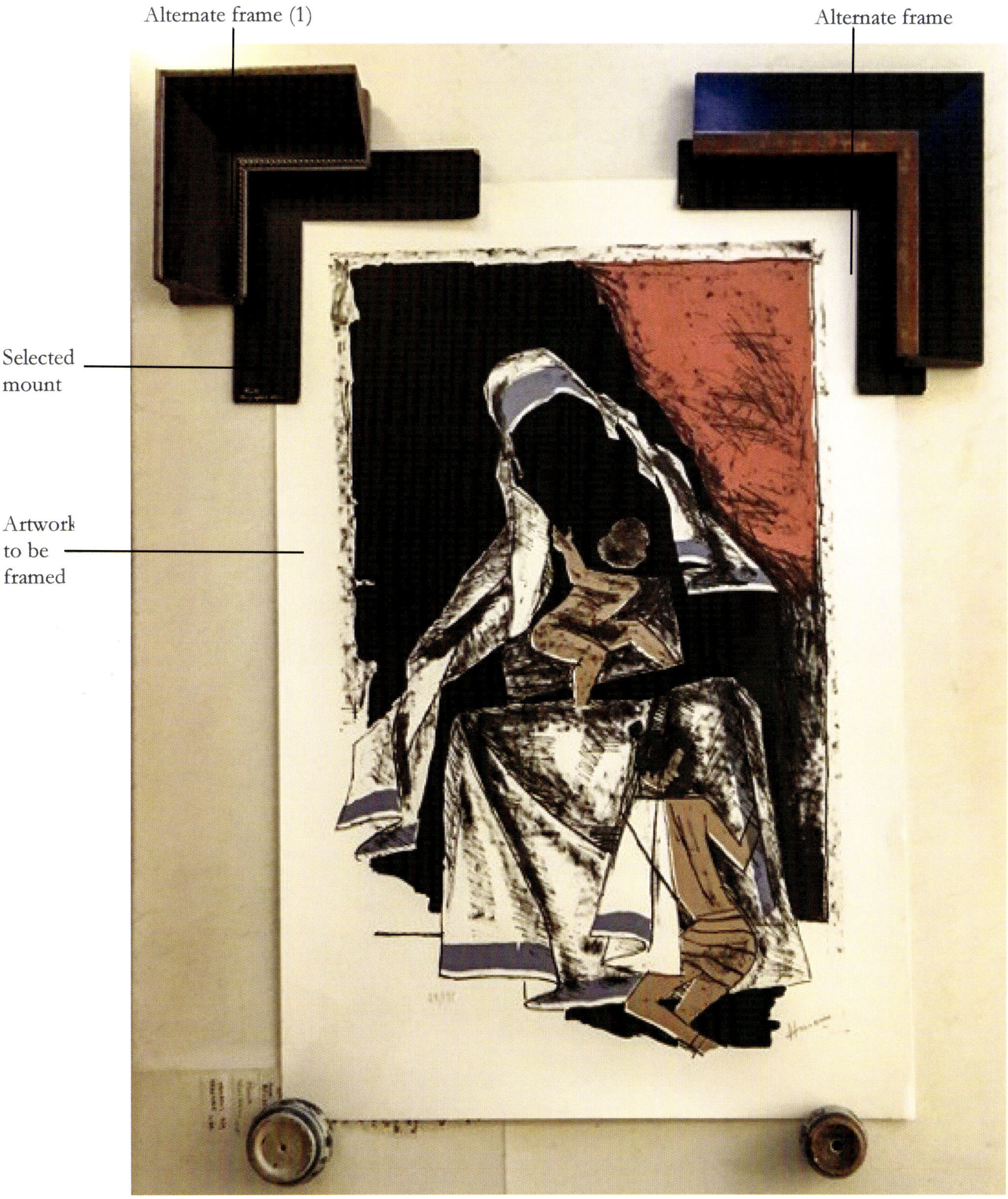

Artwork with a dark gray mount and different frames being tried out.

A

B

9cm

8.25cm

Two variations of frames, in size and color:

a. Frame is wider (9cm), with a gold and dark gray color
b. Frame is narrower (8.25cm), with a light gray, dark gray, and gold color

Note: The mount surrounding the artwork is in a dark gray color.

HOW TO ENHANCE THE LOOK AND QUALITY OF YOUR ARTWORK OR PHOTOGRAPH

by Jimmy F. Doctor

- Determine if your artwork/photograph actually needs any enhancement.

- Some artwork, like a contemporary piece, especially an oil-painting that is stretched over a frame, will not need any enhancement with a frame surrounding it.

- If the contemporary piece does need some life, you could consider putting a simple border, such as a solid timber or aluminum frame, with a 2mm or 3mm space between the frame and the edge of the painting.

- But if the piece needs further enhancement, you must decide how to frame it. You can also look into the possibility of using colored or white mat boards, single or double, around the artwork/photograph. This gives depth to the piece. (See the page200). The first image gives you an idea how to select the frame and the mount. Note that the color of the mount reflects one of the colors in the artwork. Also, leaving an off-white border around the artwork gives depth to the overall image, with the frames in different sizes and different gold-colored borders. Compare the artwork without the frame and with the frame and you can see the big difference the frame makes.)

- When deciding on arranging a group of different pieces of artwork/ photographs, it is difficult to compose your arrangement directly on the wall. It is easier to compose the arrangement by juxtaposing the various pieces on the floor below the area of the wall to be used. Then measure the space between the various pieces, and decide on the distance from the floor to the bottom and top of the frames, and transfer them to the wall.

- In the event that there is a possibility of a constant change of artwork, and drilling holes in the wall becomes a problem, you can decide on using a wall or ceiling track system. This helps you to mount a track directly to the wall, to the ceiling, or directly to the ceiling and tight to the wall. The track is either in aluminum or in steel, and is in a "J" shape. The aluminum version can come in aluminum alloy in an anodized version or can be powder coated to match the color of wall or ceiling.

- If you have a metal wall, you can have magnetic tracks that can be directly attached to the wall. In the event that you are forbidden to drill holes in the wall, you can have tracks with continuous sticking strips on the back of the track that are glued to the wall.

- Do note that the artwork will need to be hung on a hooked slider, to be slid along the J-shaped track, and hung on wires with a hook at the end. The wires should be 1mm or 2mm-thick, and can be made of steel or a transparent plastic cable.

DATA SHEET

DESCRIPTION:
TABLE SETTING FOR FORMAL DINING

SHEET NO: OF
TOTAL QTY:

ILLUSTRATION:

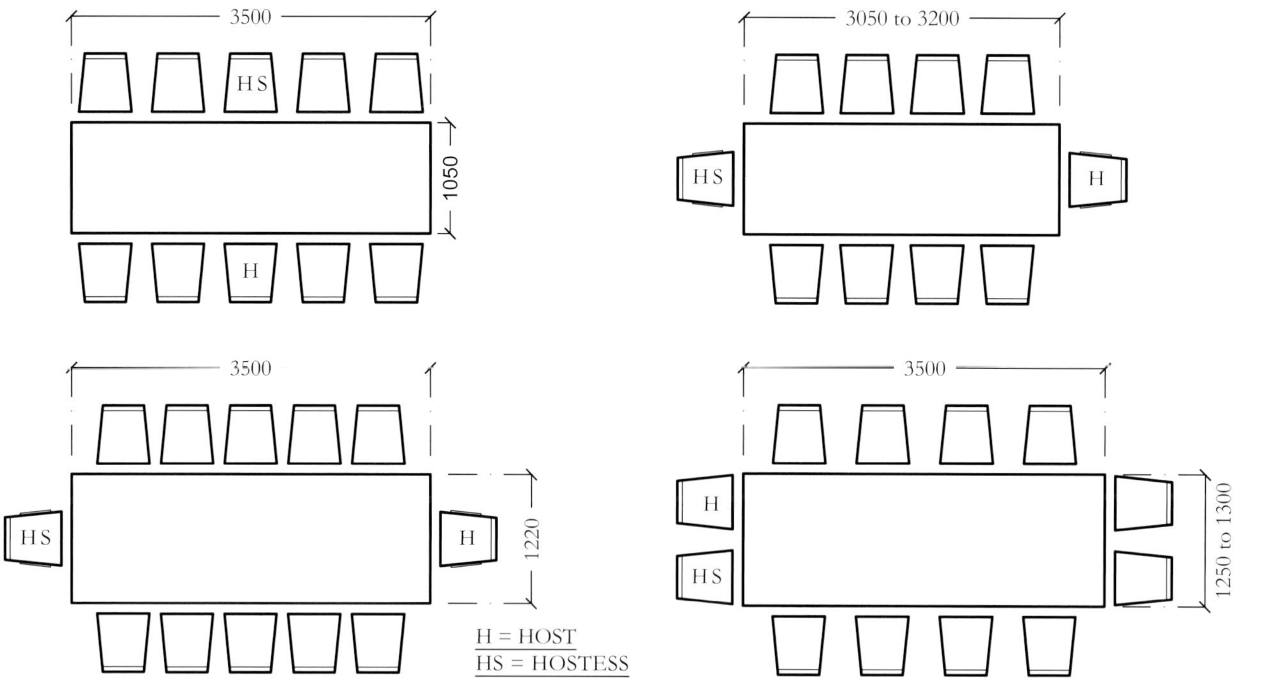

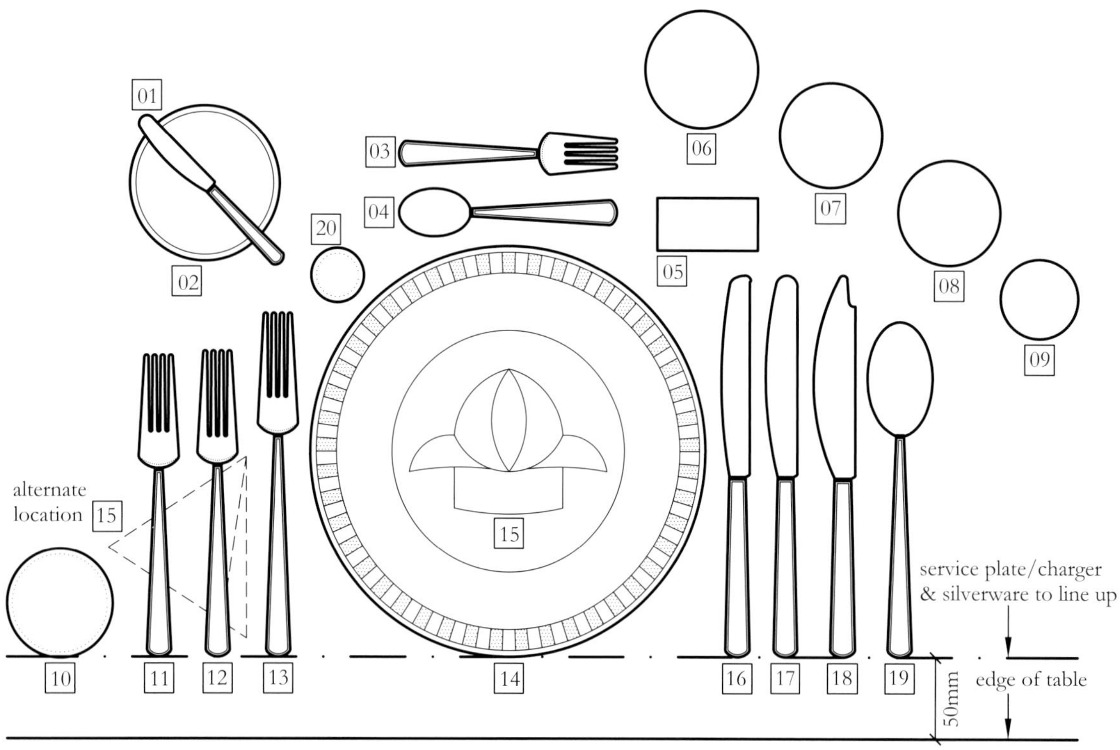

09 champagne flute or sherry glass
10 salad, dessert or side plate
11 salad fork
12 fish fork
13 dinner fork
14 service plate or charger
15 napkin
16 salad knife
17 dinner/steak knife
18 fish knife
19 soup spoon

TABLE SETTING LEGEND

01 butter knife
02 bread plate
03 dessert fork
04 dessert spoon or dessert knife
05 name/place card
06 water goblet
07 white wine glass
08 red wine glass
20 alternative location of vertical napkin arrangement

PROJECT TITLE:

DRAWING TITLE:
VARIOUS SEATING LAYOUTS FOR FORMAL DINING AND FORMAL TABLE SETTING FOR CHINAWARE AND STEMWARE

DRAWN BY | CHECKED | DATE
PROJECT NO | SCALE
DRAWING NO | REVISION △

address 1
address 2
address 3
postal code
email address

Interior Designers

CHAPTER 18

TABLE SETTING GUIDE FOR FORMAL DINING AND DINING TABLE ETIQUETTE

1. General table setting guide for formal dining and
2. Dining table etiquette
4. Food service etiquette
5. Wine tasting etiquette

DIMENSIONS

Generally a good size formal dining table, for eight persons should be at least 1050mm wide by 3500mm long by 750mm high. If the room is big, you can increase the width of the table to 1200mm or even 1350mm and, length could be increased to 700mm for every person seating along the length of the table (check the feasibility of bringing the table into the space). If the table is wider than 1050mm, then the host and hostess can be placed at either end, and the rest of the seats may be spread out. You can provide more space for diners by having a chair placed at either end of the table.

Chairs should be at least 510mm wide by 550mm deep by 460mm high (seat height). A captain's chair for the host and hostess at either end of the table could have arms and be 550mm wide x 550mm deep x 460mm high (seat height) but only applies for single seating at either end. For wider tables with two chairs at the ends, do not use chairs with arms.

FORMAL TABLE SETTING

Generally, it is good practice to use a table-cloth. Traditionally, this should be white, thick, starched and ironed. It should drop over the edges of the table by about 300mm, just about touching the knees of the diner.

Although white linen is considered to be part of an elegant formal setting, nowadays, colored, patterned or lace table cloth are acceptable and can be used with contrasting colored napkin to an elegant effect.

A formal table setting is always symmetrical, but if you have an odd number of guests, place the old seat as a central setting see diagram below.

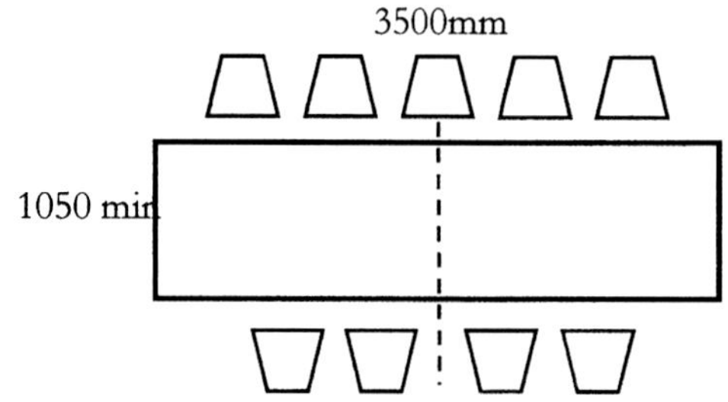

TABLE SETTINGS AND PLACEMENT

Formality dictates symmetry. If you have an odd number of guests, follow the above dictum. All table settings should be laid central to the arrangement of chairs. The center-piece, appropriately, should be laid exactly in the center of the table, in both directions. Candlesticks or candelabras should be evenly distributed, as space permits, to symmetrically balance the tablescape. Do not crowd the table and be careful that decorations do not obstruct guests' vision across the table.

SETTING OF DINNER PLACEMENT

PLATES

Service plates: central to the table placement is the service plate also known as charger. It serves as an under-plate for the placement of the courses served to the guest, up to the main course. It is removed only before the entrée is served, at which point the previous course's plate and the charger are removed together. This plate can be more decorative in color and pattern or may indicate a commemorative occasion. It is about 330mm to 360mm round. It can be in bone china, porcelain, metal or stoneware.

Dinner plates. They are normally round, 250mm to 300mm in diameter and are usually either white or off-white, but can be any color and pattern. They can also be square or oblong, such as Japanese sushi plates.

Salad, dessert and side plates can be from 100mm to 230mm in diameter and are placed 50mm from the edge of the table on the left of the forks.

Bread-and-butter plates can be from 150mm to 180mm diameter and are placed above and left of the service or charger plate.

PLACING OF CUTLERY/SILVERWARE

To make it easy for the guest to understand which piece of silverware to use for which course, follow the gourmet's rule: outside-in. This means that the outside silverware (in relation to the charger) is used first, then the next and so on.

There should be no more than three pieces of silverware on each side of the charger at any one time. Forks are placed on the left and knives (or spoon when required) are placed on the right of the charger.

Dinner fork: the largest of the forks, the dinner fork, is placed on the left of the charger and the other smaller forks are placed left or right of this main fork, depending on the order of the day's menu. The tines of forks should face upwards.

The fish fork: when a fish dish is served, it is placed on the left of the dinner fork, as the fish dish will be served before the entrée.

Salad fork: if salad is served as the first course of the evening, the salad fork will precede the fish and dinner forks on the left. If it is served after the entrée, it will be placed closest to the charger, and right of the dinner fork.

Dinner knife: the largest of the knives, the dinner knife, is placed on the left of the charger and the fish knife, specially shaped, is placed on the right of the dinner knife. When a steak is served, then dinner knife is replaced by a steak knife. If a salad is served first, a salad knife will be the first knife on right of the charger and left of the dinner knife.

The smallest of the knives, the butter knife or spreader, is placed on the butter plate, at a diagonal 45-degree angle, the blunt blade facing downwards.

A soup or fruit spoon is placed on the right of the knives, if soup or fruit is served first.

PLACING OF GLASSES

All glasses are to be placed above the knives and spoon, and to the right of the charger. They should be placed in the order they will be used, the water goblet first, red wine glass, white wine glass, and the champagne flute or sherry glass.

NAPKINS

Normally, a napkin is placed on top of the charger. If space permits, it can also be placed to the left of the forks, and if you are short of space, it should be placed under the forks. Another method is to roll the napkin and make a tower with a towel ring at the bottom of the rolled towel. Make it stand on the left top corner of the charger, the towel ring will hold it upright.

SALT AND PEPPER SHAKER

A few salt and pepper-shaker sets, should be spread across the table, so guests can easily reach them. Pass the salt and pepper shakers together.

DESSERT SPOON AND FORK

The dessert spoon (or dessert knife) is placed on the table above the charger, in a horizontal position with the handle on the right. If a knife is used, the blade should face the charger.

The dessert fork is placed above the spoon or knife, with the tines facing up, and handle on the left.

BELL

A small silver bell should be placed on the right hand of the hostess's seating area, to call the butler or helper. A neater way, if practical, is to provide a small push-button under the top of the table, which is electrically connected to the kitchen, and within easy reach of the hostess. In the future, there will probably be a remote-control button, without the encumbrance of electrical wiring.

The following explanation of Western dining etiquette offers an explanatory guide to why table settings are so designed.

TABLE ETIQUETTE AND GOOD TABLE MANNERS

At a formal dinner, when does one start eating? Etiquette demands that you wait until everyone has been served and the host or hostess wishes you, "Bon appetite" as a signal to start.

Before starting to eat, place your napkin on your lap. Napkins generally are square; fold it in two diagonally, before putting it on your lap.

If you are leaving the table for nature's call etc., then excuse yourself and place your napkin on the back of your chair. At the end of your meal, do not fold the used napkin in a neat fold, but leave it unfolded. If you fold the napkin, it will indicate to your hostess that you are inviting yourself to the next dinner, and this will be considered rude.

HANDLING YOUR SILVERWARE/CUTLERY

Forks are always placed on the left and knives on the right of the charger. When eating, hold your fork in your left hand, and your knife in your right hand.

It is good manners to spear your food with your fork and bring it to your mouth.

If you are speaking to a guest next to you, or you have not finished eating, place your fork, tines up, with the knife on top of the fork, and both at 45-degree diagonally crossed over each other. This will signify to the butler/helper that you have not finished eating, and your plate/cutlery should not be removed from the table.

When each course is finished, place the fork and knife parallel to each other, the fork on the left tines up and knife next to it on the right, and centered on the bottom edge of the plate. The helper will then remove your plate.

SEATING ETIQUETTE

For a formal dinner, each seat will have a name card assigned to each chair so follow the seating order. If a name card is not assigned, then wait for the hostess to assign you a seat.

FOOD SERVICE ETIQUETTE

Normally for a formal dinner, food will be brought to the table, course by course, by a butler or helper. Food is served from the left of the diner, and after the course is finished, the empty/used plate is removed from the right of the diner. The same will apply if the food is brought to the diner on a platter or bowl.

In the event that the occasion is not too formal, the host/hostess will bring the food on a platter or bowl, pass it to the guest closest to her, who will help himself/herself to the food and in turn pass it on to the guest on the right, and the food will then be passed around the table. At the end of the course the host/hostess will remove the used plate from the right side of the guest, with some guests helping out.

Bread is normally brought to the table in a few baskets, either in slices or buns. If you pick up the basket, offer the bread to the guest on your left and then pass the basket to your guest on the right. Butter will be individually served in a small butter plate. Put the bread and butter on your bread plate, which will be on your left and above the charger, then break off a small piece of bread, bite size, put butter on it, and eat it. It is bad manners to spread butter on the whole slice of bread, and cut it into small parts.

When eating soup, use the spoon sideways and sip from the front side of the bowl, tipping the bowl away from you to gather the soup (so as not to spill it down you) until you come to the last drops in the bowl. Then tilt the bowl backwards and away from you as you finish your soup again, so not to spill the remainder of the soup on to your lap.

WINE TASTING ETIQUETTE AND HABITS

For good, older wines, you should decant the wine from the bottle into a good, wide-based, narrow-necked decanter in order to aerate the wine.

When opening a bottle of wine, open the cork slowly and quietly, except when opening a champagne bottle, when one is supposed to make a big issue of popping the cork with a bang, as it is an occasion to celebrate.

When pouring wine from the bottle, hold the bottle from the base, and not from the neck.

When you are in company, fill all wine glasses in equal amounts, otherwise some guests will feel slighted.

Fill wine glasses to a little less than half full, so as to aerate the wine, and let it breathe.

Offer wine to your guests first, before pouring wine for yourself. When clinking glasses, touch the glasses at the bell and not at the rim of the glass, so you do not crack the glass.

If a stemmed glass is provided, hold the glass by the stem in-order not to warm the wine with your hand by holding by the bell. If the occasion is less formal, you may be provided with a stemless glass and can drink the wine by holding the bell.

When tasting wine, hold the glass with wine in front of you, then swirl the wine in the glass to aerate it, wait for a few moments while swirling the wine in the glass, then bring the glass to your nose and take a breath, smelling your wine for its subtle aroma of fruits, and taste it by filling your mouth, half full, swishing the wine subtly around your mouth to enjoy and take in the flavor.

Jimmy F. Doctor

Jimmy F. Doctor is an architect and interior designer.

Having qualified from the Department of Architecture, at the J. J. School of Art Bombay, India, he was awarded a Government Diploma in Architecture (G. D. Arch.). He also qualified from the Department of Interior Design, University of Manitoba, Canada, and was awarded a Bachelor's degree in interior design (B.I.D.). He further studied at the Pratt Institute, in New York, where he completed a special design course in interior design, with electives in jewelry design, exhibition design and architectural rendering.

He has been an associate of two of the leading interior design firms in the US and England and a senior associate of two of the leading interior design firms in Asia.

During his association with various design firms, he has provided interior design direction on various international five-star hotel projects, including:

- Hyatt Hotels in Brussels, the Caspian Sea, Tehran and Mashhad
- Sheraton Hotels in Bahrain, Brussels, Doha and Dubai
- Inter-Continental Hotel in Athens
- Regent Hotel in Kuala Lumpur
- Banyan Tree Hotel, in Phuket

He was awarded scholarships to study interior design in Canada from:

- The Bombay Parsi Punchayat Trust, Bombay-India
- The RD Sethna scholarship fund, Bombay-India
- For his design and execution of the center for the Dyslexia Association of Singapore, he was honored with a plaque, awarded to him, by Mrs. Goh Chok Tong (wife of the former Prime Minister of Singapore).

He established JFD Designs Pte Ltd in May 1997 in Singapore and is the present owner and director of the firm. His focus has been on the designing of a number of large residential homes, apartments, restaurants, clinics, offices and more in Southeast Asia.